Mischief, Morality and Mobs

Geoffrey Pearson, who died in 2013, was one of the most outstanding social scientists of the post–Second World War era. His work spanned social work, social theory, social history, criminology and sociology. In particular, his work has had a huge impact upon studies of youth, youth culture and drugs.

This collection comprises contributions from scholars producing empirical work on some of the key areas upon which Geoff Pearson established his reputation. All of the writers in this collection have been profoundly influenced by his scholarship. This collection focuses on urban ethnography, race and ethnicity, and youth and drugs. It includes chapters on boxing gyms; understanding the English Defence League; black male adults as an ignored societal group; drug markets and ethnography; and sex, drugs and children in care.

The result is a cutting-edge collection that takes readers into social worlds that are difficult to access and are complex, yet utterly normal. Overall this is an exciting and fittingly challenging tribute to one of the UK's most important scholars, which will appeal to scholars and students of criminology, sociology, social history and research methodology—in particular ethnography.

Dick Hobbs is currently Professor of Sociology at the University of Western Sydney, Emeritus Professor at the University of Essex, Visiting Professor at Goldsmiths College and an Associate Fellow at the Royal United Services Institute.

Routledge Advances in Ethnography
Edited by Dick Hobbs, *University of Essex* and
Les Back, *Goldsmiths, University of London*

Ethnography is a celebrated, if contested, research methodology that offers unprecedented access to people's intimate lives, their often hidden social worlds and the meanings they attach to these. The intensity of ethnographic fieldwork often makes considerable personal and emotional demands on the researcher, while the final product is a vivid human document with personal resonance impossible to recreate by the application of any other social science methodology. This series aims to highlight the best, most innovative ethnographic work available from both new and established scholars.

Mischief, Morality and Mobs

Essays in Honour of Geoffrey Pearson

Edited by Dick Hobbs

Routledge
Taylor & Francis Group
LONDON AND NEW YORK

First published 2017 by Routledge

2 Park Square, Milton Park, Abingdon, Oxfordshire OX14 4RN
52 Vanderbilt Avenue, New York, NY 10017

Routledge is an imprint of the Taylor & Francis Group, an informa business

First issued in paperback 2019

Library of Congress Cataloging-in-Publication Data
Names: Hobbs, Dick, 1951– editor. | Pearson, Geoffrey, honoree.
Title: Mischief, morality and mobs : essays in honour of Geoff Pearson / edited by Dick Hobbs.
Description: New York, NY : Routledge, 2017. | Series: Routledge advances in ethnography | Includes bibliographical references.
Identifiers: LCCN 2016010189 | ISBN 9781138679733 (hardback) | ISBN 9781315544960 (e-book)
Subjects: LCSH: Sociology. | Criminology. | Youth—Social conditions. | Violence. | Drug abuse.
Classification: LCC HM585 .M57 2017 | DDC 301—dc23
LC record available at https://lccn.loc.gov/2016010189

ISBN: 978-1-138-67973-3 (hbk)
ISBN: 978-0-367-37109-8 (pbk)

Typeset in Times New Roman
by Apex CoVantage, LLC

To Geoff's family:
His wife, Marilyn
Children, Kate, Joe, James and Saul
Grandchildren, Joseph, James, Halo and Mylo
And great-grandson, Marley

Contents

SECTION FOUR
Geoff's Final Publication 223

Notes on Contributors

Daniel Briggs is Professor of Criminology at the Universidad Europea in Madrid. He is the author of *Deviance and Risk on Holiday: An Ethnography of British Tourists in Ibiza* (Palgrave MacMillan, 2013) and *Crack Cocaine Users: High Society and Low Life in South London* (Routledge, 2012); co-author of *Riots and Political Protest* (Routledge, 2015); *Culture and Immigration in Context: An Ethnography of Romanian Migrant Workers in London* (Palgrave MacMillan, 2014) and *Assessing the Impact and Use of Anti-Social Behaviour Orders* (Policy Press, 2007); and editor of *The English Riots of 2011: A Summer of Discontent* (Waterside Press, 2012). He is currently writing a book on drug distribution in Madrid and undertaking ethnographic research on illegal border crossings into Spain.

Andrew Davies is a Reader in History at the University of Liverpool. He is the author of *The Gangs of Manchester* (Milo Books, 2008) and *City of Gangs: Glasgow and the Rise of the British Gangster* (Hodder and Stoughton, 2013), along with a series of articles on the history of gangs, crime and violence in urban Britain.

Charlie Edwards currently works for the British Government. He was Director of National Security and Resilience Studies Group at the Royal United Services Institute (RUSI) between 2013 and 2015. Prior to joining RUSI he was a Research Leader at the RAND Corporation, focusing on defence and security, and was Deputy Director for Strategy and Planning in the Office for Security and Counter-Terrorism in the Home Office. He has conducted major research and analysis projects for the European Commission, European and Canadian Governments, and the US Administration.

Jon Garland is a Reader in Criminology in the Department of Sociology at the University of Surrey. His main areas of research are in the fields of hate crime, rural racism, community and identity, policing and victimisation. He has published six books: *Racism and Anti-Racism in Football* (with Mike Rowe); *The Future of Football* (with Mike Rowe and Dominic Malcolm), *Youth Culture, Popular Music and the End of 'Consensus'* (with the Subcultures Network) and (all with Neil Chakraborti) *Rural Racism, Responding to Hate Crime*: *The Case for Connecting Policy and Research*, and *Hate Crime: Impact, Causes, and Consequences* (now onto its second edition). He has also had numerous journal articles and reports published on issues of racism, the far right, hate crime, policing, cultural criminology and identity.

Mark Gilman has spent more than 30 years working in addictions research, policy and practice. Mark is the Managing Director of Discovering Health (www.discoveringhealth.co.uk), a company providing consultancy services to commissioners and providers of recovery-oriented systems of addiction care. Mark has a first degree in Organisation Theory and an MA in the study of Drugs, Crime and Social Deviance. Until July 2015, Mark was the Strategic Recovery Lead for Substance Misuse in Public Health England and advised NHS England and the UK Ministry of Justice on the implementation of the substance misuse elements of the 'Through the Prison Gate' programme.

Dick Hobbs is currently Professor of Sociology at the University of Western Sydney, Emeritus Professor at the University of Essex, Visiting Professor at Goldsmiths College, and an Associate Fellow at the Royal United Services Institute. His most recent books are *Lush Life: Constructing Organised Crime in the UK* (Oxford, 2013), and *Policing the 2012 London Olympics: Legacy and Social Exclusion* (with Gary Armstrong and Richard Giulianotti—Routledge, 2016).

Calum Jeffray is a Research Fellow within the National Security & Resilience studies programme at the Royal United Services Institute (RUSI). He conducts research and analysis on a broad range of subject areas, including cyber security, surveillance, counter-terrorism and counter–violent extremism, and organised crime within the UK. He has undertaken research projects on behalf of the European Commission as well as the British, Canadian and Danish governments. Before joining the Institute, Calum organised security and defence conferences for an international events company. He completed his MPhil in International Relations at the University of Cambridge, where his dissertation examined the role of international organisations in improving cyber security. He also holds a first-class MA in French from the University of St Andrews.

Deborah Jump is a lecturer in criminology at Manchester Metropolitan University, and has more than ten years' experience working in youth justice as both a practitioner and service manager. She has implemented sporting programmes such as Splash and Positive Futures, and was the recipient of a Winston Churchill Memorial Fund grant evaluating the impact of sporting programmes on communities in the United States. Deborah's current research focuses on sport and desistance from crime, and she has recently completed an ethnography looking at the impact of boxing on young offenders' attitudes towards violent crime. She has published on qualitative research methods and national sporting policy evaluation.

Brendan Marsh is a final-year PhD research student in Queens University, Belfast. His self-funded ethnography seeks to understand the role of violence in the relationships, interactions and transactions in the illegal drug market in Dublin. Brendan has worked in various positions in Dublin with young drug users, addicts and people seeking recovery from addiction.

Kenny Monrose is visiting lecturer in Sociology at the University of East London. He spent many years as a 'black' London taxi driver before graduating both as an undergraduate and post-graduate in criminology at Middlesex University, London. He obtained an MA in criminological research and a PhD in sociology at the University of Essex. His doctorate examined narratives of second-generation African British Caribbean men in post-industrial East London. His research interests include ethnicity, race and gender, criminal justice, organised crime and criminological theory.

Alice Sampson is a criminologist and co-director of the Centre for Social Justice and Change, School of Social Sciences, University of East London. Alice specialises in community-based research and the prevention of violent crimes against women, children and minority ethnic groups, and understanding how social policies and institutions can better contribute to improving the lives of those who are most oppressed.

Daniel Silverstone is head of the John Grieve Centre for Policing and the head of the criminology subject area at London Metropolitan University. His research interests include organised crime, 'gangs' and the policing of organised crime.

Matthew Taylor has studied at both London South Bank University and the University of Kent. His interests include illicit drug markets and subcultural movements, such as the London free party scene. Matthew's first publication focused on the importance of friendship and trust within drug distribution circles. His current research looks at interactions between security and police at illegal raves in London. Matthew hopes to conduct future research on raves in mainland Europe.

James Treadwell is a lecturer in Criminology at Birmingham Law School, University of Birmingham. He researches and teaches in the areas of Criminology and Criminal Justice, with particular expertise in topics of professional and organised crime, violent crime and victimisation. He is the author of *Criminology* (Sage) and the revised and updated *Criminology: The Essentials* (Sage). He edited (with Matt Hopkins) *Football Hooliganism, Fan Behaviour and Crime: Contemporary Issues* (Palgrave Macmillan) and authored (with Simon Winlow, Steve Hall and Daniel Briggs) *Riots and Political Protest: Notes from* *the Post-Political Present* (Routledge). He was the first criminologist to undertake empirical research with former military personnel in UK prisons (for the Howard League for Penal Reform) and has recently been undertaking prison ethnography on violence and bullying.

Jenni Ward is a senior lecturer in criminology at Middlesex University, London. Before joining Middlesex, Jenni was an academic researcher at Goldsmiths College and Imperial College. Jenni's earlier research centred on young people growing up in state care, illicit drug use and youth transitions to adulthood; research she jointly held Economic and Social Research Council (ESRC) and Home Office funding awards with Geoffrey Pearson. Her current research is on 'lay magistracy' and transformations to summary justice in the lower criminal courts, criminal court sentencing and drug law enforcement. She is the author of several journal papers, the book *Flashback: Drugs and Dealing in the Golden Age of the London Rave Scene* and is writing a book for Routledge's 'Frontiers of Criminal Justice Series'.

Andrew Wilson is senior lecturer in criminology at Nottingham Trent University. He is the author of *Northern Soul* (Willan, 2007). His research has centred on drugs and on community policing issues, with emphasis on the inter-relationship between the responses to social problems and its impact on marginalised groups. After leaving school with no qualifications at the age of 15, he spent the next ten years involved in subculturally related crime. He sits on the Welsh Government's Advisory Panel on Substance Misuse.

Geoffrey Pearson

Published Work

I Books and Monographs

G. PEARSON (1975) *The Deviant Imagination*, Basingstoke: Macmillan. 258pp.

G. MUNGHAM and G. PEARSON eds. (1976) *Working Class Youth Culture*, London: Routledge. 167pp.

G. PEARSON (1976) *Het Ongekamde Denken*, Amsterdam: Boom Meppel. 262pp.

G. PEARSON (1983) *Hooligan: A History of Respectable Fears*, Basingstoke: Macmillan. 275pp.

G. PEARSON, M. GILMAN and S. McIVER (1987) *Young People and Heroin*, Aldershot: Gower. 65pp.

G. PEARSON (1987) *The New Heroin Users*. Oxford: Blackwell. 194pp.

G. PEARSON, J. TRESEDER and M. YELLOLY eds. (1988) *Social Work and the Legacy of Freud*, Basingstoke: Macmillan. 236pp.

G. PEARSON and A. DAVIES eds. (1999) *Histories of Crime and Modernity*. Special issue of the *British Journal of Criminology*, 39(1), 174.

A. MARLOW and G. PEARSON eds. (1999) *Young People, Drugs and Community Safety*, Lyme Regis: Russell House, 170pp.

G. PEARSON ed. (1999) *Drugs at the End of the Century*. Special issue of the *British Journal of Criminology*, 39(4), 189pp.

G. PEARSON and D. HOBBS (2001) *Middle Market Drug Distribution*. Home Office Research Study 227, London: Home Office, 82pp.

J. WARD, Z. HENDERSON and G. PEARSON (2003) *One Problem Among Many: Drug Use Among Care Leavers in Transition to Independent Living*. Home Office Research Study 260, London: Home Office, 82pp.

II Research Reports

G. PEARSON (1978) *Public Attitudes Towards Vandalism: A Report to the Crime Prevention Panel of Bradford Police*, Wakefield: West Yorkshire Police.

G. PEARSON, M. GILMAN and S. McIVER (1985) *Young People and Heroin: An Examination of Heroin Use in the North of England*. Research Report No. 8, London: Health Education Council.

G. PEARSON and D. LAISTER (1988) *Hammersmith and Fulham Drug and Alcohol Survey: Final Report*, London Borough of Hammersmith and Fulham.

H.S. MIRZA, G. PEARSON and S. PHILLIPS (1991) *Drugs, People and Services in Lewisham: Final Report of the Drug Information Project*, London: Lewisham Safer Cities Project.

D.E. LAWRENCE, G. PEARSON and C. AINA (1992) *Black Offenders Project: Report to the Inner London Probation Service*, London: Goldsmiths College.

K. PATEL, G. PEARSON and F. KAHN (1994) *Outreach Work Among Asian Drug Injectors in Bradford: A Report to the Mental Health Foundation*, Bradford: Bridge Project and London: Goldsmiths College.

G. PEARSON (1994) *UK Government's Drug Misuse Research Agenda: Drug Misuse and Family Life, Lifestyle, Employment and Crime*. Position paper commissioned by the Home Office Research and Planning Unit.

G. PEARSON (1995) *Drug Treatment and Crime Reduction*. Research review commissioned by the Department of Health Task Force on Services for Drug Misusers.

G. PEARSON (1995) *Exploration of the Untreated Condition*. Review commissioned by the Department of Health Task Force on Services for Drug Misusers.

E. BURNEY and G. PEARSON (1995) *Crime, Mental Health and the Inner City: The Experience of the Islington Mentally Disordered Offenders Project*. A report to the Mental After-Care Association and the Inner London Probation Service, London: Goldsmiths College.

G. PEARSON (1996) *Drug Prevention Among Racially and Culturally Diverse Groups: An Action-Research Strategy*. Commissioned by the Central Drugs Prevention Unit, Home Office.

G. PEARSON (1996) *Drug Misuse and the Environment: A Research Review*. Commissioned by the Advisory Council on the Misuse of Drugs Working Group on Prevention, Home Office.

III Chapters in Books

G. PEARSON (1972) 'Comment on N. Moray, "Models in Experimental Psychology"', in T. Shanin (ed) *The Rules of the Game: Cross-Disciplinary Essays on Models in Scholarly Thought*. London: Tavistock.

G. PEARSON (1974) 'Prisons of Love: The Reification of the Family in Family Therapy', in N. Armistead (ed) *Reconstructing Social Psychology*. Harmondsworth: Penguin.

G. PEARSON (1975) 'Misfit Sociology and the Politics of Socialization', in I. Taylor, P. Walton and J. Young (eds) *Critical Criminology*. London: Routledge.

G. PEARSON (1975) 'The Politics of Uncertainty: A Study in the Socialization of the Social Worker', in H. Jones (ed) *Towards a New Social Work*. London: Routledge.

G. PEARSON (1976) 'In Defence of Hooliganism: Social Theory and Violence', in Department of Health and Social Security, *Violence*. London: HMSO.

G. PEARSON (1976) '"Paki-Bashing" in a North East Lancashire Cotton Town: A Case Study and Its History', in G. Mungham and G. Pearson (eds) *Working Class Youth Culture*. London: Routledge.

G. PEARSON (1976) 'Making Social Workers: Bad Promises and Good Omens', in R. Bailey and M. Brake (eds) *Radical Social Work*. London: Edward Arnold.

G. PEARSON (1977) 'Devianza e Politica', in M. Ciacci and V. Gualandi (eds) *La Construzione Sociale della Devianza*. Milan: Il Mulino.

G. PEARSON and J. TWOHIG (1977) 'Ethnography Through the Looking Glass: The Case of Howard Becker', in S. Hall and T. Jefferson (eds) *Resistance Through Rituals*. London: Hutchinson.

G. PEARSON (1978) 'Welfare on the Move, 1945–1975', in Open University, *Social Work, Community Work and Society*, Block 1, Course DE206. Milton Keynes: The Open University.

G. PEARSON and L. HEMINGWAY (1978) 'Psychiatry and Society', in Open University, *Social Work, Community Work and Society*, Block 7, Course DE206. Milton Keynes: The Open University.

G. PEARSON (1979) 'Goths and Vandals: Crime in History', in S. L. Messinger and E. Bittner (eds) *Criminology Review Yearbook*. Los Angeles: Sage Publications.

G. PEARSON (1979) 'Resistance to the Machine', in H. Nowotny and H. Rose (eds) *Counter-Movements in the Sciences: Sociology of Science Yearbook 1979*. Dordrecht: Reidel.

G. PEARSON (1981) 'Goths and Vandals—Crime in History', in D. F. Greenberg (ed) *Crime and Capitalism: Readings in Marxist Criminology*. Palo Alto: Mayfield.

G. PEARSON (1982) 'The Sociology of Deviance and Social Control', in A. Hartnett (ed) *The Social Sciences in Educational Studies*. London: Heinemann.

G. PEARSON (1983) 'The Question of Social Change: Crime and Cultural Dislocation', in Centro Internazionale di Richerche e Studi Sociologici Penali e Penitenziari di Messina, *Cultura e Criminalita: Anomia, Alienazione e Delitto*. Milan: Dott A. Giuffre Editore.

G. PEARSON (1984) 'Falling Standards: A Short, Sharp History of Moral Decline', in M. Barker (ed) *The Video Nasties: Freedom and Censorship in the Media*. London: Pluto.

G. PEARSON (1986) 'Developing a Local Research Strategy', in P. Wedge (ed) *Social Work: Research into Practice*. Birmingham: BASW.

G. PEARSON (1986) 'Perpetual Novelty: A History of Generational Conflicts in Britain', in D. Dowe (ed) *Jugendprotest und Generationenkonflikt in Europe im 20 Jahrhundert*. Bonn: Verlag Neue Gesellschaft.

G. PEARSON (1987) 'Short Memories: Street Violence in the Past and in the Present', in E. Moonman (ed) *The Violent Society*. London: Frank Cass.

G. PEARSON (1987) 'From Hooliganism to Heroin: The Social Context of Violence', in *Facing the Future: Report of a Seminar on Inner City Crisis*. Wakefield: HM Prison Service.

G. PEARSON (1987) 'Social Deprivation, Unemployment and Patterns of Heroin Use', in N. Dorn and N. South (eds) *A Land Fit for Heroin? Drug Policies, Prevention and Practice*. Basingstoke: Macmillan.

G. PEARSON (1987) 'Drug Use and Misuse', in The Open University and the Health Education Authority, *Drug Use and Misuse*. Milton Keynes: Open University Press.

G. PEARSON, M. GILMAN and S. McIVER (1987) 'Becoming a Heroin User and Heroin Using Careers', in T. Heller, M. Gott and C. Jeffery (eds) *Drug Use and Misuse. A Reader*. New York: John Wiley.

H. BLAGG, G. PEARSON, A. SAMPSON, D. SMITH and P. STUBBS (1988) 'Inter-Agency Cooperation: Rhetoric and Reality', in T. Hope and M. Shaw (eds) *Communities and Crime Reduction*. London: HMSO.

G. PEARSON (1988) 'Substance Abuse', in E. Monck (ed) *Emotional and Behavioural Problems in Adolescents: A Multidisciplinary Approach to Identification and Management*. London: NFER-Nelson.

G. PEARSON (1988) 'The New Heroin Problem in Britain', in G. A. El Azayem (ed) *Proceedings of the Cairo World Congress for Mental Health*. Cairo: World Federation of Mental Health.

G. PEARSON (1988) 'Custody for Juveniles: The Way Ahead', in *Diversion from Custody: The Proceedings of a Seminar*. London: The Children's Society.

G. PEARSON (1988) 'Developing a Local Research Strategy', in B. Broad (ed) *Enquiries into Community Probation Work*. Cranfield: Cranfield Press.

G. PEARSON (1988) 'Britain: A Violent Society?', in Open University, *Social Problems and Social Welfare*, Block 5, Course D211. Milton Keynes: The Open University Press.

G. PEARSON (1989) ' "A Jekyll in the Classroom, a Hyde in the Street": Queen Victoria's Hooligans', in D. Downes (ed) *Crime in the City: Essays in Honour of J. B. Mays*. Basingstoke: Macmillan.

G. PEARSON (1989) 'Social Work and Unemployment', in M. Langan and P. Lee (eds) *Radical Social Work Today*. London: Hutchinson.

G. PEARSON (1989) 'Heroin Use in Its Social Context', in D. T. Herbert and D. M. Smith (eds) *Social Problems and the City*. Oxford: Oxford University Press.

G. PEARSON, A. SAMPSON, H. BLAGG, P. STUBBS and D. SMITH (1989) 'Policing Racism', in R. Morgan and D. J. Smith (eds) *Coming to Terms with Policing*. London: Routledge.

G. PEARSON (1989) 'Women and Men Without Work: The Political Economy is Personal', in C. Rojek, G. Peacock and S. Collins (eds) *A Haunt of Misery: Critical Essays in Social Work and Helping*. London: Routledge.

G. PEARSON (1990) 'Drugs, Law Enforcement and Criminology', in V. Berridge (ed) *Drugs Research and Policy in Britain*. Aldershot: Gower/Avebury.

G. PEARSON (1990) 'Identifying Social Risk Factors', in H. A. Ghodse, C. D. Kaplan and R. D. Mann (eds) *Drug Misuse and Dependence*. New Jersey: Parthenon.

G. PEARSON (1991) 'Drug Problems and Social Work', in P. Carter, T. Jeffs and M. K. Smith (eds) *Social Work and Social Welfare Yearbook 3*. Milton Keynes: Open University Press.

A. SAMPSON, D. SMITH, G. PEARSON, H. BLAGG and P. STUBBS (1991) 'Gender Issues in Inter-Agency Relations: Police, Probation and Social Services', in P. Abbott and C. Wallace (eds) *Gender, Sexuality and Power*. Basingstoke: Macmillan.

M. GILMAN and G. PEARSON (1991) 'Lifestyle and Law Enforcement', in P. Bean and D. K. Whynes (eds) *Policing and Prescribing: The British System of Drug Control*. Basingstoke: Macmillan.

G. PEARSON (1991) 'Drug Control Policies in Britain', in M. Tonry (ed) *Crime and Justice: A Review of Research*, vol. 14. Chicago: University of Chicago Press.

G. PEARSON (1991) 'The Local Nature of Drug Problems', in T. Bennett (ed) *Drug Misuse in Local Communities: Perspectives Across Europe*. London: The Police Foundation.

H.S. MIRZA, S. PHILLIPS and G. PEARSON (1991) 'Drug Misuse in a South London Borough', in T. Bennett (ed) *Drug Misuse in Local Communities: Perspectives Across Europe*. London: The Police Foundation.

G. PEARSON, J. DITTON, R. NEWCOMBE and M. GILMAN (1991) 'MDMA/Ecstasy: New Wave of Drug Use', in *Drug Misuse in Britain 1991: National Audit of Drug Misuse Statistics*. London: Institute for the Study of Drug Dependence.

G. PEARSON (1992) 'Drugs and Criminal Justice: A Harm Reduction Perspective', in P. A. O'Hare, R. Newcombe, A. Matthews, E. C. Buning and E. Drucker (eds) *The Reduction of Drug-Related Harm*. London: Routledge.

G. PEARSON (1992) 'The Role of Culture in the Drug Question', in G. Edwards, M. Lader and C. Drummond (eds) *The Nature of Drug and Alcohol Problems*. Society for the Study of Addiction Monograph No. 2. Oxford: Oxford University Press.

G. PEARSON, H. BLAGG, D. SMITH, A. SAMPSON and P. STUBBS (1992) 'Crime, Community and Conflict: The Multi-Agency Approach', in D. Downes (ed) *Unravelling Criminal Justice: Eleven British Studies*. Basingstoke: Macmillan.

G. PEARSON (1992) 'Misunderstanding Foucault', in A. Still and I. Velody (eds) *Rewriting the History of Madness: Studies in Foucault's Histoire de la Folie*. London: Routledge.

J. AWAIAH, S. BUTT, N. DORN, K. PATEL and G. PEARSON (1992) 'Introduction', in J. Awaiah, S. Butt and N. Dorn (eds) *Race, Gender and Drug Services*. ISDD Research Monograph No. 6. London: Institute for the Study of Drug Dependence.

G. PEARSON, H. S. MIRZA and S. PHILLIPS (1993) 'Cocaine in Context: Findings from a South London Inner-City Drug Survey', in P. Bean (ed) *Cocaine and Crack: Supply and Use*. Basingstoke: Macmillan.

G. PEARSON (1993) 'Varieties of Ethnography: Limits and Possibilities in the Field of Illegal Drug Use', in H. F. L. Garretsen, L. A. M. Van de Goor, C. D. Kaplan, D. J. Korf, I. P. Spruit and W. M. de Zwart (eds) *Illegal Drug Use: Research Methods for Hidden Populations*. Proceedings of EV Invited Expert meeting. Rotterdam: Nederlands Institut voor Alcohol en Drugs.

G. PEARSON (1993) 'Talking a Good Fight: Authenticity and Distance in the Ethnographer's Craft', Foreword to D. Hobbs and T. May (eds) *Interpreting the Field: Accounts of Ethnography*. Oxford: Clarendon Press.

G. PEARSON and M. GILMAN (1994) 'Local and Regional Variations in Drug Misuse: The British Heroin Epidemic of the 1980s', in J. Strang and M. Gossop (eds) *Heroin Addiction and Drug Policy: The British System*. Oxford: Oxford University Press.

G. PEARSON (1994) 'Youth, Crime and Society', in M. Maguire, R. Morgan and R. Reiner (eds) *The Oxford Handbook of Criminology*, 1st edn. Oxford: Oxford University Press.

G. PEARSON (1995) 'Moral Panics, Moral Dilemmas and Moral Progress', in P. Neate (ed) *Scare in the Community: Britain in a Moral Panic*. London: Community Care Press.

G. PEARSON (1995) 'The War on Words: Reflections on the American War on Drugs', in N. South (ed) *Drugs, Crime and Criminal Justice*, vol. 1. Aldershot: Dartmouth.

G. PEARSON (1995) 'Drug Problems and Criminal Justice Policy in Britain', in N. South (ed) *Drugs, Crime and Criminal Justice*, vol. 2. Aldershot: Dartmouth.

G. PEARSON (1995) 'Drugs and Deprivation', in J. W. T. Dickerson and G. V. Stimson (eds) *Health in the Inner City: Drugs in the City*. Supplement to the *Journal of the Royal Society of Health*. London: Royal Society of Health.

G. PEARSON (1995) 'City of Darkness, City of Light: Crime, Drugs and Disorder in London and New York', in S. MacGregor and A. Lipow (eds) *The Other City: People and Politics in New York and London*. New Jersey: Humanities Press.

G. PEARSON (1997) 'Victorian Boys, We Are Here!', in K. Gelder and S. Thornton (eds) *The Subcultures Reader*. London: Routledge.

J. WARD and G. PEARSON (1997) 'Recreational Drug Use and Drug Dealing in London: An Ethnographic Study', in D. Korf and H. Riper (eds) *Illicit Drug Use in Europe*. Amsterdam: University of Amsterdam.

G. PEARSON (1999) 'Madness and Moral Panics', in N. Eastman and J. Peay (eds) *Law Without Enforcement: The Marginal Contribution of Law to Mental Health*. Oxford: Hart Publishing.

G. PEARSON (1999) 'Drug Policy Dilemmas: Social Exclusion, Partnership and Targeting Resources'. in A. Marlow and G. Pearson (eds) *Young People, Drugs and Community Safety*. Lyme Regis: Russell House.

A. DAVIES and G. PEARSON (1999) 'Introduction' to *Histories of Crime and Modernity*, Special issue of the *British Journal of Criminology*, 39(1).

G. PEARSON (2001) 'Drugs and Poverty', in S. Chen and E. Skidelsky (eds) *High Time for Reform: Drug Policy for the 21st Century*. London: Social Market Foundation.

G. PEARSON (2002) 'Victorian Boys, We Are Here!', in Y. Jewkes and G. Letherby (eds) *Criminology: A Reader*. London: Sage Publications.

G. PEARSON (2002) 'Youth Crime and Moral Decline', in J. Muncie, G. Hughes and E. McLaughlin (eds) *Youth Justice: Critical Readings*. London: Sage Publications.

G. PEARSON and M. GILMAN (2005) 'Drug Epidemics in Space and Time: Local Diversity, Subcultures and Social Exclusion', in J. Strang and M. Gossop (eds) *Heroin Addiction and the British System*. London: Routledge.

M. LAWRENCE and G. PEARSON (2007) 'Forever Young: Not Psychoanalysing Bob Dylan', in C. Bainbridge, S. Radstone, M. Rustin and C. Yates (eds) *Culture and the Unconscious*, London: Palgrave.

G. PEARSON (2007) 'Drug Markets and Dealing: From "Street Dealer" to "Mr. Big"', in M. Simpson, T. Sheldrick and R. MacDonald (eds) *Drugs in Britain: Supply, Consumption and Control*. London: Palgrave.

G. PEARSON (2009) '"A Jekyll in the Classroom, a Hyde in the Street": Queen Victoria's Hooligans', in A. Millie (ed) *Securing Respect: Behavioural Expectations and Anti-Social Behaviour in the United Kingdom*. London: Policy Press.

G. PEARSON (2011) 'Perpetual Novelty: Youth, Modernity and Historical Amnesia', in B. Goldson (ed) *Youth in Crisis? 'Gangs', Territoriality and Violence*. London: Routledge.

G. PEARSON (2012) 'Everything Changes, Nothing Moves: The Longue Durée of Social Anxieties about Youth Crime', in D. Briggs (ed) *The English Riots of 2011. A Summer of Discontent*. Hook, Hampshire: Waterside Press.

IV Journal Articles

G. PEARSON (1973) 'Social Work as the Privatised Solution to Public Ills', *British Journal of Social Work*, vol. 3, no. 2 [Reprinted in P. Halmos et al. eds., *Welfare in Action*, London: Routledge, 1978.]

G. PEARSON and J. TWOHIG (1976) 'Ethnography Through the Looking Glass: The Case of Howard Becker', *Working Papers in Cultural Studies*, vol. 7/8. [Reprinted in S. Hall and T. Jefferson eds., *Resistance through Rituals*, London: Hutchinson, 1977.]

G. PEARSON (1976) 'Eighteenth Century English Criminal Law: A Review Article', *British Journal of Law and Society*, vol. 3, no. 1.

G. PEARSON (1977) 'Goten und Vandalen: Verbrechen in Historischer Perspektive', *Kriminologisches Journal*, vol. 9, no. 4.

G. PEARSON (1978) 'Leisure, Popular Culture and Street Games: A Broken Dialogue Between Youth and Age', *Youth and Society*, no. 30.

G. PEARSON (1978) 'Coths and Vandals: Crime in History', *Contemporary Crises*, vol. 2, no. 2. [Reprinted in S. L. Messinger and E. Bittner eds., *Criminology Review Yearbook*, Los Angeles: Sage, 1979; and in D. F. Greenberg ed., *Crime and Capitalism: Readings in Marxist Criminology*, Palo Alto: Mayfield, 1981.]

G. PEARSON (1980) 'Resistenza Alle Macchine', *La Questione Criminale*, vol. 6, no. 1.

G. PEARSON (1981) 'Youth and the Streets: A Historical Note on the Contemporary Preoccupation with Troublesome Youth', *Leisure Studies Quarterly*, vol. 2, no. 4. [Reprinted in the YMCA Youth and Community Work course, distance learning materials.]

G. PEARSON (1983) 'From Hooligans to Heroes', *New Society*, vol. 64, no. 1076. [Reprinted in Open University, *Preparing for the Social Science Foundation Course*, The Open University, 1985.]

G. PEARSON (1983) 'The Barclay Report and Community Social Work', *Critical Social Policy*, vol. 2, no. 3.

G. PEARSON (1984) 'Hooligans in History', *History Today*, vol. 34, May, Supplement.

G. PEARSON (1984) 'Present Tense, Past Perfect: The History of Street Crime', *Christian Action Journal*, Summer 1984.

G. PEARSON (1985) 'Lawlessness, Modernity and Social Change', *Theory, Culture and Society*, vol. 2, no. 3.

G. PEARSON (1986) 'Heroin and Diversity', *Drug Questions: Institute for the Study of Drug Dependence Research Register*, no. 2.

G. PEARSON, M. GILMAN and S. McIVER (1986) 'Heroin Use in the North of England', *Health Education Journal*, vol. 45, no. 3.

G. PEARSON, M. GILMAN and S. McIVER (1987) 'Responses to Heroin Misuse: Working Together', *Druglink*, vol. 2, no. 1.

G. PEARSON (1987) 'Tid Och Otid, Da Och Nu: Ungdomsvaldets Historia', *Uppväxtvillkor*, no. 2/1987.

G. PEARSON (1988) 'Hooligans and Youthful Crime: "Permissiveness" and Tradition', *Social Studies Review*, vol. 3, no. 4.

A. SAMPSON, P. STUBBS, D. SMITH, G. PEARSON and H. BLAGG (1988) 'Crime, Localities and the Multi-Agency Approach', *British Journal of Criminology*, vol. 28, no. 4.

G. PEARSON (1988) 'The Roots of Violence', *British Medical Journal*, vol. 297, 26 November 1988.

G. PEARSON (1989) 'The Street Connection', *New Statesman and Society*, 15 September 1989.

G. PEARSON, M. GILMAN and P. TRAYNOR (1990) 'Cyclizine Misuse: The Limits of Intervention', *Druglink*, vol. 5, no. 3.

G. PEARSON (1990) Translation with an Introduction of B. Le Gendre, 'La Drogue Dans Tous Ses États', *International Journal on Drug Policy*, vol. 1, no.4.

G. PEARSON (1990) 'Crime and Criminology in Israel', *British Journal of Criminology*, vol. 30, no. 2.

G. PEARSON, H. S. MIRZA, N. DORN, J. AWIAH, S. BUTT and S. PHIL- LIPS (1990) 'Black People and Drug Use', *British Journal of Addiction*, vol. 85, no. 11.

G. PEARSON (1990) 'Misunderstanding Foucault', *History of the Human Sci- ences*, vol. 3, no. 3.

G. PEARSON, J. DITTON, R. NEWCOMBE and M. GILMAN (1991) 'Every- thing Starts with an "E": An Introduction to Ecstasy Use by Young People in Britain', *Druglink*, vol. 6, no. 6.

G. PEARSON (1992) 'Drug Problems and Criminal Justice Policy in Brit- ain', *Contemporary Drug Problems*, vol. 19, no. 2. [Reprinted in N. South ed., *Drugs, Crime and Criminal Justice*, vol. 2. Aldershot: Dartmouth, 1995.]

G. PEARSON (1992) 'The War on Words: Reflections on the American War on Drugs', *Journal of Research in Crime and Delinquency*, vol. 29, no. 3. [Reprinted in N. South ed., *Drugs, Crime and Criminal Justice*, vol. 1. Aldershot: Dartmouth, 1995.]

G. PEARSON (1993) 'Pharmacology and Fashion: The Uses and Misuses of Cultural Relativism in Drug Policy Analysis', *European Journal on Crimi- nal Policy and Research*, vol. 1, no. 2.

G. PEARSON (1993) 'Youth Crime and Moral Decline', *The Magistrate*, vol. 49, no. 10. [Reprinted in J. Muncie et al., eds., *Youth Justice: Critical Readings*, London: Sage, 2002.]

G. PEARSON and D. E. LAWRENCE (1995) 'Race and Ethnic Monitoring: How Not To Do It', *Criminal Justice*, vol. 13, no. 1.

G. PEARSON (1995) 'Crime and Social Exclusion' *Criminal Justice Matters*, no. 18.

E. BURNEY and G. PEARSON (1995) 'Mentally Disordered Offenders: Find- ing a Focus for Diversion', *Howard Journal of Criminal Justice*, vol. 34, no. 4.

G. PEARSON (1995) 'The Quantitative-Qualitative Dispute: An Unhelpful Divide, But One To Be Lived With', *Addiction*, vol. 99, no. 6.

G. PEARSON and K. PATEL (1998) 'Drugs, Deprivation and Ethnicity: Out- reach Among Asian Drug Users in a Northern English City', *Journal of Drug Issues*, vol. 28, no. 1.

G. PEARSON (2000) 'Une Semi-Profession Bat en Retraite? Histoire de la Formation Professionelle des Travailleurs Sociaux en Grande-Bretagne', *Vie Sociale*, no. 2/2000—Mars–Avril.

G. PEARSON (2000) 'Substance Abuse and the Family', *Current Opinion in Psychiatry*, vol. 13.

G. PEARSON (2001) 'Normal Drug Use: Ethnographic Fieldwork Among an Adult Network of Recreational Drug Users in Inner London', *Substance Use and Misuse*, vol. 36, nos. 1&2.

G. PEARSON and M. SHINER (2002) 'Rethinking the Generation Gap: Attitudes to Illicit Drugs Among Young People and Adults', *Criminal Justice*, vol. 2, no. 1.

S. M. BIRD, G. PEARSON and J. STRANG (2002) 'Rationale and Cost-Efficiency Compared for Urine or Saliva Testing and Behavioural Inquiry among UK Offender Populations: Injectors, Arrestees and Prisoners', *Journal of Cancer Epidemiology and Prevention* (formerly the *Journal of Epidemiological Studies*), vol. 7, no. 1.

G. PEARSON (2002) 'Introduction: Crime and Criminology in China', *British Journal of Criminology*, vol. 42, no. 2.

G. PEARSON and D. HOBBS (2003) 'King Pin? A Case Study of a Middle Market Drug Broker', *Howard Journal of Criminal Justice*, vol. 42, no. 4.

G. PEARSON and D. HOBBS (2004) 'E is for Enterprise: Middle Level Drug Markets in Ecstasy and Stimulants', *Addiction Research and Theory*, vol. 12, no. 6.

G. PEARSON (2006) 'Disturbing Continuities: "Peaky Blinders" to "Hoodies" ', *Criminal Justice Matters*, Autumn, no. 65. [Reprinted in the *Guardian*.]

G. PEARSON (2007) 'Lead Editorial: Policing Cannabis in the United Kingdom', *Addiction*, vol. 102, no. 8, pp. 1175–1177.

G. PEARSON (2008) 'Évolution des Problèmes Liés à la Toxicomanie et des Politiques Relatives aux Drogues au Royaume-Uni', *Deviance et Société*, vol. 32, no. 3, pp. 251–266.

G. PEARSON (2009) 'Entwicklungen von Dropenproblemen und Drogenpolitik in Großbritannien'. *Soziale Probleme*, vol. 1, no. 2, pp. 37–56.

Geoffrey Pearson

Research, Consultancy and Other Professional Experience

1973–1976   Visiting Lecturer, Department of Health and Social Security, Social Work Services Development Group, Seminars on Violence.

1974–1976   Consultant, NACRO Inter-Professional Crime Prevention Conferences and NACRO Research Group.

1978–1988   Associate Editor, *Children and Youth Services Review* (USA).

1979   Consultant, Social Science Research Council Psychology Committee, Working Group on Juvenile Crime.

1980–1994   Editorial Board and later Associate Editor, *Contemporary Crises: Crime, Law and Social Change* (USA).

1980–1989   Visiting Lecturer, Police Staff College, Bramshill. Junior Command, Intermediate Command and Senior Command courses.

1981–1987   Editorial Board, *Critical Social Policy* (UK).

1985–1986   'Young People and Heroin Use in the North of England', funded by the Health Education Council, £24,000.

1985–1987   'Crime, Community and the Inter-Agency Dimension', funded by the Economic and Social Research Council, £96,898.

1986   Consultant to ESRC research initiative on Drugs and Addictions, responsible for the position paper on 'Law Enforcement, Criminological and Penal Aspects'.

1986–1989   Council Member, Central Council for Education and Training in Social Work.

1986–1989   Academic Advisor to the 'Drug Enforcement Strategies and Intelligence Needs' research project, undertaken on behalf of the National Drugs Intelligence Unit and the Association of Chief Police Officers, funded by the Police Foundation.

1986–1992   National Council, British Society of Criminology.

1987–1988   Member of the Church of England Children's Society Advisory Committee on Penal Custody and Its Alternatives for Juveniles.

1987–1988   'Drug and Alcohol Survey', funded by the London Borough of Hammersmith and Fulham, £19, 365.

1987–1989   Consultant to the Mental Health Foundation, 'Drug Abuse Research Team' project, 'Problematic Drug Use in SW5'.

1988–2008	Member of the Council of Management, Bishop Ho Ming Wah Association, St. Martin-in-the-Fields, London.
1988–1998	Editorial Board and Associate Editor, *British Journal of Criminology*. (Subsequently, Editor-in-Chief.)
1989–1991	Research Consultant, 'Black Outreach Drugs Services' project, Institute for the Study of Drug Dependence, funded by the Home Office.
1990–1995	Editorial Advisory Board, *Prison Writing*.
1990–2000	Editorial Board, *International Journal on Drug Policy*.
1990–2013	Editorial Board, *Howard Journal of Criminal Justice* (UK).
1990–1992	Member of the Human Behaviour and Development Research Development Group, and the Evaluation Steering Committee, Economic and Social Research Council.
1990	'Drug Information Project', commissioned by the Lewisham Safer Cities Project, funded by the Home Office, £24,900.
1990–1992	'The Development of Community Mental Health Services in Poland', in collaboration with the Copernican Jagiellonian University, Krakov, funded by the Wates Foundation, £44,000.
1991–1992	'Black Offenders Project', commissioned by the Inner London Probation Service, funded by the Islington Safer Cities Project and the Home Office, £27,000.
1991–1993	'Insight: Young Offenders Project', funded by the Home Office and the Halley Stewart Trust, £55,750. (With D. E. Lawrence.)
1992–1994	Research Consultant, 'Asian Drug Injectors Outreach Project', Bradford Bridge Project, funded by the Mental Health Foundation and the Home Office.
1992–1998	Commissioning Panel and Steering Committee of the Economic and Social Research Council research programme 'Crime and Social Order'.
1992–1995	Member of the Research Programmes Board, Economic and Social Research Council.
1993–2007	Vice-Chair, Institute for the Study of Drug Dependence, later DrugScope.
1993–1995	'Islington Mentally Disordered Offenders Project', commissioned by the Inner London Probation Service, funded by the Islington Safer Cities Project and the Mental After-Care Association, £49,000.
1994	Research Consultant to the UK Government's Drug Misuse Research Agenda, on 'Drug Misuse and Family Life, Lifestyle, Employment and Crime', funded by the Home Office Research and Planning Unit.
1995–1996	Member of the Steering Group of the Parliamentary Office of Science and Technology, 'Common Illegal Drugs and Their Effects'.

1996	Research Consultant to the Central Drugs Prevention Unit of the Home Office, on 'Accessing and Engaging with Racially and Culturally Diverse Groups'.
1996	'Drug Misuse and the Environment: A Research Review', commissioned by the Advisory Council on the Misuse of Drugs Working Group on Prevention, Home Office.
1997–2000	Member of the Independent Committee of Inquiry into the Misuse of Drugs Act 1971, sponsored by the Prince's Trust and the Police Foundation.
1998–2006	Editor-in-Chief, *British Journal of Criminology*.
1998–1999	Editorial Board Committee, American Society of Criminology.
1998–2000	Independent Member of the Official Steering Group of the Cabinet Office Cross-Cutting Review of Government Expenditure on Drugs.
1998–2000	Member of the Advisory Council on the Misuse of Drugs Working Group on Reducing Drug Related Deaths.
1998–2000	'Patterns of Drug Use Among Young People in Care', funded by the Economic and Social Research Council, £99,660. (With T. Newburn.)
1999–2004	Commissioning Group, Department of Health Policy Research Programme, Drug Misuse Research Initiative.
2000	'Middle Market Drug Distribution', funded by the Home Office, £86,629 plus travelling expenses, etc. (With D. Hobbs.)
2001–2002	Steering Group, Lambeth Cannabis Warning Pilot Scheme, Metropolitan Police Authority.
2001–2003	'Drug Use Among Care Leavers in Transition to Independent Living', funded by the Home Office, £65,000. (With J. Ward.)
2004	'Tracking Drug Users Leaving Care', Economic and Social Research Council small grant, £24,000. (With J. Ward.)
2005	Member of the Foresight Brain Science, Addiction and Drugs Project, Department of Trade and Industry.
2006–2013	Joint Editor, with Dick Hobbs, of Crime Ethnography Series/ Routledge Advances in Ethnography.
2009–2010	Chair, Independent Commission into the Future of Social Services in Wales, Welsh Assembly.

Introduction
Geoffrey Pearson 1943–2013

Dick Hobbs

Amongst the cacophony of cant and ignorance masquerading as social commentary that followed Britain's 2011 riots, there were few credible voices of
understanding, let alone attempts to place the youthful violence, nihilism and
looting within anything approaching historical perspective. Yet as the usual
clichés were rolled out about the riots being without precedent, and a sure
sign of a radical and dangerous departure from the subservience of the past,
the carefully modulated tones of a 68-year-old ex–grammar school boy from
Accrington came once again to the fore.

Geoff Pearson was born in Manchester, the only son of a Co-op worker and
a local Labour Party activist, and educated at Accrington Grammar School,
where he gained an astonishing five A Levels, including Maths and Further
Maths. At Cambridge University he studied Moral Sciences (philosophy and
psychology), before gaining a Postgraduate Diploma in Sociological Studies
at Sheffield University in 1965. He stayed in Sheffield, first employed as a
social worker, and from 1967 to 1969 as a Psychiatric Social Worker/Mental
Welfare Officer during which time he trained as a psychiatric social worker at
the London School of Economics.

Much of Geoff's early academic career was in social work education and
training, first, from 1969 to 1971 as a Lecturer in Social Work at Sheffield
Polytechnic, and then for five years at University College, Cardiff. While at
Cardiff, Geoff published his first major work, *The Deviant Imagination* (1975).
About a year before he died Geoff expressed to me his 'embarrassment' with
this book, an emotion inspired by his belief that social science should above all
else be empirically based. However, revisiting the book after 40 years confirms
that Geoff's analysis of his own work was due to a typically self-deprecating
tendency. *The Deviant Imagination* has an intellectual breadth exceeding that
of more celebrated products of the National Deviancy Conference (NDC).
Geoff explored the background assumptions and ideological foundations of
a wide range of theories, and while social work, welfare and anti-psychiatry
were themes of the NDC, few of its affiliates articulated their strategic importance to the establishment of deviance as a credible academic space, preferring
a heady cocktail of leftist essences that was to establish an enduring manifesto
for the sociology of deviance within the expanding British university sector.

Geoff located amongst this radical political 'soup' of the 1960s and 1970s, 'snatches of Marx, a romantic mysticism, some shreds of democratic pluralism, and a politically untutored wish to better the condition of all people, everywhere' (1975: 143), while simultaneously highlighting the influence of libertarians such as Thomas Szasz. In doing so he flagged some contradictory aspects of the NDC era, an era which within contemporary criminology is often reduced to a simplistic Handbook friendly karaoke.

Geoff was well qualified to address psychiatry, anti-psychiatry and social work, and with an explicit focus upon *social practice* he provided a rigorous and wide-ranging critique of the complex, contradictory and largely ignored theoretical arguments implicit to what was to become the orthodoxy of the sociology of deviance. He also unpacked some of the influential social theories that were to be subsequently popularised during the next 40 years. Long before the academic community deified Foucault, he offered a distinctly pragmatic, non–fan-boy utility of 'the archaeology of knowledge', and most significantly in relation to his subsequent career, *The Deviant Imagination* established historical precedents for many contemporary policies and social attitudes relating to welfare recipients, working-class culture and youthful hedonism. Writing of the threat to the early industrial city posed by the 'residuum' and the 'dangerous classes', Geoff made a connection between the notion of deviance and 'the dangerous energies of King Mob', that over time allowed him to segue into the publication for which he is best known.

In 1976 Geoff Pearson joined the University of Bradford where he was a Lecturer in Sociology, later a Senior Lecturer, and then Reader in Applied Social Studies, and it was while he was at Bradford that he published *Hooligan: A History of Respectable Fears* (1980). Written at the height of Thatcherism, and with the Prime Minister's more rabid acolytes lining up to stomp on a social science community poorly equipped for a ruck, *Hooligan* emerged during a fractious decade that was bookended by urban riots in the UK. Influential Thatcherite heavy hitters such as Norman Tebbitt and Sir Keith Joseph lashed out against the social sciences, and sociology in particular bore the brunt of right-wing hostility. The landslide electoral victory that followed the Falklands War also marked a shift by established right-wing historians to popularise versions of history that supported and enforced Imperialist narratives. This shift is expertly explained by D. G. Wright in a 1983 review of *Hooligan* for the *London Review of Books*, where he foresaw '. . . students and schoolchildren subjected to appropriately uplifting selections from British history, perhaps including our boys shinning up the Heights of Abraham, marching boldly from Kabul to Kandahar and yomping across Goose Green. Efforts will no doubt be made to convince bored and alienated youth that Mrs Thatcher's Cabinet stands in direct line from liberty-loving Saxon monarchs, bold Elizabethan privateers, sober Puritan possessive individualists, earnest penny-pinching Victorian shopkeepers and those resolute chaps who, ignoring the fainthearts, went with the flag to Pretoria and defeated the General Strike' (Wright, 1983).

Well, timing is everything, and with the devastating riots of 1981 fresh in the mind of the British electorate, and with Tory attack dogs such as Rhodes Boyson berating 'mindless sociologists' and social workers, for a combative socialist such as Geoff the timing was perfect. *Hooligan* is concerned with the eternal recurrence of a form of cultural pessimism that regards youth crime as a threatening departure from the stable traditions of a 'golden age' of peace and tranquillity. Whether the triggers for youth deviance were regarded as music hall, gangster movies or rock and roll, Geoff identified a connected vocabulary of respectable fears stretching back to Victorian times and beyond. The book demonstrates that the fear of young people has a long history, and that there is a link between economic and social confidence and the prevalence of moral panics. However, Geoff does not fetishise the notion of moral panic, and his rendition is lodged firmly in his ability to locate historical evidence linking youth deviance to an accelerating trajectory of reaction that should be linked to economic and social conditions rather than the false memories of a golden era. This era is always about 20 years earlier, when youths were unambiguously obedient, knew their place, and respectable people could walk the streets.

Crucially, Geoff Pearson did not deny youth crime and violence; his thesis is that youth crime tends to be regarded as extraordinary, a radical departure from the tranquility and stability of the past. Unlike the diluted rendition of moral panic that is a mere replacement for 'I don't believe you', as in 'it's just a moral panic', Geoff Pearson uses the term correctly as part of a process of amplification and reaction. Following on from his 'King Mob' chapter in *The Deviant Imagination*, Geoff, using some beautifully edited extracts from contemporaneous writers, and from the archives of nineteenth- and early twentieth-century newspapers, locates a long connected history of youth crime, with people responding to each real episode by reminiscing about a 'golden age' of peace and tranquility.

Hooligan will remain highly relevant as long as society continues to disinter the notion of a 'golden age' whenever youthful violence erupts. In addition, as a child of the Co-op and local activism, Geoff was always careful not to glamorise or celebrate youth deviance, identifying such romantic tendencies as part of the subjectivist politics that sought out political heroes to enliven otherwise mundane research findings. Neither does his work deny that youth and the communities that spawn them have undergone huge changes. For as he noted in an interview in the wake of the 2011 London riots, 'although we need a bottom-up process of re-integration, built around families, schools and communities . . . the problem remains: how do you re-integrate people who were not integrated in the first place?' (Sinclair, 2011)

The nostalgic imaginings that Geoff critiqued in *Hooligan* were completely absent in *The New Heroin Users* (1987), where the carefully collected individual histories of users that form the book's core explode key myths involving 'drug fiends' and 'evil pushers', and instead emphasise a huge range of experiences amongst a demonised group who were heavily concentrated in areas already suffering unemployment, poor housing and poverty. Importantly, rather than the clichéd depredation and destitution, the book stressed mundane repetition, typified by a drab and stressful lifestyle preoccupied with locating the next £5 'bag' of heroin. Some of the interviews with users and their families are unbearably poignant, and it is Geoff's empathy with the downright bloody ordinariness of their plight which established him as the UK's most humane and authoritative commentator on drug use and drug policy.

Eschewing the mannered disdain for policy that is a feature of other more self-consciously radical scholars, Geoff engaged in a wide range of policy debates, both in the UK and abroad, serving on key committees, Inquiries and editorial boards with something approaching a relish. In particular, as Harry Blagg notes, Geoff had a huge impact on social work teaching and, through both his lecturing and as an advocate for the profession, 'he defended some fundamental social work values in the face of attempts to de-professionalise social work and hand it over to "patch"-based volunteers' (Blagg, 2013), a theme he was to return to shortly before he died.

Geoff moved to London in 1985 as Professor of Social Work at Middlesex Polytechnic during which time he was a member of the Council for Education and Training in Social Work. He worked on a number of projects, including a critical study of multi-agency policing that was written in the wake of the Scarman Report.

His final career move was in 1989 to Goldsmiths College as Wates Professor of Social Work. By this time his research interests were mainly focussed on drug misuse and crime, and for eight years he was Editor-in-Chief of the *British Journal of Criminology*, and his title at Goldsmiths was subsequently changed to Professor of Criminology. Geoff was a member of the Runcimann Inquiry into *Drugs and the Law* that reported in 1999, and he went on to carry out with the author of this paper a study of Middle Market Drug Distribution, more of which is presented later, and three studies of young drug users in care. Importantly, Geoff was highly effective at nurturing scholars of crime and deviance such as Mark Gilman, Alice Sampson, Jenni Ward, Dan Silverstone, Andrew Wilson, Dan Briggs and others, encouraging them to dig out stories of marginalised and ignored individuals and groups, and whenever possible let them speak for themselves.

A Personal Note

I met Geoff in late 1985 when I was completing my PhD and working as a very junior researcher. I was amazed to find that he treated me as an equal. He was interested in my work, findings and methodology, and in the ethical conundrums common to any rookie ethnographer. His advice regarding the possibility of coming to the attention of the police as a result of writing up ethnographic fieldwork was, 'If in doubt, leave it out'. While during the past 30 years I have not always taken his advice, being given license by someone of Geoff's standing to divert from the self-conscious piety that all too often accompanies the outpourings of apprentice ethnographers was most welcome, and I have passed this on to many graduate students suffering from post-fieldwork angst. Some of them even took it.

Subsequently Geoff became a friend whose laid-back style and socially engaged but academically rigorous approach was always pitted with incidents and experiences from beyond the university sector. He retained a group of friends made up of working-class drinking pals from Shepherds Bush who provided light relief from the everyday pomposity of university life, as well as a source of uproarious stories. His family and friends were afforded high priority, and were important sources of both comfort and knowledge. Geoff possessed social skills that are rare in a profession that celebrates an unworldly priestly nihilism, and as a consequence he was comfortable in a wide range of settings and amongst a variety of individuals which, coupled with his awesome breadth of intellectual interests, enabled him to wear his scholarship lightly. He found people interesting.

Geoff had the ability to return from a night out, a family holiday or the school run with his granddaughter with detailed, poignant and well-told stories. In a bar in New Orleans the especially tactile bonhomie of his new-found drinking companions alerted Geoff to the fact that they were actually a team of professional pickpockets whose demonstrative patting, clasping and hugging was no more than a prelude to the subtle liberation of his cash and credit cards. You do not have to be a professor of criminology to know that New Orleans is a dangerous place, and a rapid exit from the bar may well have aggravated the 'dippers'. In a bid to avoid any unpleasantness Geoff retreated to the sanctuary of the gents toilet, an establishment consisting of no more than a urinal and a basin where, in an effort to cut his losses, he proceeded to re-distribute his worldly possessions all over his clothing in various shirt, jacket and trouser pockets. While in the process of performing this crime prevention procedure, one of Geoff's new friends decided to empty his bladder, and on entering the toilet witnessed Geoff frantically stuffing dollars into every available pocket. Back in the bar the drinks flowed and the 'dippers' were, if anything, even more tactile as they crowded around their mark, but Geoff felt that while some of his possessions would be lost, not all of the small stashes would be extracted, and their loot would be relatively meagre. When the session finally ended and Geoff was walking back to the hotel alone, he found that the team had not only located all of his hidden cards and cash, but also that they had been returned to their original locations. On the walk home he encountered the aftermath of a fatal police shooting. Barely four hours later, he wove these adventures into a hilarious yet relevant and academically immaculate conference presentation on urban crime.

The 'Middle Market Drug Distribution' project (Pearson and Hobbs, 2001) was funded by the Home Office, and Geoff's enthusiasm, knowledge and ability to engage with cops, spooks, civil servants and Home Office scientists, along with our luck in being assigned an atypically engaged Home Office liaison officer, ensured the success of the project. This was during the post-cold war, pre 9/11 period when the security services, if not seeking work, were certainly available for 'non-attributable' interviews. I have particularly fond memories of Geoff interrogating a Home Office scientist on the crucial issue of tracing the DNA and purity of drug seizures at various stages of the market, and how such data could be used by academic researchers with regard to understanding importation and distribution networks. We spent one morning with some Customs 'country experts' whose outpourings were so fascinating and detailed that we both forgot to take notes. This resulted in many hours in the pub trying to unwrap what these and other experts were actually saying, while making comparisons with data that we were simultaneously gleaning from offender interviews (Pearson and Hobbs, 2003; 2004). He was a joy to work with.

For Geoff empirical research was important, and we were both struck by how, largely as a result of the emergence of mass higher education in the UK, publishers were ignoring ethnographies, which are typically produced by young scholars and initiated as a PhD thesis, in favour of textbooks and handbooks. Partly to address this problem, Geoff and I started the *Crime Ethnography* series with Willan Publishing, which after Routledge bought Willan out, became the *Advances in Ethnography* series with a far wider range of concerns across the sociological spectrum. As will become apparent from reading the following chapters, Geoff was extraordinarily supportive to rookie authors faced with the daunting task of turning a PhD thesis into a book. The gentle and highly respectful way that he coaxed the best out of these authors showed a sensitive side to a man whose telephone manner could, on a bad day, make him sound like a spurned bailiff. Indeed, his trademark gravelly tones resulted in Geoff being hired to provide the voiceover for a police reality video.

Although he retired in 2008, his inquisitiveness and natural affinity with blighted communities led to Geoff chairing the *Independent Commission on Social Services in Wales* that produced a highly critical report in 2010. Just six months after a Conservative regime was ushered into power on a punitive austerity ticket, Geoff's pithy, direct and precedent critical voice rings out of his introduction to the report:

> Social services unlike the NHS are not, and never have been universal services. They evolved essentially from the post war welfare state reforms of the National Assistance Act of 1948 and its provisions for 'Part III accommodation' for older people and from the Children Act, which themselves derived from the Poor Law institutions, orphanages and workhouses of an earlier age. It is to be hoped that the current UK Government's commitment to a 'Big Society' does not involve a return to Samuel Smiles and Self Help and the Dickensian Bleak House.
>
> (Welsh Local Government Association, 2010: 4)

There was no trick or sleight of hand with Geoff Pearson, no mystique to his craft as an academic, or indeed to the way that he led his all too short life. Geoff was the most sociable of men. He liked people, and people liked him.

This Collection

My apologies to those who would have liked to have made a contribution to this book but were not asked, to those who expressed a real desire to write a chapter but as a result of work or family pressures were unable to, and to those who feel that not every aspect of Geoff's scholarship is represented in this volume.

It is a common characteristic of this kind of publication to invite the great and the good: big-name scholars from prestigious universities who proceed to write about themselves, or compose ludicrous sycophantic arse-licking prose about the book's subject. However, this would denigrate what Geoff was all about. He was a warts and all kind of man who, despite the richness of his scholarship, and the esteem in which he was held, had no time for the self-aggrandizing reflex that accompanies so many academic careers. This was after all a man whose retirement party was packed with secretaries, researchers and friends. The guest of honour was Halo, his 4-year-old granddaughter.

This collection is made up of scholars producing empirical work on some of the key areas upon which Geoff Pearson established his reputation. Most, but not all of the writers worked with Geoff in some capacity, were students of his or their work was examined by him. All of the writers in this collection have been profoundly influenced by his scholarship. Some are established writers, while some are at the very early stages of what may or may not turn out to be an academic career. I think that Geoff would have liked that.

Although this collection is organised into themes reflecting Geoff's major interests, it is bookended by two stand-alone chapters. As an hors d'oeuvre we have a chapter written by a new scholar whose only obvious connection to Geoff is Manchester. However, Deborah Jump's paper is exactly the kind of engaged, edgy and original ethnography that Geoff championed. As a woman working in a male boxing gym in working-class Manchester, and via vivid description and interview data, Deborah engages with masculinity, violence, the body, class, race and a whole range of key issues affecting contemporary urban life.

Section One: Race

One of Geoff's early and most important publications was concerned with the contextualisation of racist violence in Lancashire (Pearson, 1976), and in this section James Treadwell and Jon Garland, utilising outstanding ethnographic fieldwork with the *English Defence League*, provide an update on the enduring political nature of racist violence in the UK. James and Jon also address the failure of both the left and the discipline of criminology to address ideologies and actions that contradict comfortable class stereotypes. Alice Sampson, a one-time colleague of Geoff, refers to Geoff's seminal writings on deviance and uses this material to provide a unique focus upon government policy within the context of Muslim extremism. While Alice brings to the fore some of the more valuable work to emerge from the sociology of deviance, Kenny Monrose, another new scholar, points out a major failing of both the sociology of deviance and its successor criminology. The obsession with the usual youthful subjects can come at the expense of studies addressing a wider age range, and as Kenny indicates, adult notions of deviance should be understood in terms of cross-generational class and racial oppression.

Section Two: Youth

Particularly via *The Deviant Imagination, Hooligan* and *Working Class Youth Culture* (Mungham and Pearson, 1976), Geoff's influence on youth scholarship has been especially profound. Consequently this section could have easily been expanded into an edited collection in its own right. The chapter written by Andrew Davies, who co-edited with Geoff an influential Special Issue of the *British Journal of Criminology* (Pearson and Davies, 1999), is an overview of the concept of hooliganism and its related scholarship. In this fine-grained paper, Andrew considers some problems of methodology, and revisits Geoff's original work, confirming its status as an academic classic and its excellence as a critique of class relations. As he explains in his introduction, Andy Wilson's PhD thesis was examined by Geoff Pearson, and in his chapter Andy makes a case for a revival of subcultural theory. Given the growing preoccupation with gangs, this is no mean feat, and he achieves it by teasing out the more resilient qualities that made subcultural analysis so important during the 1960s and 1970s, and critiquing the notion of the gang from the perspective of a potent fusion of his own life experience and scholarship. Matt Taylor is a postgraduate student whose interests—squatting, illegal parties and informal and formal control—create the kind of ethnographic cocktail that would have appealed to Geoff. Matt's paper, that stands outside the subculture/gang orthodoxy, is a vivid account of a contested cultural and economic environment that thrives under the radar of the media, policy makers and the majority of the academic community.

Section Three: Drugs and Illegal Markets

How illegal markets operated became one of Geoff's major interests, and the papers in this section address different aspects of this constantly evolving commercial sphere. Charlie Edwards and Calum Jeffray offer a detailed analysis that unpacks some increasingly normalised areas of illegality that pose some unique threats to consumer well-being that need to be considered alongside those of the recreational drug trade, as well as those emanating from the legal alcohol and tobacco industries. Geoff Pearson was the co-examiner of Dan Silverstone's PhD thesis, and in his paper Dan provides an update on the concept of the Middle Market, and carefully addresses the stodgy rhetoric that is often utilised to address illegal markets. Market analysis was close to Geoff's heart, and Dan's paper neatly puts some big clichés of criminology in their place. In a paper derived from his ongoing Dublin-based ethnography, Brendan Marsh presents a vivid portrait of the multifarious roles played by violence within drug markets. Brendan's paper confirms Geoff's faith in the abilities of ethnography to shine some light on inconveniently embedded, often unpleasant societal alcoves. Dan Briggs is another scholar directly influenced by Geoff. The biographical approach that he has adopted for his paper on drug markets perfectly captures the impact that Geoff had, particularly in relation to early career academics. His ready availability alone set him apart from most of his peers, and Dan shows how these personal qualities merged with his scholarship to create a unique sphere of influence. While Mark Gilman's paper also stresses the importance of individual biography in shaping academic research, it also highlights Geoff's prowess as a talent spotter. The paper draws on Mark's experience as both a friend and colleague of Geoff, and reports back from a chaotic frontline of drug use and treatment where some of the UK's most marginalised individuals can be found blagging, complaining, explaining and laughing.

Section Four: Geoff's Final Publication

Finally, we conclude with a stand-alone previously unpublished paper authored by Geoff Pearson and Jenni Ward. Jenni's PhD was supervised by Geoff, and she worked with him and Tim Newburn on a project looking at the plight of young people in care. This paper focuses upon the exploitation of this vulnerable group, and it is fitting that Geoff's final publication should bring together some of his key academic and personal concerns, in particular: youth, drugs, social work, social policy, inequality and social justice.

Geoff Pearson was a unique man, and a remarkable intellectual. While his personal beliefs were forged in working-class Lancashire, his professional and academic footprint can be found across five decades of historical, sociological, criminological and social work scholarship. And he could play the piano.

All that we could possibly achieve with this book was to attempt to pay tribute to a wonderful scholar and his body of work. The fact that these tributes are interwoven with references to his many personal qualities is testimony to a life well lived.

References

Blagg, H. (2013) Remembering Geoff Pearson. *Criminal Justice Matters*, vol. 93, Iss. 1.

Pearson, G. (1975) *The Deviant Imagination*. Basingstoke: Macmillan.

Pearson, G. (1976) '"Paki-Bashing" in a North East Lancashire Cotton Town: A Case Study and its History', in G. Mungham and G. Pearson eds., *Working Class Youth Culture*. London: Routledge.

Pearson, G. (1987) *The New Heroin Users*. Oxford: Blackwell.

Pearson, G. and Davies, A. eds. (1999) Histories of Crime and Modernity. *Special Issue of the British Journal of Criminology*, vol. 39, no. 1.

Pearson, G. and Hobbs, D. (2001) *Middle Market Drug Distribution.* Home Office Research Study 227. London: Home Office.

Pearson, G. and Hobbs, D. (2003) King pin? A case study of a middle market drug broker. *The Howard Journal of Criminal Justice*, vol. 2, no. 4, 335–347.

Pearson, G. and Hobbs, D. (2004) 'E' is for enterprise: Middle level drug markets in ecstasy and stimulants. *Addiction Research and Theory*, vol. 12, no. 6, 565–576.

Mungham, G. and Pearson, G. eds. (1976) *Working Class Youth Culture.* London: Routledge.

Sinclair, I. (2011) Reaction to the Riots: Interview with Geoffrey Pearson https://ianjsinclair.wordpress.com/2015/02/05/reaction-to-the-riots-interview-with-geoffrey-pearson/.

Welsh Local Government Association (2010) *From Vision to Action: The Report of the Independent Commission on Social Services in Wales.* Cardiff: Welsh Local Government Association.

Wright, D. (1983) Great Tradition. *London Review of Books*, vol. 5, no. 19.

1 They Didn't Know Whether to 'Fuck Me or Fight Me'

An Ethnographic Account of North Town Boxing Gym

Deborah Jump

Boxing is—to borrow Goffman's terminology—'where the action is', a universe in which the smallest of actions becomes 'fateful', which is both exciting and problematic for the individuals involved (1967:174). Referring to my recent ethnography conducted in an inner-city boxing gym in the north of England, this chapter illustrates core observations from fieldwork in the 'North Town' boxing gym, and reflexively comments on the intricacies and personal relationships of the men in this social world. During the six months that I spent in the field of amateur and professional boxing it became increasingly evident that the gym was an important, exciting and valuable space for the men who attended. I therefore reflect on the appealing nature and social hierarchy of boxing for the men in this study, and discuss how the gym seemingly offers routes into employment while providing status-affirming attributes for those who attend. Secondly, I examine how the structured activity of the gym environment has the potential to promote desistance from crime, by detaining and incapacitating men when they may otherwise be involved in criminal behaviour.

Drawing on classical ethnographic research techniques (see Hobbs 1995; Bourgois 1996; Anderson 1999), I aim to give a strong experiential sense of the physical and social environment in which this research was situated, and of the role I played in shaping it. I aim to recreate and illustrate the habitus[1] of these men and bring alive their social world and subjective stories. Having previously worked in youth offending services for close to ten years I became particularly interested in how sport was being used as a vehicle for change via a diversionary activity that was being promoted to young men who found themselves constantly in contact with the youth justice system. Seeing the same young men return weekly led me to believe that 'nothing works' (Martinson 1974), and overcoming this cynicism became increasingly difficult. I became determined to find out why this might be the case, and therefore applied for PhD funding to explore the reason why young men seemed keen to take up the sport of boxing, and also why the authorities deemed this to be a good idea. Moreover, I wanted to understand if and how the sport of boxing could potentially contribute towards a process of desistance for young men, and whether it influenced the way in which they viewed and understood violent behaviour.

The basic question for any qualitatively oriented researcher is to ask how one can represent the viewpoints of the subjects he or she studies, and how to comprehend the production of social reality in and through interactive processes. In this research I sought to understand how members of the gym related to one another and what interactive processes formed their mutual understandings. In short, I was interested in the ways in which 'legitimate' (celebrated) violence was constructed, how it was viewed, and how it was practiced and rehearsed by men who boxed. Furthermore, I was interested in whether the collective and subjective meanings of those who participated in boxing contributed towards a process of desistance from 'illegitimate' (criminalised) violence.

In exploring these ideas I employed an ethnographic approach. This method has long been viewed as an effective and sophisticated technique for analysing social worlds from the 'inside' as it starts from a theoretical position of describing social realities and their making (Adler and Adler 1987). A common feature of ethnography is participant observation, and I relied upon this method to observe the climate and habitus of the boxing gym. It is the job of the ethnographer to gain access to people's everyday thinking and interpret their actions and social worlds from their point of view; therefore, adopting this method assisted in my quest to understand what the gym meant to these young men and their trainers, and also how the relationships formed could potentially influence motivations and behaviour in and outside of the boxing ring.

This method further allowed me to observe the boxers in their natural setting, while encouraging me to stay close to the field and the world it represents. More importantly, it allowed me to develop an integrated set of theoretical concepts from the data collected, specifically those that related to my research ideas mentioned previously. Accordingly, the theoretical framework of both ethnographic research and grounded theory assisted in the unpicking of actions and meanings for these men, and therefore allowed me to explore what elements these men assigned to specific actions. Additionally, it facilitated my understanding surrounding the culture of the boxing gym, and also, how the inherent discourses of competition and masculinity potentially transposed into the wider community when men left the premises.

Gaining Access to North Town

Woodward (2004:4) posits that: 'Men's boxing gyms are very difficult to access for women'; however, previous work experience in the field of youth work gained me access to these arenas as former colleagues acted as gatekeepers. According to Coffey (1993:94) the sponsorship or use of gatekeepers in gaining access to the field 'is the ethnographer's best ticket into the community', and these were essential components in the research.

Previous ethnographies in boxing gyms have mostly been conducted by men acting as participant observers (Sugden 1996; Beattie 1997; De Garis 2002; Wacquant 2004). In fact, the small amount of boxing research that has been conducted by women (Woodward 2008; Trimbur 2009) has generally been non-participatory and focused on issues of race and ethnicity. My research, while technically non-participatory, was actually that of someone who 'hangs around', a 'researcher-participant' (Gans 1962); therefore, I did seek to embrace the overall culture of the boxing gym as I felt this was important to maintaining access and understanding the lives of these men.

Sugden (1996:201) argues that: 'It is only through total immersion that she or he can become sufficiently conversant with the formal and informal rules governing the webbing of the human interactions under investigation, so that its innermost secrets can be revealed'. While I acknowledge the benefits that 'insider' status can provide, I would also argue that full participation is not tantamount to producing knowledge and, as such, I am inclined to concur with Morgan (1992:87), when she states that: 'Qualitative research has its own brand of machismo with its image of the male sociologist bringing back news from the fringes of society, the lower depths, the mean streets', and further align with Wheaton (2002) when she suggests that very few ethnographies of boxing acknowledge gendered identity as part of their research, highlighting that maleness often passes unquestioned in these particular environments.

Notwithstanding, it was imperative that I was viewed as someone who played an active role in the gym, and I soon discovered that small amounts of participation were crucial to developing trust among the participants. Accordingly, I decided to dress in sportswear and assist and participate in the day-to-day activities of the gym. It was during these participatory moments that I was able to forge relationships with the men, as they appreciated the effort I had made to understand their social world and the importance that the sport had to their lives. Indeed, it was during the holding of the pads/participation in light sparring, or by sweeping the floor that I was able to schedule interviews and negotiate access to their lives.

Before commencing the interviews I 'hung around' the boxing gym for a period of two weeks. I became familiar with the faces in attendance and spoke informally to many of the men who seemed curious by my presence. I began by interviewing the trainers as I felt it important to begin with those who ran the gym because boxing gyms have strict hierarchal structures and the trainers and professionals are classed as being at the top. It was important to be respectful to the cultural standing of the gym members and begin with those deemed to be most experienced and influential. This was a wise move on my part as other men began to follow suit after the trainers had already been interviewed, as they reported feeling 'safer' about talking to a researcher once the trainers had 'checked me out'.

Most of the interviews were conducted during the day at the boxing gym, as the evening sessions were very crowded and noisy. Most men wanted to train hard and I did not want to stand in their way (literally and figuratively); therefore I organised the interviews around their training schedules and often met them after their lunchtime workouts. The changing rooms proved to be a good place for the interviews to be conducted as they were away from the ring and the deafening sound of the bell. Furthermore, the showers were housed in a different section and this allowed me access without worrying about breaching the men's privacy. Most of the men were responsive and found my research intriguing, whereas a few declined to 'go on record' but would offer me vignettes and anecdotes of their lives and boxing careers. I wrote most of these down, and incorporated them into my thinking and field notes. These short accounts, although not on tape, offered me a chance to think deeper about my subject area and helped build a rapport with the men in whose social world I had immersed myself.

Reading books and boxing magazines helped increase boxing knowledge, as the men would often test my understanding of the weight categories or terminology used in the sport. Hence, I was able to follow the trajectory of the interview naturally as the men discussed prior champions they had defeated, or boxing techniques that they had employed in winning. I soon became a known presence and on a first name basis with gym trainers and members. They began to allocate me boxing tasks such as becoming the 'spit bucket' holder as the men spat their gumshields into a bucket after a bout. The holding of the bucket and the passing of hand-wraps and gloves became second nature after a while; all the time offering either congratulations or condolences to bruised faces and egos, as the men often left the ring either dismayed or elated. All of this was recorded, jotted down and memorised as I attempted to blend into the ethnographic background.

As a result of this immersion, I began to understand the gendered experience of the research context, and more importantly, how my involvement shaped the production of knowledge.[2] As Denzin (1989:27) has argued, 'There is no such thing as gender free knowledge' as gender is a significant factor in the research process (see also Presser 2005). Woodward (2008) argues that the sexualised positioning of a female researcher in hyper-masculine arenas such as boxing gyms is highly significant. In her research, Woodward consciously adopted a subject position that was neither threatening nor complicit in masculine discourses, finding the 'maternal figure' to be the most successful research persona.

Joyce Carol Oates (1987:73) states that a, 'Female boxer cannot be taken seriously—she is a parody, she is cartoon, she is monstrous, and had she an ideology, she is likely to be a feminist'. This resonated with me in the context of my fieldwork, as I identify as a feminist white gay woman. I suffered sexist remarks on several occasions, and while my aim was to remain as asexual as possible this did not always prove to be successful, as one boxer stated that he did not know whether to 'fuck me or fight me'. Accordingly, a sense of distancing had to be established, as my distinction as a researcher was further constituted as an outsider particularly in terms of my class, race and sexuality.

In total I interviewed 13 participants. Most of these were professionals—or retired professionals—at least, and were therefore serious about their sport. I spoke with nearly every member of the gym, spending significant periods of time in these men's company over six months, and through the taking of ethnographic field notes—what Emerson et al. (1995) refers to as 'jottings'—an understanding began to develop. These jottings helped to shape and illuminate the particular themes in this research, and this proved to be invaluable in the analytical stages of the enquiry as they helped me to reconstruct interactions, discussions and the general characterisation of the order of events. Furthermore, by taking extensive field notes, I was able to recall first impressions of settings, ideas, people, relationships and elements of interaction.

The use of Biographical Narrative Interviewing (Wengraf 2001) proved very successful after a period of trying out a few different techniques. Using this method, and particularly the opening statement of: 'Tell me the story of how you became a boxer', initiated a dialogue that most men appeared to be comfortable with. The use of this particular method allowed the men to be more open regarding the nature of their stories, and some disclosed that they had 'never told anyone this before', whereas I sensed that this may have been because nobody had previously cared to ask. In certain interviews, I felt upset at the trauma and violence experienced by some of these men, as stories of familial abuse as both victim and perpetrator jarred me, and at one point a respondent broke down as he relayed his story of manslaughter involving a fellow boxer. At other times I felt objectified by the male gaze and angered by men's often-profound misogyny.

Reflexivity from a narrative position scrutinises the researcher's process and examines how power relations are attended to both within the relationship and in the construction of the narratives. Presser (2005:2070) argues that: 'Cross gender studies of men generate unique concerns about research practice', and from a feminist perspective this argument is well known. I align with Presser, when she argues that cross gender studies simply bring the processes of gender accomplishment into plain view, as I observed men using the research situation as a further opportunity to accomplish their masculinity (Messerschmidt 2000), telling me stories of masculine accomplishments involving violence, virility and status-affirming exploits. However, I acknowledge that there is no final version, and my narrative representation and interpretations are only made possible through interpretative readings. Hence, the narrative accounts presented in this study do not resemble every boxer, nor do they resemble every man. In short, they resemble a collection of life stories. Yet, by interviewing and facilitating the construction of these men's narratives I was able to discern and analyse what violence, masculinity and desistance meant for them, both collectively in the gym environment and subjectively in their everyday lives.

Meeting 'The Boys': The Gatekeeper's Introduction

I first met Rico, my gatekeeper, when he arrived at a youth project I was managing as part of my time as a youth offending worker. He was recruited as a member of volunteer staff for a local mentoring project I was involved with, but overall, his disposition reflected that of the client group we worked with. He admittedly referred to himself as 'street', and said that volunteering, as part of this mentoring project was his last chance to 'get out' of a troubled lifestyle. According to Rico what 'saved' him was boxing. He had turned his back on gang violence after seeing his friend killed in a fight over 'something stupid to do with drugs and money'. After witnessing this shooting, Rico was determined to do 'something else'. The local boxing gym—North Town—overlooked the estate where Rico lived, and the boxers could often be seen 'road running' around the park adjacent to the housing estate and gym. 'Knowing a few of the lads in there', Rico crossed the busy road that separated the housing estate to the gym that would become his 'life and love' for the next ten years.

Rico and I became colleagues, and over the course of three years of working together we became friends. As we were professionally tasked with designing diversionary programmes for young offenders, we started discussing the possibilities of boxing as a tool for reducing illegitimate violence. When the project ended, as funding dried up under a shift in government policy, Rico went on to train as a fireman. Regardless, we kept in touch as he said that if he was ever in 'need of a reference from someone who "got him"' then I was to be his 'go to' for this. Ironically, Rico ended up being my 'go to' as the idea of boxing as a diversionary activity never left my sights; therefore, Rico was the first person I called when I needed access to a boxing gym.

'Meet me by North Town at 1 p.m. and I'll introduce you to Marcus and Eric', said Rico. He was excited by my idea and was willing to facilitate the introductions to North Town's trainers and owners—'his boys' as he often referred to them. When I arrived Rico was already waiting for me outside— 'how's it goin' Deb?' as was often his greeting when we worked together. We embraced and then walked towards the steel door that was the downstairs entrance to the gym. Rico did not knock nor ring any form of buzzer, 'they don't hear that shit anyway, what with the music and the bell'; thus, he merely pulled out a bank card from his pocket and slid it in between the lock and the door frame. As the door sprung open we laughed and went inside. As I climbed the stairs I started to feel anxious; the gravity of the situation began to sink in, even though this was just a boxing gym in the town I grew up in, I realised that I was about to meet the men that Rico had spoken to me about when we worked together, the same men that he grew up with; those that 'changed his life for the better'.

Anyone who has walked into a boxing gym knows that it is an immediate assault on the senses, from the deafening sound of the bell instructing men to change posts from either sparring to bag-work or vice versa, or the loud music inevitably competing for space among the shouting and the rhythmic pummelling of flesh and leather. The smell is naturally one of body sweat, but intermingled with this is the faint smell of Vaseline, blood and glue from the hand-wrapping tape. It is distinctive and indicative of most boxing gyms nationally and internationally. Necessarily, there is a weighing scale in the corner near the ring and more than likely there is at least one mirror close by. The apparatuses are fundamental to the boxing gym as they reflect the hard work— the hard bodily work—of the boxers, and an orderly queue is often forming at various times of the day, as men check their weight against their fighting category—heavyweight, lightweight, bantam weight, etc. The mirror is a celebratory or commiserative reflection of a pugilist's craft. 'The mirror does not lie', according to Simon, the professional light middleweight, and indeed, it represents the male boxing ego in its full glory.

The male boxing ego forms the fabric of the space, and the essence of physical competition pumps through the veins of the men. Conversations focus on this, and the gym is littered with posters and motivational quotes spurring on the boxers. Those with highest social status are the professionals, and among this elite group the number of belts accrued and defended takes centre stage in the daily flow of conversation. Most of the professional's photographs sit alongside fantasy characters such as Rocky Balboa, or Raging Bull, and I often wondered whether men like Marcus, Simon, Frank and Ricky saw themselves as action figures or movie stars. To introduce some of these men would allow a fuller picture to develop, and I will interrogate and present snapshots of their narratives of appeal and persistence/desistance throughout this piece. Initially, however, they came as a group, the group of men waiting to meet me at the top of the stairs in North Town gym.

'Yes, Rico man', Marcus proclaimed as he grabbed Rico's hand and quickly enacted some form of complicated hand gesture that ended with bumped fists. 'Touch', each one of the professionals said, as Rico went along the group and bumped fists with Eric, Simon and Frank. 'This is Deb, who I told you about, she's safe', as I was introduced to the men by Rico. Unable to remember, or more likely through fear of embarrassing myself, I refrained from 'touching', and merely raised my hand in a hello gesture. I explained why I was there, the aim of my research, and sought their permission to come and 'hang out' at North Town. It was immediately evident that Marcus called the shots, as everybody turned to him to provide the answer. 'Sure, if you're a friend of Rico's then we trust you', Marcus answered. However, he needed additional reassurance that I was not a 'fed' (police). I told them my history of youth offending work, and how Rico and I had always wanted to explore the possibility of boxing being used as a tool in the reduction of violent crime. 'I'm telling you, boxing works!' said Eric. The others nodded in agreement, as Frank proclaimed that without boxing he would most certainly 'have not made it', stating jail or death as the alternatives. Simon professed that 'boxing saved my life', as Marcus chimed in with 'Yeah man, before boxing I'd never been nothing, never seen nothing, was nothing, you know what I'm saying?', looking to me to nod in agreement with each of the men's sentiments.

It became clear quite quickly, that these men believed in boxing as a tool to reduce violent crime, and crime more generally, as they spoke wholeheartedly about its desisting and 'life-saving' properties. I was excited to get started and told the men that I would be back on Monday with consent forms and an enthusiastic attitude, as Rico beckoned me down the stairs of the gym and out into the community that I was to live within, love and better understand over the course of my six-month ethnographic fieldwork.

First Day 'on the Job'

Monday came around and at roughly 6pm that evening I arrived at North Town gym on my motorcycle. I parked it next to the entrance and stood with the men as they waited for Marcus to arrive and open the shutters that protected the door. A black BMW pulled up alongside my motorcycle, and Marcus got out to let us all inside to train. 'Nice bike', said one of the younger amateurs as I entered the gym, and a part of me felt relieved that I was visible—someone had actually noticed me—as most of the men initially ignored me or gave a sideways glance that seemed to infer that I was not supposed to be there. Women are not commonly seen attending boxing gyms, at least not in North Town. Indeed, during my time there I never once saw another female, nor were there any facilities such as women's changing rooms or toilets. I initially identified as a PhD student researching boxing and men's understanding of violence; however, this position was not proving fruitful as nobody spoke to me on that first night, and I found myself edging closer towards the periphery as I sat on a stack of mats next to the ring watching the amateurs and professionals hit the bags and one another. As a result of this, and an ensuing fear that I would not be able to collect any data, I decided to come back the next day dressed to participate. As Monaghan (2006:235) attests, 'all fieldwork is dependent upon the researcher's bodily insertion and participation in a sometimes emotionally charged social world'; hence, on Tuesday evening I climbed the stairs of North Town dressed in sport shorts and running shoes, and equipped with an attitude telling me that I *could* and *would* succeed.

'You decided to train then?', Marcus asked as I walked through the door. I felt foolish for a second but took a deep breath and told him I could do it. Regardless, some men, particularly Marcus, were not as enthusiastic as I, and expressed their disapproval quite openly. 'I'm not getting in the ring with a girl', shouted a younger amateur as we lined up to spar, and one other older professional refused to hold the pads for me as I tried to 'partner up' and practice drills. Others were curious and had no qualms in partnering up, or indeed sparring with me, as it enabled them to use sport as a terrain for testing, proving, displaying and enhancing masculinity (Connell 1990).

Blinde and Taub (1992a:38) have argued that 'women who display athleticism are perceived to be challenging the boundaries of femininity', and when Derek, the older amateur, proclaimed that I was 'not your average girl' it solidified this very point. When I asked Derek what he meant, he stated that 'most girls don't ride motorbikes, and get in the ring with men'. Being female and participating in a male-dominated environment was certainly challenging, and at times I was more than aware of my gender positioning and sexuality. Yet, I found that my own experiential knowledge of violent youth culture as a result of my working-class upbringing, older boxing-brother, and youth work experience allowed me to 'gender-cross' more efficiently.

Hobbs et al. (2007:28) in their work on female working-class bouncers state that 'pragmatic knowledge is a deeply embedded aspect of working class life, a distinctive form of consciousness geared towards embodied performance'; therefore, I was able to adapt and embed myself in the 'quintessentially masculine habitus' (Wacquant 1995a:234) of boxing, and share a 'feel for the game' (Bourdieu 1990:62). In some respects I drew upon my habitus of 'working class femininity' (Skeggs 2004) to occupy and negotiate my continued access in the hyper masculine environment of the boxing gym, and construct an 'alternative femininity to confirm my gender as pure situated accomplishment (Mennesson 2000:56). This in turn helped me better understand the habitus of the boxing gym, while inhabiting a precarious space at the intersection of sexuality, race, femininity and class.

Identifying as a gay woman was something that I never openly disclosed to these men. I felt that this information was not appropriate for this setting, and more than likely would become salacious gossip, or further reason for the men to create distance between me as a female researcher in their homosocial world of male pugilism. Goffman (1963) suggests that the control of personal information is the key to identity management among people labelled as deviant, which my lesbianism most certainly would have been in this environment, and as Blinde and Taub (1992a:11) further identified in their research into homophobia in sport, 'concealment of information, deflection of characteristics perceived as harmful, and normalization of the stigmatized behaviour is used to manage the lesbian label'.

Accordingly, my sexuality and gender positioning were blurred and confusing for the men in this study and, as I became a known presence in the gym, men often wondered: 'how my boyfriend felt about me being in a gym with all these half-naked men?' I had to negotiate my way around such questions with tact and care, and most of the time I just laughed, as I found this to be the most useful defence mechanism in guarding my privacy and maintaining my access. In the main, however, the men accepted me—Rico had 'vouched' for me after all—and as I started showing my face each week and asking how their kids were, or who 'won at the weekend' the men started to refer to me as Deb as opposed to 'that girl'.

Boxing's Appeal: Physical Capital and Social Hierarchy

The majority of the men involved in this research invested heavily into the sport of boxing. Professional trainers, professional boxers and various amateurs said boxing symbolised—to them at least—much more than a place where you went to punch a few bags and 'let off steam'. For others, boxing was an ancillary activity to a career in the night-time economy, providing the physical capital needed to guard the pubs and nightclubs in a metropolitan city. For some men, the boxing gym was simply a place to come and hang out, constructed as a neutral space that remained a place of safety no matter what was happening in the community outside. Indeed, Wacquant (2004:31) referred to boxing gyms as 'islands of stability and order', in that they 'protect an individual from the street' and 'act as a buffer against the insecurity of the neighbourhood and pressures of everyday life'. In short, he believed that boxing gyms helped to regulate men's lives when disorder and delinquency threaten them, and this seemed to be the case for a significant amount of men in my sample, as those who grew up in the surrounding community disclosed how the gang violence that engulfed the area was 'left outside the gym doors for us to pick up after training!'

Others spoke of the boxing gym as they would a lover and discussed the sensual and erotic appeal of pugilism; disclosing how the smell of sweat, and feel of skin contributed towards the seduction of the sport:

> Once you get the boxing bug, you got it for life I'm tellin' you, you walk up them stairs and you can hear the music and it turns you on, gets your blood pumping, you can smell the sweat and gloves, I love that feeling.
>
> (Derek, 32-year-old amateur)

This is indicative of Stephen Lyng's (1998) concept of 'edgework', whereby participants combine the exhilaration and momentary integration of danger, risk and skill in the experience of boxing, and the physicality required to participate seemed only to add to the appeal. Most certainly, the physicality required to invest in the sport was a huge draw, as men honed their bodies into either moneymaking machines or defensive structures, mainly in pursuit of employment in the security industry or the professional boxing circuit.

Bouncers and professional boxers were at the top of the hierarchy in the gym, and this was quite evident in the way the gym functioned. It was not very often that those with professions such as these had to queue for equipment or want for a parking space outside, and this was due to the respect and prestige placed upon them as a result of earning a living from the crafting of their physicality. The men in these superior positions also did favours for gym attendees, such as guest lists for nightclubs and ringside seats; therefore, the regular attendees behaved in ways that maintained the bouncers and professional's exalted positions, and this hierarchy was clearly well established. Moreover, it became quite clear early on in my fieldwork that this hierarchy was based on physicality and the participant's capacity for violence, whereby those with the highest rate of physical capital had the most power. Professions that supported or employed physical capital in the day-to-day occupations that the men inhabited merely contributed towards this omnipotence, as they existed in a habitus within which violence is a normal part of everyday life. Thus, the boxing world came to be seen as a site where implicit rules of physical capital and masculine accomplishment governed its smooth running; indeed, it was seen as a place of excitement, male companionship and ruthless violent competition, and all these factors contributed towards its appeal.

Most of the men I spoke to had a personal reason for participating, whether this was getting fit and/or losing weight, or because boxing was classified as their 'life'. Others perceived themselves as contributing to, or overcoming some form of social, economic or academic barrier, and Simon, one of the successful professionals I spoke with, proclaimed that boxing 'proved I was capable of doing something, that I was worthy of something'. One of the other men, Ricky, believed that boxing was a 'good thing to channel into' and 'if you haven't got anything to put your aggression into, it goes elsewhere—thieving, fighting or robbing'.

Simon in particular was a popular professional and many of the younger amateurs were keen to be associated with him. His posters dominated the walls, and he came from a lineage of boxers, as his father was also a professional in his time. Simon was referred to as 'Junior', and the mantle of his father's success was something Simon felt he had to live up to:

> My dad was a boxer, wasn't he? A good one too after he stopped pissing around as a journeyman. He turned his life around when he quit drinking and focused on boxing. He wasn't around much, but when I turned pro I would watch all his old videos, hoping to replicate his style, hoping to be as good as him one day"

The men in the gym would talk about Simon's father with fondness, particularly the trainers, as they especially enjoyed reminiscing about the 'good old days which Simon's father was evidently a part of. One story in particular that circulated around the gym, and was often referred to, was the story of a violent outbreak among the spectators at one of Simon's father's title fights:

> It went off. Kicked right off. Made national news, on TV and all that. Some of my dad's fans travelled to see the fight down south and wore football shirts from up north; they didn't like that down there, and what with the fight and all that, it kicked off. It got dealt with at our end as we came en masse and our firm don't fuck about when it goes off.

This was a legacy in North Town gym: 'the firm's way of handling the situation when violence arose, the firm being Simon's father's friends who actively engage in violence as part of their job in the night-time economy or local men who have no qualms about rehearsing violence as part of their everyday lives. The firm's definition of 'not fucking about', according to Simon, meant retaliation and ultimately winning and, if status and televised kudos could be achieved, then even better. It was never made clear whether the outbreak impinged on Simon's father's career, but it certainly added to his, and subsequently Junior's informal status among the social world of professional boxing. Indeed, stories were important to men in the gym, especially those that spoke of triumph over hardship, or courage in the face of fear. This is likely because stories such as this confirmed and accomplished key aspects of a boxer's identity. The discourses in the gym environment supported narratives of victory, bravery and toil, and the men accomplished these attributes by relaying tales of individual and collective success, whether that of legitimate violence in the ring, or illegitimate violence outside of it.

Ricky a young 'up-comer' was keen to be included in the conversation; he wanted a legacy too. He was also keen to grab at success as soon as possible, and could not wait for 'the nice house and nice car'. Ricky's uncle was a friend of both Marcus and Eric and was the one who introduced Ricky to the gym originally. Having problems at school for fighting Ricky was excluded and sent to a Pupil Referral Unit, yet his uncle 'didn't believe in that shit' and brought Ricky to North Town instead, believing that the discipline and guidance of Marcus and Eric would be the key to 'setting him straight'. Ricky was a determined character and attended the gym every day; having left school five years ago without any qualifications he believed the gym was 'his only chance at success'. Struggling to read, evidenced by an inability to fully comprehend the consent forms I provided, Ricky in particular disparaged any form of academic or mental labour. He was completely invested in bodily and visceral forms of capital, and similar to other manual occupations—labouring under certain conditions of deskilling and casualization (Connell 1995:55)—boxers are largely defined in relation to their potentially forceful bodies. Indeed, the physical body is a boxer's economic asset, and for these men, 'bodily capital' (Wacquant 1995b), and acquired 'techniques of the [violent] body' (Mauss 1973) can be transmuted into forms of capital such as income and masculine-validating recognition. Ricky was acutely aware of this and trained to the point of exhaustion, and I often wondered how he maintained his energy and drive for such brutal sparring matches or bag drills:

> It's all about hard work. If you put in the graft no one can beat you. If you mess about and take days off, your opponent gets the edge, and I can't have that; I've got fuck all else.

Ricky was highly competitive, yet one Tuesday afternoon when sparring with Derek for an upcoming fight, Ricky disclosed that he was 'not feeling it today'. When I asked him what he meant, he started to discuss how he had not slept properly for a few days as he had been in charge of childcare and the baby had been having sleepless nights. Derek capitalised upon Ricky's mood and saw this as an opportunity to beat him physically; in the ring Ricky was up against the ropes for most of the count, taking and absorbing painful blows from Derek's gloved fist, and I distinctly remember at one point having to look away.

Prior research into the field of violence, bodily capital and hierarchical male structures (Winlow 2001) evidences that violence becomes routinised and normalised, but is also, more importantly, seductive and status enhancing (Katz 1988; Hobbs and Robins 1991). Thus, by forcefully dominating Ricky at a time of weakness, Derek demonstrated how bodily capital and the cultural 'sensual' importance of violence enables boxers to not only 'recognise and label others' but also 'grade them hierarchically' (Shilling 2001:333–7; Winlow 2001). For Derek this meant having secured a place farther up the pecking order as a result of having physically beaten Ricky, the 'upcoming pro'.

This lack of sympathy and consideration for others' personal lives is in line with Wacquant's (2004:67) observations, as he also argues that very little information regarding members' private lives is exchanged in the gym environment. There is a sense of camaraderie present, yet this is bound by competition, either through talk of football teams that the men support, or who is the most physically capable in terms of exercise regimes. For example, Eric was not pleased with Ricky for his poor performance in the ring, and I could hear him from the shower room berating him:

> You can't let no woman get in the way of your training, get her to sort the kid, you know what I'm saying, son? If we don't win the next fight, then we're never gonna get a shot at the title next month.

A shot at the title was always big news in the gym, as it meant payday for the trainers and kudos for the pros. Title fights are what make a boxer, and they are a series of intricately woven accomplishments and belts that make little sense to the layperson. However, they remain at the pinnacle of boxing success, and every professional in North Town anxiously awaited a shot at a title. This is because titles and belts are tangible assets for men who box; they act as 'cultural capital', to cite Pierre Bourdieu (1986). Cultural capital comprises a series of ideas and knowledge that people draw upon as they participate in social life and, for a social group such as boxers, the acquisition and accumulation of capital is paramount to success. Wacquant (1995a:65) describes it as 'conceiving of and caring for the use of the pugilistic body as a *form of capital*', and how they transform 'abstract' bodily capital into '*pugilistic capital*'. In other words, the body of boxers is a learning machine, an instrument, a weapon, and crucially something boxers deeply invest in to enhance their ability to succeed, as it is 'liable to produce value in the field of professional boxing in the form of recognition, titles and income streams' (ibid: 67). Further, a skilled participant in the gym, someone with ideal-typical bodily characteristics valued in this habitus, will rank higher in the social hierarchy of the field, because their appearance specifically fits with beliefs about field-specific ability.

Biography and history are also important in the gym. Your name and potential for success translated as 'your rep'—one's reputation in this social world. Indeed, reputation was hugely important; 'making a name' for oneself was prevalent across the sample, and the capacity to convert cultural capital into economic or 'workplace capital' (McDowell 1997) was significantly relevant for this social group as a whole. Interestingly, most of the men claimed to be unsuccessful in other careers outside of boxing, yet quite a few of the gym members also worked in the security industries. This was mainly the amateurs, those who supplemented their employment with boxing routines and reputations, as it enhanced their physical capital and added to reputations that relied on the ability to employ violence when necessary (Winlow 2001).

Framing Desistance: Incapacitation and the Ambivalence of the Boxer

Desistance was achieved in part by the men in the gym. It took shape in the form of incapacitation, detaining and occupying men's time when they may otherwise be involved in criminal activity. Yet, the conversations I heard and the interactions I detailed did not instil confidence within me when it came to refraining from fighting outside the gym walls. Challenges to the men's identities and status-diminishing comments, especially those of the emasculating kind, seemed to negate the desistance-promoting potential of the gym, as men would discuss having to 'defend their honour' (Ricky, 20 years old, professional), and not 'look like a pussy' (Simon, 32 years old, professional) when challenged or berated. Having said that, a distinct difference among the desistance-promoting elements of the gym existed between the professionals and the amateurs. The professionals were certainly detained for longer in the gym environment, as the monastic nature of the gym dictated dedication and constant attendance.

The stakes in terms of status and identity seemed higher for the professionals as they had more of a reputation to defend; yet, having said that, the pros generally refrained from day-to-day incidences of street violence. Professionals such as Ricky and Jonny would often talk of being involved in skirmishes after professional fights, or even backstage before stepping into the ring, whereas the amateurs seemed more inclined to engage in street-based violence when necessary. Indeed, the younger teen amateurs seemed intent on establishing identities based on violence, and boxing served as a status-promoting asset in this quest:

> Good thing about the gym is that people know you train, they walk past and see you in here; that's a good thing because it means you're less likely to get targeted.
>
> (Carl, 16 years old, amateur)

> Boxing gets me girls and respect. I love it!
>
> (Elliot, 16 years old, amateur)

Stories of violence from the boxers both young and old generally focused on bravado or reclaiming respect. In addition, the potential for violence or the threat of violence was also sufficient enough for men to be able to maintain desired identities and also ward off potential attacks. This is where boxing comes into its own—acting as a resource that allows men to achieve a semblance of violence—an outward appearance of someone 'not to fuck with'. It is this attribute, as well as the ability to actually fight, which men such as these base both their commercial value and social status upon. Or, for young men like Carl or Elliot, boxing allowed them to accomplish masculine identities based on the potential for physical violence and male virility.

Aside from men's potential for violence and the employment of this in maintaining identities and careers in security industries, actual violence was also evident. Narratives from the likes of Jonny, Ricky and Marcus all attested to the use of violence on occasion. Ricky in particular often became involved in skirmishes after professional fights, as it was common for him and his friends to go out drinking afterwards:

> Me and the lads generally go on a bender after the fight; it's tradition. I try and keep my head down but you get recognised and sometimes that isn't a good thing, especially if there's a bird involved or someone fancies a pop, you know what I'm saying . . .?

Jonny was slightly different in his approach, and was not one for going out drinking after his fights. He had a girlfriend and generally just 'chilled with her and a few mates after a fight'. However, Jonny was known for 'kicking off' backstage before the fights, especially if other contenders laughed at the fact he wore glasses. Jonny was slightly more reserved than Ricky, but nonetheless still concerned with his status and identity as a boxer. I would argue that Jonny's long-term girlfriend was one of the main reasons for his stated desistance, as the relationship proved to be another form of incapacitation not dissimilar to the gym:

> When I'm not here I'm generally at home with my girlfriend; she's studying to be a nurse. When she works nights I come down to the gym and sometimes just hang out; I don't really go out much to be honest, it's not massively my thing anymore . . .

Marcus loved to discuss how he negotiated his way around external agencies and forms of social control. He saw himself as being 'above the law', and liked to think that he 'saw through the system'. Indeed, Marcus liked to offer his opinion to other men on how to 'cheat the law', especially minor civil offences such as speeding tickets or parking fines, and his glee was evident when his advice paid off, as men would bob and weave their way around statutory legislation as they would gloved fists in the ring.

Mostly however, the men talked of how boxing saved them from lives of crime and how without the gym they would not be successful at their chosen professions. Yet, when framing this in context of the desistance literature, boxing did not prevent the men in this research from still engaging in illegal activity and illegitimate violence when the opportunity arose. Constructions of masculinity and competency centre upon bodily capital, whereby techniques and embodied hierarchies of violence ultimately translate and transpose beyond gym culture and into the communities from which these men herald. It is therefore arguable that the discourses of the boxing gym reinforce the discourses of wider structural logics that require men to reaffirm masculine valour, honour and respect. Indeed, the boxing gym speaks to these discourses and therefore forms part of a broader church of masculinity, one in which legitimate/illegitimate violence is viewed as a viable solution to a problem.

Conclusion

In this chapter I have discussed and provided a picture of my ethnography at North Town Gym. I have illustrated a small part of these boxers' lives, and it was my intention to remain authentic to their narratives and also non-judgmental in my quest to paint an evocative picture of boxing and its relationship to desistance from violence. It is commonly known that ethnographic research provides the detail to analyse the wider relationship that groups and social worlds have to larger structures, and in my research I aimed to look at the context of these men's lives in relationship to the communities and circumstances they have experienced. By undertaking participant observation in the context of both gym and street, I obtained a grounded understanding of the embodied hierarchical appeal of the boxing gym and its ability to provide economic and cultural capital to disenfranchised men.

However, previous assumptions in sporting and desistance literature argue that, while relevant, diversionary activities and sport-based programmes that incapacitate are only one element in the theory of change. Accordingly, I argue that, while boxing is undeniably a great tool for engaging men, it can actually trap them in an attendant culture of competition that dictates aggressive responses to maintain images of both masculinity and respect. This attendant culture—that is transposable between gym and street—can override the pro-social incapacitating elements that the boxing gym can offer, and reinforces the logic and discourses that evoke and trap men in habits of responding to violence. Therefore, in terms of future policy and practice, new directions need to be sought.

Notes

1 This being a set of socially learned dispositions, skills and ways of acting that are often taken for granted, and which are acquired through the activities and experiences of everyday life.
2 Denzin, N.K. (1989) *Interpretive Interactionism*, London: Sage.

References

Adler, P.A. and Adler, P. (1987) 'The Past and the Future of Ethnography', *Journal of Contemporary Ethnography*, 16(1): 4–24.
Anderson, E. (1999) *Code of the Street: Decency, Violence, and the Moral Life of the Inner City*, New York, NY: Norton.
Beattie, G. (1997) *On the Ropes: Boxing as a Way of Life*, London: Indigo, Cassell.
Blinde, E. and Taub, D. (1992a) 'Homophobia and Women's Sport: The Disempowerment of Athletes', *Sociological Focus*, 25: 151–166.
Bourdieu, P. (1986). 'The Forms of Capital', in John G. Richardson (ed) *Handbook of Theory and Research for the Sociology of Education*, pp. 241–258. New York: Greenwood Press.
Bourdieu, P. (1990) *In Other Words: Essays Towards a Reflexive Sociology*, Cambridge: Polity Press.

Bourgois, P. (1996) *In Search of Respect: Selling Crack in El Barrio*, Cambridge, UK: Cambridge University Press.

Coffey, A. (1993) 'Double Entry: The Professional and Organizational Socialization of Graduate Accountants'. Unpublished PhD thesis, Cardiff University, in L. Noaks, and E. Wincup (2004) *Criminological Research: Understanding Qualitative Methods*, London: Sage.

Connell, R.W. (1990) 'An Iron Man: The Body and Some Contradictions of Hegemonic Masculinity', in M. Messner and D. Sabo (eds) *Sport, Men and the Gender Order*, pp. 83–96. Illinois: Human Kinetics.

Connell, R.W. (1995) *Masculinities*, Cambridge: Polity Press.

De Garis, L. (2002) 'Be a Buddy to Your Buddy', Male Identity, Aggression, and Intimacy in a Boxing Gym', in J. McKay, M. Messner and D. Sabo (eds) *Masculinities, Gender Relations and Sport*, pp. 87–107. London: Sage.

Denzin, N.K. (1989) *Interpretive Interactionism*, London: Sage.

Emerson, R.M., Fretz, R.I. and Shaw, L.L. (1995) *Writing Ethnographic Fieldnotes*, Chicago, IL: University of Chicago Press.

Gans, H. (1962) 'The Participant-Observer as Human Being: Observation the Personal Aspects of Field Work', in H. Becker (ed) *Institutions and the Person:* Papers presented to Everest, C. Hughes, pp. 300–317. Chicago: Aldine.

Goffman, E. (1963) *Stigma. Notes on the Management of Spoiled Identity*, Englewood Cliffs, NJ: Prentice Hall.

Goffman, E. (1967) *Interaction Ritual*, New York: Anchor.

Hobbs, D. (1995) *Bad Business*, New York: Oxford University Press.

Hobbs, D., O'Brien, K. and Westmarland, L. (2007) 'Connecting the Gendered Door: Women, Violence and Doorwork', *British Journal of Sociology*, 58(1): 21–38.

Hobbs, D. and Robins, D. (1991) 'The Boy Done Good: Football Violence, Changes and Continuities', The *Sociological Review*, 39(3): 551–579.

Katz, J. (1988) *Seductions of Crime: The Moral and Sensual Seductions of Doing Evil*, New York, NY: Basic Books.

Lyng, S. (1998) 'Dangerous Methods: Risk-Taking and the Research Process', in Jeff Ferrell and Mark S. Hamm (eds) *Ethnography at the Edge*, pp. 221–51. Boston: Northeastern University Press.

Martinson, R. (1974) 'What Works? Questions and Answers About Prison Reform', *The Public Interest*, 35(2): 22–54.

Mauss, M. (1973) 'Techniques of the Body', *Economy and Society*, 2(1): 70–88. (Orig.1934)

McDowell, L. (1997) *Capital Culture: Gender at Work in the City*, Oxford: Blackwell.

Mennesson, C. (2000) 'Hard Women and Soft Women: The Social Construction of Identities among Female Boxers', *International Review for the Sociology of Sport*, 35: 21.

Messerschmidt, J.W. (2000) *Nine Lives: Adolescent, the Body, and Violence*, Boulder, CO: Westview.

Monaghan, L.F. (2006) 'Fieldwork and the Body': Reflections on an Embodied Ethnography', in D. Hobbs and R. Wright (eds) *The Sage Handbook of Fieldwork*, pp. 225–242. London: Sage.

Morgan, D. (1992) *Discovering Men*, London: Routledge.

Oates, J.C. (1987) *On Boxing*. London: Bloomsbury.

Presser, L. (2005) 'Negotiating Power and Narrative in Research: Implications for Feminist Methodology', *Signs Vol 3 (4) New Feminist Approaches to Social Science*. Chicago Press.

Shilling, C. (2001) 'Embodiment, Experience and Theory': In Defence of the Socio-logical Tradition', *The Sociological Review*, 49(3): 327–44.

Skeggs, B. (2004) *Class, Self and Culture*, London: Routledge.

Sugden, J. (1996) *Boxing and Society: An International Analysis*, Manchester and New York: Manchester University Press.

Trimbur, L. (2009) '"Me and the Law Is Not Friends": How Former Prisoners Make Sense of Re-entry', *Qualitative Sociology* (32): 259–277. Published Online 18th June: 2009.

Wacquant, L. (1995a) 'Pugs at Work: Bodily Capital and Bodily Labour Among Profes-sional Boxers', in Cheryl L. Cole, John Loy and Mike A. Messner (eds) *Exercising Power: The Making and Remaking of the Body.* Albany: State University of New York Press.

Wacquant, L. (1995b) 'The Pugilistic Point of View: How Boxer's Think and Feel about Their Trade', *Theory and Society*, 24(4): 489–535.

Wacquant, L. (2004) *Body and Soul: Notebooks of an Apprentice Boxer*, New York: Oxford University Press.

Wengraf, T. (2001) *Qualitative Research Interviewing: Biographic Narratives and Semi-Structured Methods*, London: Sage.

Wheaton, B. (2002) 'Babes on the Beach, Women in the Surf', in A. Tomlinson, and J. Sugden (eds) *Power Games: A Critical Sociology Of Sport.* pp. 3–21. London: Routledge.

Winlow, S. (2001) *Badfellas: Crime, Tradition and New Masculinities*, Oxford: Berg.

Woodward, K. (2004) 'Rumbles in the Jungle: Boxing, Racialization and the Perfor-mance of Masculinity', *Journal of Leisure Studies*, 23(1): 5–17.

Woodward, K. (2008) 'Hanging out and Hanging About: Insider/Outsider Research in the Sport of Boxing', *Ethnography*, 9: 536–560.

Section One

Race

2 More Than Violent Whites? From 'Paki Bashing' to the English Defence League

James Treadwell and Jon Garland

Introduction

The English Defence League (more commonly known by the abbreviation the EDL) is a street protest movement formed in the southern English town of Luton in 2009. Its members are largely white, male and, while initially drawn from the settings of organised football violence and traditional right-wing groups, are now much more frequently from a broader demographic of disaffected, aggrieved and forgotten white working-class communities (Winlow et al., 2015). The roots of the group are to be found in the disappearance of traditional forms of work and key changes in popular culture as much as in contemporary media-fuelled anxieties about Islamic terrorism, even if the manifestations of these anxieties are largely a continuation of the traditional street-based far-right violence that has long been encountered in England (e.g., see Pearson, 1976). While there are obvious differences and discontinuities between the EDL and earlier manifestations of violent inter-ethnic group tensions encountered in Britain's industrial cities (Treadwell and Garland, 2011) and while the 'English culture' that they seek to defend is mythical, the forces that have marginalised and alienated its supporters are all too real. These pressures and social shifts have created a form of anger, frustration and rage which now have no legitimate political outlet.

When Geoff Pearson began writing in the mid-1970s about 'Paki bashing' (a term that is now starkly unacceptable to most contemporary sensibilities), it was clearly partly the product of a specific time and place, as well as Pearson's own biography and background. Pearson's work on racialised, anti-immigrant violence in the north-west of England is now unfortunately an oft-overlooked contribution to British criminology. It stemmed from a concern with the history of normal people and everyday community relations that marked out, in hindsight, the not-so-halcyon period of the early British sociology of deviance, a time when social researchers were beginning to draw increasingly upon personal biography to allow for a closer interpretive understanding of the social. It is in the spirit of that endeavour that this chapter draws on our long-term research into the English Defence League, and especially the ethnographic work undertaken mainly by James Treadwell inside the organisation. Just as

Pearson drew on social research and Marxist theory to understand crime and youth subcultures, and sought to consider whether certain types of working-class adolescent, racially charged violence (in the then accepted parlance of 'Paki bashing') could be regarded as a form of politically motivated action (see Pearson, 1976); so too similar concerns framed our work, and it is in accordance with Pearson's traditions that we set out to study the EDL. Our personal motive is comparable to Pearson's, and specifically we have sought to re-introduce consideration of the 'political' nature of crime and violent conduct at a time in which the term 'politics' is frequently applied to activities that are not political at all, such as the lamentable tendency in much contemporary empirical criminology to discover politics in almost every social activity under the sun, thereby diluting the very term (Winlow et al., 2015).

In our view, then, it seems slightly odd that Pearson's work has been subject to a great deal of disparagement for its political reading of deviant activity. Tierney, for example, has heavily criticised the imbuing of such 'deviance' with political motivation, and perhaps most expressly, Pearson's choice to ascribe to the types of violent racist he encountered in Lancashire the label of 'folk hero', which, Tierney suggests, endorses the view of wider public encouragement and support for such detonations of violent racism in the working class than ever really existed. As Tierney states:

> [t]he label 'hero' is ordinarily applied to someone who achieves admiration for great deeds. The prefix 'folk' presumably indicates that the admiration comes from among the ranks of 'ordinary' people, thus a folk hero would be, literally, a hero of the people.
>
> (Tierney, 1979: 17)

Yet while this might seem a fair criticism, when seen in the light of contemporary understandings of how deviancy theory generally recognised youthful criminality as political resistance, Pearson's view of 'politics' and how political concerns are a factor in racist violence, looks much more sophisticated than, say, reading 'politics' into many contemporary forms of youthful rebellion such as urban exploring or base jumping. Indeed, while it might initially seem reasonable to criticise the new deviancy theories of the 1960s as something of a wrong turn (see Hall, 2012), it is arguable that at least with regard to the inter-ethnic violence of the Lancashire cotton town of Accrington, Pearson was indeed right and proper to consider politics (at least in part), just as it is right and proper today to consider the violence of the EDL as political. That is why for us, Pearson's work on racial violence remains a strong, useful and provocative contribution. It is because he is willing to consider the complex issues of motivation and politics against a backdrop of wider social acceptance of prejudices and intolerance that frame the more obvious explosions of violent hostility to an 'other' minority community, that his work is still important. For Pearson, as for us today, considering the socio-economic and political context is vital, and while we are not inclined to talk of members of the EDL as 'folk heroes' involved in 'crypto-political' or 'primitive rebellion', we are nevertheless keen that they are understood in a context of broader unarticulated and latent prejudices of the majority. While for Tierney such theorising might get unduly close to a wider form of 'racist complicity' (Tierney, 2010: 197) when seeking to understand contemporary reactionary violence, it still has merit. After all, most contemporary Islamophobia manifests itself in quite basic and low-level ways, and not in detonations of interpersonal violence, and yet the latter clearly thrives in a climate where the former is the more commonly shared sentiment (see Allen, 2011), as any brief read through the *Daily Star* or *Daily Mail* will likely demonstrate.

This chapter begins by outlining factors within the broader social context which may precipitate involvement in an organisation such as the English Defence League. We discuss the difficulties and dilemmas of researching, close up, those whose views we find repugnant, and also address some of the criticisms we have received for conducting research into an organisation that some believe should not be given the credence of having their views examined and then aired. We assess, via the findings from this fieldwork, why the EDL holds such appeal for some from disenfranchised white working-class communities, and why the political left has failed to hold similar appeal. Throughout we have incorporated the words of those we have researched, although the names of those we met have been altered to preserve their anonymity.

From the Lancashire Racist Lads to the Casuals of the EDL

> Simon looks around us, he is still spoiling for a fight, he starts to attempt to vocalise his anger: 'the fucking police ought to let us at them [by 'them', he means the young Muslim males gathered to oppose the EDL], we are the same, we are not child rating, soldier murdering, fucking brainwashed scum from some medieval fucking cult. I fucking hate them; I fucking hate Musrats' [he means Muslims]. He spits on the floor. 'I would love to see their fucking blood running in the streets. They are the fucking death of this country, since they started letting them in, look at how the country has got, it is that what has fucked it, that and the fucking idiots that let it happen. . .'.

> [Later in the day] Simon and Ginge have already exchanged words and are arguing again; I [James Treadwell] decide not to intervene. Simon is full of alcohol and cocaine and is spoiling for a fight, even though he has already hit several people today. Robbie tries to play peacemaker and asks, 'What's up lads?' Simon looks at Ginge and says, 'I have had enough of this prick's fucking moaning'. Ginge quickly and somewhat thoughtlessly responds: 'Who are you calling a prick?' It's enough of a challenge to give Simon the excuse he has been looking for and without a further word, he turns round quickly and punches Ginge once, hard in the face. His fist lands with a mix of a thud and a slap, but it breaks Ginge's nose.

Why do the people at society's margins, often those from its poorest communities, turn on one another? Why is the violence of these young men so frequently targeted against those who are similarly precariously positioned and disadvantaged? Whether it is young men quite like them from the same ethnic group, or those demarked by difference because of race or religion, a stark fact of violence is that it largely involves young males positioned precariously at the bottom rungs of the social ladder. Is there a complicity and public support for some forms of violent crime? It seems to us that Pearson's argument on the 'Paki bashing' of the 1960s is that rather than view the racist violence as just simply a meaningless individual pathology, it should in part at least be considered as a potentially rational, purposeful response (at least in the point of view of the perpetrators); and in order to reach this point, Pearson suggests that it is necessary to understand their behaviour in light of the socio-economic changes taking place in that area of Lancashire at the time of the violence and wider community feelings. Just as that was true then, for us it remains utterly true now.

Perhaps, following Pearson's lead it is possible to look at the broader context in which some forms of violence occurs and the socio-economic, political and cultural drivers of such actions while avoiding the danger of drifting into any 'romanticisation of deviance'—and specifically of working-class violence. It was essentially towards that end that we became involved in an ethnography of the EDL in 2009. It is now, after hours and days spent amongst core supporters of the group in several regions of the UK that we can say that the EDL is an avowedly violent organisation (irrespective of its public claims to passivity on the part of its official spokespeople). For the most part, it has directed that violence at the Islamic (and perceived Islamic) communities, the police (Treadwell, 2014) and not infrequently in our experience, at one another (the example just given is only one of several incidents James witnessed where members violently assaulted one another). Its emergence and character have been well charted elsewhere (Treadwell and Garland, 2011), and the growth of the organisation now means that we feel more comfortable in giving less detail about the group's origins. Suffice to say that our unique position is being able to talk from the inside about what the EDL is, based on hours of ethnographic research undertaken within the group at demonstrations, events, in pubs and bars and at meetings.

As a society we must force ourselves to understand what would push somebody to be involved in a movement like the EDL, to attend their meetings, to take to the streets and to believe that there is a need for such a group. We believe that our understanding of the EDL must be a cold and considered one based not on narrow condemnatory judgements of the individuals taking part, for individual motives are doubtlessly a complex interplay of the psychosocial (see Treadwell and Garland, 2011; Gadd, 2011) but driven instead by a consideration of what the contemporary moment, and what our societal structures, institutions and processes have done to facilitate the situation we now face. It is not simply a matter of understanding racist individuals. The problem is that the EDL comprises not just violent whites. Moreover, the mocking tone adopted by some populist left-wing and liberal commentators conceals the recent failures of the left to engage successfully with the working class. If they had done more to recognise the frustrations of those in the EDL or taken seriously the causes or consequences of their marginalisation, then the EDL and other right-wing organisations would undoubtedly have less appeal (see Hardy, 2014; Winlow et al., 2015).

Moreover, beyond that, such narrow dismissal ignores the precariousness and exclusion at the heart of some people's experiences that in some cases underscores the drive toward pyrrhic and pointless manifestations of violence at street demonstrations (see Treadwell and Garland, 2011). While we might rightly see the violence of the EDL as futile and nasty, so too we ought to understand how it arises out of individual schema and attitudes. We all have ingrained beliefs and ideas that shape our frameworks for understanding the world, and these beliefs become embedded and influence how we interpret our daily experiences and interactions, a manner that some would term 'habitus'. Indeed, that very term is one that is used to denote the manner in which acquired schemata, sensibilities, dispositions and taste are a complex result of embodying social structures.

If our world view has been constructed by the *Daily Mail*, the *Sun*, Facebook, the *Daily Star* and the occasional glimpse of the UK Border force on Sky television, and if we have never been taught to question, to critique; if we have no confidence in politics (and let us face it, in this age of insipid post-politics, who truly does have?) and our experience of education has been absent of critical content; if we are told that our unemployment is a direct consequence of increased immigration; that Muslim terrorism constitutes the most obvious and pressing societal threat or that Muslims are the only people with the potential to be 'extreme', then it becomes more understandable that the EDL would be an attractive option.[1] They have tapped into the frustrations and anxieties of those white working-class groups in a manner like no other.

Seen this way, the EDL offers explanations, and explanations that increasingly are rejecting and critical of the prevailing and dominant ideology. The organisation offers a brotherhood (or sisterhood for that matter), something to feel valued for and something to be involved in, irrespective of their massively flawed arguments, alcohol- and cocaine-fuelled meetings and racist ideologies. It offers a vision, even if it is reactive, angry, intolerant and violent. The EDL knows that there are people who do not like them; they feel alienated, many of its supporters feel marginalised and pissed off.

Yet we were aware from the outset that some would see such an attempt to understand the EDL as a fool's errand. Why does such an organisation need understanding at all—after all, Tierney's original criticism still stands, as does not the EDL only speak for a small segment of the working class? Beyond that, does simply considering the EDL as 'political' grant members attention that they are best denied? When considering whether to research the EDL we did seriously consider these views and whether what we were contemplating sat comfortably within our own ethical framework. Now, having undertaken extensive fieldwork within the organisation, we feel our approach has enabled us to gain a rare insight into its members' views, opinions and motives. It therefore means, as we detail in the following discussion, that we can say as credibly as anyone that the EDL leadership's self-articulated claims that the organisation is merely expressing the concerns of ordinary patriotic British citizens is rather undermined when there is clear evidence that the leadership and a large section of its membership consist of racist, violent hooligans spoiling for a fight.

Inside the EDL

To understand the EDL it is necessary to get close to them as a group, and the concern with such proximity should not just be at the potential for offering a platform for views that many find distasteful. Of course, Pearson was a veracious defender of qualitative methods, and in particular the ethnographic method. From the outset and the very inception of the EDL the lead author of this piece, James Treadwell, was in a unique position to gain access. Having said that, access to the EDL and its often violent street demonstrations and protests, while a potentially useful research opportunity, was also one that was to prove complex and difficult. Yet for those willing to take the inherent risks involved, it provides an excellent method for gathering real data at the coalface and for gaining a unique insight into the perceptions, attitudes and viewpoints of the group under study. Ethnographers occupy a privileged yet complicated narrative and discursive position. This is something Pearson recognised when he memorably noted:

> Ethnography is often said to be a way of 'telling it like it is', looking at the social world of the subject as it is seen 'from the inside'. Some perceive, [as he further argued] . . . it is not, and never can be that. . . . In my view, the ethnographic text cannot 'betray' the experience of the field since the vital opposition of authenticity and distance means that the experience of fieldwork is never quite as 'real' as it is sometimes supposed to be. . . . What is required of a good ethnographer is neither full membership nor competence, but the ability to give voice to that experience, and to bridge the experiences of actors and audiences.
>
> (Pearson, 1993: xviii)

Of course, what is also missing from this is consideration of ethnography's ability to provide evidence of individual acts that taken together might perhaps paint a broader picture of social transformation. It could be argued that social science has always been less than comfortable with the notion of knowledge generated from ethnography, and as a method, it is still too frequently lambasted for its macro focus. Yet it was always James's intent that his ethnography was grounded in the 'lived experiences' of the participants and the primary commitment was in undertaking research that would attempt to provide that detail of the nature and character of the English Defence League and those who participated in its demonstrations, and the lives behind them, to produce a form of comprehension of the EDL's violence that was not about empathetic understanding.

Yet a further point that really ought to be examined is that the EDL emerged in the UK in 2009, just after the onset of the 2008 global financial crash. Importantly, it also materialised in the wake of new and more frequently articulated concerns about national decline, the precariousness of national identity and perceived threats to traditional values and ways of life that pre-dated the 'credit crunch'. Increasingly, this 'threat' is placed by the far right at the door of Islam. However, the decision to actively participate in and give a voice to a group such as the EDL has not proved popular with everybody. For example, at a British Society of Criminology conference, in a plenary session we were asked:

> Why are you trying to understand these people, why are you doing research on them? We know why they do what they do; aren't you just serving to legitimise their grievances?

There are several responses to this, but the first is to raise the question of value. Would any other form of qualitative research be challenged on its intrinsic value on the instinctive belief that we may know what people are going to say? Would a similar argument be made about, say, victims of domestic violence? Is it not dangerous that social researchers act as subjective filters defining which social groups are worthy of academic scrutiny? While we had little sympathy with much of the simplistic, naïve and racist sentiments and viewpoints we heard while researching the EDL, it nevertheless could be argued that there is as much academic value in studying them as any group. We certainly did not consider ourselves racist or a harbinger of far-right attitudes, and James never felt at risk of 'going native', as the ideology and values of the EDL were and remain extremely alien. While we did not like many of their views, seeking to understand the generation of racist anxieties is not the same as condoning them.

In contrast to the regurgitation of common arguments concerning the character of the EDL, we have continually made the case that the rather simplistic branding of the organisation as far right misses much of the more complex dynamics at play in the reality as manifest and encountered on the streets (Garland and Treadwell, 2010). Furthermore, we have also argued for the value of speaking to those involved in the EDL so as to expose hidden practices that underscore the public face of the organisation and also the human motivations that inform them. Nowhere were we more convinced of this than when it came to the violence used by EDL members and the meanings attached to it. Yet this has not always been the case with academic research on the EDL. Take, for example, the assertion of Northampton academics that, 'Responding to a sense of powerlessness by "performing" an empowered, male identity through street protests and violence, however, is an ultimately unfulfilling channel for such frustrations' (Jackson and Feldman, 2011).

How can we possibly comprehend whether such actions are unfulfilling without speaking to those involved? We have argued, for example, that at the core of understanding a violent member of the EDL is to recognise the sense of psychological fulfilment that they get from their violent offending (Treadwell and Garland, 2011). For example, one of our subjects hardly comes across as unfulfilled when he described his feelings after committing a violent assault (punching and kicking a young Asian man) while at an EDL demonstration with the statement, 'I was proud afterwards. It made me feel like I'd made a stand' (Treadwell and Garland, 2011: 630). We might rightly ask, of course, a stand against what? But uncovering 'unpalatable' views and behaviour, and asking questions of them, is rightfully the place of social science.

More Than Just Violent Whites

Our data would suggest that the roots of the EDL are to be found in the disappearance of traditional forms of work and key changes in popular culture as much as in contemporary anxieties about Islam. Against this backdrop, the omnipresent 'other' is that of Islam and its adherents, although it needs to be mentioned at the outset this is a rather monolithic and ill-informed understanding of Islam. However, in this respect, EDL supporters are not that separate from the tabloid press, the British government and the mass of the populace who seem to believe that a 'Muslim' is a fixed and unified identity, rather than a wholly disparate category of person. Yet, while the EDL is concerned about Muslims and Islam, and talks about both as a source of anxiety, foremost in members' thoughts is worry over the decline in their own communities, the acute sense of loss, abandonment and betrayal, which manifests itself in forms of anger:

> Fucking Labour and Liberal middle-class pricks have abandoned this country to a tide of fucking lazy, worthless immigrants from Muslim lands that have no respect for English countries and fucking English heritage and values. . . . Now my country doesn't look like my country anymore. Pubs are turning into fucking mosques while these Muslim cunts, they won't work, they won't integrate. The men are fucking grooming and abusing poor white girls while claiming to be decent and upstanding and putting their women in fucking veils. It's all Pakistanis, Bangladeshis, Somalis, what does that tell you?. . . . they are all fucking Muslims, that is what they have in common. They are ripping off benefits and living in five-bedroom houses while we go without. They are all morally upstanding citizens, until you look at who is riding round in Mercs and Audis selling all the smack around here. The police won't touch them in case they are called racist, yet they all want fucking sharia law.
>
> (Danny, EDL member from the Midlands)

The stereotype of the 'paki' which is contradictory as many stereotypes, finds him sitting down at home (where he lives in filth with at least a dozen others in a couple of rooms) . . . weary from his day of labour at the dole office. He is dirty, promiscuous and cheeky, but he also keeps himself to himself and does not mix at all. . . . 'He kills goats and chickens in the back yard, his children pee on the flagstones, he has a large family, and he depresses the price of property wherever he goes. He contrives to filch people's jobs and yet batten social security at the same time. The police are on his side, and he has been granted immunity from the law of the land by the Race Relations Act'.

(Pearson, 1976: 65–66)

Just as the riots in Bradford, Burnley and Oldham in 2001 signalled the rage of some young British men of Pakistani and Bangladeshi heritage who feel denied access to futures, so too for some young men of what was once the white working class; there is a similar growing feeling of resentment that has few legitimate outlets. Yet while the Bradford riots spurned drama and discussion, the EDL is frequently regarded as a nasty social problem best ignored,[2] members' grievances a simple invention.

Indeed, while Pearson might be accused by Tierney of being rather too simplistic in his drawing of community segregation in English towns and cities in the 1960s, now with the benefit of hindsight the long-standing segregation, in housing policy, in education, in many aspects of life between different ethnic groups is something of a given. A generation of Pakistani and Bangladeshi British-born men are now growing close to their white counterparts, with little contact other than through uncertain glances on the street. Mutual distrust has increased and festered. In his ethnography of working-class life Charlesworth (2000), for example, notes the profound sense of social change in 1990s Rotherham (a city now synonymous with inter-ethnic community tension in the wake of child sexual abuse scandals) that emerged as a result of economic restructuring, and highlights how this breaking-down process began as a product of neoliberalism. From the 1980s onwards mass unemployment or more precarious forms of employment outside of traditional industry became the norm for many of Rotherham's residents. This fundamentally served to break the bond between work and community. Those who could still find employment were often forced to travel farther afield and took up roles within increasingly atomised workplaces. Charlesworth suggests that the solidarities of family and of work, once the cornerstone of working-class experience (underpinned by a culture of trade unions and education), were washed away through the institution of free market economics, producing a fractured anomie and concomitant social problems (see also Patel, 2014). What was left was a feeling of ambiguity:

For the working class, themselves, for whom the economically marginal and socially excluded are family members and neighbours, they have to deal in the most palpable way with the decline of their own economic role and social position. Since the early 1980s the gradual decline of the culture of the working class has been one of the most powerful, telling developments in British society.

(2000: 2)

Yet it is not such changes that are foremost in the concerns of EDL supporters; instead, Islam seemingly became a proxy for such anxieties. Indeed, frequently Islam and 'Muslims' were given as the foremost concern of EDL members as if there were no greater pressing social problem:

These Muslims who blow themselves up are brain-washed to think they will be getting fucked by a host of virgins for killing and maiming our soldiers, and now, we have hundreds who secretly support them over here. Muslims hate and despise our way of life; they support those who rape and abuse women and kids, who behead the likes of us in the blink of an eye and our government don't police them, it's us. They are more worried about a few of us football lads when it kicks off on the streets. If you live in some posh middle-class gaff you won't see this, but I live on a council housing estate surrounded by people who have nothing in common with Muslims, and there is no way I will ever accept them.

(Ian, EDL supporter from the South East)

I can see what has happened to this country . . . we are fed up with people coming here thinking they can get everything they want and build their stupid mosques and then try and dictate to us; why should we tolerate this? Some people might sit back and say nothing, only because they are scared to speak up. I fucking tell you, I am not. I will fight, I'll do more time, I don't care, I am not letting these Muslims ruin my country anymore.

(Steve, EDL supporter from North England)

What was apparent is that not infrequently the testimony from those inter-viewed about Muslims was one that mirrored the wider mainstream media. Frequently, EDL members followed a script set by the *Sun*, *Daily Star* and *Daily Mirror*, a concern with a monolithic Islam seen as universal, violent and intolerant. It was responsible for 'political correctness', it was banning nativity plays and secretly undermining working-class traditions. We heard frequent complaints about how 'the system was now set-up to privilege "Muslims"' while black and white Britons were marginalised.

Conclusions

EDL supporters' dislike of Muslims and Islam is not imagined. In our research we commonly found negative perceptions of Muslim or Islamic immigration coupled with a list of grievances directed at Islam, including (not exclusively) accusations of welfare benefit fraud, sexual exploitation of young white females and profiteering through 'heroin jihad' while receiving preferential treatment from the criminal justice system. These fears were amplified by frustration at what they saw as society's tacit acceptance of violent Islamism that was occurring at the same time as deep concerns about lack of jobs and access to affordable housing which exemplified the exclusion of the lower strata of the white working class. Indeed, many EDL members used a language and examples where anything perceived to be at the advantage of 'them' was to the detriment and disadvantage of 'us'. The Islamic 'other' was a community that existed in solidarity and unity, a feature no longer encountered routinely amongst the marginalised English working class. The emotion that typified the EDL's entire discourse and response to this acute experience of loss was that of anger. It was at street demonstrations and flash demonstrations where that anger was most apparent and frequently turned into violence.

At root, there is an assumption that Muslim communities possess the lost spirit of solidarity and brotherhood precisely because white working-class communities do not, that they are privileged and protected in a way that the white working class is not and that they receive some form of perverse advantage. This is nonsense, of course, in both respects (see also Winlow et al., 2015). Many supporters of the EDL have never experienced anything other than the present; faced with personal experiences of social exclusion that they do not fully comprehend or understand, they turn on others near to them, and often these others are similarly socially excluded. They certainly do not recognise global neoliberal capitalism as a source of their woes and problems, or the source of shared oppression. Indeed, it ought be remembered that the targets of most of the aggression of the EDL, young Bangladeshi and Pakistani (often Islamic) men, live lives that are marked by an intensified global surveillance, cultural pathologisation and social and racial exclusion, against the same backdrop of limited opportunity (Pantazis and Pemberton, 2009).

Presently, there is much evidence of the historical continuity of class-based structural constraints on working-class Pakistani and Bangladeshi men. Their collective profile includes the highest levels of unemployment and over-representation in low-skilled employment, over-representation in prisons, over-representation in poor housing, high levels of poor health and lowest levels of social mobility (e.g., see Martin et al., 2010; Barnard and Turner, 2011; Garner and Bhattacharyya, 2011). In this respect, they are much like the lower-class white working men in the EDL. The existence of the EDL clearly suggests that there is an abundance of dissatisfaction among England's white working class. However, the nature of the EDL's discourse bears witness to the failure of the left to engage with the working class, symbolise their frustrations and capitalise upon the revolutionary potential that exists in marginalised neighbourhoods. Instead, in their desperate attempt to understand their position, the angry white men of the EDL grasp the regressive politics of ethnic hatred and in so doing ignore the fundamental causes of their grim circumstances.

Many of our respondents had encountered what they believed to be representatives of the left at EDL demonstrations. These angry working-class men recounted tales of being deprecated, vilified and psychically attacked by representatives of the political left. How can we understand this situation in which the left is in conflict (and sometimes violently) with elements of the traditional working class? Is this simply a traditional clash of ideologies, in which the egalitarian left attacks the fascists of the far right? Can we not say that, when the left denounce the EDL at their demonstrations, they are in fact appraising an inverted mirror image of their own political failure? Does the mere fact that the EDL has grown so quickly in a time of significant economic turmoil reflect the failure of the left to symbolise the anger and dissatisfaction of the traditional white working class, and their failure to lead the working class towards an encounter with their true enemy (see also Winlow et al., 2015)?

Of course, such questions so frequently fall away from the remit of criminology. They are difficult and complex. It is not easy to answer why it is that the most marginalised people in the social strata turn on one another when the going gets tough. Geoff Pearson got that. His description of racist violence as 'a sad and hopeless rage' found during 'moments of cultural and economic dislocation' seems pretty timeless (Pearson, 1976: 69–75).

Notes

1 See Hardy, 2014, for a further discussion of anger, alienation and the use of 'inappropriate' racist vocabulary by young white working-class people.
2 Take, for example, the condemnation of the EDL after the UK riots in 2011, when Prime Minister David Cameron in the House of Commons stated, 'The Hon. Gentleman speaks not only for his constituents, but, frankly, for the whole House in deprecating the English Defence League and all it stands for. On its attempt to say that it will somehow help to restore order, I have described some parts of our society as sick, and there is none sicker than the EDL' (Busher, 2012: 251).

References

Allen, C. (2011) 'Opposing Islamification or Promoting Islamophobia? Understanding the English Defence League', *Patterns of Prejudice*, 45 (4): 279–294.

Barnard, H. and Turner, C. (2011) *Poverty and Ethnicity: A Review of Evidence*, York: Joseph Rowntree Foundation.

Busher, J. (2012) '"There Are None Sicker than the EDL": Narratives of Racialisation and Resentment from Whitehall and Eltham, South London', in D. Briggs (ed) *The English Riots of 2011: A Summer of Discontent*, London: Waterside Press, pp. 237–256.

Charlesworth, S. (2000) *A Phenomenology of Working Class Experience*, Cambridge: Cambridge University Press.

Gadd, D. (2011) 'Murderer, Mad Man, Misfit? Making Sense of the Murder of Zahid Mubarek', *Journal of Psycho-Social Studies*, 5 (1): 139–162.

Garland, J. and Treadwell, J. (2010) '"No Surrender to the Taliban": Football Hooliganism, Islamophobia and the Rise of the English Defence League', *Papers from the British Criminology Conference*, 10 (1): 19–35.

Garner, S. and Bhattacharyya, G. (2011) *Poverty, Ethnicity and Place*, York: Joseph Rowntree Foundation.

Hardy, S. (2014) 'Developing Themes on Young People, Everyday Multiculturalism and Hate Crime', in N. Chakraborti and J. Garland (eds) *Responding to Hate Crime*, Bristol: The Policy Press, pp. 141–154.

Jackson, P. and Feldman, M. (2011) *The EDL: Britain's 'New Far Right' Social Movement*, Northampton: The University of Northampton.

Martin, J., Heath, A. and Bosveld, K. (2010) *Is Ethnicity or Religion More Important in Explaining Inequalities in the Labour Market?* Sociology Working Papers, Paper Number 2010–02, Oxford: University of Oxford.

Pantazis, C. and Pemberton, S. (2009) 'From the "Old" to the "New" Suspect Community Examining the Impacts of Recent UK Counter-Terrorist Legislation', *British Journal of Criminology*, 49 (5): 646–666.

Patel, T. G. (2014) ' "We'll Go Grafting, Yeah?": Crime as a Response to Urban Neglect', *Criminology & Criminal Justice: An International Journal*, 14 (2): 179–195.

Pearson, G. (1976) 'Paki-bashing' in a North East Lancashire Cotton Town: A Case Study and Its History', in G. Mungham and G. Pearson (eds) *Working Class Youth Culture*, pp. 48–81. London: Routledge and Keegan Paul.

Pearson, G. (1993) 'Forward', in D. Hobbs and T. May (eds) *Interpreting the Field: Accounts of Ethnography*, pp. vi–xx. Oxford: Clarendon.

Tierney, J. (1979) *Politics and Deviance: The Political Status of Working Class Delinquency*, Durham thesis, Durham University. Available at Durham E-Theses Online: http://etheses.dur.ac.uk/10106/

Tierney, J. (2010) *Criminology: Theory and Context* (3rd edition), Oxon: Routledge.

Treadwell, J. (2014) 'Controlling the New Far Right on the Streets: Policing the English Defence League', in N. Chakraborti and J. Garland (eds) *Responding to Hate Crime*, Bristol: Policy Press, pp. 127–140.

Treadwell, J. and Garland, J. (2011) 'Masculinity, Marginalisation and Violence: A Case Study of the English Defence League', *British Journal of Criminology*, 51 (4): 621–634.

Winlow, S. (2014) 'Some Thoughts on Steve Hall's Theorizing Crime and Deviance: A New Perspective', *Journal of Theoretical and Philosophical Criminology*, 6 (2): 168–193.

Winlow, S., Hall, S., Briggs, D. and Treadwell, J. (2015) *Riots and Political Culture*, London: Routledge.

3 From 'Paki Bashing' to 'Muslim Bashing'

UK Extremism Policies Considered[1]

Alice Sampson

Introduction

In this essay I draw principally on Geoff Pearson's work on deviance that he wrote more than 30 years ago to illustrate its usefulness for assessing social policies. Using his analytical and sociological approach I assess the UK Coalition government's extremism policy. It is remarkable that his approach for assessing contemporary social issues remains pertinent and insightful, and how it exposes troubling aspects of the extremism agenda. I am pretty certain that Geoff would be very agitated by some of the research on terrorism and responses to extremism by professionals because characterisations of, and reactions to, extremism have to a great extent fallen into the traps that Geoff warned policymakers and researchers about. By applying Geoff's approach to a current policy concern the case for a policy re-think is clear and its contribution to informing policymakers and practitioners how to improve policies and practices apparent. As shown in this essay, research, debates and responses to extremism have in many ways reached a cul-de-sac and a critical sociological analysis is able to progress debates and improve our responses.

The intention is not to remain slavishly loyal to Geoff's approach but rather to use it as a method of thinking about how extremism is conceptualised as a social problem, and its implications for understanding policy and practice. Much of Geoff's earlier work was focussed on white working-class boys and men, and a broader perspective is incorporated into this essay that recognises class issues are complex and remain highly relevant to an analysis, as does the portrayal of women and girls. Nor is the academic literature on extremism, radicalisation and terrorism systematically reviewed but rather issues pertinent to a critical social policy analysis and those which Geoff considered vital for researchers to explore, are drawn on. Policy documents are analysed and findings from research in inner city areas are used selectively to illustrate the value of Geoff's analytical approach. Between November 2013 and April 2014 more than 200 participants from a wide age range, from different ethnic and cultural backgrounds and of different and no faith, who were residents, from community organisations and community leaders, and political activists, participated in focus groups and interviews. While we did not talk to self-proclaimed jihadist extremists, interviews were conducted with 'right-wing' nationalists and those who are or have been in contact with 'extremists'.

Research and Policy Traps

Geoff's work on deviancy, hooligans and 'Paki-bashing' identifies two related factors that explain how research and debate reaches an impasse. Firstly, Geoff argued research informed by abstract thinking is at too high a level to generate useful practical information for policymaking and practice. This type of research develops high-level hypotheses which 'closes down debates', as its high level of abstraction uses few 'facts' and borders on speculation and, without discussions based on actual experiences and practices, errors are not detected and rectified. Thus, Geoff emphasised that debates should be informed by theories that arise from empirical research in communities that are rooted in everyday realities and experiences shaped by local histories and cultural experiences (Pearson 1975: 208).

Two reviews of the academic literature on terrorism recognise that research has been unable to identify effective preventive strategies and inform policymakers or practitioners about what works and what might be counter-productive (Borum 2011; Schmid 2013: iv). Yet researchers have continued to be preoccupied with searching for universal and agreed definitions of terms such as radicalisation, extremism and terrorism and maintain a belief that 'the lack of clarity and consensus with regard to many key concepts . . . still present an obstacle that needs to be overcome' (Borum 2011; Schmid 2013: iv and 38). Further, a belief by researchers and policymakers that identifying root causes facilitates the development of effective de-radicalisation programmes is also identified as a priority in the search for a 'silver bullet' solution (Borum 2011).

Insufficient research that focusses on understanding 'social meanings', analyses of political and moral discourses, and perhaps most of all, a critical edge and boldness invokes a temporary or permanent suspension of conventional morality. This would be perceived by Geoff as the greatest failing of research on terrorism (Matza 1969; Pearson 1975, 1976, 1983). Indications are apparent that some research on terrorism adopts and works within dominant discourses; for example, by placing terrorism in a military context with descriptions such as the 'war on terrorism', and the militarisation of violence with phrases such as 'tactics of violence' (see, for example, Schmid 2013: iv). Categorical statements such as 'extremists are never democrats' would also concern Geoff (Schmid 2013: 10). The uncritical use of well-used phrases such as 'counter-terrorism' or 'de-radicalisation' are indicative of the binary framework that Geoff urged researchers to move away from to better understand the complexities of social issues and the importance of gaining insiders' accounts to 'throw off the shackles of a pre-defined and officially categorised social reality' (Pearson 1975: 65).

By exposing reification, deviance is revealed as a socially constructed event that requires researchers to analyse the social process of labelling to understand how society is an active partner in producing the phenomenon called deviance. In his research on 'Paki bashing' Geoff challenged 'common sense' notions that there must be something wrong with criminals and the idea that all efforts must be focussed on eradicating deviancy as if it is a contagious disease like malaria. Rather Geoff argued for a greater understanding of how deviants and hooligans are socially constructed and conceptualised (Pearson 1975, 1976, 1983).

But what can we learn from this approach that is different; what are the implications for policy and practice? By raising awareness of the 'normalisation' of the dominant discourses about the 'war on terror' and 'evil terrorists' by listening to extremists and understanding responses to extremism in local neighbourhoods, alternative explanations can be articulated and discussed and the effects of policies and practices assessed.

To explore these possibilities this essay is structured as follows: a condensed resumé of Geoff's approach and a brief outline of the UK Coalition government's concept of extremism is described. Attention is drawn to how policies can be politically used by agencies to assert their moral authority and how imagining terrorists shapes policies. The remainder of the essay discusses how the extremism agenda is implemented in local areas, with what effect and for whom. A complex picture emerges of successfully marginalising some groups, as intended by the policy, but with consequences unlikely to be intended. Key issues of significance for central government, such as community tensions and tolerance, are largely dismissed locally and ascribed different meanings in local communities. Policies that are considered to reduce community tensions locally, such as access to affordable housing, jobs with prospects and a better police response to hate crimes, are overlooked by central government in their responses to extremism.

Geoff's Critical Sociological Approach

If we assess the UK's Coalition policy on extremism using Geoff's method of critical sociology, then some uncomfortable truths are identified as follows:

Rejection of Positivism and Determinism

Geoff clearly articulated the role of social scientists in the concluding chapter of *Deviant Imagination* where he emphasised that we should 'act responsibly and critically on the question of how social problems are defined . . . and should also interrogate the society which defines the deviant imagination as a waste-product' by calling on researchers to understand 'misfits' who are not given a place in society (Pearson 1975: 203). Through his historical and cultural analysis of hooliganism and deviancy, Geoff shows how an appreciative understanding of hooligans and their violent actions reveals ordinary human beings who exercise choice (Matza 1969; Pearson 1976). In his analysis Geoff linked the practice of deviance control to both moral and political aspects of how state agencies responded to these deviants. He found that professionals make decisions and respond to 'misfits' within the moral and political discourses of their time and use a dominant scientific discourse that is itself underpinned by powerful ideologies that label deviants and hooligans as different and deficient, and who 'need to be put right' (Pearson 1975: 207).

Geoff lamented the dominance of scientific-technical discourses and how professional technicians who included criminologists, social workers, psychiatrists and psychologists perceived deviance control as a scientific matter. Geoff perceived that these technicians claim to 'know' what is best to eliminate deviance by constructing definitions of normality, and that 'ideologies wrap themselves up in scientific disguise' and are deeply problematic (Pearson 1975: 206). Technicians claim that deviance arises from 'monstrous conditioning' or bent genes and that deviants are essentially 'unlike other men' (Pearson 1975: 207). Patterns of stigma are constructed by professionals and passed on to their clients who conform and in doing so acquire the labels that are ascribed to them by society and by professionals (Pearson 1975: 75). In these ways society and professionals can amplify deviancy and contribute to its increase.

Labelling

Through his research Geoff demonstrated how the unquestioning of social rules led to a reified conception of social order and those who were not compliant with, nor accepted the official view of social reality were labelled as deviant. In his studies Geoff described how 'deviants' held attitudes and behaved according to an alternative and equally plausible set of norms. This perspective is central to Geoff's thesis that deviance and hooliganism are not mindless acts but rather, when historical and cultural contexts are considered and an analysis of societies' responses taken into account, can be understood as rational actions (Pearson 1975, 1976, 1976a,1983).

Relationships between social deviance and social order and the separation of 'them' and not 'us' leads to attempts to rationally control deviants in ways which are neither logical nor meaningful to them. It is wrongly assumed that by leading a life outside societal norms they are under-socialised and/or they are pathological as their lives are lawless, immoral and unnatural and therefore 'can be explained away in thought and swept away in practice' (Pearson 1975: 10).

Using the labelling approach enables us to understand how communities and authorities scapegoat where there are uneasy histories of mutual suspicion, complex hostilities, and differences in culture, religion and lifestyle. Scapegoating can be accompanied by 'moral panics' when reactions of the media and government inflame volatile situations. In the 1970s, for example, through the influence of national policies, race became central to British politics and with immigration controls came an increase in National Front activities, and an initial problem became amplified and 'justified' an increase in the use of punishment and control by central government and the police (Pearson 1976a).

Violent Acts as Self-Expression and Resistance

In his discussions on violence in northern towns in the 1970s, Geoff discussed how in the context of social tensions and economic inequalities violence was inherent in social situations but only 'sparks' occasionally (Pearson 1976). As Geoff illustrated in his study about his home town of Accrington, 'these troubled sentiments crystallised into "Paki-bashing" ' which was class-based, and embedded in cultural hostilities and indiscriminate racism and social inequalities (Pearson 1976). In these places fears about changing economic circumstances and depressed wages manifest themselves in street fighting and brawls outside pubs. 'Sexual edginess' was also inherent in the violence (Pearson 1976). Geoff also described how 'mugging' was a political act by young black Africans and an expression of their alienation and marginalisation from society (Pearson 1976: 217; Hall 1978). The police in particular represent the moral authority of the state and are aligned with society's position on what is considered 'right' and 'wrong' and a dynamic occurs; political resistance challenges the moral authority of state agencies, agencies respond with ever-increasing strategies of control, mistrust grows and moral panics ensue (Pearson 1976). Violence escalates, Geoff argued, where agencies and services, who are intermediaries between the state and communities, do not listen and understand what is being expressed through violent actions and therefore they are prone to further inflame volatile situations.

Extremism and the UK Coalition Government

In this section I outline the UK government's approach to extremism and identify how they have constructed and defined extremism as a social problem and how these characterisations enable the government to claim that they are protectors of our society and are used by the police to reassert their moral authority.

Conceptualising Extremism

Two speeches by David Cameron, one in 2011 in Munich and the other in 2014 to the United Nations General Assembly, set out the UK government's position on extremism. These speeches express a consistent belief that Islamist extremism is a political ideology quite separate from religion, and that 'defeating' this extremist ideology, the root cause of terrorism, is the responsibility of governments and societies across the world. All forms of extremism—extremist beliefs, thoughts and violence—are to be actively confronted and 'passive tolerance' that allows law-abiding citizens to be left alone is unacceptable and to be replaced by 'active muscular liberalism' that promotes freedom of speech, worship, democracy and equal rights. Emphasis is placed on 'defeating the ideas that warp so many minds at their root', described as 'evil', and legitimacy is claimed for taking an uncompromising approach in the UK by introducing new state powers to ensure the safety and security of UK citizens, and participating in the international air strikes against the Islamic State of Iraq and Levant (ISIL) in September 2014 (Cameron 2011, 2014). A counter-terror bill in autumn 2014 proposes increased powers for the police to seize passports of suspected jihadists travelling abroad, and only allow fighters wishing to return to Britain back into the country if they consent to face trial, home detention or regular police monitoring. The continuing escalation of a punitive policy proposed by the Coalition government may itself be perceived as arising out of an extreme ideology, a violation of human rights and extreme scapegoating.

In his Munich speech Cameron identified young men as typical extremists: 'we should acknowledge that this threat comes overwhelmingly from young men who follow a completely perverse and warped interpretation of Islam and who are prepared to blow themselves up and kill their fellow citizens'. His analysis of how they become terrorists is also clearly articulated; it starts with an identity problem that has arisen from a tolerance towards the growth in social difference and diversity in the UK. This 'state of affairs' within our society leads to feelings of rootlessness and as a result young people search for something to believe in and a sense of belonging and find extremist ideology that radicalises them into becoming terrorists. In response to these processes Cameron argues that extremist ideology must by confronted 'in all its forms' and that people should not live apart but have 'a clear sense of shared national identity, open to everyone' (Cameron 2011, speech in Munich).

This position adopted by Cameron is one that Geoff warned against and, through his writings, Geoff showed how the position adopted by Cameron typically leads to ever-increasing social controls and an amplification of the problem. By defining extremism as a binary problem—war/peace and evil/good—a lack of neutral ground is created and space for moral indignation and moral panics, making it difficult to undertake critical analyses and discussions of the problem. By defining terrorists as 'evil', morality is reified and this inhibits practice and enables agencies to justify an increase in controlling actions and to present themselves as a unified group—police officers, social workers, psychologists, lawyers and judges included—to justify their punitive actions. For, as Geoff described, where morality is reified it becomes routinized, objectified and not subject to individual interpretation and acts as 'glue that binds together professional ideology' (Pearson 1975: 69). Thus, in his speeches Cameron invokes a strong sense of moral indignation that legitimatises the authority of agencies to actively 'defeat' extremism and mandates them to take action.

The UK government's definition of extremism reflects the sentiments portrayed in Cameron's speeches and is described in the Home Office Prevent strategy as:

> vocal or active opposition to fundamental British values, including democracy, the rule of law, individual liberty and mutual respect and tolerance of different faiths and beliefs . . . preventing terrorism will mean challenging extremist (and non-violent) ideas that are also part of a terrorist ideology.
>
> (Prevent 2011)

The Prevent programme is centrally monitored with targets set nationally, restricting the ability of local authorities to respond to local circumstances and, by implication, adopts the 'we know best' attitude of those in authority that Geoff warned against.

How the Extremism Agenda Can Be Used and Abused

For Geoff integral to assessing social issues are societal responses, including analyses of responses to policies. Both policies and their implementation locally affect understandings of social issues in some way; for example, by escalating social problems so they become a 'moral panic' or by changing how they are conceptualised so that the issue is no longer considered to be a social problem. Geoff emphasised the importance of understanding the politics of deviance control and how responses to some policies can be used by agencies to deflect attention away from difficult issues and to assert or re-assert their moral authority (Pearson 1975: 77). The use of the media by the police provides an example of these processes in practice, as follows:

Cameron's (2014) speech was delivered at a time when the competencies of the police are being increasingly questioned and challenged and the police are, like all other services, experiencing a reduction in their budgets which they vociferously resist. The following analysis of one week of reporting in the *Guardian* newspaper in November 2014 is illustrative of how the police are able to reassert their moral authority through their extremism-related activities and to deflect attention away from failures and poor practices that threaten their credibility. This is achieved, in part, by issuing press releases in a manner that justifies their actions. The police drew attention to the creation of the ISIL state and fighting in Syria and described them as contributing to a 'step change' in their terrorism prevention activities. They released detailed information about arrested suspects and statistical data on terror-related arrests for the last year, none of which is common practice for arrests for other crimes. This high-profile media coverage was preceded by articles reporting on findings of the Independent Police Complaints Commission (IPCC), that found the police had failed to act on 2,300 allegations of suspected paedophiles and the Hillsborough Inquest critical of the inaction by police officers at the time of the tragedy when 96 football fans were killed (*Guardian* 14/10/14). The following day details of arrested terror suspects were released again (*Guardian* 15/10/14), followed by a rebuttal from the police over accusations that Manchester police were accused of covering up failings to arrest gangs of Asian men abusers by disbelieving girls who reported crimes with claims that child sexual exploitation is a 'hidden' crime (*Guardian* 16/10/14; see also Jay 2014). For the following two days the police again sought to reassert their moral authority by describing Syria and ISIL as a 'game changer'. They released information—some of which was repeated from earlier in the week—on extremist suspects and the escalating threat of extremist attacks with: data that included 218 terror-related arrests this year and 100 Syria-related 'preventive activities';

police officer statements about the problem of young, impressionable and sometimes vulnerable individuals being drawn into extremism; further repetition of information on arrested young men, as well as details of families of 'British jihadists' who had been arrested (*Guardian* 17/10/14 and 18/10/14). While the police like other agencies have limited, and declining, resources, they can choose how they allocate their resources, which activities to prioritise and make different decisions about what crimes to prioritise.

Imagining Terrorists and Shaping Policies

Geoff emphasised how deviancy is imbued with symbolism that enables people to be stigmatised and how societal reactions and imagination can re-brand social problems as evil. He also argued that these social processes have the power to re-order and imagination turns fantasies into concrete realities, often in response to a threat to a traditional social order (Pearson 1975: 60). In a similar way, Bharucha identifies the symbolism of appearances as 'signs', such as beards and dress, and argues that they lend themselves to demonisation and that these 'signs' are used to construct Muslims as 'Other', and imagining them as terrorists. He argues counter-terrorist agencies similarly use fantasies of terrorists to normalise Muslims as terrorists and as a 'springboard' for imposing sanctions and punishment (Bharucha 2014: 71–80). Perhaps belief in Islam and the migration of Muslims across the world is perceived by some as a signifier of a new global order that threatens traditional British values and way of life?

Geoff argued that punishment is the expected societal response to deviants because they are perceived to be violating consensual norms, and sanctions are put in place to 'bring them back into line' (Pearson 1976). Deviants are perceived as inadequate and incompetent, as sick people in need of psychologically based policies with individually based solutions delivered by professionals who know best (Pearson 1976). Indeed, the search for an extremist personality and the labelling of suspects as vulnerable people and unusually susceptible to extremist ideology are all part of imagining individuals with psychological problems who are 'not one of us'. The use of psychological profiling to identify who is susceptible to radicalisation is compatible with technical discourses and remains integral to the imagining of terrorists.

Government responses to Muslims who are leaving the UK and going to Syria provides an example of how the imagining of Muslims as 'terrorists' is detrimental and confrontational towards Muslims and their communities, and how alternative explanations are overlooked. The police and media describe those suspected of leaving the UK for Syria as Muslims, and give their 'country of origin' as Bangladesh or Somalia, for example, rather than describe them as British, and not mentioning their faith. A presumption is made that radicalised young men are leaving to fight as jihadists and young women are leaving to marry jihadists, rather than for humanitarian reasons or that women are taking up arms to support the Kurdish Women's Protection Units, to which Western countries are providing weapons (see, for example, *Guardian* 30/9/14 and 2/10/14).

Despite claims by the police that Muslims are leaving every week for Syria and the Islamic state, and the media report that about 500 in total have left, the reality is that only two people have been convicted for Syria-related terror offences; both were employed married men with respectable jobs, one as a youth worker and the other as a teacher, aged 30 and 31 years old at the time of the convictions, and one was a father of young children. Other families have described the humanitarian work of their siblings, and how they are normal teenagers from caring families. These alternative perspectives draw attention to how there may be a range of motives and explanations and that those which are overlooked are those which represent normal behaviour. Some of these young men and women may find the idea of living in a caliphate as an exciting and romantic adventure (*Guardian*, 30/9/14). As Geoff argued, such possibilities should not be overlooked or dismissed by researchers, policymakers and practitioners just because the dominant social order disapproves. In their interviews with convicted terrorists a motive was indeed to find excitement, danger and romance (Bartlett et al. 2010: 12). A policy silence seems to exist about responding to reasons why girls and young women and men are leaving the UK to find excitement.

'Fit for Purpose' In Local Areas? The Extremism Agenda in Practice

The extremism policy of central government is implemented in areas it identifies as high risk where community tensions are expected in response to extremism and where terrorism is nurtured. Prevent programmes are introduced into these areas with the intention of maintaining laws and order and to seek out possible terrorists. By, as Geoff suggested, listening with compassion and taking critical perspectives seriously, including accounts of structural and social conditions, alternative yet logical responses to extremism can be identified from our research (Pearson 1975: 207). Using an interview style compatible with Geoff's perspective the following section describes how the central government's policy works in practice.

Central Government Policy for Local Areas

In areas that receive funding under the Prevent programme, local authorities are mandated to implement a series of interventions which are overseen and monitored by the Home Office. Local authorities are sanctioned for non-compliance and central government will 'take steps to intervene where local authorities are not taking the problem seriously' and 'make delivery of "Prevent" a legal requirement' in areas where they are particularly concerned about extremism (Cabinet Office 2013: 4).

The essence of the Coalition's policy for preventing extremism locally is outlined in a document produced by the Department of Communities and

Local Government in 2012 entitled, *'Creating the conditions for integration'*, which reflects the sentiments outlined by Cameron in his 2014 speech on the value of a 'shared national identity'. The document outlines the principles that shape local actions and states that 'Integration benefits us all, and extremism and intolerance undermine this as they promote fear and division . . . integrated communities may be better equipped to reject extremism and marginalise extremists.' (DCLG 2012: 2). Later in the document there is a commitment to strengthening common bonds through mutual tolerance and to 'marginalise and challenge extremists who seek to undermine our society' (DCLG 2012: 16). Far-right and Islamist extremists are both mentioned as a threat to integration and potential links between extremism and public disorder identified where people 'deliberately seek to inflame tensions between communities' (DCLG 2012: 23). Thus, the role of agencies and responsibilities of local communities are to promote integration in a manner that alienates extremists and prevents community tensions becoming transformed into public disorder. The linking of extremism with a fear of public disorder is reminiscent of the moral panics around 'mugging' in the 1970s (Hall 1978).

Agencies Mandated to take Action

In our research areas we found that the Home Office requirements under the auspices of the Prevent programme put local authorities under pressure to 'do something'. These demands invoke anxieties amongst implementers because of uncertainties about how best to respond to extremism and make the local area safe and free from civil unrest. One consequence is, combined with intensive media pressure on the evils of extremists, professional judgements are made in 'highly charged' circumstances. Tendencies to 'cover your own back' become stronger and reflective decision-making sidelined, all of which compound the effects of extremism policies and feeds moral panics. Interviewees working in the community sector and community leaders described how tensions between agencies are increasing, how the police are sharing little information about their 'intelligence' operations yet demand that communities co-operate, creating discord and a lack of trust.

Since, as argued earlier, identifying and engaging with 'future terrorists' is reliant on imagining terrorists, in practice agencies are left to fall back on 'conventional wisdom' about deviants and identify poor areas, vulnerable and 'at risk' young men, and above all Muslims, as suspects. This sets in motion a response that potentially criminalises those living in poor areas, some ethnic groups and young Muslim men. This is not of itself necessarily a problem if sound evidence exists that certain types of neighbourhoods produce terrorists and particular types of people become violent extremists, but reliable knowledge about predicting who might become a terrorist and where they live is not available to decision makers. Convicted terrorists are from different social classes and ethnic backgrounds, adults as well as young people, married with children; are professional, managerial, skilled and unskilled workers, and live in towns and cities throughout the UK in expensive homes and terraced houses.

Further, practitioners working in local areas are 'chasing' very few people, if any, with the focus on ideology, which is not a rule-breaking activity and does not violate any laws. With pressures to meet targets specified in Prevent delivery plans the scope for net-widening and scapegoating is increased. Children's Centres and primary schools have been incorporated into the search for future terrorists, for example. Stop and search practices by the police on the grounds of 'suspicion' have increased significantly and are often targeted at Muslims who perceive stop and search as unfair and unjust (Parmar 2011; Hussain and Bagguley 2012). Families of known jihadists are arrested 'on suspicion of commission, preparation and instigation of acts of terrorism' and many are released without charge because of insufficient evidence, yet their names and ages are reported in local and national newspapers (*Guardian* 15/10/14 and 18/10/2014). In an international study that interviewed convicted terrorists and suspects, it was found that these types of practices can cause a strong sense of injustice and through this anger interviewees said that they feel that their use of violence is legitimate against a Western society (Bartlett et al. 2010: 12–15). Violence in these circumstances is an expression of grievance and political protest that arises from local practices.

In addition we found that the confrontational approach inherent in the extremism agenda is most divisive for mothers, partners/wives and families who are considered members of 'suspect' communities. In interviews and group discussions with mothers with young children and teenagers, they explained that they do not understand extremism as it is not part of their culture, and the pursuit of extremists makes them very fearful for their children's future. They said that extremism was not a topic of conversation at home, and they did not know what their older children did when they were on their computers. A youth worker explained that many teenagers are not allowed out of their homes except to attend the mosque or activities organised by the mosque, and this is a source of great tension within families. We found that in response to their worry about extremism—and their children joining gangs—parents strictly regulate their children. In one area social workers have removed children and taken them into care because of the 'harsh' childcare practices of their parents. These women feel that social workers do not listen or understand their circumstances, and they feel that they are judged unfairly because of their ethnic group and religion. From other perspectives, their child-rearing practices may be considered as an indication of strong family values and of keeping their children safe, which are also strongly held British values. However, anxieties arising from the extremism agenda are also causing feelings of resentment in families and maybe 'rootlessness' amongst older children grows out of these tensions? They are further exacerbated by the police, who are calling on mothers to report their sons to the police if they suspect their involvement in radicalisation ('Stop you sons joining Syria war, urges Met', *Guardian* 24/4/14, pg. 1). Mothers told us that this makes them more anxious and less certain about what extremism is and how people become terrorists. Interviewees from 'suspected' communities repeatedly told us about their surprise who had left for Syria, a theme that families have reported to newspapers.

These examples from our research illustrate how the practices of agencies are creating a sense of injustice and increasing anxieties, which have marginal-ising effects. These actions and their consequences are consistent with the gov-ernment's intentions to exclude extremists from society, but they stir feelings of injustice and unfairness. Such responses may spark future civil unrest and may be encouraging a greater number of people to resort to using the internet and social media to make contact with a virtual group with shared sentiments.

Community Tensions

According to research participants, the main issue that explains increasing ten-sions in their local communities is immigration. They explained that migrants who arrive and settle in their neighbourhood add to the shortage of affordable housing and increase rents; they make it harder to find employment and they contribute to a reduction in wages as new immigrants are prepared to work for less. In some neighbourhoods young people talked about the lack of jobs 'with prospects' as well as affordable housing and how these limited opportunities locally thwarted their ambitions. Others indicated that racial discrimination and prejudice preclude them from much of the labour market, and they feel frustrated that some, most notably white British, have privileged access to employment opportunities

Local tensions arising from feelings of economic inequalities manifest them-selves as a lack of friendliness and avoidance and are expressed as general discontentment, according to research participants. Disillusionment with politi-cians and mainstream politics make them feel disenfranchised and unable to redress their grievances. Research participants also emphasised, however, that immigrants contribute to their quality of life; they bring vibrancy and diversity to their neighbourhood. The majority of our interviewees consider themselves to be nationalists and are sympathetic towards opinions expressed by right-wing activists. Self-proclaimed nationalists in our research included Muslims from Pakistan, Hindus from India, Christians from Nigeria and Jews from Poland. It is the erosion of the British way of life that is, however, of greatest concern to those living in our research areas, and immigrants who are perceived as wanting to challenge British culture and alter core British values are considered to be a significant source of community tensions. Most research participants referred to any group of immigrants who were disrespectful of English values as unaccep-table, whilst those who identified themselves as members of right-wing organi-sations such as the English Defence League (EDL) or the British National Party (BNP) explicitly expressed a strong dislike of Muslims, a perspective found in other studies which have found young EDL members scapegoat the Islamic 'other' for their feelings of marginalisation (Treadwell and Garland 2011). However, where everyday practices that symbolise 'British-ness' are violated, strain arises and serves as a reminder of unwelcome and unwanted immigrants; queuing at bus stops and Accident and Emergency waiting rooms in hospitals are examples of everyday fractious encounters.

Thus, community tensions may arise from practical issues that touch everyday lives: affordable housing, decent employment, access to services and respecting English traditional and honouring British values. Extremism is not perceived as a cause of community tensions by the overwhelming majority of our research participants precisely because it does not affect everyday lives or future prospects. For most, extremism is not a visible activity and there are few 'signs' of extremism in the places they frequent. 'Far-right' and 'Islamist extremists' and those interested in extremism communicate 'from the privacy of their bedrooms', as one interviewee expressed the frequent use of social media by these groups (Carter et al. 2014). Travel and meeting arrangements are made in private. Those wishing to travel to Syria receive documents and contacts and when they arrive at their destination are welcomed into a well-organised organisation with a clear purpose and modus operandi that gives new members clear roles, all of which eases their journey from their bedroom to a jihadist. These private arrangements have little, if any, impact locally. Interviewees who were knowledgeable about their local communities described how informal meetings take place away from mosques but their talk is 'posturing' and 'bravado' and it would be against their religious beliefs to turn to violence to air their grievances or in support of *umma*. In other communities, in places such as Cardiff and Portsmouth, friendship groups have become jihadists, but this appears to be a less typical pattern of behaviour and may increase suspicion within local areas. Increasingly, however, Muslims are seeking to redress their grievances through local politics and becoming councillors, and an increasing number are being elected.

Similarly, active far-right nationalists also communicate and organise using the dark web and difficult-to-access websites, and do not necessarily meet locally. Interviewees described how their 'street politics' strategy, based on small informal meetings, is often invisible locally as their aims are national in intention. At the time of our research, their aim was to influence national debates by influencing politicians on immigration and to secure the introduction of restricted immigration policies.

Interviewees who are affiliated with right-wing organisations spoke about how they are trying to educate members of their group who resort to violence and overtly racist behaviour in an effort to change the 'thuggish' image of their organisations in order to attract more members and to increase their influence on national politics. Interviewees expressed how they are uncomfortable with those who are violent and drunken at demonstrations and who they consider to be ignorant and use violence as a way of attaining status and creating violent right-wing subcultures (Treadwell and Garland 2011).

Nevertheless, racist graffiti and violence, often associated with right-wing perpetrators, were considered by research participants to be divisive and a source of community tensions, arising out of ignorance and fear of the 'Other',

and that education is a key preventative strategy. Yet, interestingly, the perpetrators of hate crimes receive far less media attention and fewer press releases
from the police than Muslim extremism, even though Islamic jihadists are not
considered to be a source of community tensions.

Tolerance

For the UK Coalition government, tolerance is both a key contributor to extremism, as it allows for an increase in social difference and diversity that make
young men rootless and attracted to extremism, and a policy solution through its
capacity to strengthen common bonds within communities and as a mechanism
to challenge intolerance and extremism. In our study, insights from interviewees
raised some doubts about the use of tolerance as a reason for extremism and as
a preventive measure, and our findings raise questions about adopting tolerance
as the 'silver bullet' that will eradicate extremism.

Firstly, we found tolerance towards extremism by the overwhelming majority of our research participants; they do not consider extremist ideologies to be
a crime and think that responses to ideologies should be outside the remit of the
police. Rather, interviewees think that the police should restrict their activities
to crime and respond to hate crimes as these are divisive and create tensions
within communities, as well as fear and suspicion among social groups. A lack
of fear of becoming a victim of extremism, despite media propaganda, can be
explained by, for example, well-policed EDL marches and a confidence in the
police to contain any violence. Whilst threatening during a demonstration they
are considered as a temporary disruption to everyday routines. They may be a
stark reminder of the hatred that some in society have for others but those who
marched were not thought to be local people and it was perceived that they
would leave the neighbourhood at the end of day. Atrocities such as 9/11 and
7/7 are considered by the majority of research participants, irrespective of gender, age and ethnicity of religion, to be rare events perpetrated by Muslims and
as an unequivocal statement against Western society symbolic locations, and
servants of the state—soldiers and police—are specifically selected as targets.
Thus, a terrorist event is not typically expected to happen in local residential
neighbourhoods. It seems that low levels of concern about becoming a victim
of extremism is consistent with a perception that a terrorist attack in the UK
is a rare event, even though the imagery of a terrorist attack is very powerful.
Crime, on the other hand, is often associated with high levels of fear and fear
can remain unchanged despite falls in actual crime, making it an additional
social issue and one which perpetuates worries about criminal victimisation
and an intolerance towards activities associated with hate crime. Fears and
anxieties associated with extremism are, by comparison, as illustrated earlier
in this essay, connected to agencies' practices and associated with particular
groups feeling marginalised through policy and practice.

Secondly, some interviewees were clear that central and local government
and police practices contradict the values to which the extremism agenda aspires

to promote, namely, tolerance and democratic principles. Constructing policies to eradicate extremism is considered to make for poor policies; interviewees reasoned that it will always be possible to find an extremist if agencies look hard enough but only through increased surveillance, and doing that undermines democratic principles, the very principles the extremism policy is promoting as a strategy to counter terrorism. The amplification of extremism occurs when communities are stigmatised by increased surveillance activities that include undercover 'intelligence' policing and stop and search which puts relationships between democracy and 'myth' of free speech under duress (Bharucha 2014: 8).

Thirdly, interviewees asked; 'integrated into what'? 'Why would we want to be integrated?' These questions reflected a list of concerns that illustrates different cultural and social meanings of tolerance: for example, a lack of trust between Muslims and Hindus becomes open hostility when marriages are mixed and Muslims insist that Hindus convert to Islam and can contribute to intra-community tensions (Bharucha 2014: 97); where young people socialise and develop youth cultures around alcohol and heavy drinking Muslim young people are forbidden to participate by their parents; and how some evangelical Christians condemn homosexuality as a sin and are intolerant of its acceptance under the Equalities Act. From an analysis of our interviews it is apparent that the majority of our research participants expressed a preference for the understanding, and accepting of, difference; political, social, cultural, ethnic and faith. Their attitudes and experiences demonstrated how locally many hold considered and well-reasoned perspectives that are based on everyday experiences of living in their neighbourhoods. Participants in our study had many constructive suggestions about how to create co-operation between different ethnic and cultural groups in societies and how campaigning groups that challenged discrimination and prejudice have a valuable role locally. Interviewees suggested, amongst other things, the value of mixed-faith children's centres and schools, of addressing everyday problems such as poor English language and lack of qualifications, of having wheelchair access to public buildings and initiatives to reduce feelings of alienation from formal political processes.

Moving Forward

In this essay I have used Geoff Pearson's critical sociological perspective to consider 'extremists' not as a 'pest to be eradicated' but as Geoff suggested 'an invaluable "early warning system" which alerts us to a dangerous fragmentation of social life' (Pearson 1976: 217). This method has exposed, amongst other things, that UK Coalition government reactions to extremism are more closely aligned to extreme ideologies than those living and working in local communities who, on the whole, hold more reasoned perspectives and considered responses. Indeed, our research participants expressed a preference for a more measured and thoughtful response from central government, local government and the police in particular. Further, in our research areas local people and community organisations consider that their local issues have different characteristics to those supposed by state policy. These findings show, as Geoff argued, that empirical research in local communities that listens to and respects local people is a better way to understand community tensions and fragmented neighbourhoods and has potential to develop policies and practices that improve everyday lives.

Note

1 I thank Jon Griffith for his useful comments on an earlier draft of this essay, to other researchers who were involved in fieldwork, Henry Akaluka, Sancha Cadogan-Poole and Lara Frumkin, Afsia Khanom and to all those who participated in the research.

References

Bartlett, J., Birdwell, J. and King, M. (2010), *The Edge of Violence: A Radical Approach to Extremism*, London: Demos, available at: http://www.demos.co.uk/files/Edge_of_Violence_-_web.pdf (last accessed March 2014).

Bharucha, R. (2014), *Terror and Performance*, London: Routledge.

Borum, R. (2011), 'Radicalisation into Violent Extremism 1: A Review of Social Sciences Theories', *Journal of Strategic Security*, 4(4), 7–36.

Cabinet Office (2013), 'Tackling Extremism in the UK', *Report from the Prime Minister's Task Force on Tackling Radicalisation and Extremism*, London: Cabinet Office, HM Government.

Cameron, D. (2014), 'British values aren't optional', *Daily Mail*, 15 June. Available online at http://www.dailymail.co.uk/debate/article-2658171/DAVID-CAMERON-British-values-arent-optional-theyre-vital-Thats-I-promote-EVERY-school-As-row-rages-Trojan-Horse-takeover-classrooms-Prime-Minister-delivers-uncompromising-pledge.html

Cameron, D. (2011), Prime Minister: "While Bin Laden is gone, the threat of Al Qaeda remains." Announcement to the House of Commons. UK FCO, May 3, 2011.

Carter, J., Maher, S. and Neumann, P. (2014), *Greenbirds: Measuring Importance and Influence in Syrian Foreign Fighter Networks, ICSR*, London: King's College.

Department for Communities and Local Government (DCLG) (2012), *Creating the conditions for Integration*, London: Department for Communities and Local Government.

Hall, S. (1978), *Policing the Crisis: Mugging, the State, and Law and Order*, London: Macmillan.

Home Office. (2011), *UK Prevent Strategy*, available at: http://www.homeoffice.gov.uk/publications/counter-terrorism/prevent/prevent-strategy/ (last accessed January 2014).

Hussain, Y. and Bagguley, P. (2012), 'Securitized Citizens: Islamophobia, Racism and the 7/7 London Bombings', *The Sociological Review*, 60, 715–734.

Jay, A. (2014), *Independent Inquiry into Child Sexual Exploitation in Rotherham 1997–2013*, Rotherham: Rotherham Metropolitan Borough Council, available at: http://www.rotherham.gov.uk/downloads/file/1407/independent_inquiry_cse_in_rotherham (last accessed October 2014).

Matza, D. (1969), *Becoming deviant*. Englewood Cliffs, NJ: Prentice Hall.

Parmar, A. (2011), 'Stop and Search in London: Counter-Terrorist or Counter-Productive?' *Policing & Society*, 21(4), 369–382.

Pearson, G. (1975), *The Deviant Imagination*, London: Macmillan Press Ltd.

Pearson, G. (1976), ' "Paki-Bashing" in a North East Lancashire Cotton Town: A Case Study and Its History', in ed. G. Mungham and G. Pearson, *Working Class Youth Culture*, London: Routledge and Kegan Paul, pp 48–81.

Pearson, G. (1976a), 'In Defence of Hooliganism, Social Theory and Violence', in ed. N. Tutt, *Violence*, London: HMSO, pp 192–220.

Pearson, G. (1983), *Hooligan: A History of Respectable Fears*, London: Macmillan Press Ltd.

Schmid, A. (2013), Radicalisation, De-Radicalisation, Counter-Radicalisation: A Conceptual Discussion and Literature Review, International Centre for Counter-Terrorism—the Hague, available at: http://www.icct.nl/download/file/ICCT-Schmid-Radicalisation-De-Radicalisation-Counter-Radicalisation-March-2013.pdf (last accessed April 2014).

Treadwell, J. and Garland, J. (2011), 'Masculinity, Marginalisation and Violence', *British Journal of Criminology*, 51, 621–634.

4 Shame, Scandal and Respectability Amongst the Children of the *Windrush* Generation

A Scholarly Omission

Kenny Monrose

African Caribbean men in Britain are often defined as being a problematic social category. Father deficit and unmarried female-headed families often dominate discourses on black British culture. However, a common observation within ethnographic studies concerning black men is that often there is a police or crime story to tell. This is perhaps the case as officially presented statistics inform us that black men in Britain are chronically criminalised and subjected to a disproportionate level of criminalisation by enforcement agencies, facts that can be validated and verified within much British sociological literature spanning several decades (Pryce, 1979; Gilroy, 1987; Cavidino & Dignan, 1992; Bowling & Phillips, 2002; Glynn, 2014). Whilst these findings can perhaps leave an impression for some that a preponderance of black men engage in crime, what is often omitted from this deliberation is the fact that an overwhelming glut of men of African Caribbean descent wilfully choose to shun or cease criminal participation, and are instead commonly influenced by strategies that are aimed at blocking any potential criminal drift, by virtues of structures cemented within Caribbean cultural identity (Monrose, 2013). Central to these strategies are concepts of respectability, propriety and notions of shame, instilled by parents in order to avert dishonour of one's family and community—factors which the newly arrived West Indians took extremely seriously. The following remarks are not only singularly applicable to the paradigms which exist with sociological enquiries on race and ethnicity, but are equally relevant in the investigation of issues related to social stratification and class structure.

Introduction

In this chapter I investigate the issue of criminal commission, in relation to the notions of shame and sense of respectability within the shared values of the newly arrived migrants from the Caribbean to Britain. The arrival of the Empire *Windrush* at Tilbury dock in Essex on 22 June 1948 was arguably the most visible and significant migration of black people to Britain from commonwealth territories. On board the vessel were nearly 500 passengers, drawn from various West Indian islands, who had sojourned in order to help rebuild the mother country back to her former glory after the ravages of the Second World War. This chapter, which draws upon data collated from my doctoral thesis, examines how factors centrally positioned within offered narratives have affected the liaison between African British Caribbean (ABCs) men and criminal justice. The voices presented throughout provide a factual and rich account of the inner workings of an under-researched assemblage, which despite the often negative representations, remains a vibrant part of modern British society. The concepts of respectability and the associated notions of shame become a valuable asset by which the criminal preclusion and desistance of the post-*Windrush* generation can be understood. The impact and influence of empire and post-colonialism within West Indian culture[1] is stressed, particularly in the areas of education and religion, as these variables act as the conduits by which adopted social action is modified and maintained. Narratives related to criminal pathways are also presented in order to inform the reader of the lived experience of racial prejudice and discrimination for black men, which in some cases prompted a drift into crime. The accepted guidelines in reference to social conduct meant that little tolerance was given to acts of crime or any deviation from these proscribed cultural norms. As the post-*Windrush* generation found their place in Britain, additional broader social factors emerged that diluted and made notions of respectability extremely difficult to maintain. The problematic nature of obtaining employment and accommodation, the persistence of criminalisation from a demonstrable racialist criminal justice system and media and education systems which liberally disseminated negative representations of blackness proved to be challenging at best. These issues worked in tandem with the often unreasonable expectations of sons by parents, who frequently failed to acknowledge the lived reality of oppressive status of their offspring. Therefore, we see some young black men embrace an alternative way of life, in order to forge informal forms of respectability, and as a result cast aside the notions of shame with which they were raised, in what they regarded as a hostile and unwelcoming Britain. For some, this led to nihilistic behaviourisms, such as a conscious (or unconscious) collusion with the frequent negative representations of black masculinity, and has resulted in an abandonment of some of the impelled Caribbean values with which they were raised, and the usually acquiescent posture possessed by their parents to racism. Finally it is important to remember that despite the arrested and sometimes fragmented structure of the black family unit, the post-*Windrush* generation of African Caribbean men in Britain were brought up in respectable homes, equipped with high moral codes of decency, which is a common thread that runs throughout this chapter.

Caribbean Respectability

> For my dad it was all about the family name. Do not disrespect or shame the family name.
>
> (King)

Respectability occupies noteworthy space within West Indian culture, and is explicably linked with colonial ideals of Britishness (Pryce, 1979; Bourne, 2010).This also dominates socio-historical discourse related to hierarchical structures and class stratification in Britain. The Anglophone or British West Indian territories often promoted Britishness within the core institutions that they governed. The acquired schema of social conduct within British dominions was dictated by the instep of the British Empire. Britishness for the West Indian meant respectability, tied up in duplicitous ideals of affability, decency and lawful obedience. These idealistic aspirations laid an infrastructure upon which a formation of an imposing colonial-inspired cultural identity was developed and maintained. Therefore, Caribbean migrants fervidly frowned upon any traits of idleness, frivolity or criminality, particularly in children. Migration to the mother country was serious business, not a trivial jaunt or quest for meaningless adventure. Faro, now a retired pensioner in the Caribbean island of St Lucia, reflects on the primary purpose of his countrymen's arrival to London:

> We came here to work hard and make a good foundation for our self and for our children. We didn't have time for any papishow.[2]
>
> (Faro)

It is also important to remember that most *Windrush* arrivals were often the most skilled and law-abiding citizens from their respective islands, who were without spot or blemish in regard to criminality, knowing that this may blight authorisation to travel (Phillips & Phillips, 1998). Therefore, Britain arguably obtained the most respectable, gifted and talented citizens that the British West Indian territories had to offer (Sewell, 1997).

> The average Jamaican who came on the *SS Windrush* on 24 May (from Kingston) was not destitute. The destitute man did not have £28.10 (the passage cost). One or two might be unemployed, but they were from a family background of support. So they were above average as far as income was concerned.
>
> (Phillips & Phillips, 1998: 59)

Windrush arrivals entered Britain possessing these highly flavoured Victorian and Edwardian moral standards and principles that were firmly grounded within a synergy of colorialism and, of course, religiosity. To be regarded as a well-thought-of and respectable individual, these exacting assumed characteristics were of paramount importance. For example, regardless of personal privation, elders stressed the need for their sons to be seen as well-brought-up, well-groomed and neatly attired individuals. Steve, a 55-year-old Antiguan who arrived in Britain at age 11, reflects on the importance of respectability whilst growing up in the Caribbean. He states that it was considered shameful for a child to be seen in public with uncombed hair and shoddy garb—pride in personal appearance was essential.

> Back home you had to comb your hair, and have clean fingernails. That was important, and it still applied when we came over here too.
>
> (Steve)

British-born Fire adds to this:

> As a youth you couldn't dress like a waste man like some of them boys do today, with their trousers half way down their arse—our parents weren't having it. Look back to the footage of the West Indians coming off of the *Windrush*. Look how they dressed in their sharp seamed suits, and felt hats. My old my man always wore a brimmed hat when he left the house. Even if he was only going down to the bookies. He always looked respectable and smart—a proper dandy.
>
> (Fire)

Additionally, more so than attire, any brush with authority, however minor, was looked upon with scorn, and considered shameful. It was not uncommon for a family to severely reprimand, or in some cases disown a son for a criminal conviction, regardless of guilt or innocence. The mere possibly of a son's involvement with criminality was enough to draw wrath:

> My old man believed all the hype the boy them (police) said about me, so he kicked me out the house and refused to speak to me in public. I was a disgrace to him.
>
> (TT)

TT's comments highlight that parents often upheld a police accusation levelled at their sons. This too was similar within school. For the Caribbean parent, a teacher's assessment of their child was infallible, and schoolteachers were fully aware of this, often using it to their advantage. A retired schoolteacher mentioned:

> We didn't have to discipline the West Indian kids too much; all we had to do is tell their parents. That was punishment enough for most of them.
>
> (Retired schoolteacher)

Now as adults, informants are still visibly disturbed by the lack of emotional support that their fathers provided, particularly in reference to law enforcement and education:

> My dad is white rum and betting shop man, an old-fashioned West Indian you know. Anything that was said about us black boys by a white person

he believed them, and we would get beaten and catch hell for it. This made me hate white people more than I did already.

(Rambo)

Shame, Discomfiture and Ignominy

Closely tied to respectability is the often muted issue of shame. The notion of shame is a prominent and central feature that typified communities in the Caribbean. These smaller communal-based clusters were dependent on close communal attachments, and this proved to be a valuable asset in crime prevention. Like respectability, notions of shame were one of the key qualities that the *Windrush* arrivals carried with them upon entering Britain. Notions of shame were wholly dependent upon the micro interactions and taught rigid relationships of Caribbean life. This meant that sanctions imposed by relatives, friends or a personally relevant collective had a more forceful effect on criminal behaviour than sanctions imposed by legal authority:

We grew up over here seeing so many negative images of black people all over the place, and most of it had to do with crime. Our parents didn't want us to fall in that type of bracket. We as youngsters knew that we had to behave ourselves or else we would quickly be labeled a criminal and that would bring down shame on not only the family but us as a community. There was a lot of pressure on us as youngsters to toe the line.

(Stopper)

If you turned to crime in my house then kiss your sorry black ass out the door. Being West Indian, and being a criminal brings shame and scandal on your family.

(Colin)

So the question arises, how useful were these notions and sensibilities in the lives of the post-*Windrush* generation? For those I exchanged with in the field, shame invoked the expression of dishonour, disapproval and hurt from family and loved ones. This was an attempt to summon feelings of compunction and penitence, by highlighting the transgression of the accepted mores of the collective. Hubert, a pensioner, states:

He's ashamed of him, and you can't blame him; I would feel shame too. Look at the kind of things his son's been involved with. His father came all the way from where he came from and look, he can't go back home. Everyone will shake their head and scandalize him because they see how his bad son has turned out—that is why every day you see him walking round with his head down like he's hiding from people.

(Hubert)

Individuals who held pronounced criminal pathways, such as Blacker and Arthritis, mentioned that they encountered an acute crisis of conscience with regard to the shame and injury they had brought upon their families as a result of their criminal drift:

> I was inside looking out. My old man came to visit me (in prison) and was just bawling; I'd never seen him bawl like that before. He was bawling bad, and it made me bawl too. I said, 'I can't make them (his parents) go through this shit anymore'. Even when I was involved in those shootings, and was in hospital, I lied and told them I got stabbed to lessen the blow.
>
> (Blacker)

> When I was doing what I was doing I didn't feel no way. But trust me, when I saw the damage these things caused my family, I must admit I did feel shame.
>
> (Arthritis)

Religious Respectability

> It is written in the Bible that for us to bring up a child in the right way, they have to get to know God, and that means going to church and reading the Bible.
>
> (Miss Marie)

Religion plays an important role in this debate as it is was maintained as an apparatus via the expected and accepted notions of shame, and sense of respectability were upheld and transmitted:

> The church was the main thing; the whole island was really religious. When I was younger I went to church and Sunday school and constantly referred to things in a Biblical way. I had to go to church every Sunday whether I liked to or not. That was the regime in our household and that went for everybody; that's how it was in Jamaica.
>
> (Stopper)

Du Bois (1907) considers religion as being an integral part of the function of diasporic black communities. For Du Bois, religion resides at the core of black cultural modality and behaviour. Herskovits (1990) concurs, by suggesting that blacks are an overwhelmingly religious people, for whom religion transcends any other form of social expression. For the post-*Windrush* generation, religion was vital in their upbringing, as religious or 'church' participation equated to being an upstanding member of community, and socially respectable (Beckford, 2000):

> The home was a typical (St) Lucian home, so the Catholic business ran things. It played a large part. Baptism, communion, confirmation—all

Catholic. So it was church every Sunday. Between me and my parents the understanding was you had to go church without anything being said. You couldn't turn around and say you wouldn't go church. It was expected. From the age of 6 and 7 church was part of your routine.

(Arthritis)

We also notice that religious involvement provided a level of newly found status. For example, Pryce (1979) notices that domestic workers were transformed into Sunday school teachers, and bus drivers became pastors, meaning that those who occupied low status employment in the 'white world', once within the 'church', secured an elevated status within their communities. This suggests that church attendance and public displays of religiosity are not always directly linked to an individual's faith or belief, but has more to do with issues related to community and social obligation than with spirituality (Herberg, 1956). Although a majority of informants no longer regarded themselves as churchgoers, many still hold strong religious/spiritual beliefs, and clearly understood the reasons why their parents forced them to attend 'church':

That was something that was decided for me. 'You are going to church'. So I went to Sunday school and church on a regular basis. It was something that I was forced to do because like a medicine it was supposed to be good for me.

(Gee)

Colin, who was raised a Jehovah Witness, states that although he is not a direct member of the congregation anymore, he attempts to live his life in accordance with the strict religious manner in which he was brought up:

Religion played a fairly big part in my life, and taught me the right from wrong, and how to be respectful.

(Colin)

Despite religious instruction being a mandatory rite of passage for this assemblage, their experience of it varied greatly, meaning that some were involved as acolytes, altar boys or choir members, and others simply experienced a superficial involvement by means of youth clubs, for example, or when it overlapped into education, where the relationship between church and school became seamless. During the '70s and '80s it was difficult for black youth to avoid interaction and involvement with the 'church', as many public spaces which were available (youth clubs, sports teams, etc.) were organised by religious groups. Whereas white working-class youth were able to access alternative pastimes, such as army cadets or cub scouts, black youth, particularly those located within densely populated urban areas such as Newham, relied heavily upon the church for extracurricular activities.

Parents were, of course, happy with this, as it fortified their conviction that involvement within the church aided personal development. However, although religion and 'church' within the context of ABC life acted as a social stabiliser, and religious patronage provided benefaction to community members, easing the psychological resentment of the alienation and racial discrimination which existed within wider society, not all forms of religious observation were deemed respectable. Some beliefs, to which a significant number of black youth gravitated, became a concern to parents and community elders, who found these religious movements to be retrograde and offensive—Rastafari being the case in point.

As the social consciousness of ABCs and ideas surrounding identity of their newly acquired political status grew, questions regarding the religious regimes they were grown into were raised. The increasing input and popularity of reggae music, which was infused with the doctrine of Rastafari, acted as a repository of knowledge of cultural identity. This both empowered and informed a vast number of marginalised black males in Britain. Rasta was comfortable answering the questions that parents, priests, pastors and preachers felt uncomfortable simply listening to. Reggae and Rastafari for black British youth rode in tandem with the development of an updated collective consciousness, helping cement a more balanced and cohesive understanding of their existence in Britain, opposed to their parents' futile ideals of respectability:

> It was all about Rasta in the seventies for us. Dr Alimandado, Burning Spear, Big Youth, Peter Tosh and Bob Marley—they gave us a message that we hadn't heard before and it felt good. The music and message kind of healed us.
>
> (Fire)

Rastafari, although shunned by their parents, was for second-generation ABCs the benchmark by which respectability was now to be measured:

> The Rasta man was a man to be instantly respected amongst his peers, and feared by the authorities because he believed in standing up for his rights. If you saw a Rasta man on the street you would big him up, because respect was always due to the dread.[3]
>
> (Fire)

Rastafari, however, was openly held in contempt by elders, as they saw it as something corruptible and corrosive to the future of their youngsters. Indeed, Rasta, which was seen in the Caribbean, particularly Jamaica, as early as the 1930s, was outlawed and forced to employ a subterranean existence. Fifty years later the knotted hair and bearded faces of the Rastamen were still vehemently frowned upon by elders, who could not understand why vast numbers of their youngsters would wantonly place themselves in a position of 'disadvantage', and ignore conforming to the strong sense of respectability and decency that they had painstakingly attempted to cultivate:

> I just don't know why all these young boys neglect themselves and turn to nasty Rasta. When we first came to England you don't see how we dressed nice and decently in our tie and jacket? These Rasta's boys are worthless pieces of dirt. What English man will give them a job looking like that?
>
> (Fitz)

Being Rasta was considered as being the most shameful and dishonourable thing an ABC could do—akin to being criminal:

> I remember my grandmother telling me not to come round her house again because I was Rasta and grew locks. That day she threw me out her house. I had to sleep in a graveyard that night.
>
> (K)

Being a Criminal

> To have once been a criminal is no disgrace. To remain a criminal is the disgrace.
>
> (Malcolm X)

As mentioned on opening, one of the more common themes within sociological literature relevant to race in Britain surrounds the criminalisation of black men, and their consequent connection and over-representation within the various branches of criminal justice. For some, this suggests a black male predilection and propensity toward criminality, despite volumes of empirical data suggesting otherwise, and literature which highlights black men rejection of criminality (Liebow, 1968; Duneier, 1992; Anderson, 1999). As sociologists we are aware that the raison d'être and correlations of offending are multifarious, and this is a fair assessment, as the motivational factors for committing crime can vary from individual to individual. However, one of the more striking parallels to emerge from my own data collection concerning the minority of black males with criminal pathways surrounds issues tied to social and cultural exclusion. As we know, once an individual *perceives* exclusion, a disconnect emerges that can result in acts of deviance and or rebellion, which in some instances can lead to crime (Merton, 1938; Deleuze & Guattari, 1980; Agnew & Passas, 1997; Young, 1999). Whilst my data does not promise to account for the experiences of *all* African Caribbean men in Britain in terms of crime, it is representative enough to provide a sufficient understanding of criminal drift and criminal participation.

Even though respectability tied to notions of shame were encouraged domestically for the post-*Windrush* generation, it proved to be extremely difficult for some to uphold these values outside of the home, as the very institutions which they were heartened to be part of in order to secure respectability, spurned them. For their parents respectability surrounded employment, education and lawfulness. However, their sons were often denied just treatment in the spheres, and this made maintaining these ideals extremely difficult. For example, Gillborn (1990; 1995) notices that the education system in Britain had in place regimes which enforced stereotypes of 'black' male behaviour, such as an emphasis on sport and art, as opposed to the traditional modes of academic excellence such as science, mathematics and literature. For some this highlighted the often insidious nature of racial prejudice and discrimination within schools:

> The level of the blatant racist abuse that some of the teachers gave us was incredible. They would call us 'nigger' and 'Black Bastard' and all kinds of stuff. It became normal at school. 'Go on get over there you Black Bastard'. 'Shut your black lips when you look at me'. 'Come on Golly—hurry up'! Even got us to read some of those racist Enid Blyton books! Parents didn't know half of what we went through, and what was the point of telling them? They'd never believe us anyway.
>
> (K)

As K mentions, these types of regimes were too frequently left unchallenged by parents who had failed to fully engage with school governance. As a result, some sons believed their parents negated their personal and parental responsibly for their replete education, by supposing that these destructive and clearly racist organizations held the best intentions for the children. A conclusive and uncomplimentary report by the Newham Monitoring Project gives a valid and pensive account of the manner in which school governance in respect to black children was viewed:

> The local authority also saw black children as a threat to the social cohesion of the school (they could only be integrated in small numbers), and this was further reinforced by the corralling of black children into special schemes: withdrawal classes for Asian children with language difficulties, and schools for the educationally subnormal (ESN) for Afro Caribbean children perceived to have behavioural problems.
>
> (Newham Monitoring Project, 1991: 24)

Because of issues related to cultural capital and cultural reproduction within the classroom, black students were commonly written off as *educationally subnormal*. Such labelling, which is highlighted by Coard (1971), exposes the scandalous regimes which existed in schools regarding the treatment of black schoolchildren. The shortcomings of the model of assimilation within British education was questioned at what was a politically sensitive period of British education, and prompted a number of commissioned reports and the introduction of an integrationalist model of teaching amongst some local education authorities. Integration as opposed to assimilation supposedly meant that open-mindedness and tolerance of the cultural needs of black students was adopted, so that their academic attainment and experience within the classroom would improve (Mullard, 1982). Instead however, like the model of assimilation, the integrationalist method possessed a number of significant flaws. This framework, unlike before, explicitly encouraged black students to focus on lifestyle, sports and music and the acceptance of academic mediocrity opposed to excellence. For example, Blacker, now middle aged, provides us with a solid reflective account of the educational experience as a black adolescent male in Newham at this time, and the consequences that this had later on in life:

> I asked questions at school, but got no answers. They kicked me out of school because they couldn't deal with me and my questions. When I was 13 my older brother turned Rasta, and told me to ask my teachers questions about religion. Believe me king the next day I couldn't waits to ask them. The teachers couldn't answer me, and I wasn't accepting it. It just added fuel to the fire. So I pressed and pressed until the teachers said, 'Why are you pressuring me? Get out my class'. That kind of attitude from teachers is what I rebelled against. They should have told me to go to the library or something, but no—just kicked me out.
>
> (Blacker)

Being expelled from the formal educational system at the age of 14 resulted in Blacker spending most of his time loitering on the streets of East London. Inevitably, he made acquaintances with those in a similar position who had been excluded from school, or those who were slightly older and unemployed. Blacker idled away his time in amusement arcades, drug dens or simply 'on ends', as no positive alternative spaces were open for those like him who were decanted from formal systems of education. He believes his drift into crime was inescapable once expelled from school. What made things increasingly alienating for Blacker was that no other establishment in Newham afforded him a second chance of schooling, which patently arrested his development and planted in him a seed of resentment for all rules and institutions. The education system, Blacker believes, regarded him as a lost cause, and beyond redemption:

> I got excluded 11 times, and then finally expelled permanently—I was 14. So that period is when it really went wrong. I was interviewed at every school in the area, but got rejected. Nobody wanted to take me in. I guess being excluded so many times made me too bad to handle.
>
> (Blacker)

Expulsion impinged on his self-confidence, and self-respect, which in turn led him to seeing crime as a strategy to be employed in order to refurbish what he regarded were the now crumbling building blocks of his personal identity:

> That's when I really hit it (crime). I was full time. It was something that I just felt I had to do. I was coming out my yard, and roaming the streets looking for something to commit.
>
> (Blacker)

Crime acted as an outlet for the frustrations and his feelings of injustice. However, more importantly, Blacker believed crime allowed him to replenish the respect he had lost as a result of being deemed a social outcast:

> I had had already lost the plot, I didn't care. When I got kicked out (of school) I really started hitting crime hard.
>
> (Blacker)

Therefore, although his educational development was stunted, his street-level respect from peers soared, and having respect on the street, for a young black male within an alarmingly deprived urban environ, was of major significance at this time (Majors, 1993; Anderson, 1999; Bourgouis, 1995):

> Society didn't care about me, so fuck it; I didn't care about society. I tried to be respectable, I grew up in a respectable home, but society didn't respect me.
>
> (Blacker)

By breaking into cars, *Blacker* quickly found how easy it was to make money:

> Breaking into cars and taking stereos—I was doing that from I was 10. Once I learnt it I thought 'Rarse this is the easiest lick'. I was breaking into the cars right outside my house. Money for old rope! Money to squander! I couldn't take the money home and say to my mum, 'Here mum, here's a score'. I had to spend it. So I would buy a draw of weed, play in the arcade, and feast on fast food. It was good living at the time, and I had respect from people around me, because I had something going on, and always had a bit of money on me.
>
> (Blacker)

As well as hitting back at the society which he felt rejected him, one of the main objectives for Blacker was to 'live good', and gain access to easy money. As stated, this had the dividend of being valued by his peer group as an 'earner', which was a paramount prerequisite in gaining respect on the streets of East London. Once gained, respect was cherished, protected and cultivated by any means necessary, albeit this was not allied to the established form of respectability that was culturally encouraged. In retrospect, Blacker is aware that this period of his life was important, and had he been in school, his life may well have developed differently. His voice adopted a melancholy quality, which was tinged with sadness whilst he recollects those 'lost' years of his youth:

> Those were priceless years. If I was in school it could have changed the course of my life.
>
> (Blacker)

Colour Blue, like Blacker, is another individual who turned to crime after experiencing social exclusion. Because of a racially motivated incident in the workplace, Colour Blue had the unfortunate experience of losing his job as an apprentice for Newham council. Colour Blue still rues at this, as it was a job that he loved, and one which was much sought after and respected amongst the majority of East London men (Hobbs, 1988). This was also a profession which he knew made his parents feel proud of him. Colour Blue confessed that whilst growing up in Forest Gate during the 1980s, so prevalent was the racism which surrounded him that he failed to even notice it. As a child he accepted that white racism was 'just how life was'. He recalled regularly seeing racist graffiti liberally daubed around the council estate where he lived, and noted that very little effort was made by other residents or the local authority to eradicate it. It was simply considered part of the natural surroundings, and an ingrained fixture within the building architecture of Newham:

> I even had a big NF (national front) symbol drawn on the front wall of my house—it was there for years. It didn't even register. NF symbols were everywhere else as well, so being on my wall didn't really make a difference. Now as a man I realize the impact of seeing something that told you, you were hated every day.
>
> (Colour Blue)

As he matured, he became aware of the extent and toxicity of the racism that surrounded him:

> Getting older and moving from Forest Gate, and going to other parts of the area like Canning Town, Custom House and East Ham, I really saw how racist Newham was, and how much they (whites) hated blacks. I was shocked.
>
> (Colour Blue)

Unemployment plunged Colour Blue into world-weariness and bitterness. He was 'pissed off' and 'fed up', and consciously chose to remove himself from mainstream society, and retreated into his 'blackness' by embracing the lifestyle of Rastafari (Cashmore, 1984). What followed was not only an increased distrust of (white) society but an unswerving rebellion against many of society's established rules surrounding respectability, which he no longer saw as valid to him or his newly adopted lifestyle:

> My dad worked at Fords on a production line, but wanted me to be a doctor. He never gave me a clue, or went out of his way to find out what I had to do to become a doctor; it was just something he wanted me to do. When I told my teacher I wanted to be a doctor when I grow up, she laughed at me—what chance did I ever have?
>
> (Colour Blue)

Colour Blue viewed society and his parental expectation of him being respectable by means of employment and occupation as an additional burden to the
casual level of racism he experienced daily:

> I was just fed up of it. All the crap and having to deal with the white man
> and his laws. For what?
>
> (Colour Blue)

To counter unemployment and redundant occupational status, he turned to
crime. He makes no excuses for his criminal drift, as he believes that he was
forced into illegal activity in order to subsist. Criminal participation was something which he was wholly unrepentant for:

> I had to survive. I tried to do it the right way, but the Babylon[4] wouldn't let
> me, so I had to find my own way.
>
> (Colour Blue)

Desistance and Cessation

So a question arises. Given the experience of exclusion which correlates in
the drift from respectability towards a shift into criminality, what then acted as
the spur for desistance and cessation of criminality in the lives of these individuals? This is a significant area for investigation, as it perhaps offers some
broader explanation of why some refuse and reject a criminal pathway in the
first place, and can shed light on the role which notions of shame and respectability have within core and long-term life choices. For Blacker his choice was
simple; becoming a father and husband induced what he described as spiritual
awakening that highlighted newly acquired responsibilities and the need to be
considered as respectable for his soon-to-be-acquired family:

> What stopped my crime more than anything else was the birth of my
> daughter. When my wife was pregnant I was touched by what I can only
> describe as a spiritual force that just changed me. I felt the baby inside
> my wife's stomach and just thought 'Wow, this is me. Someone who is
> entirely reliant on me'. I felt a bond straight away. I said, 'I'm not going
> back to jail again'. Before I was prepared to go to jail for foolishness like
> money and drugs. Now I'm not prepared to go back to jail, and walk away
> from my daughter.
>
> (Blacker)

Similarly, Kay describes the formal bonds of family commitment as prompting
him to give up crime:

> I was doing a blag (an armed robbery) in a post office, and I got trapped
> in the building. I had the money in one hand, and a shotgun in the other,

but knew the police were on their way to get me. I don't know how I did it, but I hid, and then managed to get out of there without being caught. That was the closest I've been to being sent to prison, and remember I was doing armed robbery for a long time. I suddenly realized what the implications of a lengthy sentence would be. At the time Maggie (Thatcher) and her lot was handing out ten-year sentences like jelly tots—I didn't want one. Loads of people around me were getting a ten or fifteen (years) for crap. I didn't want to be away from my family for that long, so I stopped—simple as that.

(Kay)

Here we notice the significance of formal social bonds which are tied to the ideals of respectability (Reckless, 1950; Hirschi, 1969; Braithwaite,1989). Both Kay and Blacker saw a prison sentence as a hindrance to their roles as fathers and husbands, and were aware that crime would compromise these roles by the harsher penal sentencing structures which were being imposed. For them detention meant isolation from loved ones, and the inevitable feelings of shame and dishonour that would be brought on by incarceration and estrangement from family. It is as though the core issues of shame and respectability never truly piqued them until they were responsible for a family of their own. Before fatherhood, the roadman mantra which they were in accord with was 'he, who has nothing, has nothing to lose'. Now however, as fathers and husbands, their behaviour is scrutinized, and evaluated. Blacker for example, who was victim of a shooting, showed how the thoughts of retribution and revenge that haunted him for an extended period were dealt with. He quickly realised the long-term carnage that a reprisal could potentially cause:

Being shot whilst my wife was pregnant gave me a whole new perspective on things, and made me look at myself, and what I was doing in a different way. I had to make a change, and make some difficult decisions.

(Blacker)

The matter of drug usage also has a place within this debate, as involvement with drugs on any level was considered an appalling and reprehensible act in the eyes of traditional West Indian culture. Drugs were not only stigmatized by police but, more importantly, by the elders. However, in the eyes of black youth, the use of drugs such as cannabis was seen simply as a form of cultural expression, devoid of any sinister attachments that the older generation spoke of (Becker, 1963):

Weed smoking was part of me, and my culture. Cokeys (whites) went to the pub, down fifteen pints, eat a kebab, go home and piss in the wardrobe. Next day they'd say what a great night out. We'd rather smoke a spliff (a cannabis cigarette), listen to some tunes, and just chill. That's how we as black men flexed.

(Fire)

Why cannabis was the drug of choice is open to speculation; however, it can be suggested that it is linked in part to black British youth culture in the 1970s and '80s, which was markedly influenced by the music of the period, as it often carried cannabis usage as a significant theme:

> We West Indian guys would listen to reggae when I was coming up, and the reggae was talking about weed.
>
> (Rambo)

As previously remarked, reggae music had a forceful impact on the cultural identity and consciousness of blacks in Britain in the 1970s and 1980s (Gilroy, 1987; Bradley, 2000; Henry, 2006). Rebellion, resistance and black cultural references were typical themes within the genre, and this, informed by the spiritual aspect of Rastatfari, spoke of 'the herb' (cannabis) as being 'the healing of nations'. Youths read this as meaning it was able to provide relief from the exploitive nature of the ills within the mechanisms of Babylon (4), and placed cannabis usage at the epicentre of black British youth culture. Of this convention Colour Blue states:

> I guess that's what this Babylonian system would call criminal activity, but under who's jurisdiction are they judging it? They call it crime; I call it survival. I don't class weed as a drug. If you want drugs go to the doctor and he will give it to you.
>
> (Colour Blue)

As inoffensive and harmless as drugs like cannabis were professed to be amongst those who used and distributed it, there were those for whom it acted as a pathway to involvement with so-called hard, or more harmful, drugs. L is one such example. For a number of years L was a successful entrepreneur, and an established nightclub owner. His success saw him burgeon financially, and benefit from a high level of celebrity, and street-level respect. However, he found the demands of maintaining this lifestyle difficult, once crack cocaine became part of the landscape:

> I was the life and soul of the party. I had swag; I had the girls, the houses, the cars, and money *and* the influence—the full belly! I had it all, but the truth is I couldn't handle it. Getting it is easy—keeping hold of it is a different thing. You get roped in with the wrong people, and then you start to wobble. I never ever thought I would fall as far as I did. All my money, my cars and my houses went up in smoke.
>
> (L)

Crack abuse had led L into a position which placed him in considerable danger, both in terms of his health and at the hands of criminals. Quickly he became aware of the need to re-examine his lifestyle. Embarrassment, resulting from the depths to which he had fallen, was coupled with the unrelenting internal feelings of shame that he had poured out on those who were close to him. L describes the levels to which he sank:

> I moved from East London to South London, which as you know is not an easy thing to do, and thought nobody would know me over there, but the crack made me forget just how popular I really was. I was living *in* a crack house. Did you hear what I said, Ken? I wasn't visiting the crack house; I was living there, and when members of the community found out I was there they would just mock and jeer me. That hurt, but didn't stop me though. I had no shame man—I just loved to get high. I could easily spend £500 a day on crack, seven days a week. My habit was so bad that the dealers used to fight each other to sell to me, because they knew they could bathe (awash with cash) off me. Man I sold everything I had, and knocked (stole from) everyone around me. What really did it for me is when I got caught stealing the pillowcases from my mum's bed to go and buy crack. My sister caught me and cussed me out. She called me all kind of horrible names that day.
>
> (L)

L finally decided to stop using crack when, as he states, he 'hit rock bottom', and realized that his life had spiralled out of control. He had become homeless, penniless and friendless. All that remained were the clothes he stood in and, in his own words, 'his crack pipe'. L was desperate and moved away from London to look for a new start, believing that being away from 'certain people and influences' would help. Unfortunately, his drug-fuelled criminality continued whilst being located elsewhere, but this time the consequences were far worse. Being an outsider in a new city meant L found it easier to again rip people off. However, he soon discovered that this type of behaviour held in store potential for some very serious ramifications with members of the criminal underworld. L admitted he was associating with some overtly villainous people who were connected to even more iniquitous and sinister individuals:

> There are certain people you just shouldn't mess with—I mean the heavy-duty faceless and nameless ones who run things, and fly low. With the crack coursing through me though I wasn't thinking straight, and was scamming these people. Luckily I woke up one day and realized what I was doing, and just who I was involved with (and I) decided to leave town.
>
> (L)

L made for Scotland; however, this time he sought help and a positive solution for his addiction. He joined an evangelical church, received baptism and is now a fully committed Christian. He believes that it was God who helped him turn his life around:

> Ken, I was on skid row It was God who turned my life around. I conduct a food ministry, and I've found myself a beautiful wife now. The respect

that I had on the street meant nothing, but the respect I now have being part of the church and a community means everything.

(L)

Like L, Blacker explained in detail his experiences with crack cocaine, and makes particular references to the cycle which induced him to abuse the drug:

No friend of yours would give you crack! If a 'friend' gives you crack he's not your friend, especially if he smokes it himself; he knows that shit is just nasty.

(Blacker)

Blacker revealed that his first experience of taking crack was with a gang he associated with:

I was hanging out with these guys I used to thieve with, and they started smoking the fucking thing in front of me. Next thing I know I'm trying it. That was my first taste. This was the early days of crack in the 1980s. It was disgusting, horrible; it makes you crave. Imagine the same night we went out to hit (burgle) another drum (house) just to get money to buy more crack. We hit the drum off at nine (o'clock), went back to our place at ten–ten thirty, smoked till midnight, and then out again to lick off another drum to buy more rocks—pure fucking madness. With all the money we got, I was left with a tenner in my pocket—the rest got smoked off.

(Blacker)

Blacker considered himself fortunate that he did not become fully immersed in the cycle of crack and crime because, as he claimed when speaking about his criminal activity, it was the financial gain to 'live good' which motivated him more than anything else. He quickly came to the realisation that using crack meant that he would face too many disadvantages, loss of money being one of them, and reasoned that dealing crack was better than using it. This view is shared by Arthritis, who dealt crack although never admitted using:

Nothing like crack money, let me tell you. Crack has small amount of cocaine in it; the majority of the other ingredients are dirt cheap. Why do you think crack dealers can bathe? It's a load of money for minimum outlay. Let's say I buy a key (kilo) of good-quality cocaine for 30 bags (£30,000)—you know how many rocks I can get out of that? If I wash a minimum amount of cocaine to make rock, I can easily double my money.

(Arthritis)

Comparable to some, Arthritis also holds negative peer group pressure as accountable for his criminal drift. However, unlike the others, he mentioned that being part of a crime-centred street gang actually assisted in curbing his criminal exploits. Arthritis possessed a long-held desire to realise his academic potential, and the need to obtain a high-quality education. He explains:

> I always wanted a good education, not just any kind of community college education, but a good respectable education. My moment of clarity came when I was chatting to a friend, and he was telling me about all the bird (prison sentences) he had done. I was horrified, and thought 'you know what, you ain't got no fucking prospects in life. There's no future for you other than doing more and more bird'. I realized that in a few years that would be me too, because I'm doing the same stupid shit as him. I had to fix up. So I applied to do a degree in business and economics at a Russell uni. I did the degree, and then went on to do an MBA. Now look, I work for a blue chip company, making money like when I was slinging rocks. Straight honest money is sweet, bro.
>
> (Arthritis)

This adds an additional twist to an already complex topic. Although Arthritis initially maintains that he became involved with crime to gain the respect of his peers, over time he noticed that the respect which he initially sought would inevitably lead to self-destruction, by way of lengthy prison sentences. This was not the real authentic type of respectability he desired. For him the ultimate form of respect was bound up in notions of formal respectability. Being respectable in the eyes of mainstream society, akin to that encouraged by his parents, which through reflective analysis, did in instances play a significant role in the cessation of his criminal activity.

Final Thoughts

> Crime prevention begins at home. I didn't commit crime because of the shame it would bring down would be worse than any prison sentence, and being from a tight West Indian family, I'd catch hell.
>
> (Fire)

Respectability and shame as an approach toward criminal preclusion was and still is a central feature in the lives of the post-*Windrush* generation. A solid work ethic, personal discipline and decorousness that were inculcated en bloc during the Caribbean colonial period were transported to Britain by the *Windrush* arrivals, who then raised their children with similar values. However, for the current generation of ABCs, who have become a minority black group (sub-Saharan ethnicities currently dominate black classification in the UK), we see that the ideals which were germane to *Windrush* arrivals slowly transform, deviate and maintain a new trajectory. These ideas are now loaded with new features related to identity and masculinity where traditional elements of shame and respectability are no longer as valued, or as relevant, as previously:

> It's my Nan and Granddad really. It would bother me more letting them down than it would my parents. I can't explain it, but it's like I'm closer to them in that right and wrong thing. It's like they don't expect me to get in trouble like, but my parents now, kind of half expect it 'cos they know what being on road is all about and what can happen.

> (Daryl)

The decreased potency of shaming and traditional modes of respect has meant that the post-*Windrush* generation's children have lost sight of the core affirmative Caribbean values which over the past three decades have been slowly diluted:

> Look at how some of these ratchet youths get backed up and defended by their parents nowadays.

> (TT)

It seems the view of respectability and shame is now inverted and rotated full circle, where a culture of blame, opposed to shame, thrives and is left untamed.

Notes

1 West Indian. Here I specifically use the term *West Indian* opposed to Caribbean, as it was the British Empire which defined a significant portion of the region as the *West Indies*, and arguably the cultural and collective consciousness of post-colonial populace at this time was based upon notions of *Britishness* grounded in Victorianism.
2 Pappishow. An Eastern Caribbean colloquial term for playfulness, silliness or stupidity.
3 Dread. Typically a Rastafari, but commonly asserted toward one who wears dreadlocks.
4 Babylon. The colonial and imperialist power structure which has oppressed black people. Also frequently used to describe the police.

References

Agnew, R. & Passsas, N. (1997) 'The Nature and Determinants of Strain: Another look at Durkheim and Merton', in R. Agnew, and N. Passas (eds), *The Future of Anomie Theory*, Boston: North Eastern University Press.

Anderson, E. (1999) *Code of the Streets: Decency, Violence and the Moral Life of the Inner City*, New York: Norton.

Becker, H. (1963) *Outsiders: Studies in Sociology of Deviance*, London: Free of Glencoe.

Beckford, R. (2000) *Dread and Pentecostal*, London: SPCK.

Bourgouis, P. (1995) *In Search of Respect: Selling Crack in El Barrio*, Cambridge: Cambridge University Press.

Bourne, S. (2010) *Mother Country: Britain's Black Community on the Home Front 1939–45*, Gloucestershire: The History Press.

Bowling, B. & Phillips, C. (2002) *Racism Crime and Justice*, Harlow: Longman.

Bradley, L. (2000) *Bass Culture: When Reggae Was King*, London: Penguin.

Braithwaite, J. (1989) *Crime, Shame and Reintegration*, Cambridge: Cambridge University Press.

Cashmore, E. (1984) *The Rastafarians*, London: Minority Rights Group.

Cavidino, M. & Dignan, J. (1992) *The Penal System: An Introduction*, London: Sage.

Coard, B. (1971) *How the West Indian Child Is Made Educationally Sub-Normal in the British School System: The Scandal of the Black Child in Schools in Britain*, London: Karia Press.

Deleuze, G. & Guattari, F. (1980) *A Thousand Plateaus: Capitalism and Schizophrenia*, Minneapolis: University of Minnesota Press.

Du Bois, W. E. B. (1907) *The World and Africa: An Inquiry into the Part which Africa Has Played in World History*, New York: The Viking Press.

Duneier, M. (1992) *Slim's Table: Race, Respectability and Masculinity*, Chicago: Chicago Press.

Gillborn, D. (1990) *Race, Ethnicity and Education*, London: Unwin Hyman Ltd.

Gillborn, D. (1995) *Racism and Antiracism in Real Schools*, Buckingham: Open University Press.

Gilroy, P. (1987) *There Ain't No Black in the Union Jack: The Cultural Politics of Race and Nation*, London: Hutchinson Education.

Glynn, M. (2014) *Black Men, Invisibility and Desistance from Crime: Towards a Critical Race Theory of Desistance*, London & New York: Routledge.

Henry, W. (2006) *What The Deejay Said*, London: Nu Beyond.

Herberg, W. (1956) *Protestant, Catholic, Jew*, New York: Doubleday.

Herskovits, M. J. (1990) *The Myth of the Negro Past*, Boston: Harper & Row.

Hiro, D. (1992) *Black British, White British: History of Race Relations in Britain*, London: Paladin.

Hirschi, T. (1969) *Causes of Delinquency*, Berkley: University of California Press.

Hobbs, D. (1988) *Doing the Business*, Oxford: Oxford University Press.

Liebow, E. (1968) *Tally's Corner: A Study of Negro Street Corner Men*, Boston: Little Brown & Company.

Majors, R. (1993) *Cool Pose: The Dilemmas of Black Manhood in America*, New York: Touchstone.

Merton, R. K. (1938) 'Social Structure and Anomie' *American Sociological Review*, (3) pp 672–82.

Monrose, K. (2013) *It's Not as Simple as ABC: A Qualitative Study*, Unpublished Doctoral thesis, Department of Sociology, University of Essex, Colchester, UK.

Mullard, C. (1982) 'Multiracial Education in Britain: from assimilation to cultural pluralism' in J. Tierney, (ed), *Race, Migration and Schooling*, London: Holt, Rinehart & Winston.

Newham Monitoring Project (1991) *Forging a Black Community: Asian and Afro Caribbean Struggles in Newham*, London: NMP/CARF.

Phillips, M. & Phillips, T. (1998) *Windrush: The Irresistible Rise of Multi-Racial Britain*, London: Harper Collins.

Pryce, K. (1979) *Endless Pressure*, Harmonworth: Bristol Classics.

Reckless, W. C. (1950) *The Crime Problem*, New York: Appleton-Century-Crofts.

Ross, E. A. (1901) *Social Control: A Survey of the Foundations of Order*, London & New York: Macmillan.

Sewell, T. (1997) *Black Masculinities and Schooling: How Black Boys Survive Modern Schooling*, Staffordshire: Trentham Books.

Solomos, J. (1988) *Black Youth, Racism and the State: The Politics of Ideology and Policy*, Cambridge: Cambridge University Press.

Solomos, J. & Back, L. (1996) *Racism and Society*, Basingstoke: Macmillan.

Young, J. (1999) *Exclusive Society*, London: Sage.

Section Two
Youth

5   Histories of Hooliganism

Andrew Davies

More than thirty years since its publication in 1983, Geoffrey Pearson's *Hooligan: A History of Respectable Fears* remains both required reading for sociologists, criminologists and historians and a vital point of reference for those rare media commentators willing to acknowledge the historical roots of street crime, disorder and violence in Britain's cities.[1] Working back from the wave of riots that spread from London to Liverpool, Manchester and Birmingham during the summer of 1981, Pearson showed how preceding generations of Britons had all seen themselves as uniquely troubled by lawlessness and disorder. Each generation had invoked mythical 'golden ages' in the past, with conservative social commentators across decades and even centuries issuing remarkably similar complaints about the corrosive influence of popular culture on the young, accompanied by recurring pleas for harsher punishments.

Pearson took his title from the 'hooligan' panic that gripped London during the hot summer of 1898. As he showed, 'hooliganism' was rapidly adopted as a new label for the exploits of unruly youths, whose disorderly conduct, drunkenness, assaults on the police, street robberies and gang fighting were characterised by a sensation-hungry press as both unprecedented and 'un-English' (1983: 74–7). Responses to these youthful miscreants betrayed a profound amnesia. As Pearson wryly observed, 'If Hooliganism was an entirely novel outburst as was usually supposed, then a tropical growth of gang life must have sprouted overnight' (1983: 82). Pearson took his readers on a 'tour of the quiet streets' of late Victorian London, revealing a street life that was tumultuous and frequently violent. Assaults on the police and collective resistance to arrest were commonplace, while those suspected of co-operating with the police and courts faced intimidation, if not reprisal (1983: 81–92). Youthful gang members played their part, Pearson acknowledged, but they did not act in isolation: 'Suspicion and hostility towards the law in working-class London at the turn of the century drew on much deeper funds of popular feeling' (1983: 88).

As Pearson revealed, London's hooligans were by no means unique. Their provincial counterparts—the 'scuttlers' of Manchester and Salford, 'peaky blinders' and 'sloggers' of Birmingham and 'High Rip' of Liverpool—had already earned widespread notoriety by the 1880s (1983: 98). Across England's major cities, youthful gang members adopted a common uniform: peaked caps, worn tilted over their eyes, 'flashy' scarves, bell-bottomed trousers and heavy, brass-buckled belts marked them out from their adolescent peers, while their favoured hairstyle—a close crop, with a long fringe plastered down on the forehead—startled middle-class observers (1983: 93–8). As Pearson noted, here was evidence of a well-established, working-class 'youth culture' that predated the better-known 'Teddy Boys' by seventy years (1983: 100–101, 256). In each city, youth gangs resorted to weapons, including knives, stones and the buckle ends of their belts, although Pearson was wary of claims in the popular press that London's hooligans routinely carried firearms (1983: 101–6).

Contemporary responses to hooliganism were far from uniform. At the height of the panic, in 1898, calls for hooligans to be flogged extended from the *Daily Mail* and *News of the World* to the medical journal, the *Lancet*. Commentators in the radical and socialist press took a different view: for *Reynolds's Newspaper*, the panic showed the folly of prioritising missionary work overseas above attending to social problems at home (Pearson 1983: 77–9). In the decade that followed, the troublesome figure of the hooligan provided a 'crystallising focus' for Britain's imperial, military, industrial and social anxieties. In Pearson's words: 'He loomed large in the apocalyptic discourse surrounding . . . fears of racial decline and physical inefficiency' (1983: 107). Social reformers set out both to reform the hooligan and, in some cases, to channel his instincts and energies into schemes for imperial renewal. Attempts to wean boys and lads off the streets and out of gangs hinged on the provision of sports facilities—frequently promoted by the boys' club movement, which sought to combine boxing clubs with Bible classes. Others, like Robert Baden-Powell, founder of the Boy Scouts, celebrated the hooligan's 'character'. As Baden-Powell put it in a speech to the National Defence Association in 1910, the hooligan was 'the best class of boy' (Pearson 1983: 108–11).

As D.G. Wright (1983) noted in his review of *Hooligan* for the *London Review of Books*, Pearson's findings ran counter to many of the orthodoxies then current among historians of crime and punishment in nineteenth-century England. These stressed the fall in the recorded level of indictable crime between the 1850s and the 1890s, which V. A. C. Gatrell attributed to the success of the 'coercive state' in combating traditional forms of law-breaking (Gatrell 1980: 336). Gatrell's conclusions echoed those of David Philips, who emphasised working-class acceptance of the criminal law and participation in the prosecution process during the Victorian period (Philips 1977: 285–6), and David Jones, who argued that, in both London and Manchester, people and property were notably safer by 1900 than they had been in 1850 (Jones 1982: 143, 177). As Pearson showed, contemporary commentators—especially in the press—were less confident that the war on crime had been won.

Pearson's revelation that hooliganism had a history stretching back to the late nineteenth century had been anticipated two years previously by social historian Stephen Humphries. In *Hooligans or Rebels*, Humphries noted that hooliganism was a 'constant cause of concern' between the 1880s and the 1930s, with recurring moral panics followed by prolonged campaigns to control and rehabilitate working-class youth. These law-and-order campaigns, Humphries observed, were prompted not so much by increases in delinquency *per se*, as by heightened public sensitivity to youthful law-breaking at moments of economic and military threats to national stability—notably during the 'Boer War' of 1899–1902 and the First World War (Humphries 1981: 174–5). However, Humphries' own examination of street gangs and hooliganism largely covered the early decades of the twentieth century. He made only fleeting mention of the late Victorian youth gangs that Pearson subsequently investigated in *Hooligan*.

Humphries used a series of oral testimonies to offer an account of street gangs from within. For Humphries, the illegal and antisocial acts perpetrated by youthful gang members 'grew out of resentment and hostility rooted in a shared experience of inequality and subordination.' Gang violence, whether motivated by territorial rivalry or racism, was 'self-destructive and futile in the long term' but nonetheless 'offer[ed] working-class youths momentary reprieve from their inferior social identity' (Humphries 1981: 175). Anticipating Pearson's findings in *Hooligan*, Humphries viewed attacks by street gangs on the police as an expression of a wider working-class resentment, motivated by police interference in popular leisure activities and their role in the containment of political protests and strikes (1981: 205). In contrast to Pearson, Humphries claimed that conflicts between rival street gangs were 'to a large extent ritualized and involved customary constraints that prevented serious injury.' Weapons were 'rarely used and were carried largely as symbols of defiance and resistance.' 'Serious' violence was most likely to be directed at newly arrived immigrant groups during periods of socio-economic decline (Humphries 1981: 189–96).

Historians of modern Britain were slow to build on the pioneering studies of Humphries and Pearson. The first book-length study of hooliganism focused not on London, but on St Petersburg (Neuberger 1993). Since the late 1990s, however, there has been a proliferation of English case studies—of late Victorian Liverpool, Manchester and Salford, and Birmingham, as well as London—drawing inspiration from Pearson's recognition that London's hooligans were part of a 'nationwide phenomenon' (1983: 94).[2] More recently, scholarly attention has turned to the hooligan's Australian counterpart, the 'larrikin', whose exploits—as Pearson noted—can be traced back to 1870 (Pearson 1983: 98–100; Sleight 2009; Bellanta 2012; Bellanta and Sleight 2014). Focusing on the cities of late Victorian England, this chapter surveys these new histories of hooliganism, highlighting their debt to Pearson's 'history of respectable fears' as well as to Humphries' recognition of the persistent links between youth gangs and economic inequality.

Liverpool: The 'High Rip' Gang

The first provincial case study, by Rob Sindall (1990), focused on Liverpool, where the exploits of the High Rip gang briefly made headline news during the mid-1880s. Sindall claimed that the gang first came to the attention of the judges on the Northern Circuit in 1884, when 17-year-old Michael McLean—subsequently said to be its leader—was hung for the murder of a Spanish sailor in the city's North End. Reflecting on the case two years later, the *Liverpool Echo* insisted that there was 'as much intimidation and terrorism in the portion of the city lying between Scotland Road and the river as there [was] in the most disturbed district in Ireland' (Sindall 1990: 66; Archer 2011: 185).

The High Rip's local notoriety was sealed in August 1886, when 150 of its members reportedly marched along Scotland Road to Walton Gaol, seeking retribution against a man who had given evidence against one of their associates. According to reports in the local press, their intended victim belonged to a rival gang known as 'the Logwood'. Three months later, two 19-year-old 'High Rippers' were convicted of unlawful wounding and sentenced to exemplary terms of fifteen years' penal servitude. Their victim was also said to belong to the Logwood gang (Sindall 1990: 67; Macilwee 2006: 175–8).[3]

The *Liverpool Daily Post* employed a 'special commissioner' to tour the High Rip's 'hunting ground'. The commissioner duly provided the *Post*'s readers with a detailed portrait of the gang's members and their *modus operandi*. Aged between 17 and 22, they hailed from the city's impoverished North End docklands. According to the *Post*'s investigator, the High Rip operated as a 'secret society', with new recruits swearing allegiance to the gang and its members and pledging never to initiate an attack without drawing blood. (Their distinctive 'bucko' hats must have significantly undermined the secrecy of their operations.) According to the *Post*, they levied systematic blackmail on the local dock labourers, using knives and belts with sharpened buckles to terrorise their victims (Sindall 1990: 68–9). The *Post*'s commissioner claimed that the High Rips' adversaries, the Logwood 'gang', were in fact not gang members but vigilantes—'being formed of working men who have banded themselves together to put an end to the High Rip Gang' (Sindall 1990: 69).

The *Post*'s accounts of the High Rip generated widespread alarm in Liverpool during the autumn of 1886. Its coverage did not go unchallenged, however. By late September, the *Liverpool Review* began to question the gang's existence. As Sindall observed, discrepancies in local press reports reflected the proximity of the municipal elections on 1 November. Sensational depictions of gang outrages in the *Post* and its sister paper, the *Echo*, were intended to embarrass the Watch Committee and undermine the Tory grip on the city council. The *Liverpool Review* lent its support to the Tories by playing down the allegations. In the event, the Tories increased their hold on the council (Sindall 1990: 67–8). According to Sindall, the *Review* brought the episode to a close in March 1887, declaring that stories of 'High Rip Outrages' had been 'worked up to a point of serious exaggeration for sensational poster purposes'. For Sindall, the episode was a clear demonstration of the capacity of the press to manufacture a crime scare to boost sales and embarrass the establishment (1990: 70).

The notoriety of the High Rip extended beyond Liverpool. This was largely due to the actions of one of the judges on the Northern Circuit, Sir John Day.

Confronted by several batches of alleged High Rippers at the Liverpool Assizes in November 1886, Mr Justice Day declared that he 'did not think it possible that such gangs existed.' He nonetheless arranged to tour the Scotland Road district to see for himself. His expedition was arranged by the city's Head Constable, William Nott-Bower. He set out at pub closing time with his fellow judge, Mr Justice Grantham, escorted by Nott-Bower and two detectives, and they spent two to three hours making 'a complete tour of the district'. The judges were shocked by the poverty and squalor they witnessed, but—unsurprisingly, given their escort—they saw no sign of the High Rip. At the close of the Assizes, Day declared: 'I have never seen and cannot believe that there is anything in Liverpool of the nature of an organisation of ruffians banded together against the law. All I say is that there may be, but I have seen no evidence of it' (Nott-Bower 1926: 149–50; Sindall 1990: 120–22). Day's willingness to brave the 'perils of the Liverpool slums' was widely applauded in the national as well as local press.[4]

Three months later, Liverpool witnessed renewed allegations of 'High Rip Terrorism' after four youths rampaged through the Scotland Road district, robbing shopkeepers and stabbing and kicking bystanders. The youths were tried before Mr Justice Day at the Liverpool Assizes in May 1887. All four were convicted of robbery with violence. Day caused a sensation when he sentenced them to relatively short terms of imprisonment on account of their ages (three were aged 20 and the other 19), only to pronounce that each of them was to be flogged three times with the 'cat', receiving twenty lashes on each occasion (Macilwee 2006: 166–9). Day's resort to the cat was widely credited with ending the High Rip's 'Reign of Terror' in Liverpool's North End (Nott-Bower 1926: 151; Archer 2011: 109).

This belief was unfounded—it was subsequently shown that cases of robbery with violence in Liverpool had increased, rather than decreased, after Day's resort to flogging (Radzinowicz and Hood 1986: 704)—but it was widely invoked during the hooligan panic of 1898. The *Pall Mall Gazette* was in no doubt that flogging would clear hooliganism from the streets of London in an instant, since 'there is Mr. Justice DAY's putting down of the Liverpool High Rip gang to prove to all time that the cat is effective.'[5]

The controversy surrounding the High Rip was one of a series of episodes from different cities examined by Sindall in his account of street violence between the 1850s and the 1880s. In a more systematic study of violence in Victorian Liverpool, John Archer (2011: 109) concluded that the High Rip episode was 'a heady brew of press exaggeration and sensationalism', but acknowledged that the youths involved belonged on 'the spectrum of male-on-male violence' in the city (2011: 110). Youths in the city's poorer districts routinely 'hung around on street corners, swearing and cursing, shouting lewd remarks at passing women and being generally anti-social' (2011: 183). These groups occasionally came into conflict, as in 1883, when a 13-year-old spectator named Michael Burns was fatally kicked and beaten during a fracas that erupted following a fight between representatives of the Lemon Street gang and the Regent Road gang. A detective observed that 'the lads in each street combined together in lots, or gangs, for the purpose of play; and should there be any fall-out between lads in different lots, they had a general scrimmage' (Archer 2011: 183–5). However, historians have so far uncovered few traces of these conflicts. The extent of gang formation in late Victorian Liverpool is therefore still to be determined.

Manchester and Salford: The Scuttlers

The first in-depth studies of late Victorian youth gangs focused not on London or Liverpool, but on Manchester and the adjacent County Borough of Salford (Gooderson 1997; Davies 1998; 1999; 2008; 2011). As Pearson noted in *Hooligan*, Manchester's gangs were fiercely territorial. Their fights, known locally as 'scuttles', sometimes involved several hundred combatants and were so ferocious that the civic authorities petitioned the Home Secretary for sterner measures to put them down (Pearson 1983: 94–6; Davies 2008: 201–3). Focusing on a single conurbation made it possible to trace the reported escalation (and decline) of gang formation and activity over time and to examine patterns of conflict, along with the responses of the police, judiciary and local press, in depth for the first time. Crucially, it also made it possible to compile profiles of individual gangs and their members, locating them in the context of family and community relationships as well as local labour markets.

Reports of 'scuttling' first surfaced in the Manchester press during the Franco-Prussian War of 1870–71. Rival gangs of Catholic and Protestant schoolboys staged their own 'mimic warfare' on the streets of Angel Meadow, a notorious 'slum' district to the north of Manchester city-centre (Davies 2008: 38–44). Police arrested more than 500 of the combatants over a period of twelve months, but failed to quell the violence. Quite the reverse: the conflicts spread across the factory districts that ringed the city-centre, drawing in large numbers of youths aged in their mid- to late teens. The sectarian basis of the initial conflicts was quickly eclipsed by territorial loyalties, and by the mid-1870s it was common for Catholics (most of whom were of Irish descent) to fight alongside Protestants in skirmishes between gangs from rival neighbourhoods (Davies 2008: 51, 74).

Scuttling in Manchester and Salford persisted for three decades. Utilising a sample of 250 cases tried by the local magistrates and reported in the local press, it is possible to discern clear patterns in scuttlers' backgrounds as well as in their territorial feuds and their frequent resort to violence. Almost all of the 717 young people prosecuted in these cases were convicted. They were generally aged between 14 and 19, and most lived with their parents and siblings. Without exception, they belonged to working-class households: they were the children of manual workers, and they worked in manual occupations themselves—as labourers, factory operatives, dyers, colliers, carters or street traders. It is rare, however, to find apprentices among those convicted following scuttling affrays. This is perhaps unsurprising: once they had 'served their time', apprentices stood to enter the elite ranks of skilled craftsmen with the prospect of higher rates of pay and relatively secure employment. Few of them appear to have been willing to jeopardize their future prospects by scuttling (Davies 1998: 350–2).

The most notorious gangs were clustered in the 'slums' of Ancoats in Manchester and Greengate in Salford, or in the lodging-house districts of Angel Meadow and Deansgate—the reputed haunts of 'Criminal Manchester'. However, scuttling was by no means confined to the slums. Conflicts extended to the relatively prosperous manufacturing districts to the North and East of the city-centre (Newton Heath, Gorton and Openshaw) and to the colliery districts of Bradford to the East and Pendleton in Salford. All of these localities were firmly identified as 'working-class', but they were considered 'superior' to Ancoats or Angel Meadow. Most scuttles took place in the streets to which the gangs laid claim, but on Friday and Saturday nights confrontations also took place in and around city-centre music halls and nearby beerhouses (Davies 1998: 350, 351, 362; 2008: 126).

Of those charged in this sample of 250 scuttling cases, 93.7 per cent were male (Davies 1998: 350) Gang conflicts constituted arenas in which youths could demonstrate their toughness and prove themselves as men, both individually and collectively. Public displays of aggression and daring in confrontations between opposing gangs allowed those on the brink of adulthood to derive considerable kudos and to imagine themselves as 'hard' men (Davies 1998: 356–7). Young women were rarely prosecuted following scuttles and contemporary commentators tended to depict them either as inciting conflicts between rival gangs or in auxiliary roles: as observers of male fighting prowess, as handmaidens (carrying weapons) or as witnesses, ever-ready to commit perjury on behalf of their 'sweethearts' (Davies 1999: 73). However, scrutiny of trial reports reveals that young women sometimes took an active part both in fights between rivals and gangs and in the subsequent intimidation of witnesses (Davies 1999: 79–85). In Salford, the local press was much excited by the discovery of a 'gang of female scuttlers' in 1890, but on closer inspection they turned out to be members of a long-established, and predominantly male, gang from Pendleton (Davies 2008: 250–2).

The most bitter—and enduring—feuds tended to be between gangs from adjacent districts. In Salford, the Hope Street and Ordsall Lane gangs clashed weekly over eighteen months, culminating in the trial of seventeen youths at the Salford Borough Quarter Sessions in June 1890. The two gangs' meeting places were less than five minutes' walk apart and their members were well known to each other (Davies 2008: 213–21). Contrary to Humphries' claim that weapons were carried 'largely as symbols of defiance and resistance' (1981: 193), scuttlers routinely fought with knives and belts. Stabbings were frequent enough to provoke the ire of hospital staff as well as magistrates and judges, but fatalities were rare: the local press attributed just five deaths to scuttling between 1870 and 1900. Surgeons' evidence in trials at the higher courts testified to a fighting code whereby gang members sought to scar or maim their opponents. Knife wounds were generally to the face or upper body, and fatal stabbings were met with surprise—and some disapproval—among scuttlers themselves (Davies 1998: 352; 2011: 44–5).

Police memoirs testify to the dangers posed by scuttlers to beat constables, in particular. Many scuttles appear to have taken place without police intervention, and attempts to suppress the conflicts by posting additional officers in recognised trouble spots were generally futile. As Superintendent Charles Godby of the City of Manchester Police ruefully admitted in 1871, scuttles were 'no sooner put down in one place than renewed in another.' Magistrates and judges were similarly thwarted in their efforts to curb the gangs. Hundreds of scuttlers were jailed—more than 300 in 1871 alone—and exemplary sentences of fifteen and twenty years' penal servitude for manslaughter imposed during the mid-1880s had no apparent deterrent effect (Davies 2011: 45–8).

As in London, during the hooligan panic of 1898, coverage of scuttling in the Manchester press was routinely sensationalised. News reports on clashes between rival gangs showed that injuries were generally restricted to the opposing bands of scuttlers, but editorial commentaries tended to misrepresent scuttling in terms of wholly random assaults on peaceable passers-by (Davies 2011: 49). Scuttlers enjoyed their notoriety. When John-Joseph Hillier (alias 'Red Elliott') was christened 'King of the Scuttlers' by the *Salford Reporter* in 1894, he revelled in the title. Hillier took to parading the streets of Salford and Deansgate wearing a jersey into which both his street name and the legend 'KING OF SCUTTLERS' had been sewn (Davies 1998: 362).

Reports of scuttling declined rapidly during the late 1890s. By 1898–9—the very moment that London was gripped by reports of hooliganism—only a few isolated scuttles made the 'Police Court News' columns of the Manchester and Salford newspapers. Local commentators were adamant that if scuttling had not disappeared entirely, it had significantly diminished. Senior police officers were understandably eager to claim the credit, but others attributed the demise of gang conflicts to the establishment of working lads' clubs (Davies 2011: 50–1). The first clubs in Manchester were founded in response to a reported escalation of gang violence during the late 1880s. They were built in the districts most associated with scuttling: four separate clubs opened in Ancoats alone between 1888 and 1890. The clubs quickly took root, not least by establishing football, rugby and cricket teams and promoting gymnastics, athletics and swimming. They found thousands of willing takers (Weinberger 1993: 46; Davies 2008: 291–7). Working lads' clubs did not convert the existing ranks of scuttlers. However, as the clubs grew during the 1890s they appear to have helped to reduce the numbers of new recruits into the gangs (Davies 2011: 51).

Birmingham: Sloggers and Peaky Blinders

In Birmingham, as in Manchester, conflicts between rival youth gangs were first reported during the early 1870s. According to Barbara Weinberger, Birmingham's gang conflicts originated in 'territorial wars fought between Irish and English street gangs' (1991: 408). Hostility towards Birmingham's Irish-Catholic population had intensified during the previous decade. In June 1867, Park Street in the city's 'Irish' quarter had been largely demolished during the 'Murphy' riots—provoked by an anti-Catholic tirade by the militant Protestant orator, William Murphy (Gooderson 2010: 29–33). Anti-Irish feeling was subsequently inflamed by reports of 'Fenian' activity (Weinberger 1991: 408).[6] During the following decade, Weinberger argued, anti-Irish sentiment 'offered a focus and a target for the frustrations of inner city youths which . . . became institutionalized in gang warfare' (1991: 408–9).

Weinberger offered two further explanations for the reported upsurge in street disturbances and 'gang warfare' in Birmingham from around 1873–4. The severe recession that followed the economic boom of the early 1870s threw thousands of unemployed—and disenfranchised—youths onto the streets (1991: 410–11). At the same time, aggressive police campaigns against drunkenness and street gambling met with fierce resentment in the city's working-class districts. Young men featured prominently in the communal disturbances that ensued (Weinberger 1991: 412–14; 1981: 227–8). Weinberger contrasted the vigour of municipal campaigns to reform 'public manners' with the indifference shown by the civic authorities to the 'welfare or rights of a section of the community who had no power or votes . . . and for whose behaviour they had nothing but disdain' (1991: 414). Echoing Humphries' account in *Hooligans or Rebels*, Weinberger concluded: 'However misconceived, gang warfare at least gave the participants a chance to acquire some local power and prestige which was denied them at any other level of public life' (1991: 417).

Weinberger's account of the emergence of Birmingham's youth gangs drew upon her wider study (1981) of crime and policing in the city in the ten years that followed the 1867 Reform Act. In a more comprehensive analysis—based on 143 incidents reported in the local press between 1870 and 1900—Philip Gooderson (2013) drew a series of parallels between the 'slogging' gangs of late Victorian Birmingham and the scuttlers of Manchester and Salford. Slogging, like scuttling, drew on local traditions of prize-fighting and workplace violence (Gooderson 2013: 65). Girls and young women were less active in Birmingham's gang conflicts than in Manchester's—Gooderson's sample of 284 sloggers included only four females (2013: 67). The majority of sloggers were aged in their late teens, and their occupations closely reflected the structure of the local economy: around half were iron or brass workers, with smaller numbers employed in the manufacture of guns, jewellery and pearl buttons (2013: 67–70). Only 15 per cent of those in Gooderson's sample were unskilled labourers (2013: 69).

Gooderson cautiously accepted Weinberger's claim that Birmingham's gang conflicts originated in sectarian antagonism (2010: 83–4, 110–11; 2013: 69). However, he rejected the link posited by Weinberger between gangs, poverty and 'marginalisation' (2013: 78). According to Gooderson (2013: 65–6), slogging appears to have increased during periods of prosperity (such as the early 1870s, the mid-1880s, and especially from 1888–91), diminishing during economic downturns (after 1874, and again from 1892–5). Moreover, Gooderson stressed that in Birmingham—as in Manchester—the ethnic basis of gang conflicts was quickly superseded by territorial rivalries, with most feuds occurring between gangs from adjacent districts (2013: 72–4). In Birmingham, again as in Manchester, gang conflicts spread across the conurbation during the 1870s and 1880s, before reportedly diminishing in the late 1890s (Gooderson 2010: 88–96, 165–6, 192; 2013: 66, 73–4). Gooderson ascribed the decline of slogging to a number of factors, invoking the growth of 'adult-approved' football as an alternative source of excitement among working-class youths along with a belated triumph by the local 'forces of law and order' (2013: 79).

During the 1890s, Birmingham's gang members—formerly known to each other as well as to the civic authorities as sloggers—were rechristened 'peaky blinders'. In local lore, the term is sometimes held to refer to the practice of stitching razor blades into the peak of their caps (Davies 2006: 108). In reality, it derived from the fashion of pulling the peak of a cap, or hat, low over one eye (Bramwell 1991: 47). As Arthur Matthison recalled (1937: 63), the peaky blinder wore:

> Bell-bottomed trousers secured by a buckle belt, hob-nailed boots, a jacket of sorts, a gaudy scarf and a billy-cock hat with a long elongated brim. This hat was worn well over one eye, hence the name 'peaky blinder'. His hair was prison cropped all over his head, except for a quiff in front which was grown long and plastered down obliquely on his forehead.

This was instantly recognisable as a gang uniform, whether on the streets of Birmingham, Manchester or London, even if the peaky blinder's boots distinguished him from the scuttler with his Lancashire-style clogs (Pearson 1983: 96–7; Gooderson 2010: 216).

Late-Victorian social commentators were as much concerned with male violence towards women as with the problems posed by warring youth gangs (Hammerton 1995; D'Cruze 1998). They rarely connected the two. Historians have tended to maintain this distinction, with studies of gangs and hooliganism making only fleeting references to violence within courtship or marriage. A rare case study (Davies 2006) examined the conviction of James Harper, an 18-year-old Birmingham metal polisher, and an alleged peaky blinder, for the manslaughter of his former 'sweetheart', Emily Pimm, in November 1898. Refusing to accept that Pimm had jilted him, Harper repeatedly assaulted her in the street over a period of ten weeks before knocking her down and stamping repeatedly, and fatally, on her head (Davies 2006: 113–14).

In commentaries on the case in the local press, both gang membership and male brutality towards women were denounced as problems of the city's 'slums' (Davies 2006: 108, 115–16). Close inspection revealed that neither the perpetrator nor the victim in this case confirmed to the stereotypes of the 'peaky' and his 'moll' that were applied to them (Davies 2006: 116–18). Yet these stereotypes performed an important ideological function, distancing the problem of violence from the mainstream of civic life and thus preserving the veneer of English civility whilst masking the extent of male violence within courtship as well as marriage (Davies 2006: 118–19).

London: The Original Hooligans

Historians were surprisingly slow to build on Pearson's pioneering account of London's hooligan panic of 1898. When they did turn their attention back to the capital, their focus was not so much on the youthful perpetrators of violence and disorder themselves as on the symbolic importance of the figure of hooligan in debates on social welfare reform that followed the Boer War of 1899–1902. In an essay published in 1992, Seth Koven noted that the 'very existence of the hooligan' affirmed the need for wholesale state intervention to ameliorate the conditions of life among Britain's urban poor (1992: 383–4).[7] As Koven revealed, many of the self-styled 'experts' on hooliganism to emerge in the wake of the panic of 1898 were Oxford or Cambridge graduates who had lived in university settlements in the slums of London during the 1880s and 1890s (1992: 376). Their earnest attempt to 'create nation and community through vertical bonds of comradeship across class lines' had faltered, but their experience of working with 'rough lads' gave them a degree of authority as social reformers as well as social commentators (1992: 365–6). In several cases—notably Hubert Llewellyn-Smith, Robert Morant and C. F. G. Masterman—they used this authority to considerable effect as architects of the Liberal welfare reforms of 1906–11 (1992: 380).

Writing more directly in response to Geoffrey Pearson, Bill Schwarz (1996: 106–7) posed the question: why did the hooligan panic erupt at the close of the nineteenth century? If recurring anxieties about young men, street disturbances and criminality have such a long duration—as Pearson showed—why did the term 'hooligan' resonate so powerfully at this particular historical moment? To Schwarz, the rapidity with which the term entered the English language owed something to the growth of state intervention in family life during the late nineteenth century: the increasing regulation of childhood and the practices of motherhood created new arenas for intensified public concern. This was exacerbated by the rapid growth of the press. Mass circulation newspapers—notably the *Daily Mail*, first published in 1896—were eager to denounce criminals and hooligans, while simultaneously revelling in 'the grisly details of each new barbarity' (1996: 107–9).

More than anything, however, Schwarz attributed the timing of the hooligan panic to the protracted, and contested, process through which Britain edged towards mass democracy. Following the 1867 Reform Act, working-class men came to be recognised 'as real or potential members of the political nation', pressing for—and in some cases securing—the vote on the one hand, and receiving compulsory schooling and the benefits of culture (including parks, museums and libraries) on the other. As the political nation slowly became more inclusive, new structures of exclusion were devised to screen out those who wilfully resisted these civilising processes. The 'concept of the hooligan', Schwarz concluded, 'was produced by the concept of the citizen, hooliganism working as the discursive Other of citizenship' (1996: 118).

In the first full-length study of the hooligan panic and its repercussions, Ian Livie closely echoed Pearson's account, noting how the press cast hooliganism as a distinct threat both to British civility and racial purity and to the capacity of the state to maintain public order (2010: vi, 13–55). Livie showed how the 1898 panic prompted evangelical moral reform groups to take an increasing interest in delinquency among working-class juveniles. The Salvation Army, in particular, turned the hooligan crisis into a crisis of faith as well as 'moral health' by linking hooliganism to 'vices' common among city youths such as smoking, gambling and intemperance (2010: 98). Salvationists' fears for the physical and spiritual health of the urban poor were widely shared in official circles, as demonstrated by the publication in 1904 of the *Report of the Inter-Departmental Committee on Physical Deterioration* (Livie 2010: 145).

Campaigns by the Howard Association provided further impetus for reform in the wake of the hooligan panic. The Howard Association lobbied for the introduction of separate juvenile courts along with the expansion of the Borstal system to house a new category of offender—the 'juvenile-adult' aged between 16 and 21 (Livie 2010: 202–11). These reforms were implemented by the Liberal government in 1908 with the passage of the Children's Act and the Prevention of Crime Act. In Livie's account, the Children's Act was the 'culmination of a decade of social agitation' following the hooligan panic of 1898. As such, it 'was ultimately as much an expression of conservative fears of moral decay as it was a product of a progressive agenda to create a new safety net for children and young persons' (2010: 245–7).

Geoffrey Pearson's comment that hooligan was a new label for youths previously known more loosely as 'street arabs', 'ruffians' or 'roughs' (1983: 75), has recently been borne out by Drew Gray in a case study of 'gang' murder that took place ten years before the hooligan panic. On the evening of 24 May 1888, a group of 'Tottenham Court Road Lads' set out for Regent's Park to avenge a 'kicking' suffered by one of their number the previous night. They were searching for 'the Marylebone chaps'. When they found Joseph Rumbold, a 22-year-old printer's machinist, promenading with a young woman and another couple, they set upon him and Rumbold was fatally stabbed. (It is unclear whether Rumbold belonged to a gang: Gray suspects that 'he was simply unfortunate in being in the wrong place at the wrong time.') George Galletly, aged 18, was convicted of Rumbold's murder. He was sentenced to death at the Old Bailey, although he was subsequently reprieved on account of his youth (Gray 2013: 562–5).

Gray argues that the killing—an exceptional event—was systematically misrepresented by the press. While newspapers routinely exaggerated the extent of youth-gang violence, the *Pall Mall Gazette*, in particular, used the 'Regent's Park murder' as ammunition in its campaign to oust the Chief Commissioner of the Metropolitan Police, Sir Charles Warren (Gray 2013: 569–72). The editor of the *Pall Mall Gazette*, W. T. Stead, had targeted Warren since the brutal suppression of demonstrations by socialists and the unemployed in Trafalgar Square the previous year (Gray 2010: 141–3). Stead's relentless exposure of the state of crime in the capital—including a feature on the 'Bandit Gangs of London' published in October 1888—heaped pressure on Warren, whose reputation was severely damaged by his force's continuing failure to apprehend 'Jack the Ripper'. Warren resigned in November 1888, two days after the death of Mary Kelly, the 'Ripper's' final victim (Gray 2013: 566, 572).

In the first systematic study of youth gangs in late nineteenth century London, Heather Shore (2015) has recently revealed that metropolitan gang conflicts first came to the attention of the higher courts (and the press) during 1882 following the death of Frederick Wilmore, a 19-year-old carman, during a clash between the 'City Road Boys' and the 'Lambeth Chaps' on the Thames Embankment (Andersson 2013: 57–8; Shore 2015: 7–9, 11). This was a decade later than the first reports of scuttling in Manchester and slogging in Birmingham. Wilmore's death prompted a series of articles on 'the fighting gangs of London' in the *Pall Mall Gazette*, which warned its readers that while such gangs were not a new presence on the capital's streets 'the new generation of the savages of the slums is more combative and more inclined to organization than its predecessor' (Shore 2015: 7).

Shore traced forty-one 'gang-related' affrays reported in London between 1882 and 1912. Of the ninety-seven defendants in these cases, ninety-six were male (Shore 2015: 7). Like the scuttlers of Manchester and Salford, most were aged between 16 and 19 and employed in semi- or unskilled manual occupations. Many of London's gang members worked as costermongers or labourers. Few held apprenticeships (Shore 2015: 7, 15–16). In London, however, as in Manchester and Birmingham, there was no simple correlation between gang membership and slum life. The districts most noted for their gangs—Clerkenwell, Hoxton, Islington, Somers Town and Lambeth—were predominantly working-class, but socially mixed: the circumstances of their inhabitants ranged from 'lowest class' to 'poor' to 'fairly comfortable', according to Charles Booth's poverty map of 1898–9. As Shore concluded, London's gang members were not the 'savages of the slums', or even members of a 'criminal class', but 'working-class youths from poor to respectable working-class areas' (2015: 10–11, 22).

As reports of scuttling rapidly declined in Manchester during the late 1890s, concern with youth gangs in London intensified. Indeed, the hooligan panic of 1898 was preceded by reports of a 'Pistol Plague', or 'Revolver Mania', in the capital the previous year. Whereas scuttlers seldom resorted to firearms, almost half of the cases in Shore's sample involved the use of pistols or revolvers (2015: 17–19).[8] Shore found that an outbreak of 'something akin to gang warfare' between factions from City Road, Somers Town, Clerkenwell and parts of East London during 1907–8 attracted much less press attention than similar episodes during the 1880s and 1890s. Even a fatal stabbing inflicted by one of the 'Nile Boys' in City Road in April 1907 generated remarkably little interest (Shore 2015: 6, 19, 26).

Conclusion

As Pearson (1983: 94–8) pointed out, the hooligan panic of 1898 was only one manifestation of a broader concern with gang formation, violence and disorder during the late nineteenth century. Case studies of Liverpool, Manchester and Salford, Birmingham and London have confirmed many of Pearson's findings, while providing new insights into patterns of gang activity along with profiles of the participants and insights into the responses of the police, judiciary and local authorities. Some important common findings emerge from these local studies. Across England's major cities, members of youth gangs tended to be male, working class and aged in their mid- to late teens. Only in Manchester and Salford, where female factory workers were a boisterous presence in the street life of working-class districts, do young women appear to have played an active part in gang conflicts. Contrary to assertions by some Victorian social commentators, gang members were not all slum-dwellers and nor were they 'unemployable'. Few went on to have criminal 'careers'. However, gang membership was not universal among working-class youths, and apprentices seldom appear to have joined the ranks of scuttlers, sloggers or hooligans. This is significant: those working-class youths with relatively secure economic prospects seem to have resisted the lure of the gangs.

There are further similarities in the patterns of violence. In Manchester and Salford, Birmingham and London, feuds between rival youth gangs were largely territorial. Fatalities were rare, but weapons were routinely used to inflict severe injuries—confirming another of Pearson's findings in *Hooligan*. In each city, police and magistrates struggled to suppress outbreaks of gang violence to the fury of the local press, whose allegations of police ineptitude and judicial impotence were at times as fierce as their condemnations of the perpetrators. Sensational newspaper reports appear to have significantly bolstered the reputations of prominent gang members.

Reports of gang activity in Liverpool only partially fit these wider trends. Although Archer uncovered evidence of 'scrimmages' between groups of youths from neighbouring streets in the city's North End, historians have so far found notably fewer traces of gang conflict in Liverpool than in the other major English cities. Moreover, the most notorious of Liverpool's gangs—the High Rip—was associated with robbery with violence rather than territorial skirmishing. This raises questions about the structural factors that shaped patterns of gang activity (Gillis 1974: 66). It is possible that, in Liverpool, territorial affiliation was at least in part eclipsed by the city's deeper sectarian animosities (Neal 1988), while the lack of industrial employment in this port city appears to have fostered a more widespread resort to petty theft, street robbery and 'levying'—demanding money with menaces—especially in the North End dockland districts (Macilwee 2006: 162–9; Archer 2011: 112–14).

Recent research into youth gangs and hooliganism in late Victorian England has been dominated by local case studies. One of the tasks awaiting future historians is the development of a more integrated, comparative analysis. This will need to address the startling contrast in periodization that has emerged from the plethora of recent case studies. In Manchester and Salford, as in Birmingham, gang conflicts reportedly escalated during the early 1870s, and persisted for three decades before declining during the late 1890s. In London, by contrast, concern with violent youth gangs surfaced later—in the early 1880s—but peaked in 1898–9, at the very moment that scuttling and slogging appeared to have declined. This raises some important questions. Did trends in youth violence over time vary from city to city, and if so, why? Alternatively, were the reported local escalations (and diminutions) of gang conflict more apparent than real? Did the local press in Manchester and Birmingham lose interest in youth gang violence after 1900—as Shore suggests might have been the case in London by 1907–8? More comprehensive research is required for each of the major conurbations for the period from 1860 to 1914, not least to determine the extent to which youth violence persisted beyond the phases of public concern with gangs.

Future research needs to extend beyond the major cities and across the class divide. To what extent were territorial gangs formed across urban England during the late Victorian period? And were the problems posed by disorderly youths more easily dealt with in smaller towns, where perpetrators were more likely to be recognised by police and passers-by? Equally, historians of crime need to turn their attention to outbreaks of disorder among middle-class and aristocratic youths. During the late Victorian period, as today, the punishment of young people was often made to fit the person as much as the crime. While scuttlers, sloggers and hooligans received tough sentences from an unforgiving judiciary, the Lord-Justice General, Baron Robertson, signed a letter to *The Times* in 1894 in defence of members of the Bullingdon Club, who had been sent down from Oxford following a drunken disturbance in which every window was smashed in Peckwater Quad at Christ Church.[9] In any other context, prosecutions for wilful damage would surely have followed.[10] The line between youthful criminality and 'high jinks' is worth exploring, not least since—to paraphrase Geoffrey Pearson—the 'problem' of youth has always been the problem of the children of the poor (1983: 208).

Notes

1 In 2007, *Hooligan* was voted one of seven 'iconic studies' in British criminology (Soothill and Peelo, 2007: 481–3). For media recognition of the book's enduring relevance, see Toynbee (2007; 2011).
2 For a slightly later episode in Glasgow, peaking in 1906, see Davies (2013: 17–23).
3 Sindall appears to have conflated two separate episodes in the reported feud between the two gangs: see Macilwee (2005: 175–8).
4 See, for example, the *Morning Post*, 16 November 1886.
5 *Pall Mall Gazette*, 10 September 1898.
6 The Fenian movement grew out of the Irish Republican Brotherhood. As MacCraild (1999: 138–42) pointed out, during 1867 and 1868 the British press was 'racked by reports, many of them bogus, of Fenian activities, including imminent insurrection'.

7 Here Koven developed one of Pearson's observations in *Hooligan* (1983: 107).
8 As Shore notes, Gooderson (2010: 265–7) found that reports of assaults involving firearms also increased in Birmingham during the late 1890s.
9 *The Times*, 3 July 1894. The Lord-Justice General was Scotland's most senior judge.
10 For prosecutions for wilful damage at the Oxford Police Court during the 1890s, see Gillis (1975: 102).

References

Andersson, P. (2013), *Streetlife in Late Victorian London*. Basingstoke: Palgrave Macmillan.

Archer, J. (2011), *The Monster Evil*. Liverpool: Liverpool University Press.

Bellanta, M. (2012), *Larrikins*. St Lucia: University of Queensland Press.

Bellanta, M. and Sleight, S. (2014), 'The Leary Larrikin: Street Style in Colonial Australia', *Cultural and Social History*, 11/2: 263–83.

Bramwell, B. (1991), 'Public Space and Local Communities: The Example of Birmingham, 1840–1880', in G. Kearns and C. Withers, eds, *Urbanising Britain*. Cambridge: Cambridge University Press.

Davies, A. (1998), 'Youth Gangs, Masculinity and Violence in Late Victorian Manchester and Salford', *Journal of Social History*, 32/2: 349–69.

Davies, A. (1999), '"These Viragoes are No Less Cruel than the Lads": Young Women, Gangs and Violence in Late Victorian Manchester and Salford', *British Journal of Criminology*, 39/1: 72–89.

Davies, A. (2006), 'Youth, Violence, and Courtship in Late-Victorian Birmingham: The Case of James Harper and Emily Pimm', *History of the Family*, 11/2: 107–20.

Davies, A. (2008), *The Gangs of Manchester*. Preston: Milo Books.

Davies, A. (2011), 'Youth Gangs and Late Victorian Society', in B. Goldson, ed., *Youth in Crisis?* London: Routledge.

Davies, A. (2013), *City of Gangs*. London: Hodder & Stoughton.

D'Cruze, S. (1998), *Crimes of Outrage*. London: UCL Press.

Gatrell, V. (1980), 'The Decline of Theft and Violence in Victorian and Edwardian England', in V. Gatrell, B. Lenman and G. Parker, eds, *Crime and the Law*. London: Europa.

Gillis, J. (1974), *Youth and History*. New York: Academic Press.

Gillis, J. (1975), 'The Evolution of Juvenile Delinquency in England 1890–1914', *Past and Present*, 67: 96–126.

Gooderson, P. (1997), 'Terror on the Streets of Late Victorian Salford and Manchester: The Scuttling Menace', *Manchester Region History Review*, 11: 3–11.

Gooderson, P. (2010), *The Gangs of Birmingham*. Wrea Green: Milo Books.

Gooderson, P. (2013), '"Noisy and Dangerous Boys": The Slogging Gang Phenomenon in Late Nineteenth-Century Birmingham', *Midland History*, 38/1: 58–79.

Gray, D. (2010), *London's Shadows*. London: Continuum.

Gray, D. (2013), 'Gang Crime and the Media in Late Nineteenth-Century London: The Regent's Park Murder of 1888', *Cultural and Social History*, 10/4: 559–75.

Hammerton, A. (1995), *Cruelty and Companionship*. London: Routledge.

Humphries, S. (1981), *Hooligans or Rebels?* Oxford: Basil Blackwell.

Jones, D. (1982), *Crime, Protest, Community and Police in Nineteenth-Century Britain*. London: Routledge & Kegan Paul.

Koven, S. (1992), 'From Rough Lads to Hooligans: Boy Life, National Culture and Social Reform', in Andrew Parker et al., eds, *Nationalisms and Sexualities*. New York: Routledge.

Livie, I. (2010), 'Curing Hooliganism: Moral Panic, Juvenile Delinquency, and the Political Culture of Moral Reform in Britain, 1898–1908', unpublished PhD thesis, University of Southern California.

Macilwee, M. (2006), *The Gangs of Liverpool*. Wrea Green: Milo Books.

MacCraild, D. (1999), *Irish Migrants in Modern Britain*. London: Macmillan.

Matthison, A. (1937), *More Paint, Les Vanity*. London: Heath Cranton.

Neal, F. (1988), *Sectarian Violence*. Manchester: Manchester University Press.

Neuberger, J. (1993). *Hooliganism*. Berkeley: University of California Press.

Nott-Bower, W. (1926), *Fifty-Two Years a Policeman*. London: Edward Arnold.

Pearson, G. (1983), *Hooligan*. Basingstoke: Macmillan.

Philips, D. (1977), *Crime and Authority in Victorian England*. London: Croom Helm.

Radzinowicz, L. and Hood, R. (1986), *A History of English Criminal Law and its Administration from 1750. Volume 5: The Emergence of Penal Policy*. London: Stevens & Sons.

Schwarz, B. (1996), 'Night Battles: Hooligan and Citizen', in M. Nava and A. O'Shea, eds, *Modern Times*. London: Routledge.

Shore, H. (2015), *London's Criminal Underworlds, c. 1720–c. 1930*. Basingstoke: Palgrave Macmillan.

Sindall, R. (1990), *Street Violence in the Nineteenth Century*. Leicester: Leicester University Press.

Sleight, S. (2009), 'Interstitial Acts: Urban Space and the Larrikin Repertoire in Late-Victorian Melbourne', *Australian Historical Studies*, 40/2: 232–50.

Soothill, K. and Peelo, L. (2007), 'Constructing British Criminology', *Howard Journal*, 46/5: 476–92.

Toynbee, P. (2007), 'Election Battle Lines are Set Over Crime and Punishment', *Guardian*, 28 August.

Toynbee, P. (2011), 'How Sad to Live in a Society that won't Invest in its Young', *Guardian*, 19 August.

Weinberger, B. (1981), 'Law Breakers and Law Enforcement in the Late Victorian City: Birmingham 1867–1877', unpublished PhD thesis, University of Warwick.

Weinberger, B. (1991), 'L'Anatomie de l'Antagonisme Racial et de la Violence Urbaine: Les Bandes à Birmingham dans les Années 1870', *Déviance et Société*, 15/4: 407–18.

Weinberger, B. (1993), 'Policing Juveniles: Delinquency in Late Nineteenth and Early Twentieth Century Manchester', *Criminal Justice History*, 14: 43–55.

Wright, D. (1983), 'Great Tradition', *London Review of Books*, 5/19: 13–14.

6   The Same Old Song?

The Contemporary Relevance of Subcultures

Andrew Wilson

Introduction

The cocktail of concerns that swirls around the head of any doctoral candidate about to enter the final examination had been spiked by a comment my then employer, Professor Mick Ryan, made after I told him the names of my examiners. He had not heard of Simon Frith, the external examiner, but the name 'Geoff Pearson' produced a visible reaction. Like a dodgy builder calculating just how high he can pitch the estimate without losing the job, he paused as if searching for the best way to deliver the bad news. Eventually he arrived at a well-weighted estimate, 'Ah, Geoff'. . . he can be rather contrary'. The failure to elaborate on what form of contrarian this implied made the prospect of facing an unknown quantity for the external and a 'disagreeable' internal more daunting. After reflecting on the contrarian in Pearson's work, the going against the flow of condemnation, asking awkward questions, looking to qualify assumptions, exposing mythologies and adding historical perspective, I could see room for optimism in the qualities I admired.

Like any keen student of sociology in the 1980s I had good knowledge of Pearson's work. In fact, I attended the 1996 National Deviancy Conference primarily to hear his talk on researching heroin use in the north of England (Pearson 1986). I have a vivid recollection of a presentation enlivened with the accounts and characteristics of participants that I recognised from my own involvement in the South Yorkshire drug scene. The empathetic presentation should have prepared me for the warm welcome to the viva, though maybe not for the anxiety dispelling announcement that 'you have passed . . . now that's out of the way we can have a relaxed conversation about the thesis'. I was too shocked at passing to deliver meaningful conversation—that's my enduring memory.

There are two reasons for mentioning the encounter. One is to emphasise the way that the methodology of the thesis, 'essentially that of oral history, informed both by theoretical considerations and the candidate's own past involvement in the northern soul scene' (Pearson 1999) had much in common with Geoff's prescription for ethnography, that is, 'telling it like it is' as seen from the 'inside' and 'telling stories as people might tell these stories themselves' (Pearson 1993: viii). This will involve some self-revelation that goes against Geoff's advice when I was struggling to find the right level of personal involvement to add to the introduction to *Northern Soul* (Wilson 2007), the book based on the PhD published in the ethnography series he co-edited with Dick Hobbs. His good advice to 'avoid self-disclosure because people will use it against you' probably explains why I currently have an academic job. It has, however, come at the cost of being 'gagged' by self-censorship, hiding or masking insights afforded by real experience while tolerating the odd casual offensive assumption of academics (not always in their capacity as anonymous peer reviewers).

Consequently I am notable by my absence from the book, appearing only as the knowing author translating the experience of others into a contextualised narrative, leaving little to indicate where I "belong" in the story. The distance between author and subject may have provided insulation from past misdemeanours to stop them being used to undermine good intentions, but it has also allowed for misinterpretation. Feminist research has proved adept at taking up Le Guin's (1989) call to 'offer your experience as your truth' or to 'use yourself to get to culture' (Pelias 2003: 372), but the personal in criminology can appear crass, un-academic or disturbing (Ancrum 2011; Cohen 1979). Distancing my "self" from the text of *Northern Soul* may have helped avoid such criticism but it came at the loss of hiding influences and connections that would have gained from the presence of a more central character. The reason for taking centre stage here is not to fill gaps in the *Northern Soul* story or to add entertainment or embarrassment to a subcultural plot, but to use the experiences to illustrate how the subcultural contours of the 1970s resonate with contemporary youth formations. In the spirit of Pearson it makes sense to pick up the continuities, the historical similarities to add perspective to our current fears and to argue that the concept of subculture offers an antidote to the current trend towards the reification of gangs.

Finding a Subcultural Fit

> The more vociferously a term is trumpeted in public, the more contestable it is under scrutiny.
>
> (Gitlin 1995: 126)

There is no doubting the relevance of my personal experience of subcultures, delinquency and crime, not least because just about all of my offending occurred within a subcultural (or gang) context. Unpicking the strands of influence is no easy task. Looking back over the life-course raises the problem of trying to restore balance to the 'distilled memories' (Wilson 2009) and sifting through a repertoire of narratives (Sandberg 2010) used to explain, excuse or entertain. This admission could be seen as a weakness but I can, like others who have negotiated a path through the criminal justice process, distinguish the "self" presented for differing effects (Taylor 1985: 129). The difficulty applying a clearly constructed identity to myself, or perhaps being acutely aware of the need to re-negotiate identity, helps to explain why my book was reticent on the theoretical literature on identity. The lack of engagement was picked up by Patrick J Williams in his review of *Northern Soul* (Williams 2009); he later speculated that the omission may have stemmed from the perception that 'writing about subcultural experience is *always* about identity, at least implicitly' (Williams 2011: 129). His point has commonsensical appeal to those who have a repertoire of images they can invoke to add stylised flesh to the concept. The tie between the two concepts, subculture and identity, became stronger the more subculture has been moved from delinquent gangs towards stylistic groupings regarded by theorists as a positive (more often than not positive in both a personal and theoretical sense). This captures something of the shift from regarding subculture as a conceptual tool for understanding gangs as the product of reaction formation to create a solution (Cohen 1955; Downes 1966) to the style being interpreted as a magical recovery of community (Cohen 1997), leading to an interpretation of subculture as a form of 'resistance' (Hall and Jefferson 1976; Hebdige 1979). I will return to the merits of both strands later.

It is instructive that the most recent debate about the value of the concept of subculture has taken place away from criminology (Bennett 2005; Blackman 2005; Hesmondhalgh 2005; Shildrick and MacDonald 2006). Among the many derogatory terms like 'yob' and 'chav' used to single out working-class youth the term 'gang' has been elevated to describe collectives that were previously located within subcultural identities. For the uninitiated a simple way to understand the split is to think of subculture as something a friend may be involved in and the gang as something 'they' (people not like us) join. The years of bad publicity make it easy to appreciate the tarnished image of the gang but the apparent disappearance of subculture from the lives of delinquent youth is more of a puzzle. Blackman's (2014) well-researched history of the concept followed the scholarly trail to reading of styles at the Birmingham Centre for Cultural Studies (Hall and Jefferson 1976; Hebdige 1979) without asking how subculture become divorced from the gangs. The question is worth asking not least because the answer helps to explain why scholars such as Bennett and Hesmondhalgh discount subculture as a useful way to conceptualising music-based scenes. It is not difficult to think of examples that illustrate their point. Applying subculture to a grouping that exhibits a modicum of distinctiveness without generating the cohesiveness provided by cultural context (the bonds formed through shared social background) or the situational factors that encourage group solidity such as fear of arrest or censure, the concept appears more as an empty shell lacking a bonding substance. A key theme to *Northern Soul* was to understand how people with anti-drug attitudes were converted to drug use. This required appreciation of the way the scene created contextual normalisation, that is, the extent that 'the subculture shaped and moulded how people construct their social worlds and how it impacted upon their deviance and understandings of deviance and control' (Wilson 2007: 11). This helps to explain how someone, such as a privately educated economics graduate son of a senior police officer, could think it a good idea to commit a chemist burglary with a former borstal boy. Clearly for him, like many of the other buyer/dealers in the study, the move into the drugs economy was not just driven by opportunity advanced by the subterranean economy (Densley and Stevens 2015) in the absence of a legitmate career. His case may be an extreme example but it captures the way that music or club scenes that contextually normalise drug use compromise otherwise law-abiding people by forcing them to have as much interest in avoiding arrest as those engaged in more serious criminal activity. This marks the point at which such scenes cross over into subcultures, a point where people move beyond the full protection of the law without necessarily subscribing to the moral code of violence that surrounds drug market transactions for the simple fact that most deals are conducted on a blend of trust, obligation and reciprocity. This may be a simplification of a process; nevertheless it illustrates the problem of isolating style, music and social life from the cultural backgrounds of the consumers, and failing to recognise that the universal labels of consumption mask deeper differences than those seen in the supermarkets of style (Polhemus 1997).

The distancing of 'consumers' from the subcultural distinctions in the leisure sphere has been matched by the extraction of the subcultural core into units of criminal justice concern called 'gangs'. The reification of gangs, however, has not just distanced gang members from the leisure sphere, apart from appearances as predatory characters dishing out violence and exploiting clubgoers, they have been completely divorced from the parent culture. The oddity is that when we, that is, some members of the northern scene, carried switchblades, dealt drugs, rolled (mugged) people and dressed in leather jackets that mimicked the black urban style represented in Blaxploitation films, it failed to dent the image of northern soul as 'the next big thing'. So incidents such as the police discovering a sawn-off shotgun at the home of one of my accomplices, a firearm he had taken to an all-nighter to intimidate lads he had a dispute with, the incident passed without media comment. It is easy to dismiss these isolated events as being comparable with the later over-reaction to rap (Klein 2011; Kubrin and Nielson 2014) because it lacked the severity of violence. But it is equally valid to point out that, as Hall et al. (1978: 155) did in the case of the over-reaction to the black mugger, folk devils appear more threatening when their outgroup status is defined by ethnic identity. It may invite over-simplification to ask whether the benign response to *Northern Soul* would have been the same if the ethnic mix of its participants had been the reverse of the small proportion of Afro-Caribbean and majority white British. Would the arrest of a black youth who admitted taking a shotgun to a club to threaten people have made the news in the middle of the mugging panic? There is no need to repeat the points on the reification of gangs made by scholars such as Hallsworth (2011) or to dwell on the differences of opinion on this issue (Hallsworth and Young 2008; Pitts 2008; Pitts 2012; Hallsworth

2014). There is some merit to both positions, not least because gangs can only be adequately conceptualised as occupying a position on a continuum that remains little changed since Yablonsky (1959) made the point more than fifty years ago. There remains value to Yablonky's claim that the middle ground of the gang continuum is occupied by near groups that lack the formal structure conferred on it by 'misconceived theories', many of which were 'derived from the popular and traditional image of gangs held by the general public as reported in the press' (1959: 109). There is also little doubt that 'some' gangs move along the continuum (Densley 2014) though they do not always move to progressively worse. Recently a police force I worked with was so baffled by the dissolution of a gang that had been involved in serious criminality, including a fatal shooting, that they wanted research to discover why. The issue at stake is not denial of the existence of extreme gang violence (Shute 2013) but the way the extreme is used as the guiding principle that draws low-level gang formations into the risk paradigm and exaggerates the prevalence of violence through tenuous connections to gangs and guns. As someone who has experienced police over-reaction to reputation and tenuous connections in the shape of armed officers breaking down doors to make an arrest, I am acutely aware how easily reputations can be distorted to justify extreme police responses. And how difficult it is to challenge the image the police portray.

This is not to dismiss or underplay the reality of some threats; it is more an appeal to restore a sense of perspective to assessments based on misleading categorisations. Comments, such as one made recently by a gang prevention worker who warned that the gang member we were lined up to interview did not 'see himself as gang member', should sound alarm bells. It is perhaps not so surprising that the police should find the world full of verifications once they began looking for 'confirming instances' (Popper 1962: 35). The tendency to follow a confirmatory logic when assigning actions or friendship links into gang or organised crime categories undermines the value of flow-chart–guided decision making (Tarrant 2008: 23). This was captured well by the risk assessment carried out by Nottingham police that found they had almost as many gang members as Birmingham, a city with a population three times its size. Research on Manchester's gang database by Patrick Williams (2015) highlighted the problem of soft targeting and bias. He found that forty of the 172 people listed as gang members had no previous convictions, while thirty-nine of those who did had not been convicted in the previous three years. The fact that almost 90 per cent of those listed as gang members were Black Asian and Minority Ethnic (BAME) people suggests that the consequences of both soft and hard targeting has a disproportionate effect, one that notably runs counter to findings from earlier gangs research that found little evidence to support this kind of bias (Aldridge and Medina 2008). Whatever the merit in the argument that over-representation should direct attention to the socio-economic and prejudicial factors that create the problem (Hallsworth 2008), the looping effects (Hacking 1995) generated by construction of gangs are an inseparable part of the process. The Metropolitan Police gang and criminal network flow chart (Tarrant 2008) offers insight into the way interpretation of the range of actions and effects listed is open to tainted judgements. The absence of the need for hard evidence has perhaps encouraged use of the term 'nominal' because it captures opaque status of the individuals perceived to be associated with a gang, proving a code for individuals bearing an indefinable status: a gang 'something' or 'other'.

There is, however, nothing new in the tendency of the police to escalate individuals and their crimes to the highest level. We appear culturally geared towards newsworthy exaggeration, but the move towards publicised policing has ratcheted up the process. Within this context there is logic to discourse that promotes youth groups to gangs and gangs to organised crime networks because it serves the symbolically important function of filling what the police perceive as a justice gap created by lenient sentencing (Ashcroft 2011) as well as providing justification for more resources. Austerity may add impetus to the current dramatization of evil (Tannenbaum 1938) discourse but escalation of seriousness has a longer history. The northern scene provided a good example of the process after a series of loosely connected drug arrests were collated to produce a court case involving thirty-three individuals from across the north of England. The *Yorkshire Post* reported a case that:

> . . . [L]ifts a curtain on a society of people maintaining widespread contact with each other and using one another to obtain drugs for themselves. . . . There was a number of ringleaders. These were certain people who travelled many miles to these all night parties . . . to barter and exchange the drugs they had stolen. Those who had the hard type class A drugs . . . left over from the raids on chemists . . . would exchange them with hard-drug addicts for soft drugs.
>
> (Johnson 1975)

The escalation worked by imposing a veneer of organisation and structure complete with 'ringleaders' on a loose network engaged in largely chaotic drug deals. The organised image justified the harsh sentences, vindicated the work of the regional drug squad and promoted misunderstanding about the drug trade. When the activities are set against the 'increasingly vague' (Lea 2007) definition of 'organised' crime, it becomes easy to justify the flow from subcultural activities to the organised networks on the flow chart (Tarrant 2008). The point here is simply that the escalation of seriousness is not new but the institutionalisation of the processes through the often ill-constructed categories of organised crime has added an insidious dimension (see Hobbs 2013).

The Separation of Gangs from the Wider Community

It appears no coincidence that the growth of the term 'nominal' has taken place in the wake of the British Prime Minister's pledge to launch 'A concerted, all-out war on gangs and gang culture' (Cameron 2011). The funding to cities with a perceived gang problem was awarded in proportion to the number of young people in the population, a simplistic guide to an initiative that lacked strategic direction (Shute, Aldridge and Medina 2012). There is little doubt that the saturation of 'confirming instances' of gang activity presented in the 2011 riots gave a boost to the gangs industry. A senior police officer in one of the riot-affected areas gave a good example of the effects when expressing shock that they did not know of the existence of the 'gang' that threw rocks at a police station. There was little room for doubt that the youths might not be gang members because only a gang member would throw rocks at a police station. These commonsensical attributions have been bolstered by growth of predictive tools, including software that saves time by calculating risk based on associations, previous offences and insults posted on the internet (Kelion 2014). The pseudo-scientific tools gain credibility when combined with lurid comments by consultant criminologists commenting on gangs exploiting naïve young teenagers by packing them off like Oliver Twist to hawk crack cocaine many miles from home only to be beaten on their return if they failed to sell their rocks. The story may have a basis in 'a' reality but what shaped the narrative: was it the story of someone caught selling; how generalizable is this case? The vox pop categorisations offer a pick and mix set of images that blend the 'real' and 'fake' participants to feed two sides of the looping process: by adding substance to what it is to be a gang member and offering a clear image of the need to control this exploitative entity. For one group it may be an image to live up to; for the other it confirms the worst fears about gangs as a symptom of immigration and broken Britain.

Prime Minister Cameron's speech made a clear distinction between the good 'law-abiding majority' and the bad 'thugs who make people's lives hell' (Cameron 2011). As Cohen (1988: 62) pointed out, this kind of rhetoric 'serves to exaggerate its [in this case the gang] badness (its atypicality) in comparison to a hypothetically overnormal population'. The trick of hard crime narrative is the way the stories about stabbings, shootings and drug busts have been seamlessly stitched into the move towards taking soft crime seriously. So perceptions of nuisance-related behaviour is also used as an interpretative framework to identify the gang as the problem social group (Blackman and Wilson 2014). The significance is not just in the way the gang has become the lightning rod for a range of fears but more the way that the process has been accompanied with the gang being detached from the host community. Skinheads did not provoke the sympathy of middle-class, hippie-orientated academics but the analysis located both the style and attitudes within working-class culture. This link to the past was extended into many other aspects of the lifestyle; whether through the previous generation of Mod or the earlier Teddy Boys, the values resonated with those of the parent culture. There is room for argument about the precision of the continuity but that matters less than the general point that gangs were seen as part of the community and not as a parasitic alien entity. In this view the importance of friendship networks, of the children and parents, the reciprocal relationships, the black economy (whether counterfeit and stolen goods, or drugs) and the many other interactions that shape neighbourhood relations are missing from the story. This is not to ignore the fact that some gangs cause significant problems within communities; I encountered enough examples during the course of research to appreciate the reality of the problem (Lupton et al. 2002; Wilson et al. 2002; Bottoms and Wilson 2004). The same projects also produced a counter view with examples of gang members keeping order, sanctioning drug users who commit local crime and stopping the sale of heroin on the estate. This observation does not come with a recommendation for sainthood but it does point to a more nuanced moral universe than presented by Cameron, the media or the consultant criminologists who thrive on exaggerated differences. Making sense of the nuances is a difficult task. There is no easy correlation between a gang's location on the continuum and its absorption within or dislocation from the wider community. Clearly these aspects are as much related to the nature of the community as they are the status of the gang. Not just the economic status of the area but also the other important markers of neighbourhood health such as transience, housing demand, single-parent households and long-term unemployment; in short, all the factors that undermine the collective efficacy of neighbourhoods (Sampson, Raudenbush and Earls 1997; Pattillo 1998; Bottoms and Wilson 2006). It is perhaps not so surprising that conditions of multiple marginality (Vigil 1988; Vigil 2003), the fractures or interstitial gaps, create fertile ground for the formation of subcultural capital and enterprise (Hobbs 1988; Pearson and Hobbs 2003; Hobbs 2013). This can be taken further with appreciation that any system of exchange is founded on the principle that the two parties have something to gain from the transaction: this forms the basis of a relationship of trust that is bounded by moral principles that set the parameters of what is and what is not acceptable Of course, as with any market, there will always be people looking to sell products that are inferior to what is claimed and people looking to obtain the goods at a lower price. That applies in the drug market but not on anywhere near the scale that commentators suggest: most drug deals end in mutual satisfaction (Coomber 2006).

On the one hand the good versus bad rhetoric picks up a frequently observed division within poorer neighbourhoods (Elias and Scotson 1965; Sennet 1970). But the ranking of 'problem families' or groups who are 'not like us' tends to mask moral contours shaped by both specific and general justifications for illegal activities (Downes 1966; Hobbs 2013). Any comprehensive understanding of a gang has to locate it within its social universe, not just the constellation that surrounds the action focus of its members, but also the elements that relate to biography where 'some of solidarities are largely hidden' (Spencer and Pahl 2006: 45). The action focus of the gang perspective has drawn the research attention away from the important contextual details that help to prevent exaggeration and over-generalising the negative attributions. That is not to say gang research always fails to pick out nuances or correct the crude views. The recent research by Windle and Briggs (2015) showed that, rather than drug dealing being a gang activity, it was carried out by members individually in a way remarkably similar to dealing on the 1970s soul scene. Another example is the research by Garot (2010: 3) which countered the 'reductionist fallacy' and often absurd claims about the inevitability of apocalyptic violence in response to low-level insults (Fiske and Rai 2014: 283). Garot's accounts of 'face saving' manoeuvres and the compromise of 'lumping it' to protect social ties and prevent an issue escalating presents an account of gang-involved youth that is seldom told. Appreciation of this form of equivocation helps to distinguish why some interactions escalate into conflict and others dissipate, a distinction that is lost when action is explained as the product of gang status, respect or machismo without registering the nuances not just in the observed action but also in how these constructs play out. Sometimes a street-savvy reputation can shape unwanted expectation, obligation and responsibility such as the nomination to sort out drug supplies mentioned earlier. The fact I was asked to 'sort out a problem' for an old friend while carrying out my doctoral research illustrates the enduring legacy of a good 'bad' reputation (Wilson 1999).

Subculture offers an appropriate concept to pick out the blurred boundaries as long as researchers look beyond the surface action and reputations of the participants. Any valid explanation needs the detail required to make sense of contextual imperatives and appreciate the nuances involved not just in the motivation of action but the grading of the moral contours of action. In this respect the concept is engaged most usefully when it addresses groups that are bound by something more substantial than style of dress or musical tastes, though both of these may have symbolic value in the process (Thrasher 1927: 290). Reaching towards a definition for subculture, however, risks repeating the mistakes present in the reification of gangs by simply substituting one concept for the other. The fact that involvement in some form of delinquency is the prime catalyst for elevating the status of a youth group to that of the gang and that this is the same substance that is seen to engender cohesion in subcultures, the parallels are obvious. The difference is that the study of subculture should avoid defining the group by its activity and instead look to explain why the activity occurs: to document and explain the properties of the wider cultural influences that help us to make sense of individual choices. This is not to argue that gang research fails to ask these questions, or to provide well-weighted answers— some of it does—but using the term as the organising principle invites mistakes. For instance, when Skinheads borrowed from the imagery of Italian-American gangsters, or the northern scene adopted African-American street attitudes, it would have appeared ridiculous to suggest that it constituted a threatening cultural transmission. Racial similarity may help to make the borrowing easier to imagine but in responding to gangs as if each are or have the potential to be 'the real thing' invites the kind of injustices that make 'gangs' a reality.

Reflection

We think of these kinds of people as given, as definite classes defined by definite properties . . . [but] They are moving targets because our investigations interact with the targets themselves, and change them. And since they are changed, they are not quite the same kind of people as before. The target has moved. That is the looping effect. Sometimes our sciences create kinds of people that in a certain sense did not exist before. That is making up people.

(Hacking 2007).

In 2007, before an interview for what would have been my first academic post, I phoned Stan Cohen for his response to the 'what is criminology' question I had been set for the presentation. His response virtually repeated what Geoff Pearson (1983) set out to achieve in *Hooligan*:

You need to keep sight of the academic history of criminality, the intellectual history and apply it to understanding contemporary events . . . you need to link it to the political. Criminology has become too pragmatic, too focused on short-term solutions with no history of ideas. You have to look at the big picture, ask how they fit. Understand the play between sociological problems and social problems . . . the headlines. Keep people aware of the differences, the tension, try to resolve the tensions/contradictions.

There is little doubt Pearson's attempt to set concerns about the moral decline of young people in context and to expose the problem of recounting the behaviour of previous generations through distilled memories fits Cohen's vision for criminology. There is no satisfactory way to compare and rank past behaviour but even attempting to do so is to miss the point. On the one hand is the observation that the phenomenon capturing the attention is always composed of groups that are defined as much by their socio-economic status as their style and activity. On the other, it is less obvious material around the nature of the activity, the response of the authorities and the shaping of sentiment towards the phenomenon. What is important about history is that it reveals both the continuities and changes. The latter is likely to invoke a reflex reaction in some observers that 'change' is the point: these gangs are not like the ones in the past; they have more lethal weapons, they are more organised and so on. There is little doubt that gangs operate in a different environment today than they did in the past; it no longer makes sense to turn up at a bank with a balaclava and sawn-off shotgun, or to hold up the security van. The drugs industry has had a significant impact on de-skilling villainy, leaving heists like Hatton Garden to senior citizens (Withnall and Gallagher 2015). The Hatton Garden ensemble, what the media is calling a crew, reflect the way groups were often shaped through a combination of close friendships and loose connections to do a specific job. The drugs business may involve similar arrangements at the top end but as the trade moves towards the consumer it invariably demands regular contacts and established networks. This statement of the obvious is worth making because it illustrates the banality of the soft-fix label 'drug gang' to groups of young people in which one or two of their number sell drugs

(Windle and Briggs 2015) and the easy escalation to organised crime network when this involves moving drugs between centres. As pointed out previously, the vast majority of drug deals are completed to the mutual satisfaction of both parties—buyers do not have to look down the barrel of a gun to be convinced of the need to part with their money.

So how has the gang become symbolic of broken Britain? As with any mythologising process there is a reality to the gang image. Resources such as friendship network, reputation and access to weapons are protective factors that facilitate trade and help ward off predators. When problems do occur it invariably invites comparison with gangs in America, an image gang members in the UK are often willing to play up to as they act out the prevailing cool images; how seriously they play the role depends on location on the gang continuum and the characteristics of place and personality. It is worth reiterating the last point because it leads to the central problem of the gang construct: the over-generalisation. This is where cutting a path through the competing explanations becomes difficult without unintentionally adding to the perceived pathology of the bearers of the characteristics (Williams 2015). In some respects I would hope that my own experiences, whether as a fit with the 'life course persistent' offender category or through the subcultural shaping of criminal action, or current status as lecturer would offer an antidote to the poison of pathological assumptions. The racialisation of subculture, however, introduces a range of problems that go beyond the scope of this chapter. What is clear is that the extraction of gangs from their subcultural context, that is, both the subculture of style and leisure and the subculture of locality, allows for a reification of the entity that facilitates its definition as a policing concern. The fact involvement in crime is a key attribute to most definitions of gang justifies its policing status without any pause of consideration of the implications of escalating the seriousness of 'adolescent limited offending' (Moffitt 1993). This, more than gang members appearing in photographs with fingers pointing towards an LA gang guise, is at the heart of an Americanisation of gangs. Two developments signify this process. One is the racialisation of the gang construct that Williams describes which has led to the over-identification of BAME groups and individuals as gang members, or more pointedly, as criminally involved gang members.

The second is iniquitous sentencing with the use of the doctrine of joint enterprise to secure criminal conviction of co-participants, the most glaring example. The fact that just about every conviction adds another family to the protest group campaigning against application of this doctrine should have added another alarm bell to the one sounded by the slippery gang flow chart. The defence of joint enterprise by former Justice Minister Grayling (2015) in his letter to the Chair of the Justice Committee, Sir Alan Beith, shows remarkable indifference to the flaws in the categorisation of people. 'It is worth emphasising that the law on joint enterprise only applies when a group of people are already engaged in criminal activity (sometimes very serious criminal activity) and in the course of that activity another offence is committed.' This is conviction by reputation, whether grounded or spurious. The families and friends campaigning against the injustice is a clear sign of the loss of proportionality. The fact that 80 per cent of those sentenced under the doctrine are from BME backgrounds makes it difficult to separate the strength of the offender's 'foresight' from the foresight constructed in the minds of the jury. The identification of gangs as a racialised problem plays out without the checks and balances needed to add perspective or qualify the images. So perceptions are played back as evidence to support the artificial distinction between gangs and the 'law-abiding majority' whose drug use is distanced from the issue, creating a rhetorical reality with taken-for-granted 'reasonable assumptions' about what we 'know' (or think we know) (Edmondson 1984: 14). Those with the power to forgive and forget their own transgressions can be accommodated as long as the image of the other is associated with the worse aspects of gangs and the drugs trade. So making up people as different, as driven by a more selfish, less caring principle becomes part of a looping process that taints perceptions (Lee 2007: 76). American research has shown the link between the emphasis the authorities give to 'policing' disadvantaged minorities and the effect this has on 'colouring' negative public perceptions of immigrant groups and undesirable neighbours (Bobo 2001; Quillian and Pager 2001; Rumbaut and Ewing, 2007 cited in Sampson 2012). Other studies illustrate the way this over-policing affects the wider community by promoting subcultural pathways of resistance (Goffman 2014).

If I apply this to my experiences I can pick out the interaction between social background factors and the events that nudged me towards what could be termed 'street socialisation'. But following that strand of influence ignores the important part played by the criminalisation of amphetamine use in 1964. An event that puts that in perspective came after an IRA prisoner was briefly detained in Armley prison. I recall it because he provoked thought about the parallels between his political justification and my status as a prisoner of 'conscience'. I reasoned that amphetamines were illegal because a political decision was made to change the status of the drug: one day the drug may be legal again. Whatever the naiveté of the thought, or whether the reasoning was simply an attempt to neutralize the moral bind (Matza 1964), it captured the substance that links those northern soul days with the contemporary problem of gangs. The most notable changes, the wider acceptance of drug use and its cultural accommodation (Measham, Newcombe and Parker 1994), should point to the issue of supply being less contentious. Instead, most of the criminals listed on the National Crime Agency most wanted list in 2015 appear for drug-related offences. This pattern seeps through the criminal rankings where the differing layers and substances are merged and packaged as a gang or organised crime problem. Amphetamines offer an excellent insight to processes involved in the creation of a criminal market for a drug and the unintended consequences of changes (Wilson 2008).

This is not to reduce the issue of gangs to simply a matter of the legal status of drugs. Only a naïve person would suggest that changing the drug laws would eradicate the problems surrounding gangs; in fact it could be argued that the loss of an equal opportunities employer of the magnitude of the drug market could provoke more crime that is acquisitive. There is no doubt that violence has a part to play in maintaining standards in the moral economy of poorer neighbourhoods (Thompson 1971; Karandinos et al. 2014). The cases of excessive or inappropriate violence attract the attention, which may add to the function of violence as deter (Jacques, Wright and Allen 2014) or rank risk, but ratio of deals to violence support the view that actual violence tends to be the response of last resort (Pearson et al. 2001: 43). The infrequent outbursts of violence in response to competition can stem from police disruption of the drug market (Lupton et al. 2002; Moeller and Hesse 2013) or from its use to rob drug dealers (Jacobs 2000). The general rule is that high-profile violence is not good for business (Pearson et al. 2001: 42). This view was used by the police in Nottingham after a spate of shootings early in 2000 to disrupt the drug trade by setting up armed road blocks to 'send a clear message to stop the violence' (Lupton et al. 2002; Wilson et al. 2002). This pragmatic management of the problem, behave or else, reveals the gap between the rhetoric around drugs and the recognition that it is not a problem the police can resolve. Governments have created a genuinely free-enterprise commodity market that is self-regulated. There is a link between violence and the drug market in the UK, but it is difficult to separate the precise nature of the link from the other violence-promoting influences occurring at the neighbourhood level. This includes violence related to community policing drug-related behaviour. The drug market and community research previously cited produced a number of examples that support findings from Walklate's (1998) Salford study showing how the established 'firms' had a pivotal role in distributing community justice to those who broke the 'community dogma' (Elias and Scotson 1965) on not thieving from your own. The existence of this form of sentiment is important in that it shapes the moral contours even if breaking the rule is frequently justified. As Whiteley and Whiteley (1964) pointed out, 'The best indication of an individual's standards is neither what he does nor what he says that he and other people ought to do, but what he is ashamed of and what he is proud of having done or not done'. What often misleads observers is that influence of subcultures on morality makes it difficult to elicit an admission of shame for some transgression of conventional laws. Violence, for example, is not simply justified as a technique of neutralisation, it is justified with the terms of maintaining standards by sanctioning transgressions (Thrasher 1927; Fiske and Rai 2014). That is not to argue that the violence is always proportionate or equitable. As much as I subscribe to Pearson's call to 'tell stories as people might tell these stories themselves' there are times when the stories are tilted towards audience expectations, making the criminologist an unwitting or willing contributor to the mythologised image of the gang (Katz and Jackson-Jacobs 2004: 92).

References

Aldridge, J. and J. Medina. 2008. *Youth Gangs in an English City: Social Exclusion, Drugs and Violence: Full Research Report ESRC End of Award Report*. Swindon: ESRC.

Ancrum, C. 2011. "'Knowing the Dance': The Advantages and Downfalls of a 'Criminal Biography' in Teaching Criminology in Higher Education." *Enhancing Learning in the Social Sciences* 3(3):1–21.

Ashcroft, L. 2011. *Crime, Punishment & The People*. London: House of Lords.

Bennett, A. 2005. "In Defence of Neo-tribes: A Response to Blackman and Hesmondhalgh." *Journal of Youth Studies* 8(2):255–59.

Blackman, S. 2005. "Youth Subcultural Theory: A Critical Engagement with the Concept, its Origins and Politics, From the Chicago School to Postmodernism." *Journal of Youth Studies* 8(1):1–20.

———. 2014. "Subculture Theory: An Historical and Contemporary Assessment of the Concept for Understanding Deviance." *Deviant Behavior* 35(6):496–512.

Blackman, S., and A. Wilson. 2014. "Psychotic (e)States? Anti-Social Behaviour and its Mind Altering Perception of Youth." Pp. 285–295 in *Anti-Social Behaviour in Britain: Victorian and Contemporary Perspectives*, edited by Sarah Pickard. Basingstoke: Palgrave.

Bobo, L. 2001. "Racial Attitudes and Relations at the Close of the Twentieth Century." Pp. 262–99 in *America Becoming: Racial Trends and Their Consequences*, edited by N. Smelser, W. J. Wilson, and F. Mitchell. Washington, DC: National Academy Press.

Bottoms, A., and A. Wilson. 2004. "Attitudes to Punishment in Two High-Crime Communities." Pp. 366–405 in *Alternatives to Prison: Options for an Insecure Society*, edited by Anthony Bottoms, Sue Rex, and Gwen Robinson Cullompton: Willan.

Bottoms, A.E., and A. Wilson. 2006. "Civil Renewal, Control Signals and Neighbourhood Safety." Pp. 63–90 in *Re-Energizing Citizenship: Strategies for Civil Renewal*, edited by Tessa Brannan, Peter John, and Gerry Stoker. Oxford: Palgrave Macmillan.

Cameron, D. 2011. "PM's Speech on the Fightback after the Riots." Gov.uk.

Cohen, A.K. 1955. *Delinquent Boys: The Culture of the Gang*. New York: The Free Press.

Cohen, P. 1997. *Rethinking the Youth Question: Education, Labour, and Cultural Studies*. Basingstoke: MacMillan.

Cohen, S. 1988. *Against Criminology*. New Brunswick: Transaction Publishers.

Cohen, S. 1979. "The Last Seminar." *The Sociological Review* 27(1):5–20.

Coomber, R. 2006. *Pusher Myths: Re-situating the Drug Dealer*. London: Free Association Books.

Densley, J.A. 2014. "It's Gang Life, But Not As We Know It: The Evolution of Gang Business." *Crime & Delinquency* 60(4):517–46.

Densley, J.A., and A. Stevens. 2014. 'We'll show you gang': The subterranean structuration of gang life in London. *Criminology and Criminal Justice* 15(1):102–20.

Downes, D.M. 1966. *The Delinquent Solution: A Study in Subcultural Theory*. London: Routledge & Kegan Paul.

Edmondson, R. 1984. *Rhetoric in Sociology*. London: Macmillan.

Elias, N., and J.L. Scotson. 1965. *The Established and the Outsiders: A Sociological Enquiry Into Community Problems*. London: Cass & Company.

Fiske, A.P., and T.S. Rai. 2014. *Virtuous Violence*. Cambridge: Cambridge University Press.

Garot, R. 2010. *Who You Claim: Performing Gang Identity in School and on the Streets*. New York: New York University Press.

Gitlin, T. 1995. *The Twilight of Common Dreams: Why America Is Wracked by Culture Wars*. New York: Metropolitan Books.

Goffman, A. 2014. *On the Run: Fugitive Life in an American City*. Chicago: University of Chicago Press.

Grayling, C. 2015. 'Joint Enterprise: Follow-Up: Government Response to the Committee's Fourth Report of Session 2014–15'. *The Law on Joint Enterprise*, edited by A. Beith. London: House of Commons. http://www.publications.parliament.uk/pa/cm201415/cmselect/cmjust/1047/104704.htm

Hacking, I. 1995. "The Looping Effects of Human Kinds." Pp. 351–83 in *Causal Cognition: A Multidisciplinary Debate*, edited by Dan Perber, David Premack, and Ann J. Premack. Oxford: Clarendon Press.

———. 2007. "Kinds of People: Moving Targets." Pp. 285–318 in *Proceedings of the British Academy*. London: OUP.

Hall, S., C. Critcher, T. Jefferson, J. Clarke, and B. Roberts. 1978. *Policing the Crisis: Mugging, the State and Law and Order*. London: Macmillan.

Hall, S., and T. Jefferson. 1976. *Resistance through Rituals: Youth Subcultures in Post-War Britain*, London: Hutchinson.

Hallsworth, S. 2008. "Street Crime: Interpretation and Legacy in Policing the Crisis." *Crime, Media, Culture* 4(1):137–43.

———. 2011. "Gangland Britain? Realities, Fantasies and Industry." Pp. 183–97 in *Youth in Crisis?: 'Gangs', Territoriality and Violence*, edited by B. Goldson. London: Routledge.

———. 2014. "Gang Talking Criminologists: A Rejoinder to John Pitts." *Youth and Policy* (112):35–43.

Hallsworth, S., and T. Young. 2008. "Gang Talk and Gang Talkers: A Critique." *Crime, Media, Culture* 4(2):175–95.

Hebdige, D. 1979. *Subculture: The Meaning of Style*. London: Methuen.

Hesmondhalgh, D. 2005. "Subcultures, Scenes or Tribes? None of the Above." *Journal of Youth Studies* 8(1):21–40.

Hobbs, D. 1988. *Doing the Business: Entrepreneurship, the Working Class, and Detectives in the East End of London*. Oxford: Clarendon Press.

———. 2013. *Lush Life: Constructing Organized Crime in the UK*. Oxford: Oxford University Press.

Jacobs, B.A. 2000. *Robbing Drug Dealers: Violence Beyond the Law*. New York: Aldine De Gruyter.

Jacques, S., R. Wright, and A. Allen. 2014. "Drug Dealers, Retaliation, and Deterrence." *International Journal of Drug Policy* 25(4):656–62.

Johnson, P. 1975. "How the Soul-Scene Pushers Were Trapped." *Yorkshire Evening Post*. Leeds: T.C. Sumner.

Karandinos, G., L.K. Hart, F.M. Castrillo, and P. Bourgois. 2014. "The Moral Economy of Violence in the US Inner City." *Current Anthropology* 55(1):1.

Katz, J., and C. Jackson-Jacobs. 2004. "The Criminologists' Gang." Pp. 91–124 in *The Blackwell Companion to Criminology*, edited by C. Sumner. Maiden: Blackwell Publishing Ltd.

Kelion, L. 2014. "London Police Trial Gang Violence 'Predicting' Software." BBC.

Klein, A.A. 2011. *American Film Cycles: Reframing Genres, Screening Social Problems, & Defining Subcultures*. Austin: University of Texas Press.

Kubrin, C.E., and E. Nielson. 2014. "Rap on Trial." *Race and Justice* 4(3):185–211.

Le Guin, U.K. 1989. *Dancing at the Edge of the World: Thoughts on Words, Women, Places*. New York: Grove Press.

Lea, J. 2007. "What is Organised Crime?" http://www.bunker8.pwp.blueyonder.co.uk/orgcrim/3801.htm

Lee, M. 2007. *Inventing Fear of Crime: Criminology and the Politics of Anxiety*. Cullompton: Willan Publishing.

Lupton, R., A. Wilson, T. May, H. Warburton, and P.J. Turnbull. 2002. *A Rock and a Hard Place: Drug Markets in Deprived Neighbourhoods*. London: Home Office.

Matza, D. 1964. *Delinquency and Drift*. New York: John Wiley.

Measham, F., R. Newcombe, and H. Parker. 1994. "The Normalization of Recreational Drug use Amongst Young People in North-West England." *British Journal of Sociology* 45(2):287–312.

Moeller, K., and M. Hesse. 2013. "Drug Market Disruption and Systemic Violence: Cannabis Markets in Copenhagen." *European Journal of Criminology* 10(2):206–21.

Moffitt, T.E. 1993. "Adolescence-Limited and Life-Course-Persistent Antisocial Behavior: A Developmental Taxonomy." *Psychological Review* 100(4):674.

Pattillo, M.E. 1998. "Sweet Mothers and Gangbangers: Managing Crime in a Black Middle-Class Neighborhood." *Social Forces* 76(3):747–74.

Pearson, G. 1983. *Hooligan: A History of Respectable Fears*. London: Macmillan.

———. 1986. "The New Heroin Users." Paper presented at the National Deviancy Conference, Central London Polytechnic, March.

———. 1993. 'Talking a Good Fight: Authenticity and Distance in the Ethnographer's Craft', Foreword to D. Hobbs and T. May (eds) *Interpreting the Field: Accounts of Ethnography*. Oxford: Clarendon Press.

———. 1999. "PhD Examiner Report." edited by London School of Economics. London: University of London.

Pearson, G., and D. Hobbs. 2003. "King Pin? A Case Study of a Middle Market Drug Broker." *The Howard Journal of Criminal Justice* 42(4):335–47.

Pearson, G., R. Hobbs, S. Jones, J. Tierney, and J. Ward. 2001. *Middle Market Drug Distribution*. London: Home Office.

Pelias, R.J. 2003. "The Academic Tourist: An Autoethnography." *Qualitative Inquiry* 9(3):369–73.

Pitts, J. 2008. "Describing and Defining Youth Gangs." *Safer Communities* 7(1):26–32.

———. 2012. "Reluctant Criminologists: Criminology, Ideology and the Violent Youth Gang." *Youth and Policy* 109:27–45.

Polhemus, T. 1997. "In the Supermarket of Style." Pp. 148–151 in *The Clubcultures Reader: Readings in Popular Cultural Studies*, edited by S. Redhead, D. Wynne, and J.O'Conner. Oxford: Blackwell.

Popper, K.R. 1962. *Conjectures and Refutations: The Growth of Scientific Knowledge*. London: Routledge & Kegan Paul.

Quillian, L., and D. Pager. 2001. "Black Neighbors, Higher Crime? The Role of Racial Stereotypes in Evaluations of Neighborhood Crime". *American Journal of Sociology* 107(3):717–67.

Rumbaut, R.G., and W.A. Ewing. 2007. *The myth of immigrant criminality and the paradox of assimilation: Incarceration rates among native and foreign-born men*. Immigration Policy Center, American Immigration Law Foundation.

Sampson, R.J. 2012. *Great American City: Chicago and the Enduring Neighborhood Effect*. Chicago: University of Chicago Press.

Sampson, R.J., S.W. Raudenbush, and F. Earls. 1997. "Neighborhoods and Violent Crime: A Multilevel Study of Collective Efficacy." *Science* 277(5328):918–24.

Sandberg, S. 2010. "What can 'lies' tell us about life? Notes towards a framework of narrative criminology." *Journal of Criminal Justice Education* 21(4):447–65.

Sennet, R. 1970. *The Uses of Disorder: Personal Identity and City Life*. New York: Alfred A. Knopf.

Shildrick, T., and R. MacDonald. 2006. "In Defence of Subculture: Young People, Leisure and Social Divisions." *Journal of Youth Studies* 9(2):125–40.

Shute, J. 2013. "Family Support as a Gang Reduction Measure." *Children & Society* 27(1):48–59.

Shute, J., J. Aldridge, and J. Medina. 2012. "Loading the Policy Blunderbuss." *Criminal Justice Matters* 87(1):40–41.

Spencer, L., and R.E. Pahl. 2006. *Rethinking Friendship: Hidden Solidarities Today*. Princeton, NJ: Princeton University Press.

Tannenbaum, F. 1938. *Crime and the Community*. Boston: Ginn.

Tarrant, M. 2008. *Gangs, Group Offending and Weapons: Serious Youth Violence Toolkit*. London: Metropolitan Police.

Taylor, L. 1985. *In the Underworld*. Oxford: Blackwell.

Thompson, E.P. 1971. "The Moral Economy of the English Crowd in the Eighteenth Century." *Past & Present* (50):76–136.

Thrasher, F.M. 1927. *The Gang: A Study of 1,313 Gangs in Chicago*. Chicago: University of Chicago Press.

Vigil, J.D. 1988. *Barrio Gangs: Street Life and Identity in Southern California*. Austin: University of Texas Press.

Vigil, J.D. 2003. "Urban Violence and Street Gangs." *Annual Review of Anthropology* 32:225–42.

Walklate, S. 1998. "Crime and Community: Fear or Trust?" *British Journal of Sociology* 49:550–69.

Whiteley, C.H., and W.M. Whiteley. 1964. *The Permissive Morality*. London: Methuen.

Williams, J.P. 2009. "Northern Soul: Music Drugs and Subcultural Identity." *Canadian Journal of Criminology and Criminal Justice* 51(4):547–49.

Williams, J.P. 2011. *Subcultural Theory: Traditions and Concepts*, Cambridge: Polity Press.

Williams, P. 2015. "Criminalising the Other: Challenging the Race-Gang Nexus." *Race & Class* 56(3):18–35.

Wilson, A. 1999. "Urban Songlines: Subculture and Identity on the 1970s Northern Soul Scene and After." Unpublished PhD thesis in *Sociology*. London: London School of Economics and Political Science (University of London).

———. 2007. *Northern Soul: Music, Drugs and Subcultural Identity*. Cullompton: Willan Publishing.

———. 2008. "Mixing the Medicine: The Unintended Consequence of Amphetamine Control on the Northern Soul Scene." *The Internet Journal of Criminology* 1–22.

———. 2009. "It's an Ill Wind That Blows No Good: How Bad Luck, Poor Resources and Missed Opportunities Made (Negative) Turning Points in the Drift to Crime." Unpublished conference paper in *British Society of Criminology Annual Conference: A "Mirror" or a "Motor"? What is Criminology For?* University of Cardiff, British Society of Criminology.

Wilson, A., T. May, H. Warburton, R. Lupton, and P.J. Turnbull. 2002. "Heroin and Crack Cocaine Markets in Deprived Areas: Seven Local Case Studies." *CASEREPORT19*. London: London School of Economics.

Windle, J., and D. Briggs. 2015. "Going Solo: The Social Organisation of Drug Dealing within a London Street Gang." *Journal of Youth Studies* (ahead-of-print):1–16.

Withnall, A., and P. Gallagher. 2015. "Hatton Garden Heist: Police Arrest Three Pensioners and Six Others Following Raids." *The Independent*. London.

Yablonsky, L. 1959. "The Delinquent Gang as a Near-Group." *Social Problems* 7(2):108–17.

7   Illegal Rave Security

Keeping Trouble Out of the London Free Party Scene

Matthew Taylor

Introduction

Urban free parties are of criminological interest in themselves: they are unlicensed, unregulated and held in venues that have been 'borrowed' from their owners. These events are self-policed according to their own moral laws, rather than the laws of the state, with security arrangements used to help enforce these moral codes and safeguard against the risks of gang infiltration, police intervention, violence and theft. Despite this, the majority of recent research on 'raves' looks at the limited categories of drug use and/or supply within events, with most focus on ecstasy use, and more recently on ketamine and poly-drug use (Chinet et al., 2007; Riley, Morey, and Griffin, 2008; Fernández-Calderón et al., 2011). The majority of research that goes beyond this drugs focus is outdated and focused on the rave 'heyday' of the late 1980s and early 1990s (Redhead, 1997; Hemment, 1998; Maylon, 1998), often centring on the early Acid House scene. Whilst the research base on legitimate bouncers and security is still relatively thin, there is almost no research at all, past or present, on security arrangements at free parties, except for a short section in Chatterton and Hollands (2003).

This study acts to fill part of this rave research void. Its core aims are to understand these events' security structures and self-policing practices. It seeks to compare the role of free party security to that of security used in legitimate venues. The study constitutes primary research, combining evidence from free party participants, including organisers, security and bar staff, and offers some comparison to existing research on pub and club security.

The responses depict a close-knit free party community that whilst at times affected by high levels of robbery and violence at events, currently has extremely low levels of these issues, largely because of the implementation of paid security. However, in this scene, it is not only the paid security who takes on the role of protecting those attending, but also the organisers and those in attendance themselves. The essay examines how the free party security personnel were introduced into free parties and the differences between their model of internal regulation and that of the typical security or 'bouncers' found in clubs.

The main findings are that the studied section of the illegal rave scene has its own security arrangements that suit its culture and environment. Rave security personnel tend to use less violence compared with legitimate event security and have a greater focus on resolution of disputes. The findings show that rave security staff assume a greater duty of care and take on specific additional roles that stem from the events being illegal, such as dealing with the police or with the building owners. There are also additional tasks created through the use of disused buildings such as keeping those attending free from hazardous areas. It is argued that many of these differences relate to the fact that free party security have emerged out of the 'self-policing' policies of earlier raves (Chatterton and Hollands, 2003).

It is useful to understand the history and development of the rave scene when considering its security practices as they are underpinned by the values of the rave culture itself. Illegal raves take multiple forms across the UK. Events vary from small outdoor gatherings to entire illegal festivals that are made up of multiple independent sound systems. Urban illegal raves such as are the focus of this study tend to take place in disused buildings or on industrial scraplands. These can vary from small parties in disused pubs, shops or nightclubs to events spanning entire industrial estates or warehouse complexes. These indoor events are often labelled 'squat parties' as organisers claim squatters' rights on the buildings used to justify their occupation.

The term 'rave' is used unquestioningly throughout this paper but it is worth noting that 'rave' is an ambiguous term used in different contexts to describe various types of events (Fernández-Calderón et al., 2011). This paper is specifically focused on the 'free party' section of the illegal rave scene; the term 'free party' typically denoting events where there are increased levels of freedom without the constraints of the legal club scene (Chatterton and Hollands, 2003). It also often assumed to mean free of entry cost; however, urban free parties often charge a small fee to cover costs such as security, which are not required at rural free parties. Free parties differ from the more commercialised urban illegal raves which typically charge £15 to 25 entry fee. The latter are loosely described as 'pay parties'.

Illegal raves are commonly cited as one of the most important and long-running subcultural movements seen in the UK (McDermot et al., 1993). Despite long-standing police harassment of organisers, and specific anti-rave legislation being put in place, thousands still attend these events every weekend—illustrating this, just whilst this paper was being written, three separate events with attendance of more than 1,000 reached the media headlines (*The Mirror*, 18/06/14; *The Daily Mail*, 26/05/14; *Sutton Guardian*, 09/05/14).

Although at times reaching the headlines, these events are typically hidden in nature and make up a secret section of the wider night-time economy (Hobbs et al., 2003). They are considered oppositional and undesirable in the eyes of the state (Hill, 2002), occurring in the peripheries of the urban city, areas associated with the 'other' (Chatterton and Hollands, 2003). Free parties challenge the sanitised mainstream night-time economy which is heavily supported by local councils who give prominence to leisure providers in city developments, seeking to cash in on their taxable revenues (Hobbs et al., 2003). In fact, free parties are largely organised by individuals looking for an alternative to this mainstream nightlife, that they consider both overpriced and excessively violent (Partridge, 2006). Profit is often not the core objective, with revenues often poured into future events (Fernández-Calderón et al., 2011).

Various values held within the free party scene have a direct impact on the nature of policing these events. Values of inclusion are core, with everyone welcome, provided they behave appropriately, and are similar to the values found in the earlier free festival movement (Partridge, 2006). The low cost of free party attendance means that people coming from all economic backgrounds can participate, in contrast to the legitimate night-time economy, where certain groups are deliberately 'priced out' (Chatterton and Hollands, 2003).

Historically, the first major electronic music raves started around 1987, with large-scale parties just off the M25 ring-road rapidly becoming common (Reynolds, 1999). However, the Thatcher government did not take kindly to these events, with raves seen as a threat to the respectable ideals of Thatcherism (Hill, 2002). This was perpetuated by mass media–induced moral panics on raves (Cohen, 1987) with headlines portraying raves as overtly sexual or drug fuelled (Hill, 2002; Critcher, 2000). Headlines such as 'Ban this Killer Music' [Acid House] (*Post*, 24 October 1998) became common (Redhead, 1997) whilst the *Daily Mail* described raves as 'a cynical attempt to trap young people into drug dependency under the guise of friendly pop music events' (*The Daily Mail*, 26/06/1989 cited in Collins, 1998: 97).

Free parties such as are the focus of this study started slightly later. In 1991 the sound systems including Spiral Tribe started to collaborate with the New Age Traveller movement in the organisation of free parties. These parties were focused on the harder sounds of acid techno rather than the acid house of earlier events, and were largely created out of the disillusionment with the profiteering of the M25 parties (Reynolds, 1999). It was a Traveller-rave collaboration that led to a real turning point for illegal raves. In 1992 there was a Spiral Tribe party on Castlemorton Common held in collaboration with New Age Travellers; the event lasted for seven days, drawing between 20,000 and 40,000 people (Reynolds, 1999: 165). The police were unable to stop it from taking place because of the high number of attendees (Reynolds, 1999). McKay (1998) argues it was the combination of the Castlemorton rave and the Twyford Down road protests that led to the implementation of the 1994 Criminal Justice Act. This act allowed police to break up any event with more than 100 in attendance provided the music was 'wholly or predominately characterised by the emission of a succession of repetitive beats'.

Some of the reviewed literature suggests that the passing of the 1994 Act totally curbed the illegal rave scene, pushing it almost entirely into legitimate licensed events. What actually took place is, whilst large sections of the illegal rave scene 'swallowed the poisoned pill of respectability' (Maylon, 1998: 199) and moved towards legal events, free parties continued and moved in the opposite direction, being driven further underground. A number of texts look at the rave scene; one of the most relevant to this text is Molly Macindoe's extensive photo-documentation of the London squat party scene in the 2000s which visually demonstrates that, whilst largely absent from the academic literature, large-scale urban raves continued to take place well after the implementation of the Criminal Justice Act.

Security

The majority of the relevant research on the rave scene simply covers key events or legislation as does the foregoing section of the essay; few papers look at the internal workings of the events themselves, such as security arrangements and policies. Whereas there is a growing body of research on the role of security within the legitimate night-time economy, there is very little existing research on the security at free parties. Here the essay looks at existing research on both legitimate event security and free party security.

Drawing on the work of Bowden (1978), Lister (2001b) describes legitimate security or 'bouncers' as 'the latest in a long line of "hard men" who are hired to protect (physically) the commercial interests of corporate capital' (p: 246). From this we can immediately draw differences between free party security and legitimate security; rather than protecting the interests of corporate entities such as the pub and club chains who dominate the legitimate scene, free party security protects the interests of small and autonomous groups of organisers who operate outside the law (Chatterton and Hollands, 2003).

Rigakos' (2004) study based on his ethnographic fieldwork with bouncers in Canada highlights the fact that an important part of a bouncer's role is to keep 'dangerous populations' out of the venues. He demonstrates that 'risk identities are negotiated on the door' (p: 1), with bouncers turning away any clientèle they consider troublesome or a risk to the venue. The findings of Hobbs et al. (2003) support this, stating that pub and club security may keep individuals queuing or waiting outside the venue in order to assess their temperament before deciding on letting them in. As well as deciding on individuals' entrance based on perceived risk, Hobbs et al. (2003) suggest that security is also employed to implement selective door policies based on assumed suitability for the venue. Different venues will have different desired clientèle, with security typically deciding who is, and who is not, right for the venue (Rigakos, 2004). In this respect bouncers play an exclusionary role, deliberately denying access to certain individuals or groups (Chatterton and Hollands, 2003). These practices of exclusion are often based on factors including dress code, race, style and economic capital (Chatterton and Hollands, 2003; Hobbs et al., 2003). This mirrors the findings of Nayak (2006) who found that his subjects were deliberately restricted from entering pubs and clubs because of their clothing preference. As free parties are deliberately inclusive, these practices of exclusion by security are less likely to apply, although the secretive nature of the scene is itself arguably exclusionary, or at least exclusive (Chatterton and Hollands, 2003).

A further key finding in the majority of research on legitimate security is their association with violence, or at least the ability to inflict violence when required (Lister, 2001b; Winlow et al., 2001; Hobbs et al., 2003). Hobbs et al. (2003) suggest that bouncers are often quick to use violence, whilst using post-hoc neutralisation in the justification of their actions. Whilst the willingness to use violence will vary from individual to individual, Winlow et al. (2001) argue that most legitimate security will originate from backgrounds where the ability to use violence is deemed a valued commodity rather than a last resort (Winlow et al., 2001). Furthermore, a local reputation for violent conduct is often considered advantageous (Winlow et al., 2001). 'I'm going to fucking punish you if you raise your hands' (p. 149) is a quotation from one of the security staff interviewed (Hobbs et al., 2003), illustrating the willingness of some security personnel to take actions well beyond the minimum physical intervention required. Here it is worth noting that the publications just cited may well now be somewhat out of date: 2003 saw the introduction of Security Industry Authority (SIA) licensing for door security that was partly aimed at removing violent individuals from the trade and providing training to door security.

Compared with the number of studies on legitimate security, free party security research is limited, Chatterton and Hollands (2003) being the only detailed offering within the reviewed literature, with other texts only offering brief descriptive comments. Chatterton and Hollands argue that the role of regulation in free parties and alternative scenes tends to be undertaken in a more democratic manner than in the legitimate night-time economy, which they suggest is largely governed by security in a condescending and patriarchal manner. Rietveld (1993) states that the use of heavy security in the raves of Dream and Sunrise in 1988 deterred people from attending their future events (p. 48), showing that hard-line security within this type of event is often seen as undesirable and likely impacting on the free environment offered. Returning to Chatterton and Hollands, they argue that alternative events, including free parties, are more likely to police themselves without the need for formal security. Moreover, they propose that the majority of alternative events occur in fringe locations, which may limit their potential for violence from unwanted [violent] clientèle coming across the venue by chance; thus, less security may be required than at the more centrally located legitimate events. Chatterton and Hollands also argue that the use of drugs at these events is likely to be a factor that reduces violence when compared with the alcohol-focused mainstream venues, again changing the dynamic of the security requirements of events. Whilst overall there is little research directly on the topic of this essay it does seem from the available literature that security personnel in the free party scene are likely to regulate events in a significantly different way from those found in legitimate clubs and pubs. The findings of this paper act to explore these differences.

Methodology

In conducting this study, a total of twelve interviews were undertaken, six with events organisers, two with security, two with DJs and two with female crew members. These data have been further supported by informal conversations and time spent with those involved in the party scene, though only information specifically given for the research has been included because of ethical considerations. All party-involved participants were taken from a convenience sample, or snowballing employed from this convenience sample. The core research tool utilised was semi-structured interviews. All interviews were recorded and transcribed.

Participants were interviewed at a location of their choice; it is considered that this is likely to aid the free flow of information. The interview process went smoothly: all interviews were completed in full with all questions answered. This would have been an unlikely outcome if the researcher had not been known to the party participants as some relatively sensitive questions on the rave scene were asked.

In terms of this existing relationship, the researcher has more than ten years' involvement in the illegal rave scene. It is essential to question how this existing relationship may have affected the research and its findings. It is increasingly argued that there is a need to consider not only the participants in research, but also the connections the researcher has with them (Finlay, 2002). It is accepted that, for many, pre-involvement within the area of research would be considered counter-productive, lacking analytical distance. However, typical research methods fall short in the study of criminality because of the levels of secrecy present (Pearson et al., 2001). When looking at the rave scene, secrecy is not only employed by the individuals involved to minimise their personal chances of prosecution, but also to 'protect the scene', with particular suspicion of researchers and authors because of the long-standing history of police investigations and media demonisation of the rave scene (see Redhead, 1993). Thus, a researcher on this subject must not only ensure anonymity to participants, but also assure them that the sensitive information will not be shared with mainstream media or the police, a factor arguably involving a greater deal of participant-researcher trust than a typical drug study for example. Thus, gaining operational information directly from organisers and security is considered realistically only achievable through a person already known to those involved. As was argued by Winlow et al. (2001) in their study of bouncers, the advantages of researcher-participant shared cultural background holds more positive than negative attributes, with an outsider researcher likely to encounter high levels of suspicion and mistrust (Holdaway, 1983 cited in Winlow et al., 2001).

There is a risk that some cultural norms may be overlooked, and similarly that existing knowledge may influence the research to some extent; however, additionally to the advantages of access already discussed, there are the advantages of a shared understanding in languages and terminology used. Taking into account the potential concerns of lack of analytical distance, great care was taken during the research process to ensure that all researcher-participant interactions were undertaken on a formal (but friendly) basis, drawing clear lines of these interactions being research-based.

There were various ethical considerations. The core concern was the protection of participant identities to avoid police detection. Safeguarding against this, participants were each allocated a synonym, their real name not being recorded. They were requested not to mention any names or identifying information during interviews. Consent was taken verbally. After the interviews had been transcribed, the tapes were erased. Ethical approval was granted by the University of Kent before fieldwork commenced.

In terms of limitations, this study would have benefited from a larger sample. Furthermore, this study only looked at one part of the London illegal rave scene, a scene that comprises a number of quite separate groups. A further study would benefit from widening the subject group to include London's multi-genre pay parties and the psy-trance scene, both of which have distinctively different security arrangements and door policies.

Research Findings

To start the findings, some general information and insight is included; it is important to understand the security of these events within the context of the events themselves, with this specific section of the rave scene likely differing from that covered in other research. The events which are the subject of this study have rooms dedicated to certain music styles, with the majority having a room predominantly playing acid techno, a music that has long-standing attachments to the London free party scene, often referred to as 'London techno'. This techno room would typically have the largest crowd. Other rooms consist of hardcore, jungle, drum and bass, and hardtek. Those attending are largely aged between 20 and 40, a noticeably older crowd than is seen in the newer generation of London pay parties. Attendees come from a wide variety of backgrounds; often more than half of those attending are from continental Europe, mainly Italy, but also France, Spain, Poland and Portugal. Those loosely identifiable as punks, New Age Travellers and 'hippies' are also present. In terms of venues, disused buildings are the focus, with legitimate clubs very rarely utilised. At times the venues are squatted and lived in, allowing multiple weekends of parties to take place before court eviction orders are served. Typically, however, buildings are acquired on the night and subsequently abandoned. Venues are often warehouse-type buildings although many other building types are also utilised, especially since the Olympic developments that wiped out much of East London's dilapidated warehouse stock favoured by organisers: anything empty, non-residential and large enough for purpose is targeted. Typically between 300 and 1000 people attend, with the larger events housing up to 30 separate sound systems, drawing as many as 5,000 people, especially on the key London rave dates of Halloween and New Year's Eve. Events start around midnight and run at least until early afternoon. A small fee is typically charged, usually five pounds, to cover security and running costs; those attending are welcome to bring their own drinks into the events.

Almost every research subject was keen to discuss what they viewed as the positive aspects of the scene. Organisers took pride in the events they organise, many suggesting their motives are partly or largely ideological:

> The moral aspects of the party, I enjoy doing it, I think I provide something which is good and helps people.
>
> (Mouldy, Organiser, 36)

Participants often stated the importance of the events in bringing together different societal groups:

> It just brings people from all sectors of society together. It brings people from far and wide to listen to music you can't find anywhere else.
>
> (Hand, DJ, 22)

Similarly, some talked about the unique kinds of music that are offered, while others were more focused on the cultural and social aspects of the gatherings and the friendships made and kept through the scene:

> I think it is a culture in itself. I think it would be a great shame to lose this unique culture: a lot of people it's about the music, but for me my favourite bit is socialising in an interesting new building.
>
> (Mouldy, Organiser, 36)

> I just see it as like having a house party, that's the logical conclusion of wanting to have music and like-minded people in a space that you control.
>
> (Small, Organiser, 27)

Unsurprisingly a significant number of party-involved participants argued the importance of the freedom experienced, in contrast to the feelings of being controlled in a nightclub. Some participants suggested that events are political in nature, enforcing personal rights to freedom. It seemed across the board that dancing in a disused building was considered more significant than just a night out:

> Well yeah I think ideologically and fundamentally I think what free parties represent is that you can make something illegal but you can't really stop people doing what they want to do. . . . You know this country belongs to the people and they'll do what they want.
>
> (Delay, Organiser, 27)

A sceptical reader may suggest that the foregoing statements, argued by participants to be the positive aspects of free parties, are merely techniques of neutralisation (Sykes and Matza, 1957), self-justifying their own profiteering from criminal involvement. However, those interviewed saw very little financial gains from their involvement, despite putting much groundwork, planning and labour into each event. Furthermore, the wages of the security employed are well below the average offered by London pubs and clubs; it can thus be argued that the ideological reasons for involvement are likely to be genuine.

Security

All those interviewed stated that the levels of violence were currently far below what might be experienced in the average clubs and pubs in town, with violent incidents in fact rare, a general contention of free parties that is supported by those such as Chatterton and Hollands (2003). The lower levels of violence are widely cited as a key reason why people choose to attend free parties (Reynolds, 1999). Three of the sample suggested that the lesser focus on alcohol consumption at these events was a contributing factor here. Despite this, all those interviewed recognised that violence, mugging and theft were real potential threats. Furthermore, many organisers suggested that a period around five to eight years previously had seen particularly high levels of these issues within this scene:

> There was definitely a point where I was thinking, Jesus it can't carry on the way it is.
>
> (Sub, Security/organiser, 40, talking on violence)

> There were a lot of people there who only came to the parties just to steal things off you, so there was a certain amount of petty theft and violence going along with that. Your mobile phone and stuff, you had to be really careful.
>
> (Jane, Crew member, 25)

> . . . gang culture has definitely played a massive part with the party scene . . . The gangs will come in and rob people . . . they will be the other side of London before you even know your phone is gone.
>
> (Purple, Organiser, 45)

> . . . they were taking a bit of a downturn . . . people were tired of having to fight crews of people, that just came to the party to rob, and yes, lots of violence. But recently it's got a lot better, if there was a violent incident at a party it would be a major thing.
>
> (Small, Organiser, 27)

Whilst none of those interviewed were entirely sure why the violence had so vastly decreased since this period, many suggested that the increased use of paid security had had a major impact. Interestingly, the implementation of security at free parties was initially seen as quite controversial, as security had typically been associated with the repressive environment of the club scene:

> I used to be very suspicious of security—first party I went to [with secu-rity] I was very shocked, I was like is this a free party or not? But now, I really rely on them.
>
> (Mouldy, Organiser, 36)

Before the implementation of security, most parties had been self-policed, with those involved (often including those attending) playing a joint role in the security of the events. This self-policing model is in line with the DIY ethos of free parties (Hemment, 1998), and avoided the use of bouncers, who were seen as unnecessarily aggressive and unreasonable in their conduct at legitimate events. The implementation of security that happened was largely an exten-sion of the ideals of self-policing, with the security used having long-standing attachments or involvement in the free party scene, rather than being hired in from outside firms as is widely described in the work of Hobbs et al. (2003) in the arrangements of many legal events:

> The security are well connected with the crews . . . they know, and were a part of what we was doing . . . they have grown up in the scene . . . it is more of a family thing, rather than a hired tool if you like, like what the clubs use.
>
> (Purple, Organiser, 45)

The use of security known within the party scene has a number of important considerations. It means the security personnel have a cultural understanding of the ethos of free parties, which allows the safety and protection of having dedicated paid security without infringing on the personal freedoms that are offered by the free party environment. The security used understands what is, and what is not deemed acceptable in terms of their actions:

> You have to understand with a squat party you are creating an environ-ment that doesn't really revolve around normal laws. It revolves around more moral laws and people's understanding of each other, so security has to reflect that. It has to allow freedom, do what they want to do, but it has to stop people from impacting on other peoples' enjoyment and experi-ence of the party.
>
> (Troll, Organiser, 29)

> Security's mandate is only to step in if someone is causing a problem to other people—there is no need to police people against themselves at a squat party.
>
> (Tig, Organiser, 27, talking on the differences from club security)

Furthermore, unlike the security observed in Lister et al.'s (2001b) study who had typically originated from backgrounds who take pride in violence, the security at free parties have largely come from within the scene, a scene which is clearly anti-violence, and thus violent dispositions are less likely.

In a similar way to the need for local knowledge, that is expressed as a key requirement for security at legitimate venues (Lister, 2001a; Hobbs et al., 2003), squat party security often utilise cultural knowledge. This cultural knowledge means that the security is better placed to recognise the signs of trouble and to know who are the more questionable characters needing to be watched at events:

> Our door staff have been in the London warehouse party scene for years and years and they know who to let in and who not to let in, but also know what type of place people are in. . . . If there is some sort of [Traveller] site issue of the moment, they should be aware of, they help us with this to a certain extent.
>
> (Small, Organiser, 27)

It was a common comment that free party security members are much less hard-line than those used in clubs and are more likely to resolve issues rather than to eject people at the first sign of trouble. There was a general belief that most issues can be resolved within the event through mediation and negotiation, without the need for eviction:

> Well, we try and sort things out on site to a certain extent. It's not just any problem kick them out of the door, we try and mediate a solution . . . rather than them causing trouble on the road.
>
> (Small, Organiser, 28)

Here it is worth noting that at free parties it may actually be easier for security to monitor individuals inside the event, rather than evicting them and having to deal with them causing problems outside and thus, drawing unwanted attention to the event. Free party security is unlikely to call the police to remove individuals as legitimate security may choose to, meaning that for free party security, observation rather than eviction may be an easier policy.

Unless absolutely necessary, the use of violence by security was not condoned and considered counter-productive: the ideals of self-policing mean that the pure numbers of those willing to help maintain the party's safe environment often allows aggressive tactics to be avoided, with often violent individuals swamped with numbers forcing them to leave. Here a DJ talks of the removal of an attendee who hit a girl in the face:

> All the sound systems turned off; a huge circle of people started to form around this guy and he got led out of the party pretty quick. He wasn't

beaten up or anything; he knew there was no getting away from this. But that is the sort of self-policing that can be achievable.

(Hand, DJ, 22)

This shows the level of support free party security have from the crowd, which is at odds with the mentality of the security being on their own against the crowd as is described by one bouncer interviewed by Hobbs et al. (2003). The approachability and friendliness levels of security were mentioned throughout the sample, with free party security described as non-confrontational, unless confrontation is required. Here a long-term organiser talks of the advantages of using women security on the front door for this reason:

What's ideal for us is women on the door . . . women who are well connected basically, to the crews. . . . They know how to handle the punters, it's not abrasive, it's not 'get out my face' . . . to a male that will come across as aggro it will put them in their place straight away, it's a great first face you see at the party. But bearing in mind there are fully grown big guys behind them all the way.

(Purple, Organiser, 46)

When asked if an event could have too much security, it was suggested by three interviewed that it was not an issue of too many security personnel, but rather an issue of the wrong type of security employed. Organiser Mouldy talks of what he describes as light touch security:

I suppose you could have too much of the wrong type of security, it's good to have a low profile. . . . I like the light touch security; I think that works with people better because they are given freedom, and they are given responsibility with that freedom.

(Mouldy, Organiser, 36)

Similarities can be drawn here to the work of Chatterton and Hollands (2003) who suggest that an internal policing model based on respect rather than the patronising and paternalistic attitudes often found in club security may, at least in the alternative scene, offer a more effective model of regulation. Furthermore, the use of the wrong type of security is not only undesirable, but is also likely to have a negative impact on the attendance of events; people attend for the free environment and thus, may be put off by heavy security as in the findings of Rietveld (1993) in the reviewed literature.

Throughout the sample it was a common contention that the security take on a greater duty of care than those in legitimate events, with security being your first point of call to look after someone who has drunk too much or taken too many drugs, as opposed to the person being thrown out for over-consumption as may be the case in legitimate clubs fearing for their licence (see Chatterton and Hollands, 2003 regarding clubs fearing for their licences). It can be argued there are advantages here in terms of risk reduction, since those at risk are looked after rather than being expelled onto the potentially dangerous streets.

This duty of care also extends to the security having added responsibilities in minimising health and safety risks. Unlike the often custom-designed clubs, that have well-thought-out situational crime prevention–type designs and extensive CCTV surveillance (Rigakos, 2004), squat parties are held in venues where there may be limited time to get to know the design of the building, with the security party in charge of restricting access to certain areas and keeping people safe. Here a security worker describes the difference to working in a club, and the process of getting to know a building:

> Well if you've been in a club, you've been there for however long so you know where all the exits are straight away. Like if you walk in as a new security guard on a new team in a club, you'll go in for a briefing, they will walk you around, they'll go, 'Right, here's this entrance, here's a trip hazard, there's the extinguishers'. When you turn up at a free party, things have been a bit, well let's just say that the time scale doesn't work out due to police moving you on, or whatever issues come up. Sometimes you walk into a building and you're blind so you have to like as quick as possible work out how to filter in the people safely, how to filter them out safely, and where are your dangers and can you block them, but you're doing all of this while you're on the run basically, all on the cuff sort of thing.
>
> (Sub, Security, 40)

Certain types of buildings were associated with increased levels of violence and theft, usually those too large, or those with areas subject to crowding such as stair wells, that may allow for easy pick-pocketing. It was generally considered by security and organisers that warehouses that are modern, ground floor and open plan are the best choice for security and safety, albeit less aesthetically pleasing than some of the older venues often used.

Interestingly, a key aspect of security's duty of care at a squat party is their duty of protecting those attending from potential attacks either by the building owners or the police:

> One of the main differences of the security of a club is that, you also, the security are also protecting you from the police and from the land owner . . . quite often the police will be hassling the security . . . so it is an extra thing to do, the more strain on the security.
>
> James, Security, 28

This can be seen as a significant difference to the role of legitimate security, such as those covered in the reviewed literature.

Security personnel are the gate holders for events both legal and illegal. Whilst club security try to keep out unwanted clientèle, in terms of dress code, attitude or estimated risk (Hobbs et al., 2003), party security members have a mandate of dealing with irate building owners, and potentially aggressive policing methods. Violent policing is relatively rare, however, arguably this rarity is a result of the negotiations that are undertaken with the police, a job that is often held by the security team:

> Personally if I'm working [running security] there's got to be at least two people who are in that team that can talk to the police, because they are going to be the first point of call you know; if you've got a door team that run away as soon as the police turn up, well let's just say they won't be working again.
>
> (Sub, Security, 40)

Similarities can be drawn here with the findings of Hemment (1998), who describes the need for protecting revellers from the police in the 'Art Lab' parties of the late 1990s in Blackburn.

In summary, free party security have reduced duties in some respects, as they allow a greater level of freedom within events so have fewer minor issues to police. Furthermore, in the current scene there is very limited violence: one organiser suggested that although security is usually employed in number, they are often standing around most of the night with little to do. However, free party security members have different and additional responsibilities to those of legitimate security documented in existing research. At times their role can be extremely active, be it removing gangs, negotiating with police or keeping people safe in poorly chosen buildings. The policy of caring for rather than evicting those over-intoxicated can certainly be seen as advantageous in terms of risk reduction. It has been demonstrated that the increased use of mediation of disputes rather than eviction has its advantages, and that giving people a little extra respect reduces rather than increases tensions inside the venue.

Discussion and Conclusion

This study shows that the rave scene, rather than dying out following the 1994 Criminal Justice Act, as claimed by some writers, still has a strong significance today, with many young people still attending events. For this reason, this type of research is important not only for the documentation of youth culture(s) and exploration of criminological interests, but also in terms of assessing the effectiveness of security strategies employed. Whilst this study has been somewhat limited by its sample size and its very specific focus, it has documented criminological topics with previously little academic focus, creating a background for more detailed studies to be conducted in the future.

This chapter has placed up-to-date information on the London free party scene into the wider picture of illegal rave-related research, which is predominantly outdated and unevenly biased towards drug-related studies. It has added new dimensions to the existing literature base on event security and 'bouncers', looking at a security model and culture that differ from those found in the mainstream urban pubs and clubs. Information has been drawn from existing research on security in the legitimate night-time economy in order to examine these differences, demonstrating the advantages of the self-policing model used within this particular scene.

Free party security has been shown to be less invasive, more approachable and generally more friendly. They are regarded as part of the scene. This allows them to operate with a great deal of support from those attending, reducing the need for violence as individuals tend to be removed by swamping with numbers, with support from revellers, rather than being tackled one-on-one. This is in a similar manner to the self-policing discussed in Chatterton and Hollands (2003), where those involved in the events also share a role in the security. Security has a greater duty of care than those in legitimate venues and additional roles of care are created through the use of disused buildings, meaning security must keep people safe. Further roles of care relate to the events being illegal, including protecting those attending from potential aggression from the police or the building owners—issues that would not be faced by legitimate security. Added to these roles are the responsibilities taken on through the caring for, rather than eviction of, those heavily under the influence of alcohol or drugs.

This security model certainly removes hostility towards security and reduces the levels of violence required to evict violent parties. However, whether these practices are transferable to the wider scene of legitimate security is doubtful; these practices arguably only work because of the closely knit nature of the groups involved in the events, aided by the lower levels of alcohol consumption. Whilst many of the key tasks are the same, free party security operate in a different manner and model to that of security in legitimate venues, with the development of security from a self-policing approach being core to understanding these differences.

References

Chatterton, P., & Hollands, R. (2003). *Urban Nightscapes: Youth Cultures, Pleasure Spaces and Corporate Power (Vol. 18)*. Psychology Press.

Chinet, L., Stéphan, P., Zobel, F., & Halfon, O. (2007). 'Party Drug use in Techno Nights: A Field Survey Among French-Speaking Swiss Attendees'. *Pharmacology Biochemistry and Behavior*, 86(2), 284–289.

Cohen, S. (1987). *Folk devils and moral panics*. 3rd edition. Oxford.

Critcher, C. (2000). 'Still Raving: Social Reaction to Ecstasy'. *Leisure Studies*, 19(3), 145–162.

The Daily Mail. (26/05/14). Emma Glanfield, 'Debacle at Devil's Dyke: Police Powerless to Intervene as Thousands Hold Illegal Rave at South Downs Beauty Spot'

Fernández-Calderón, F., Lozano, O. M., Vidal, C., Ortega, J. G., Vergara, E., González-Sáiz, F., & Pérez, M. I. (2011). 'Polysubstance Use Patterns in Underground Rave Attenders: A Cluster Analysis'. *Journal of Drug Education*, 41(2), 183–202.

Finlay, L. (2002). 'Negotiating the Swamp: The Opportunity and Challenge of Reflexivity in Research Practice'. *Qualitative Research*, 2(2), 209–230.

The Guardian. (12/7/2009). Guest, T. 'Fight for your Right to Party'.

The Guardian. (16/05/13) Travis, A. 'Legal Highs Flooding UK Pose Immense Overdose Risk, Warns Drugs Tsar'.

Hannigan, J. (2005). *Fantasy City: Pleasure and Profit in the Postmodern Metropolis.* Routledge.

Hemment, D. (1998). 'Dangerous Dancing and Disco Riots: The Northern Warehouse Parties'. In McKay (Ur.), *DIY Culture: Party and Protest in Nineties Britain*, Verso.

Hill, A. (2002). 'Acid House and Thatcherism: Noise, the Mob, and the English Countryside'. *The British Journal of Sociology*, 53(1), 89–105.

Hobbs, D., Hadfield, P., Lister, S., & Winlow, S. (2003). *Bouncers: Violence and Governance in the Night-Time Economy*. Oxford.

Lister, S., Hadfield, P., Hobbs, D., & Winlow, S. (2001a). 'Accounting for Bouncers: Occupational Licensing as a Mechanism for Regulation'. *Criminology and Criminal Justice*, 1(4), 363–384.

Lister, S., Hadfield, P., Hobbs, R., & Winlow, S. (2001b). '"Be Nice": The Training of Bouncers'. *Criminal Justice Matters*, 45(Special), 20–21.

Maylon, T. (1998). Tossed in the Fire and They Never Got Burned. The Exodus Collective. In Mckay, G. (Eds.) *Party and Protest in Nineties Britain.* Verso.

McDermot, P., Matthews, A. and O'Hare (1993). *Ecstasy in the UK: Recreational Drug Use and Social Change in Psychoactive Drugs and Harm Reduction*. Routledge.

McKay, G. (Ed.). (1998). *DIY Culture: Party & Protest in Nineties Britain.* Verso.

The Mirror. (18/06/14). Robertson, R. 'Seven Men Wanted by Police Over Illegal Party Where Teen Died'.

Nayak, A. (2006). 'Displaced Masculinities: Chavs, Youth and Class in the Post-Industrial City'. *Sociology*, 40(5), 813–831.

Partridge, C. (2006). 'The Spiritual and the Revolutionary: Alternative Spirituality, British Free Festivals, and the Emergence of Rave Culture'. *Culture and Religion*, 7(1), 41–60.

Pearson, G., & Hobbs, D. (2001). *Middle Market Drug Distribution*. Home Office Research Study 227. Home Office.

Pearson, G., & Hobbs, D. (2003). 'King Pin? A Case Study of a Middle Market Drug Broker'. *The Howard Journal of Criminal Justice*, 42(4), 335–347.

Redhead, S. (Ed.). (1993). *Rave Off: Politics and Deviance in Contemporary Youth Culture (Vol. 1).* Avebury.

Redhead, S. (1997). *Subculture to Clubcultures: An Introduction to Popular Cultural Studies*. Blackwell Publishers.

Reynolds, S. (1999). *Generation Ecstasy: Into the World of Techno and Rave Culture.* Psychology Press.

Rietveld, H. (1993). 'The Politics of Ecstasy' In Redhead, S (Eds.) *Rave Off: Politics and Deviance in Contemporary Youth Culture (Vol. 1)*. Avebury.

Rigakos, G. S. (2004). 'Nightclub Security and Surveillance'. *The Canadian Review of Policing Research*, 1, 54–60.

Riley, S., Morey, Y., & Griffin, C. (2008). 'Ketamine: The Divisive Dissociative: A Discourse Analysis of the Constructions of Ketamine by Participants of a Free Party (Rave) Scene'. *Addiction Research & Theory*, 16(3), 217–230.

Sutton Guardian. (9/05/14). 'Mike Murphy-Pyle: Warehouse Owners Warned After Illegal Rave Attracts Thousands to Beddington Industrial Estate', 45

Sykes, G. M., & Matza, D. (1957). 'Techniques of Neutralization: A Theory of Delinquency'. *American Sociological Review*, 22(6), 664–670.

Tomsen, S. (2005). 'Boozers and Bouncers': Masculine Conflict, Disengagement and the Contemporary Governance of Drinking-Related Violence and Disorder'. *Australian & New Zealand Journal of Criminology*, 38(3), 283–297.

Winlow, S., Hobbs, D., Lister, S., & Hadfield, P. (2001). 'Get Ready to Duck. Bouncers and the Realities of Ethnographic Research on Violent Groups'. *British Journal of Criminology*, 41(3), 536–548.

Section Three
Drugs and Illegal Markets

8 On Tap

Organised Crime and the Illicit Trade in Tobacco, Alcohol and Pharmaceuticals[1]

Charlie Edwards and Calum Jeffray

Introduction

HM Prison Manchester, or 'Strangeways', casts a dark shadow over Cheetham Hill, a once thriving industrial area of inner-city Manchester. The area is celebrated as one of the most diverse places in the country. The main road is lined with churches, mosques, synagogues and temples and the area is known for its Polish delis, Irish pubs, Arab sweet shops, Pakistani markets and Jamaican hairdressers. The area also hides a well-known secret. It is a hub for counterfeit clothes, drugs and organised criminality.

The district has long been associated with organised crime in general and illicit trade in particular. Small shops, warehouses and storage units, trucks and hauliers all vie for space along the back streets. The shutters on the shop fronts, however, initially suggest that trade here is far from booming. It is not until one notices the spotters and lookouts standing nonchalantly along the pavement that it becomes apparent that trade is in fact thriving. Entry into one of the many shops reveals counterfeit goods from clothing to healthcare products, cigarettes, drugs and mobile phones.

Serious and organised criminals are reaping the rewards of selling these illicit goods, in towns and cities across the country. The impact of this illicit trade in the UK is much more serious than many politicians and officials in government accept. There are plenty of reasons why this is the case: the continued focus on narcotics to the detriment of other criminal activity; the limited intelligence picture concerning certain criminal activities such as illicit trade; and a cultural mindset among the public, politicians and senior officials, which underestimates the scale, nature and impact of organised crime in the UK. Following the global economic recession, illicit trade in goods and services has also become socially acceptable among the British public, making the UK an attractive market for organised crime. In particular, the illicit trade in tobacco, alcohol and pharmaceuticals is more attractive to organised criminals than, for example, drug trafficking, given that it is a low-risk and high-value activity. The high profit margins associated with illicit trade are used to fund other organised criminal activities, a fact not widely understood by the British public.

Senior officers from police forces and from Her Majesty's Revenue and Customs (HMRC) therefore describe the emergence a 'perfect storm' in the UK. It is an alarming scenario in which relatively sophisticated, highly networked organised crime groups (OCGs) run small-scale, high-frequency operations across a diverse set of criminal and legitimate activities. Streets and communities are taken over by invisible forces. Parallel systems of governance are put in place by OCGs in areas deemed off limits to the authorities. And while much of this activity is happening in plain sight, day-to-day organised criminality takes place on the Dark Web, with illicit goods delivered to customers by legitimate multinational courier services. When challenged on the likelihood of such a scenario, the officers and officials pause: 'We're in it', they say—the question is, 'What can we do about it?'

This chapter explores the intersection between illicit trade and organised criminal groups operating in the UK, assessing the scale, methods and drivers of illicit trade, and wider trends in organised criminal behaviour. The analysis draws on a number of criminal prosecutions as case studies, as well as fieldwork conducted by the authors between October 2013 and November 2014, including interviews with representatives from government, law enforcement and industry organisations.

Organised Crime and Illicit Trade in the UK

Serious and organised crime represents a significant risk to the UK, and tackling it is currently a major priority for government and law-enforcement agencies. In a speech in June 2014, the Home Secretary claimed, 'The facts are stark. Organised crime costs the UK at least £24 billion a year. There are over 5,300 organised criminal groups that affect people in the UK today, and more than 36,000 people are engaged in these criminal activities'.

The British government's understanding of, and approach to tackling, organised crime has evolved dramatically since 2010. Historically, the police and successive governments have focused on high-end organised criminality—specifically drug trafficking. While drugs may be the most visible example of organised crime on Britain's streets and have the most immediate impact in terms of associated violence, the scale of 'hidden' organised criminality in the UK has led politicians and policymakers to consistently underestimate the severity of the situation.

The law enforcement landscape shifted as a response to the government's decision within the 2010 National Security Strategy to class an increase in the level of organised crime affecting the UK as a Tier Two risk to national security. Despite the major steps that the government has undoubtedly taken to improve its response to organised crime—including publishing a dedicated Serious and Organised Crime Strategy and establishing the National Crime Agency (NCA)—there remains no legal definition of 'organised crime' and the term remains subject to disagreement. This often acts as an obstacle to discussing the links between organised crime and particular areas of criminal activity such as illicit trade. For this chapter, we employ the definition of organised crime as set out by the UK Government's Serious and Organised Crime Strategy (2013, p.14):

> Organised crime is serious crime planned, coordinated and conducted by people working together on a continuing basis. Their motivation is often, but not always, financial gain [. . .] organised crime in this and other countries recognises neither national borders nor national interests.

Assessments by the NCA and others have found that the nature of organised crime in the UK is evolving. The NCA's National Strategic Assessment of Serious and Organised Crime (2014, p.7) found that organised groups built around a traditional hierarchy have transformed into 'loose networks where individuals, pairs or small groups bring associates and contacts together to work on particular enterprises across multiple crime types'. These networks frequently comprise ethnically and nationally diverse individuals operating across multiple jurisdictions. The internet has become a key enabler of sustaining these networks and has fundamentally changed the way OCGs operate.

It is often challenging to see where illicit trade activities fit into the organised crime threat picture. Illicit trade is defined by the World Health Organization Framework Convention on Tobacco Control (2003, p.4) as 'any practice or conduct prohibited by law and which relates to production, shipment, receipt, possession, distribution, sale or purchase, including any practice or conduct intended to facilitate such activity'. In the UK, illicit trade is frequently placed under the umbrella term of 'economic crime', which covers wide-ranging threats such as 'market abuse/insider dealing; bribery, corruption and sanctions evasion; counterfeit currency; money laundering and criminal finance; fraud against the individual, the public, private and third sectors; and intellectual property crime' (NCA 2014, p.21).

Law-enforcement officials have recognised that they tend to focus on the threats on which they have the most information. Whereas their understanding of certain risks such as narcotics, fraud and extortion are well developed, threats such as illicit trade are less well understood and therefore receive comparatively less attention. Yet the numbers associated with illicit trade are enormous. Smuggled tobacco costs governments around the world approximately $40 billion each year in lost revenue (Action on Smoking and Health 2014). The global market in counterfeit medicine is worth around $200 billion, while the illicit alcohol trade is also substantial; the World Health Organisation (2011) estimates that around 30 per cent of all alcohol consumed globally is illegally produced, or 'unrecorded'.

Because of the difficulties related to gathering evidence, however, it is often a challenge for authorities to determine the precise scale of illicit trade, particularly in relation to tobacco, alcohol and pharmaceuticals. According to HMRC, for example, the relationship between tobacco smuggling and organised crime is a 'particularly difficult issue to judge with any degree of confidence' (Home

Affairs Committee 2013, p.5). McKee et al. (2012), meanwhile, claim that 'the scale and nature of illegal alcohol production and sale are impossible to ascertain with certainty'. Finally, Reynolds and McKee (2010) note that 'by its nature, the global scale of the problem of sale of inactive or dangerous substitutes for medications by criminal organisations is difficult to assess'. The government and its law enforcement agencies do not know, therefore, the true scale and impact of illicit trade in the UK.

Information on the involvement of OCGs in these activities is equally opaque and, on the whole, few details are publicly available on the nature of these groups or the extent of their participation. This is typically referred to only vaguely in terms of 'gangs', 'groups' and 'networks'; it is not unusual to come across statements such as 'organised criminal gangs are heavily involved in tobacco smuggling' (Public Accounts Committee 2013, p.12) or 'the main threat of fraud on alcohol duty comes from organised criminal gangs' (Public Accounts Committee 2012, pp.7–8), which offer no further indication of the nature, size or methods of operation of these OCGs.

Illicit Tobacco Trade

Described by McNeill et al. (2014, p.1) as 'complex, dynamic and rapidly evolving', the global illicit tobacco industry is one of the world's foremost criminal enterprises. In 2011, an estimated 570 billion illicit cigarettes were consumed worldwide, equivalent to 11.5 per cent of total cigarette consumption. A variety of activities are covered by the term 'illicit tobacco trade', and it is important to distinguish between the following five categories, based on definition from Action on Smoking and Health (Home Affairs Committee 2014, p.39):

- **Smuggling:** The unlawful movement of tobacco products from one jurisdiction to another, without the applicable tax being paid
- **Cheap/illicit whites**: The term applies to cigarettes that are lawfully produced in one country, but manufactured specifically for smuggling into countries with higher tax rates where there is no lawful market for them
- **Counterfeiting**: The illegal manufacturing of a tobacco product, often with apparent 'trademarks', but without the owners' consent
- **Bootlegging**: The transport of tobacco products legally purchased in one country to another with a higher tax rate, in amounts beyond those reasonable for personal use
- **Illegal manufacturing**: The production of tobacco products without declaration to the relevant authorities. In some cases, they may be manufactured in approved factories, 'off the books' and/or out of normal hours; in others, they will be manufactured in unlawful covert operations.

Accurately measuring the scale of the illicit tobacco market is a problem shared by many countries, given that 'transparent, public data on illicit tobacco is limited and, in many countries, non-existent' (Joossens and Raw 2012, p.233).

The data used by HMRC is based on analyses of what is known as the 'tax gap', a calculation of total tobacco consumption in the UK minus legitimate consumption. Total consumption is calculated from the Office for National Statistics survey on smoking prevalence (with an adjustment of around 40 per cent made for under-reporting), while legitimate consumption is calculated from HMRC's own data. These official figures show that the illicit market share of cigarette consumption in the UK fell from 21 per cent in 2000 to 7 per cent in 2011, before rising to 10 per cent in 2013. The market share for hand-rolled tobacco (HRT) fell from 65 per cent in 2000 to 35 per cent in 2011, though it too rose to 39 per cent in 2013 (Home Affairs Committee 2014, p.5). In 2013, the illicit market share equated to revenue losses of approximately £1.1 billion and £1 billion for cigarettes and HRT, respectively (Public Accounts Committee 2013a; HMRC 2014).

While HMRC figures therefore show an overall decreasing trend, feedback from officers on the front line suggested that the issue of illicit tobacco remains a significant problem. It was not unusual to hear that illicit tobacco could be found 'in every corner shop in large towns and cities' or that there was 'enough tobacco rolling around communities for it to be coming from somewhere'.

Other—primarily industry—sources have proposed alternative methodologies for calculating the scale of the illicit tobacco trade which they claim provide a more accurate picture. As demonstrated in Figure 8.1, there are typically large discrepancies between government and industry data; there are also contradicting reports of trends even within the industry. In 2010, for example, the Tobacco Manufacturers' Association estimated that the illicit cigarette trade in the UK was 19 per cent of the total, compared with Philip Morris' Project

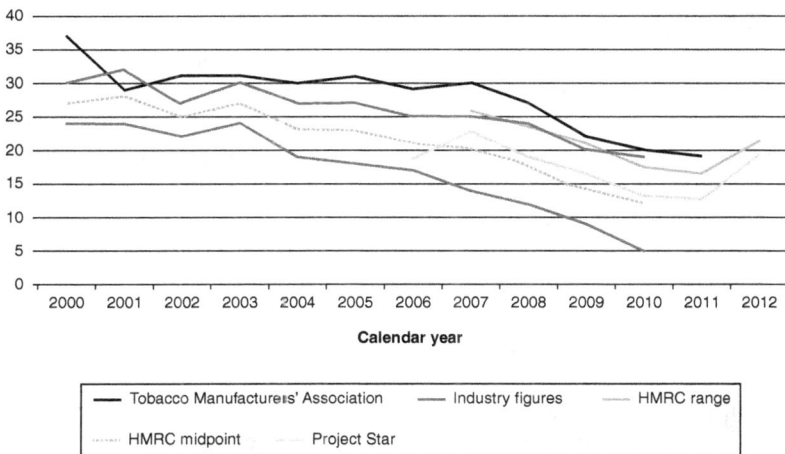

Figure 8.1 A comparison of HMRC and industry figures for non-UK duty paid market share for cigarettes, 2000–12.

Source: National Audit Office

Star estimate of 13 per cent, the Tax Payers' Alliance's estimate of 16 per cent (Home Affairs Committee 2014, p.7), and HMRC's mid-point estimate of 11 per cent (Home Affairs Committee 2014, p.84).

Despite their differences, many of the HMRC and industry reports identify common trends. Both suggest that counterfeit cigarettes and illicit whites—rather than the smuggling of genuine products into the country—account for most of the illicit tobacco market in the UK (Home Affairs Committee 2014). In HMRC's strategy for tackling illicit tobacco, it concludes that illicit whites 'represent the most significant threat to legitimate trade and tobacco revenues in the UK from large-scale organised criminality' (HMRC 2011, p.7). Industry experts generally believe that this trend is partly because non-mainstream cigarettes have become more socially and culturally acceptable, particularly in the past five years or so.

Case Study: Operation Corsica

This case concerned an importation of approximately 8 million counterfeit 'Superkings' brand cigarettes within two shipping containers. The equivalent revenue duty on the cigarettes was in the region of £1.6 million.

The OCG was made up of five members who mostly worked for front companies MSA Fireworks or Lexicon Import and Export Ltd. In December 2002, members of the group set up MSA Fireworks in order to legitimise activities in China. In April 2004, they travelled to China with £21,000 in cash and samples of branded cigarettes to give to criminals there to counterfeit. The plan was to use the company Lexicon Import and Export Ltd to import the cigarettes, but after the death of its director, the OCG stole the identity of one Ian Wallace in order to set up a new company which was ultimately used. The group carried out numerous 'dry runs' and smaller importations from Guangzhou in China to the ports of Southampton and Felixstowe (smaller seizures of counterfeit cigarettes, including Benson and Hedges, Regal and Superkings brands were made on premises associated with MSA Fireworks and its employees). The primary shipment of 8 million counterfeit cigarettes took place in September 2004. The cigarettes were concealed behind boxes containing folding camping chairs. Shipped into Southampton, the contents were allowed to be delivered to premises in Gloucestershire, where the arrests were made.

In total, the groups were ordered to pay back more than £1 million to the state. One member pleaded guilty and received a prison sentence of two years and eight months. The other four individuals pleaded not guilty but were convicted, receiving prison sentences of between eighteen months and six years.

While high-profile seizures such as Operation Corsica represent particular incidents rather than broader trends, they also highlight both the scale and professionalism of many tobacco-smuggling operations, thus giving a clue as to the magnitude of organised criminal involvement. It is estimated that 4.5 billion illicit sticks arrive in the UK each year, equating to just over 529 forty-foot containers of cigarettes slipping through the net. It is clear that OCGs invest substantial amounts of time, money and effort in gathering intelligence on the routes and methods least likely to arouse suspicion, often liaising with criminal networks overseas. Common techniques used to evade detection include combining illegitimate goods with legitimate ones, undertaking frequent dummy runs to test the response of law-enforcement agencies and 'hijacking' the import details of legitimate businesses which transport similar loads on similar routes.

The authors' research supported the theory that there are various types of criminals involved in the illicit tobacco trade from large, 'traditional' OCGs to a 'cottage industry' of more minor actors such as white-collar criminals, road hauliers and mules. Only a small number of OCGs in the UK are capable of organising the entire life cycle of the operation, from manufacture to distribution. Many others are less ambitious in scope and 'rely on the work of key facilitators, often based overseas, who engage with smaller legitimate tobacco manufacturers in sourcing the tobacco goods and associated packaging' (Financial Action Task Force 2012, p.7). Finally, some opportunistic criminals may 'simply exploit lower cross-border prices of genuine tobacco products and smuggle them to their chosen destination for sale' (Financial Action Task Force 2012, p.7).

The use of large shipping containers to smuggle cigarettes remains a challenge for authorities; at the same time, OCGs use increasingly diverse methods. According to HMRC officials, OCGs have increasingly begun to adopt the more sophisticated 'little and often' methods of consignments of Class A controlled drugs, and are able to adapt extremely quickly to the seizure techniques of law-enforcement agencies. There has consequently been a shift from using large containers to near-continent warehousing; from attempts to transport large stocks of tobacco products to first breaking them down into smaller consignments, which are then transported across the border using methods such as post and mules, before being reassembled at the destination. A more recent concern is the trend towards using fast parcel and courier services as methods of transport. It can often make more business sense for criminals to send smaller consignments and pay the higher parcel costs of private companies, given the lower chance of detection and seizure.

Drivers and Facilitators

The persistence of the illicit tobacco trade is widely attributed to the high—and increasing—level of tax on tobacco products in the UK, and the differences in price between the UK and countries in continental Europe (Figure 8.2). The

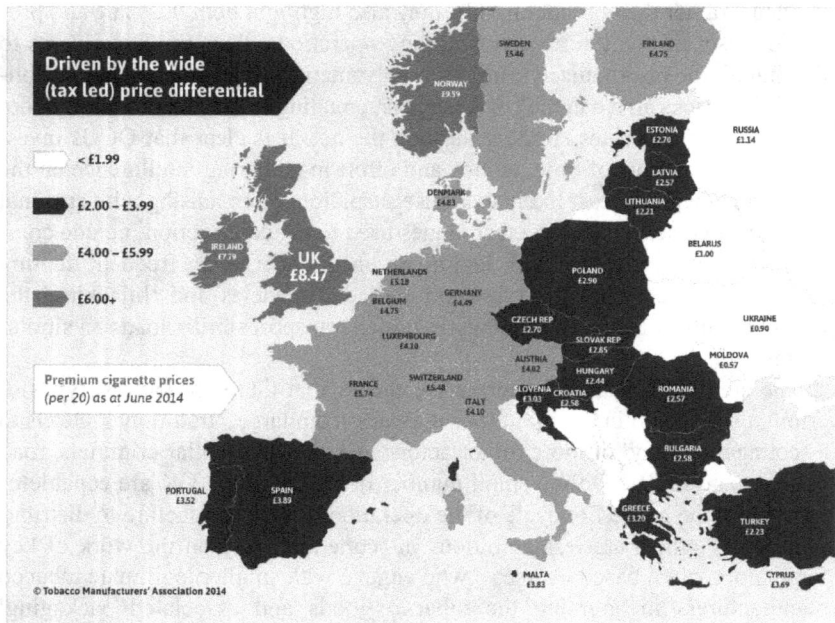

Figure 8.2 European cigarette prices, June 2014.

Source: Tobacco Manufacturers' Association

profits that can be made on duty evasion are undoubtedly the primary force driving this trade. Between 1992 and 2011, the average price of cigarettes in the UK more than tripled, while the total tax on tobacco remained at or above 75 per cent of the overall price (All Party Parliamentary Group on Smoking and Health 2013). Currently, the price of a typical pack of cigarettes in the UK is £7.98, of which 77 per cent is tax, while the typical price of a 50-gram pouch of HRT is £17.11, of which around 68 per cent is tax (data provided by a representative from the Tobacco Manufacturers' Association, April 2014). Despite its goal of lowering tobacco consumption on health grounds, this policy of high taxation has the unintended yet inevitable consequence of generating a substantial illicit market.

However, many commentators believe that blaming the problem of illicit tobacco-trading purely or primarily on tax rates is too simplistic, even deceptive. The All Party Parliamentary Group on Smoking and Health (2013, p.7) notes that making a 'simple connection between raising prices and increasing illicit trade, as the tobacco industry routinely does, is grossly misleading', while according to Joossens and Raw (2012, p.232), 'it is crucial to note . . . that the solution to this problem is not to lower tax levels, as the tobacco industry frequently claims'. Although a high tax margin may provide the initial incentive to smuggle, there are numerous other important factors that should be taken into consideration, such as 'the ease and cost of operating in a country, industry participation, how well organised crime networks are, the likelihood of being caught, the punishment if caught, corruption levels and so on' (Joossens and Raw 2012, p.232). The advent of e-commerce, low-cost airlines and globalised supply chains are also important factors to consider.

On the whole, the drivers of the illicit tobacco trade on the supply side include the desire for both legal and illegal manufacturers to increase sales and profit, the role of corruption and the capacity of law enforcement, while demand is driven by smokers looking for specific tobacco products at low prices. On the supply side, many commentators place the blame squarely on the tobacco industry; Shelley and Melzer (2008, p.46), for instance, highlight 'the willingness of many cigarette companies until recently to collude in or to overlook the smuggling of their commodities'. HMRC remains concerned about the problem of tobacco companies excessively supplying branded cigarettes to overseas markets, particularly those that are known to contain criminal networks which intend to smuggle the cigarettes into the UK.

On the demand side, the role that the consumer market plays is noteworthy. Feedback from HMRC and Trading Standards indicates that the market is increasingly consumer-driven, given that smokers are exposed to a greater variety of tobacco products than ever before, particularly from overseas. Whereas twenty years ago the illicit tobacco trade took the form of offloading large quantities of generic stock, today OCGs are more receptive to consumer demand and smuggling is increasingly done 'to order'. The complicity of smokers in the illicit trade is highlighted by Van Dijck (2009, p.167), whose research found that 'the trafficking of cigarettes is in general not seen as a very serious offence. People knowingly buying illegal cigarettes are aware of the illegality, but do not consider their actions particularly criminal. Consequently, the 'moral' threshold to step into the world of illegal cigarette trafficking is rather low'.

Illicit Alcohol Trade

There are numerous similarities between the illicit tobacco and illicit alcohol trades. As with tobacco, different categories of alcohol fraud are recognised, including illicit production, smuggling of lawful alcohol products into the UK without paying the applicable taxes, and manufacturing of counterfeit alcohol that is designed to look like a commercial product. The scale of the illicit alcohol trade has proved just as difficult to measure and HMRC once again uses tax-gap estimates. The organisation concedes that this methodology contains 'many sources of uncertainty and potential error', but remains 'sufficiently confident' over its accuracy in representing the scale of the illicit market, often corroborating results with other sources (HMRC 2013, p.3). The National Audit Office (2012, p.12) concurs but warns that the figures are inherently outdated, since 'the data required for the calculation of tax gap figures are only available about 18 months after the end of each financial period'; it also recognises, however, that the UK is 'one of the few countries to try to make such estimates'.

According to the tax gap figures, the illicit trade of beer is currently the most significant alcohol fraud in the UK, even though it is estimated to be the least profitable of the three products (Figure 8.3). The most likely explanation is that beer is the 'fastest-moving' product; consumers purchase 'units' of beer in greater quantities than wine or spirits, meaning that wholesalers and other outlets are able to sell stock more quickly. The latest estimates indicate that 9 per cent of total beer consumption is illicit (a statistic that has remained more or less constant since at least 2007), implying tax losses of approximately £550 million per year (HMRC 2013). The illicit beer market principally comprises mainstream canned and bottled beer brands, with at least one in every ten cans or bottles of beer sold on the UK market in 2009–10 thought to be UK duty unpaid (HMRC 2012). Illicit spirits, while remaining a significant problem, represent the lowest market share, at approximately 3 per cent (equating to £120 million revenue losses per year). Spirits are 'slower-moving' products, transportable in lower volumes and represent a higher risk for illicit traders (particularly after the introduction of duty stamps in 2006). However, the potential profits to be made from spirits fraud are far higher than for beer and wine (see Figure 8.3). The statistics for illicit wine show that it is a bigger problem than spirits, with an estimated illicit market share of 6 per cent and £350 million in annual revenue losses. The statistics for wine were unavailable for many years and the first estimates were only published in 2013; with the recent availability of this data on wine, the National Audit Office (2012) now estimates that alcohol fraud currently costs the UK £1.2 billion a year in lost revenue.

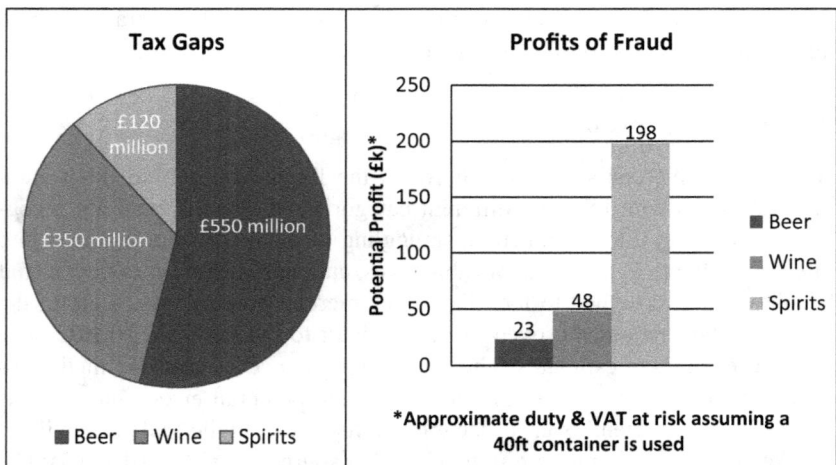

Figure 8.3 A breakdown of the estimated tax gap and potential profits by product.

Source: Her Majesty's Revenue and Customs

Operation Baygood

The eight offenders in this case were suspected of operating a plant producing, bottling and labelling counterfeit Glen's vodka. This was a highly sophisticated plant which imported counterfeit bottle caps, labels and bottles, and housed a fully operational production line.

This operation involved eight individuals: Kevin Eddishaw (central organiser behind the criminal organisation and property developer by trade); John Humphreys (foreman at the plant, managing the day-to-day running of the operation); Michael Matthews (a printer who produced the counterfeit labels); Stuart Bemrose (provided the shrink wrap machine and packaging materials); James Fyfe (foreman for the group); Wojciech Herbst (the 'chemist' who prepared the counterfeit vodka) and Mark Gyles (a driver).

The operation was based on a farm in Great Dalby, Leicestershire. While the bottles came from Leeds and the labels locally, the counterfeit bottle tops were brought in from Poland. The vodka itself was produced by adding precise amounts of bleach to denatured alcohol before mixing it with water. The source of the alcohol is unknown, though its blue colour and large volume imply that the source was industrial alcohol. When the plant was raided, several thousand litres of counterfeit vodka (more than 9,000 bottles) were discovered. In the months leading up to the discovery of the plant, seizures took place of counterfeit Glen's vodka which were later shown to have been produced there, including seizures in Blackpool, Salford and South Wales.

Dean Ironmonger and Stuart Bemrose were found not guilty; the other six were given prison sentences ranging from 12 months (suspended sentence) to seven years.

Counterfeiting cases such as Operation Baygood are relatively rare but entail significant scales of production. Cases often only come to light after some sort of incident; the most high-profile case in recent years was in July 2011, when five Lithuanian men died in an explosion at an illicit vodka distillery in Boston, Lincolnshire. Although the explosion removed much of the evidence of the extent of production, other cases point to groups producing tens or even hundreds of thousands of litres of illicit alcohol. These include cases in Cheetham Hill, where in October 2010 HMRC officers seized 25,000 litres of counterfeit vodka, and Worcestershire, where in March 2011, more than 11,400 litres of counterfeit alcohol were seized at an industrial unit.

According to HMRC, the more prevalent issue is organised criminals smuggling alcohol products into the UK in large commercial quantities, duty unpaid. The perpetrators 'systematically exploit the EU-wide excise duty suspension system which allows excise goods to move between authorised warehouses duty unpaid until released for consumption onto the home market' (HMRC 2012, p.8). The organisation of alcohol fraud is frequently much more advanced than for other types of goods, with 'complex supply chains that involve sophisticated organisation in finance, procurement, logistics, supply chain control and marketing' (HMRC 2012, p.8).

Feedback from both public- and private-sector representatives suggests that OCGs are involved at all stages of the supply chain, from the suppliers to those holding goods in duty suspense, hauliers, excise warehouses, lock-ups and cash-and-carry stores, corner shops and other outlets. As with tobacco, there appear to be a limited number of OCGs who are able to manage the process from start to finish; some may be involved in the production of counterfeit alcohol, collecting used bottles or purchasing moulds to make their own. Others are able to profit from a more opportunistic approach by exploiting weaknesses in certain parts of the supply chain, smuggling goods by sending cover loads and, if these are not stopped and checked by authorities, 'mirror' loads are sent with identical documents. The goods may then be sold cheaply to cash-and-carry stores or taken to so-called 'slaughter sites' where they are broken down into lesser volumes to be sold to small outlets. Officers from Trading Standards noted that, given the greater competition in this sector, these corner shops, international stores and local wholesalers are increasingly willing to buy cheap alcohol just to remain competitive.

Interviewees noted that OCGs were particularly adaptive and reactive in this area; as soon as law-enforcement agencies plug one gap, the market evolves and OCGs quickly learn to sidestep obstacles. One example given was the case of Bulgarian counterfeit tax strips—which were made available by OCGs even before the real versions were released.

Drivers and Facilitators

According to HMRC, the problem of alcohol fraud has grown and evolved significantly since the introduction of the European single market in 1993. The agency claims that, 'It used to centre on the smuggling of small quantities of alcohol in private vehicles and vans from the near-continent', but now 'it involves the large-scale diversion of lorry loads of duty unpaid alcohol by organised criminal gangs' (HMRC 2012, p.8).

Once again, high taxes are blamed for the rise in counterfeiting. However, a bigger issue appears to relate to the fundamental weaknesses of the EU duty suspension regime, rather than tax and duty rates. The World Customs Organization (2013) recognises this situation, highlighting the misuse of excise suspension regimes in the EU single market as a means to illicitly trade alcohol products. The technique involves, for instance, the abuse of the excise holding and movement system which allows payment of duty on goods to be 'suspended' while they circulate between registered warehouses in the EU, until the goods are released for consumption. These warehouses, also known as 'bonded warehcuses', are designed to benefit traders who import goods, offering a facility that delays duty and/or import VAT payments until traders are ready for the goods to come out of 'duty suspense', entering free circulation or the customs procedure of another EU member state. The World Customs Organisation (2013, pp.3C–31) offers a useful overview of how the illicit trade of alcohol funct ons in the UK in this regard:

> Organised criminals use this system to position large commercial consignments of popular UK beers, wines and spirits on the near continent in 'duty suspense'. These goods are subsequently diverted back into the UK under the cover of false documentation, taxes are not declared, and the illicit consignments are then sold onto wholesalers, cash-and-carries, small retailers and the leisure sector, thus undercutting legitimate suppliers.

Illicit Pharmaceuticals Trade

According to the Medicines and Healthcare Products Regulatory Agency (MHRA), the scale of organised crime involvement in the illicit pharmaceuticals trade is completely unknown. Pharmaceuticals are the easiest of the three goods to counterfeit and to transport, by a variety of methods, making it particularly difficult to assess scale. The actual number of illicit pharmaceuticals traded by criminals is often never determined, and sometimes not even known by the criminals themselves. Perhaps to a greater degree than the case of tobacco and alcohol, the illicit pharmaceuticals trade very much takes the form of a lcw-volume, high-frequency activity; there are no shipping containers, no haulage trucks and no large warehouses. Given the regulated nature of much of the industry, tablet sizes, vials and medicine packaging tend to be standardised, making the task of sourcing realistic counterfeits more straightforward.

A specific challenge with regards to the illicit trade of pharmaceuticals is achieving consensus on standard definitions, since there is no universal agreement of what constitutes an 'illicit', 'fake' or 'counterfeit' medicine, with the debate having become politically charged in recent years (World Health Organization 2013). The situation is complicated by the fact that a medicinal product may be granted a license—or market authorisation—by authorities in one country (thereby making it legal in that jurisdiction) but may not be granted one in another country (thereby making it unlawful to trade in that medicine). Kamagra, for example, is an erectile-dysfunction treatment produced primarily in India where it is legal; however, it has not been granted market authorisation in the UK and many other nations, where its trade remains illegal. The term 'illicit' is therefore used in this chapter to refer to products that are counterfeit (contravene the intellectual property rights of the patent-holder), unlicensed (not market-authorised for sale in the UK) or substandard (genuine products which do not meet quality specifications set for them).

The use of the terms 'pharmaceuticals' and 'medicines' can also be problematic, as what may be termed a 'medicine' in one country may not be considered as such in another country. It is also unclear to what degree products such as homeopathic remedies and even new psychoactive substances (NPS) would fall under this category. These disagreements are a major obstacle to co-ordinated action to combat the issue, which is particularly serious given the major health concern surrounding illicit medicines. As Finlay (2011, p.1) notes, although the counterfeiting of, and trafficking in, all manner of products is on the rise globally, 'no other bogus product has the capacity to harm or even kill its consumer as do illicit pharmaceuticals'.

Since 2008, Operation Pangea has involved a week of co-ordinated international operations to tackle the supply of counterfeit, illegal and substandard medicines, and in which HMRC, the Border Force, and MHRA all participate. These operations focus on suspending illegal websites, disrupting payment services and intercepting illegal medicines in the postal system. During Pangea VII, which took place in May 2014, the operations seized illegal pharmaceuticals worth more than £18.6 million worldwide and resulted in the closure or suspension—through domain name or payment facility removal—of 10,603 illegal online websites selling counterfeit and unlicensed medicines (MHRA 2014). What is perhaps most noteworthy for British authorities is that nearly half of the 8.4 million doses of illegal drugs were seized in the UK.

As illustrated in Figure 8.4, the most common types of illicit pharmaceuticals are so-called 'lifestyle' medicines, most notably for the treatment of erectile dysfunction—Viagra consistently tops the list of most commonly

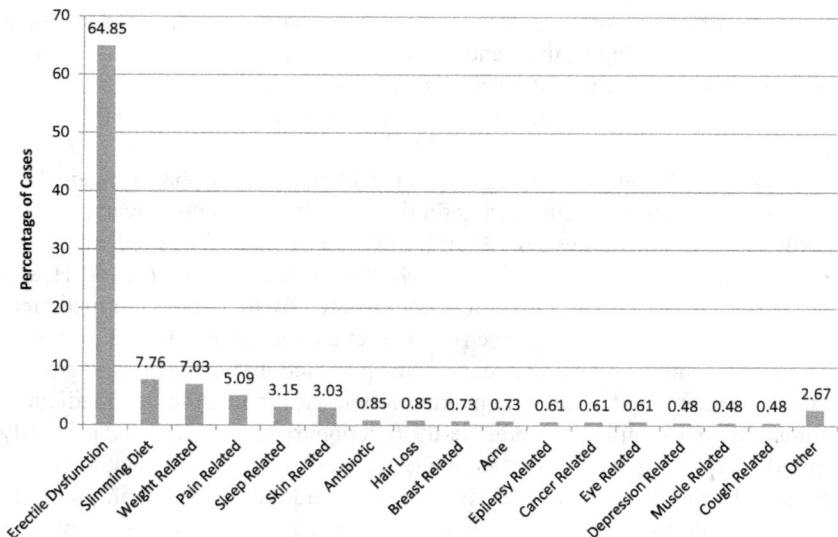

Figure 8.4 Types of products investigated by the MHRA, April 2013–March 2014.

Source: Medicines and Healthcare Products Regulatory Agency

counterfeited product—and obesity and steroids, as well as human growth hormones misused by body builders.

Despite their comparatively small percentages, the trade clearly extends beyond lifestyle drugs to more critical and potentially lifesaving medicines, including antibiotics, antiretroviral drugs, and cancer and infertility treatments. Counterfeiters are also responsive to market needs, illustrated by the counterfeit doses of the antiviral drug, Tamiflu, that were discovered at the height of the 2005 bird-flu scare, for example (Clark 2008).

The lack of available evidence also makes it particularly difficult to judge the extent of organised criminal activity, as well as to gauge whether the problem is increasing or decreasing. As illustrated by Figure 8.5, the estimated value of the seizures of illicit pharmaceutical products rose exponentially during the first six iterations of Operation Pangea, but fell from £12.2 million in 2013 to £8.6 million in 2014. The data look at the value rather than the volume of products, however, and does not indicate whether variations are a result of the number or value of pharmaceuticals available on the illicit market, or the effectiveness of the operation and wider efforts of law-enforcement agencies.

As well as being identified as a target country for illicit pharmaceuticals, the MHRA (2012, p.6) notes that the UK is also being used as a 'transit and fulfilment centre for orders placed on websites hosted and operated from other countries, thereby giving the impression to the end consumer that the product supplied originated from the UK'. These medicines are more likely to be seen as originating from a 'trusted' source and therefore less likely to arouse suspicion when transported overseas. The MHRA also notes that falsified medicines are very rarely manufactured in the UK, with just one known case since 2003. Most of the medicines seized as part of Operation Pangea VII were 'unlicensed' drugs, the majority of which were authentic pills, repackaged to

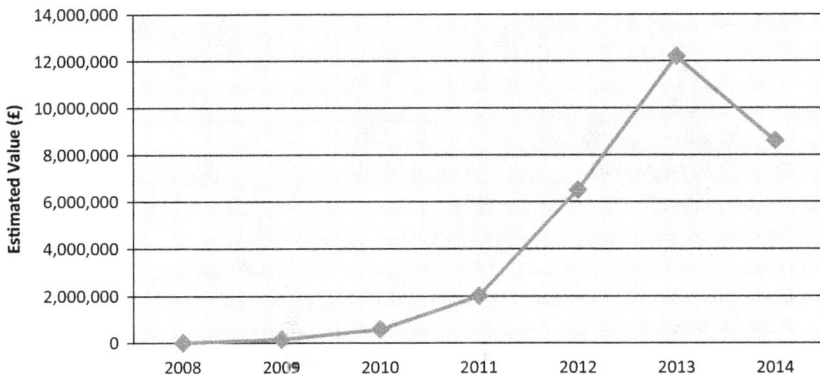

Figure 8.5 The estimated value of seizures of illicit pharmaceutical products in the UK during Operation Pangea.

Source: Medicines and Healthcare Products Regulatory Agency

conceal the fact that they are outdated, stolen, made by a manufacturer other than the one on the label, or intended for sale in other countries; only 2.6 per cent were outright fakes.

The authors' research suggests that, as with tobacco and alcohol, there are various 'levels' of organised criminal involvement in the illicit pharmaceuticals trade, from the 'cottage industry' of opportunistic individuals to more structured OCG activities taking place on an industrial scale. MHRA identifies three categories of criminal actors involved in the trade: pseudo-entrepreneurs and businessmen with a working knowledge of the pharmaceutical environment; organised criminals operating within an established criminal network; and opportunistic, multi-commodity trading individuals who identify a niche way to make quick money via internet sales—as demonstrated by Operation William, for example.

Case Study: Operation William

This case involved Mahomed Bacai, a Portuguese national, and his wife, Hina Bacai, living in Surrey. They are known to have been part of a larger network operating online across the UK, Netherlands and India.

Investigations began in January 2011 after a seizure at the Coventry postal hub by what was then the UK Border Agency. This ultimately led to the discovery of an enterprise operated by Bacai from his home, involving the distribution of unlicensed and prescription-only medicines (in addition to Class C controlled drugs). Officers confiscated vast amounts of counterfeit and unlicensed medication for erectile dysfunction, antihistamines, analgesics, hormones and diet pills, as well as benzodiazepines, a Class C controlled drug. The total value of the seizures was more than £1.7 million.

The medicines would be sent via post from India and China to various postboxes in London and the surrounding area. Bacai would then employ courier companies to collect the parcels and deliver them to his home (or occasionally, to the homes of relatives), where he would make up the orders and forward them to customers, in the UK and the Netherlands, either by post or private courier. Bacai set up at least seven mailboxes in false names using false identification documents (supplied by his brother-in-law). This was evidently a low-volume, high-frequency operation; when investigators visited the mailboxes, at least two, and up to ten, parcels containing medicines were awaiting collection in each case. Bacai communicated with other members of the network via Skype; in particular, with an individual based in New Delhi and another contact in the UK known as Noor. In lieu of payment for his work distributing medicines, Noor sometimes provided Bacai with large quantities of Golden Virginia tobacco.

Bacai pleaded guilty to five offences, resulting in a total prison sentence of three years and eight months.

Drivers and Facilitators

While commentators such as Townsend (2009) fear 'sophisticated counterfeiting syndicates are increasingly targeting Britain's network of high-street chemists, hospitals and GP surgeries', most illicit pharmaceuticals appear to be sourced directly by consumers over the internet via 'online pharmacies'. On the whole, the internet plays a much more prominent role in facilitating the illicit trade of pharmaceuticals than that of tobacco or alcohol. The MHRA claims that incidents of falsified medical products entering the UK supply chain have actually reduced since 2007, and notes that, while incidents of falsified medical products reaching pharmacies are relatively rare, 'access to falsified medical products is more common through unregulated websites' (MHRA 2012, p.2).

The common market in the EU is also held to be an important contributing factor in the illicit pharmaceuticals trade. A commonly used term in this area is 'parallel trading', in which products available cheaply in one part of Europe can legally be shifted to another with higher prices. In itself, there is nothing illegal or wrong about properly conducted parallel trading; as much as 25 per cent of Britain's NHS prescriptions arrive via this route, and an estimated 90 per cent of Britain's pharmacies have some products that have come via parallel trade (Clark 2008). However, the system is also open to abuse. The fact that medicines can legally be repackaged is a particular vulnerability; while it is designed to ensure packaging is in the correct language, it allows alternative products to be inserted. Many industry stakeholders believe that the UK is often a major transit point in parallel trading, as the products are seen to come from a credible source and thus reassure buyers.

Organised Crime and Illicit Trade

The previous sections detail subtle differences between the illicit tobacco, alcohol and pharmaceuticals markets. In particular, the methods for making the most profit for organised criminals differ in each case. The illicit tobacco trade is largely concerned with selling illicit white cigarettes to individuals; the illicit alcohol trade mostly consists of taking products out of duty suspense without paying the appropriate taxes, and selling them on to cash-and-carries and other small distributors; and the illicit pharmaceuticals trade focuses its efforts on the internet, selling both counterfeit and unlicensed medicines to consumers online. Despite these differences, there are three major themes common to illicit trade in general, and to that of tobacco, alcohol and pharmaceuticals in particular:

1 Illicit Trade is Considered a Relatively Low-Risk, High-Reward Crime

A comparison is often made between illicit trade in lawful products such as tobacco and alcohol, and the trade in illicit products such as narcotics and arms. The former carries a lower risk of detection by authorities, and sanctions for offences are typically less severe; the profits that can be made, however, are often just as substantial. These profits are often the end goal, but are just as likely to be used to fund further criminality.

Commercial gain is undoubtedly the biggest driving force behind illicit trade, and while it is recognised that the connection made between tax rates and illicit trade may be a simplistic one, it is important to consider the role of market and economic forces, particularly in a trade bloc like the EU. An often overlooked fact is that while initiatives such as free trade zones and bonded warehouses are designed to facilitate trade, they do so for all types of trade, both licit and illicit.

Within the UK, trade growth, health and tax policies all have a significant impact on illicit trade. The UK government must consider this in relation to its tobacco and alcohol policy. Raising the cost of tobacco and alcohol products may be one effective way to discourage excessive consumption of these products on health grounds, but the fact that it also generates a market that is illicit is not often recognised by policymakers. Such tax policies need to reflect consumer affordability, tax rates in neighbouring countries or within a trade bloc and the ease of administration and enforcement. Either such policies need to feature the means to mitigate an increase in illicit trade, or alternative strategies to address the issue need to be considered.

Another key driver of illicit trade is demand from consumers and their willingness to purchase counterfeit and non-duty paid goods; the reason why illicit trade in tobacco, alcohol and pharmaceuticals is such a significant issue is that there is a market for such products in the first place. Surveys examining the UK public's perceptions of illicit trade reveal that the public sees illicit trade in tobacco, alcohol and pharmaceuticals as more pervasive in British society than the government and its agencies currently understand. However, while the public recognises the significant scale of illicit trade, the statistics also reveal that it does not associate it with OCGs. For example, in a survey of 1,000 adults commissioned by the Scottish Government (2013) on perceptions to organised crime, a significant majority (84 per cent) considered organised crime to be a serious issue in Scotland; almost 90 per cent of all respondents, however, did not consider trade in counterfeit goods to be associated with organised crime. The widespread perception is that these are victimless crimes, perpetrated by tax-fiddlers rather than organised criminals. Businesses, and particularly small retail outlets, are also complicit in their willingness to sell on stock that is bought cheaply from illegitimate sources, again not fully appreciating the consequences of their actions.

Throughout the authors' research, stakeholders from all backgrounds agreed that tackling illicit trade could only be done by lowering the rewards available to criminals by addressing this market demand, as well as by raising the risk by improving enforcement and introducing stricter penalties. Frequent complaints are that current sanctions against tobacco smugglers are not strong enough, and do not target the correct people. As Steven Allen, senior global security director at Pfizer, noted in 2008:

> The chances of detection are pretty low and the penalties don't really fit the crime. If you are bringing in cocaine or heroin, you are going to go to prison for the rest of your life. At the moment if you are smuggling in Viagra you may get a slap on the wrist and a fine.
>
> (Clark 2008)

The fear is that weak criminal sanctions affect the risk/reward calculation made by OCGs and do not currently act as a deterrent. If the likelihood of being prosecuted is low and the most serious consequence of being caught is the loss of the contraband (and the majority get through successfully), then there is no real disincentive for groups or individuals to stop their activities. Given the challenges involved in reducing the potential profits from the trade, many believe it is crucial to make penalties more severe, thereby increasing the risk associated with the activity.

HMRC has argued that the UK has 'relatively punitive sanctions for tobacco fraud', although it concedes that 'there are significant profits to be made, notwithstanding the sanctions we have in place, so the balance of risk and reward is one that [criminals] will factor into their decisions' (House of Lords Select Committee on the European Union 2013, p.6). In recent years, HMRC has also begun to question the effectiveness of prosecutions compared with civil sanctions; in many cases, civil action can have a more disruptive effect on OCG activities, particularly when it is used to punish those 'further down the food chain'. However, levels of understanding of how and when to use such sanctions are currently poor, and HMRC's strategy to combine criminal with civil action is unclear to other government departments, let alone the public at large.

2 Illicit Trade is Increasingly a Low-Volume, High-Frequency Activity

OCGs have begun to realise that law-enforcement agencies find it much more difficult to respond to illicit trade when goods are broken down and transported in smaller consignments (although this is not always the case for smuggling alcohol). The role of quantitative and qualitative thresholds in understanding and responding to illicit trade was a key theme to emerge from the research. While 'little and often' shipments may increase costs for criminals, the fact that such consignments do not reach the authorities' thresholds means that it also lowers the chances of interception, particularly if the OCGs use a variety of routes to transport illicit goods.

OCGs frequently transport their goods along established commercial routes via shipping containers, road networks and the postal system. Maintaining an appropriate presence at all of the 140 sea- and airports across the UK and overseas where the Border Force operates remains a significant challenge for the agency. The scale and volume of the traffic passing through the UK's biggest airports (London Heathrow, London Gatwick and Manchester) and seaports (Felixstowe, Southampton and the Thames Estuary) make policing these facilities extremely difficult and resource-intensive. Given limited resources, the agency must prioritise the most high-risk ports of entry, based on periodic risk assessments, leading to inevitable vulnerabilities at ports and along routes that are less well established and less well monitored. Private courier services are one example, as are private charter flights and unmanned general aviation terminals. Approximately 90,000 inbound private international flights land at around 3,700 sites across the UK each year, ranging from international airports to unmanned locations, including helipads and farm strips (House of Commons Public Accounts Committee 2013b).

To a greater extent than authorities perhaps realise, OCGs conduct frequent 'test runs' to discover how much they can get away with transporting via a particular route, and adapt their methods accordingly, taking alternative routes if necessary. This is a major challenge to the government's response, not least because it challenges the current 'thresholds' approach designed to help prioritise cases.

Nowhere is this issue more evident than in the fast parcel and postal service sector; the NCA (2014, p.11) has noted that 'Fast parcels and postal services are used frequently for "little and often" trafficking ventures'. The Border Force reported that, while smaller individual consignments sent via post do not represent a high risk, on aggregate they are a 'massive problem'. Given the sheer scale of this sector—20,000 to 25,000 parcels pass through Coventry International Postal Hub alone every day—law-enforcement efforts are time-consuming and resource-intensive. Officers admitted that small consignments are more than likely to slip through the net, given the limited resources available and the focus on parcels above a certain weight threshold. Unlike countries such as Australia, where there are X-ray machines over all in-feed belts at postal hubs, UK facilities such as Coventry International Hub rely on intelligence-led profiling of parcels and a focus on higher-risk categories above a set threshold.

The trend towards using private couriers is already being noticed by the Border Force (and also by the Home Office, which is engaging with the industry). The sorting facilities of these private companies do not have a consistent Border Force presence and, given their commercial drive for operational efficiencies, the checks on incoming parcels may be less stringent.

3 Illicit Trade is Increasingly Diverse in its Products, Routes and Methods

As the previous point demonstrates, OCGs are able to quickly adapt to law-enforcement action and diversify their goods and techniques to further reduce risk. The internet allows OCGs to quickly identify new markets, routes and facilitators.

Collecting, sharing and analysing timely intelligence on these changes is a continuous challenge. On the whole, intelligence in this area is patchy and of varying quality and is not used in a sophisticated manner by the relevant agencies. Too much intelligence is left on 'the cutting room floor' rather than helping develop a useful strategic assessment. Reports from the National Audit Office (2012) have highlighted that HMRC, in particular, needs better intelligence on the distribution networks used by organised criminal gangs in the UK and the way in which money is transferred along the supply chain. The authors' research found that challenges remain in the collection of intelligence and its management across different organisations. Relevant agencies do not necessarily connect the dots and are therefore unable to develop a strategic intelligence picture of the illicit trade both in the UK and overseas (primarily in priority countries). HMRC recognises this challenge, and a new project focused on building and sharing intelligence is under way.

Conclusion

Illicit goods such as tobacco, alcohol and pharmaceuticals are within easy reach of consumers. These goods are in demand, available on tap, and represent a significant risk to public safety, community well-being and consumer health. The OCGs behind the activity are largely invisible to members of the public, who demonstrate complicity in their willingness to purchase what many know to be counterfeit goods. The methods of OCGs are ever-more sophisticated and evolve rapidly. Globalised supply chains and low-cost carriers have changed business models and in turn the ways in which OCGs conduct trade. Small volumes of illicit goods (to avoid detection) moved frequently (to meet demand) result in large rewards for some OCGs. The result is that the activities of illicit traders are largely hidden in plain sight, operating below the radar and on a small scale so as not to meet the threshold for law-enforcement action.

This is the modern face of organised crime in the UK: diverse, sophisticated, networked and largely invisible to the general public. The risk to the public is, however, different than in previous generations. The violence traditionally associated with serious and organised crime (for example, in the drugs trade) is no longer a key characteristic of the illicit trade in lawful goods. Instead, the trade involves bribery and corruption—both in the public and private sectors. Where once there was competition between rival gangs, there is now an incentive for co-operation in managing complex supply chains in order to improve profits. The traditional role of the 'enforcer' has been replaced by accountants, lawyers and business service providers who may wittingly or unwittingly be facilitating organised crime.

The illicit trade in tobacco, alcohol and pharmaceuticals thereby reflects the likely future trajectory of organised crime in the UK, and to counter the threat the government and relevant law enforcement agencies will have to respond to four key trends in the future:

   Acceptability: The illicit trade is widely seen as a victimless crime and the public is largely tolerant of purchasing illicit goods even if this is seen as morally wrong. While the illicit trade has been around for decades, it has become more prevalent with the onset of the global economic recession. The acceptability of the illicit trade and the tolerance shown towards the black market economy is a serious challenge to government policy to reduce organised crime.

Diversification: The second key trend this chapter has identified is OCGs diversifying their portfolio of criminal activities. Some OCGs have clearly moved away from high-risk activities (such as drug trafficking) and into cigarette smuggling. The returns on what are perceived to be low-risk, high-frequency activities are considerable. Diversification also brings OCGs into contact with each other; EUROPOL has highlighted the fact that traditional OCGs have morphed into networks of criminality, suggesting an increase in co-operation and collaboration across multiple jurisdictions.

Accessibility: A third trend reflects the evolution in global trade, and that is the accessibility of illicit goods and services, which in the UK is helped by inadequate enforcement across the EU, reduced customs controls and corruption in a number of EU member states. The internet has increased the accessibility of illicit goods and services, creating new markets in both developed and developing countries. It has also reduced the fixed and variable costs of entering international markets for consumers and OCGs. The high number of internet users and online payment systems in the UK has ensured that there is an infrastructure to support the growth of the illicit trade online.

Invisibility: The fourth and final trend is the growing invisibility of illicit trade. While many researchers and commentators have focused on the use of the internet as a major trend in organised crime (particularly cyber-crime), it is also worth noting that the internet makes organised crime less visible. With the click of a mouse, delivery by Parcel Force or FedEx, and online customer reviews, illicit trade remains unseen by communities and out of the reach of law-enforcement agencies.

The evolution of serious and organised crime raises questions about its impact on society and whether the absence of a visible threat has given way to an invisible and more corrosive danger, as communities are co-opted, governance structures are undermined and changes in the tactics of organised criminals overwhelm the agencies in charge. The government will need to tackle this challenge head-on; recognising the significant scale and impact of more 'hidden' threats such as illicit trade would be a good starting point.

Note

1 The original version of this paper was published as Charlie Edwards and Calum Jeffray, 'On Tap: Organised Crime and the Illicit Trade in Tobacco, Alcohol and Pharmaceuticals in the UK', RUSI Whitehall Paper 3–14 (London: RUSI Publications, December 2014).

References

Action on Smoking and Health. *Illicit Trade: Overview*. [Online] Available from: http://ash.org.uk/pathfinder/illicit-trade [Accessed 1 December 2014].

All Party Parliamentary Group on Smoking and Health. (2013), *Inquiry into the Illicit Trade in Tobacco Products*. [Online] Available from: http://www.ash.org.uk/APP Gillicit2013 [Accessed 1 December 2014].

Clark, E. (2008), Counterfeit Medicines: The Pills that Kill, *Daily Telegraph*, 5 April 2008.

Financial Action Task Force. (2012), *Illicit Tobacco Trade*. [Online] Available from: http://www.fatf-gafi.org/media/fatf/documents/reports/Illicit%20Tobacco%20Trade.pdf [Accessed 27 November 2014].

Finlay, B. (2011), *Counterfeit Drugs and National Security*. [Online] Available from: http://www.stimson.org/images/uploads/research-pdfs/Full_-_Counterfeit_Drugs_and_National_Security.pdf [Accessed 27 November 2014].

HM Government. (2013), *Serious and Organised Crime Strategy*, London: The Stationery Office (Cm 8715).

HM Revenue and Customs. (2011), *Tackling Tobacco Smuggling—Building on Our Success: A Renewed Strategy for HM Revenue and Customs and the UK Border Agency.*

HM Revenue and Customs. (2012), *Alcohol Fraud: Legislative Measures to Tackle Existing and Emerging Threats to the UK Alcohol Duty Regime* (Consultation Document).

HM Revenue and Customs. (2013), *HMRC Measuring Tax Gaps 2013 Edition: Tax Gap Estimates for 2011–12* (Official Statistics Release).

HM Revenue and Customs. (2014), *Tobacco Tax Gap Estimates 2013 to 2014* (Official Statistics Release).

House of Commons Home Affairs Committee. (2014), *Written Evidence to Tobacco Smuggling Inquiry*, London: The Stationary Office (First Report of Session 2014–15, HC200). [Online] Available at: http://www.parliament.uk/documents/commons-committees/home-affairs/Tobacco-written-evidence.pdf [Accessed 1 December 2014].

House of Commons Public Accounts Committee. (2012), *HM Revenue and Customs: Renewed Alcohol Strategy*, London: The Stationery Office (Sixth Report of Session 2012–13, HC 504).

House of Commons Public Accounts Committee. (2013a), *HM Revenue and Customs: Progress in Tackling Tobacco Smuggling*, London: The Stationery Office (Twenty-third Report of Session 2013–14, HC 226).

House of Commons Public Accounts Committee. (2013b), *The Border Force: Securing the Border*, London: The Stationery Office (Thirty-first Report of Session 2013/14, HC 663).

House of Lords Select Committee on the European Union. (2013), *Oral Evidence to Enhanced Security: EU Cigarette Smuggling Strategy Inquiry*, Evidence Session No.2. [Online] Available at: http://www.parliament.uk/documents/lords-committees/eu-sub-com-f/tobaccosmuggling/cHMRCoral.pdf [Accessed 1 December 2014].

Joossens, L. and Raw, M. (2012), From Cigarette Smuggling to Illicit Tobacco Trade. *Tobacco Control*. 21 (2), 230–234.

McKee, M., Adany, R. and Leon, D. (2012), Illegally Produced Alcohol: Is Increasingly Available in the UK and Will Add to Alcohol's Already Great Threat to Public Health. *British Medical Journal*. 344 (1146), 10.

McNeill, A., Iringe-Koko, B., Bains, M., Bauld, L., Siggens, G. and Russell, A. (2014), Countering the Demand for, and Supply of, Illicit Tobacco: An Assessment of the 'North of England Tackling Illicit Tobacco for Better Health' Programme. *Tobacco Control.* 23 (1) 44–50.

Medicines and Healthcare Products Regulatory Agency. (2012), *Falsified Medical Products Strategy 2012–2015.* http://webarchive.nationalarchives.gov.uk/2014 1205150130/http://www.mhra.gov.uk/home/groups/ei/documents/websiteresources/con149816.pdf.

Medicines and Healthcare Products Regulatory Agency. (2014), *UK Leads the way with £8.6 Million Seizure in International Operation Targeting Dangerous Counterfeit, Controlled and Unlicensed Medicines* [Press release]. [Accessed 22 May 2014].

National Audit Office. (2012), *HM Revenue and Customs: Renewed Alcohol Strategy: A Progress Report*, London: The Stationery Office (HC 1702).

National Crime Agency. (2014), *National Strategic Assessment of Serious and Organised Crime 2014.*

Reynolds, L. and McKee, M. (2010), Organised Crime and the Efforts To Combat It: A Concern for Public Health. *Globalization and Health.* 6 (1). Online journal: http://link.springer.com/journal/12992/6/1/page/1.

Scottish Government. (2013), *Public Perceptions of Organised Crime in Scotland* (Scottish Government Social Research).

Shelley, L. and Melzer, S. (2008), The Nexus of Organized Crime and Terrorism: Two Case Studies in Cigarette Smuggling. *International Journal of Comparative and Applied Criminal Justice.* 32 (1), 43–63.

Townsend, M. (2009), Health Fears Grow as Fake Drugs Flood into Britain, *The Guardian*, 4 January 2009.

Van Dijck, M. (2009) 'Cigarette Shuffle: Organising Tobacco Tax Evasion in the Netherlands', in P. C. Van Duyne (ed) *The Criminal Smoke of Tobacco Policy Making: Cigarette Smuggling in Europe.* Nijmegen: Wolf Legal Publishers.

World Customs Organisation. (2013), *Illicit Trade Report 2012*, Brussels: World Customs Organization.

World Health Organisation. (2003), *Framework Convention on Tobacco Control*, Geneva: WHO Press.

World Health Organisation. (2010), Growing Threat from Counterfeit Medicines. *Bulletin of the World Health Organization.* 88 (4), 241–320.

World Health Organisation. (2011), *Global Status Report on Alcohol and Health*, Geneva: WHO Press.

9 Reconsidering Middle Markets

Daniel Silverstone

This chapter draws on the work of the late Geoff Pearson, in particular the Middle Market Drug Distribution Study he and Dick Hobbs undertook for the Home Office in 2001. It argues that their three key points regarding the limited size of criminal organisations operating within middle market; the relative lack of violence and the importance of ethnicity in understanding middle market activity retain currency and are now widely supported by later work. In keeping with the applied nature of the study, the chapter then considers subsequent Home Office reactions to the threat of organised crime. It argues that despite the modest threat posed by organised crime, both academics and governments have either dismissed or overacted to it, thereby ignoring a radical and liberal solution to the problem.

The chapter draws on the inspiration gained from reading and enjoying the work of the late Geoff Pearson. I met Geoff on two occasions only, the first, at the London School of Economics, when he was external examiner for my Viva. The examination was uneventful but we did have a single heated exchange over the subject of smoking cocaine! I had pointed out that some door-staff (about whom I was conducting an ethnography) and punters smoke cocaine surreptitiously by licking their cigarettes and sticking cocaine onto it (Silverstone, 2003). Geoff disputed the likelihood of this and argued that the pharmacology of the drug means that it vaporises at a high temperature, so doubted anyone would indulge in something so wasteful. However, I insisted they did, and a disagreement ensued.

Ultimately, regardless of the physiological effect (it is acknowledged that there are stimulant effects if the cocaine is heated for long enough), it was agreed that, as with many other illicit drug practices, explanations for their use cannot be reduced to simple effects but rather have to be placed within a social context. The context was a pre-smoking ban nightclub in the late nineties when the bitter-smelling smoke of cocaine burning distinguished the smoker, a demonstration to those in the 'know' that they possessed the drug and were extravagant in their tastes. It was a visceral example of excessive consumption, which for them and many others is a key 'aspect for illegal market engagement' (Hobbs, 2013; 229).

Whilst I didn't see Geoff in those exaggerated terms, my observations of him were that he personally enjoyed life and intellectually he understood that enjoying life is an integral part of the human condition, something stimulated by, but not reduced to the manipulations of a 'Consumer Society' (Hall, 2012). His research interests and passionate following of football, in particular Manchester United, meant he would have had little truck with those puritanical scholars, who want to recast popular pastimes through the lens of psychoanalytical theory. He didn't need convoluted theoretical gymnastics to understand that people of all classes need palliative pursuits, whether they are legal or illegal, to negotiate their lives. Instead, he was keen to situate our 'vices' both within a historical context and within the structural conditions that often determine our tastes and habits.

On Methodology

The second time I met Geoff was when he was sitting on the advisory board for a project entitled, *Understanding Drug Selling in Communities: Insider or Outsider Trading* (May et al. 2005), whereas I was a researcher who later resigned indignant. Tasked with handing out leaflets to local drug dealers on parts of an estate out of bounds for local law enforcement (and now demolished), and meeting hostility, I brought with me a long-standing friend who is far larger, taller and better trained than myself. However, the project's sponsors upbraided me as he wasn't insured and I churlishly resigned. The story deserves mention, as one of the aims of the research was trying to entangle whose claims of territoriality in relation to selling drugs on the estate were to be believed. On the one hand, interviews with local drug users indicated that there were several drug-dealing networks operating within the estate, whilst on the other, interviews with the local council indicated that the area was controlled by a local street gang. It needed physical scoping to resolve.

These kinds of methodological issues are germane to researching organised crime generally and to Geoff's work in particular. Geoff preferred to get close to his respondents (Pearson, 1987; Pearson, 2013), but this chapter will focus on one study when this wasn't possible, the Home Office publication, *Middle Markets* (Pearson & Hobbs, 2001). Despite the scale of drug business in this country and its enduring nature, there have been very few studies of those involved in the upper and middle echelons of the drug trade (Dorn, Murji & South, 1992; Dorn, Levi & King, 2005; Matrix Knowledge Consultancy, 2007), with this particular study being amongst the best. Unlike his other work, this was based on prison interviews with convicted drug dealers and those policing them. The methodology was one of necessity, because the authors observed at the time, because of restrictions with British law, British scholars of organised crime have fewer methodological tools at their disposal than their European counterparts.[1] However, they rightly felt that these limitations could be overcome by triangulating law enforcement interviews with prison-based interviews and a literature review.

Clearly, beyond a literature review, neither methodology is straightforward. As Hallsworth (2013) reminds us, it is right to exercise caution when listening to accounts of what he labels 'control agents'. Yet equally, experience in and out of the academy indicates that there are numerous shrewd, well-informed and now reflective (being degree educated!) law enforcement officials. However, it is frustrating that their ability to share their insights can be restricted by secretive classification systems which, although necessary, have been criticised by those working inside this covert arena, as overly cautious and restrictive (Stanier, 2012). Equally, prison interviews can be rewarding but again, their limitations and the skills required to overcome them, need to be acknowledged: Different prison governors provide different levels of hospitality regarding interviewing arrangements, with some being conducted on wings of prisons and others in visiting rooms. Meeting someone only once, for under an hour—someone who can be from a different ethnicity, age and background—and expecting them to be frank, on tape, whilst prison officers lurk not too far away in the background is a skilled business. In both my experience and the experience of the authors of this report, for meaningful disclosure to occur, it is vital to use interviewers who understand prison slang and are familiar with the prices and mores of the drug world (Pearson & Hobbs, 2001; Hales, Lewis & Silverstone, 2003). The problem, however, can be the latter person will often fail any security clearances demanded to gain access to the former!

The Structure of the Middle Market and the Structure of Organised Crime in the UK

Despite these potential methodological limitations, this was a rare occasion when a Home Office initiative coincided with an academic imperative to produce a seminal report which successfully filled a lacuna in our knowledge concerning how the drug market works. The report came to three important conclusions, all three of which are supported by subsequent work and it is argued, apply to the wider structural characteristics and practices of organised crime in the UK. First:

> Although drug markets are hierarchical, in that transactions involve market-defined roles of responsibility, risk and reward, they are also highly flexible with the possibility for roles of supplier and buyer to be interchangeable at wholesale and middle market levels. Criminal networks involved in middle market drug distribution are typically small, with a correspondingly small number of suppliers and customers. The notion of organised crime groups as tightly organised, complex and hierarchical entities whose tentacles reach around the globe is not supported by our evidence. They are more usefully understood as networks.
>
> (Pearson & Hobbs, 2001; vi)

More recently, this conclusion has been echoed by Paoli, Greenfield & Reuter (2009; 205) in their review of the global heroin market who argue the 'academic literature, the grey literature, and other sources also that in North

America, Western Europe, and Australia, the great majority of drug deals, even those involving large quantities of drugs, are carried out by relatively small and often ephemeral enterprises'.[2] This broad conclusion is also supported by Morselli, Turcotte & Tenti (2010; 4) who reviewed the global literature on the mobility of criminal groups in an attempt to distil the broader evidence of push and pull factors to help us understand how and why criminal groups move across a variety of settings. Although they did not specifically review the literature on the size of criminals groups, their conclusion bears heavily on this question. They conclude that:

> There is little evidential support for those who claim that criminal organizations are intentionally or strategically mobilizing themselves to seize opportunities in various geographical locations across the world 'and that for a criminal group to expand is much more difficult than often believed in popular circles largely because no single criminal group can realistically do everything and be everywhere all the time'.
>
> Morselli, Turcotte & Tenti (2010; 4)

Although my recent research work regarding South East Asian crime groups in the UK is only tangentially aimed at the drugs markets,[3] it does add support to the evidence previously outlined. The growth of criminality within the Vietnamese community is worth reviewing first. During the past fourteen years, there has been a gradual increase in the domestic cultivation of cannabis (which, despite the so-called arrival of 'designer drugs', remains by far Britain's most popular illegal drug; ECMDDA, 2014), in particular the goring of 'skunk' and a move away from the importation and use of hashish, often from Morocco. This has also been evident elsewhere in Europe, where the increase in domestic cannabis production has meant new criminal actors entering what is a large market (ibid.). However, despite these changes, there hasn't been as first thought, an increase in the size of criminal groups operating within it. Research in the UK and Holland shows, in fact, as Pearson and Hobbs would have expected, that Vietnamese criminal groups also try to remain mobile and flexible and to keep their operations relatively small. There simply haven't been obvious attempts by criminal networks to carve out monopolising positions.

Instead, the vast majority of Vietnamese groups in the UK are formed of a mixture of law-abiding people forging symbiotic relationships with irregular migrants working to generate revenue. In addition, the specific question of strategic movement of Vietnamese criminal groups into cannabis production was reviewed in the Netherlands, where an increasing involvement of Vietnamese migrants in cannabis cultivation was also noticed. Dutch scholars[4] argue that there are differences between the countries and in Holland key participants are predominantly more established Vietnamese citizens, rather than irregular migrants (Schoenmakers, Bremmers & Kleemans, 2013). However, they also agree that for the most part, those involved were emergent rather than strategic actors and there was no evidence of attempts to impose a monopoly on the market.

Turning to Chinese organised crime, although there remain criminal vestiges and inflated rumours of Triad influence, their everyday activities have been significantly curtailed.[5] This is due to the Triads' hierarchical structures being too cumbersome to benefit from transnational criminal enterprises such as people-smuggling or counterfeit-cigarette selling which depend on fluid networks. In the UK, rather than the hierarchical and large structures of Triads, different networks of criminals provide niche services. The provision of illegal migratory services, the provision of illegal papers or illegal work in the UK and the provision of illegal goods from China are all delivered by separate discrete networks. Outside of these ethnic enclaves, ongoing interviews with law enforcement officials pertaining to those involved with the importation of heroin and cocaine also suggest that brokers exist, who will put a variety of criminal groups in touch with producers of drugs. Again, one of their keys to longevity is they are part of networks, characterised by flexibility rather than size (Silverstone, 2011; Dees, 2012; Wang, 2013).

The second enduring point to emerge from the Middle Markets' report was that it ignored the popular imaginings of drug turf wars and ultra-violence and instead concluded:

> Business principles are predominant in the potentially lucrative drugs market, which means that violence-avoidance is the more general rule. Violence attracts attention and is bad for business. Violence is most usefully understood as a consequence of market dysfunction and disorganization.
> (Pearson & Hobbs, 2001; vi).

Both parts of this insight have been confirmed by later work. Indeed a recent study carried out by Tzanetakis (2013; 6) on the conduct of the high-level drug business in Germany concludes, 'Using violence was rarely a means of settling conflicts. On the contrary, building relationships of trust between the actors of the network and the source of supply was mutually beneficial for both sides'. As I have found, there have been incidences of violent murders within both the Chinese and Vietnamese diaspora populations (Silverstone, 2010; 2011; Dees, 2012). However, given the amounts of money available, the lack of violence, or certainly the incidence of reported violence which takes place at the middle and higher area of the drug market, is actually remarkable.[6] Indeed, the standard mode of operation displayed, for example, by Vietnamese crime groups, is violence avoidance rather than confrontation with other criminal networks. However, for the drug business to operate in an unregulated market the threat of violence clearly exists. For example, recent research on cocaine traffickers suggests that family members or associates can be effectively held in ransom in the sending country, until receipt of large cocaine shipments (Campana, 2011). In relation to trafficking and distribution of drugs into the UK, when arrangements break down and serious violence does occur, it is likely that fatal violence happens out of this country where police corruption is more endemic and investigative resources are perhaps more crude (Silverstone, forthcoming).

Thirdly, Pearson and Hobbs (2001) make the point that ethnicity is important in understanding the structure and extent of organised crime groups: 'kinship and ethnicity in drug networks remains important, in that these are the traditional sources of trust in non-legal (that is, criminal) business enterprise' but they also point out its limitations, as 'market principles require that crime networks reach beyond these narrow and traditional means of securing and enforcing trust'. This is clearly contentious territory as there is a long-standing and disproportionate association with ethnicity and crime in traditional accounts of organised crime. However, again, it is argued that the authors strike the correct balance.

Ethnicity does need to be considered as an important variable in understanding the structure and success of drug networks or other organised crime groups[7]. This is amongst other factors such as the social economic background of the participants and the law enforcement actions of the state from which they originate, as well as the gains to be made within the grey or black economy. The operations of drug markets are often mono-ethnic until the point of distribution, so being able to converse with, and be sympathetic to difference is critical for this area of research. Regarding both the 'Chinese' and the 'Vietnamese', there is a tendency for the press to embark on 'orientalist' positions, which focus on the inflated risks posed by these different groups. For example, journalists report on 'Sex Slaves', (Lakhani, 2007) in relation to the purported rise in trafficking (CEOP, 2007) or of closed and complex hawala methods of banking, whereas the reality is more mundane. The sex business is actually ordered in ways similar to their Western counterparts, with the majority of those involved just making money in unremarkable ways (Chin & Finckenauer, 2012). Whilst as has recently been revealed regarding HSBC, there is no need to indulge in esoteric money laundering processes when you can simply deposit your ill-gotten gains via student accounts in your (Go)local bank (BBC, 2012)!

When considering how ethnicity interacts with organised criminality, the similarities across ethnicities are striking. Once past the obscuring misnomers of 'Chinese', 'East European', 'Nigerian' or indeed 'British' organised crime, the researcher must drill down to consider, what are the key mechanisms which enable trust to be sustained within illicit and transnational markets? Initially, it is often apparent that different ethnic groups will characterise the workings of trust mechanisms in their own language, often in self-aggrandising ways, and stress their importance. For example, 'Chinese' criminal respondents can characterise their networks of mutual obligations as Guanxi, whilst the 'Vietnamese' do not use this concept; they can explain their criminal success in terms of having an understanding of familial obligations which work across large families in ways which are superficially different from those which are present within the traditional understanding of the family in the UK. Yet, although it is wise to be sensitive to these cultural nuances, their impact can be exaggerated. In fact, studies of Dutch, Italian and British[8] organised crime also show family networks of obligation that stretch beyond the immediate confines of the 'nuclear' family and yet in explaining their criminal success the importance of their 'ethnic culture' is often unremarked on.

Equally, when the geography of organised crime is unpacked, the similarities between those from 'Chinese', 'Vietnamese' and European backgrounds are apparent. The spread of organised crime is not even but concentrated within specific parts of specific places (Silverstone, 2013a and b). For example, within the illegal Vietnamese diaspora in the UK, there is a predominance of criminal actors from Haiphong which is hard to explain without resorting to accounts of the city's geographical position and its historical experience. Whilst recent work on Chinese organized crime argues that illegal migrants and organised crime networks within them originate disproportionately from the province of Fujian and more specifically on the city of Futsing (Zhang, 2008; Silverstone & Whittle, 2016). In so doing there are echoes of their European counterparts, where key criminal families in key cities and ports in Liverpool or in the south of the Netherlands operate over generations (Spapens, 2012).

The Reactionary Response

As is outlined in the previous discussion, thirteen years ago, Pearson and Hobbs argued that the picture of the middle market drug economy was a nuanced one. There existed multiple business-oriented, flexible, small, often mono-ethnic groups willing and able to network with others like them across the globe. Therefore, Pearson's and Hobbs's recommendations made in 2001 were appropriately modest, that there were first 'issues of resource allocation' and second, 'also that there was perceived drift "up-stream" of anti-drug enforcement efforts, with the risk of leaving a "void" in lower and middle-levels of intelligence'(ibid., 2001; ix). Both of these suggestions were accepted by law enforcement and resolved by the formation of the 'Middle Market Drugs project, launched in 2003, consisting of a varied group of officers, aimed at dismantling networks that operate within the middle level of the class A drug market' (Metropolitan Police, 2005).

This chapter updates their analysis, to argue that the picture they painted has not substantially changed and is also likely to correspond to the workings of other traditional organised crime practices. Clearly, new actors have entered the drug market (although some still remain) as have new synthetic drugs and new legal and undocumented diaspora communities,[9] but none of these changes has meant the emergence of any (ultra-violent or not) criminal organisation able or willing to dominate/monopolise the drug market or pose an existential threat to the state. In summary, organised criminals have become more diverse in a more interconnected world as has the non-criminal population. Yet, this has not heralded an era of rising crime but rather its opposite—falling crime rates.

Yet this somewhat comforting picture does not reflect the position taken by an increasingly punitive state. During the interceding decade, successive governments have trumpeted successive organised crime strategies, each including growing numbers of organised criminals and growing fiscal losses to UK PLC[10] (HMIC, 2005; HMG, 2011; HMG, 2013). These could be dismissed as relatively harmless,[11] as fanciful estimates based on a well-intentioned desire to quantify something which, because of issues of definition and methodological weaknesses (see the Methodology section in this chapter), is ultimately impossible to quantify. Certainly, even within law enforcement there is a degree of cynicism over the accuracy of how organised crime is defined.[12] For example, do organised crime matrices in the UK include members of organised motorcycle gangs such as the Hell Angels and Banditos (Silverstone & Crane, 2016)? Or most recently, regarding the latest Impact Assessment for participatory offences for the Serious Crime Bill (released on 22/4/2014) which contains the figures, '5,500 active organised crime groups, comprising, 37,000 people'. Whilst the 'Fact Sheet', submitted two months later in June, mentions '5,300 active organised crime groups operating against the UK, comprising about 36,600 people'.[13] This is a reduction of 200 groups but only 400 people, indicating that 'group' must be defined loosely and if we use a mean figure, each group would have had two people in it! It also implies that there has been a significant amount of successful enforcement activity or un-promoted group dissolution, within only two months!

However, to dismiss the construction of threat would be to ignore the way the apparent growth of organised crime has been instrumental in changing the nature of its policing and the corresponding legislation. First, as others have argued, from the inception of the Serious Organised Crime Agency (SOCA) to the creation of the National Crime Agency (NCA) there has been an increase in the centralisation of specialised policing and an increase in the powers available to these officers. Secondly, there have been several new legal initiatives which blur the historic division between the criminal and civil law, allowing the civil law's lower burden of proof to be used to target the most serious criminals.

The first innovation of SOCA with its officers unrivalled powers and has been much remarked upon elsewhere (Bowling & Ross, 2006; Harfield, 2006; Sproat, 2014). Whilst there are long-standing criticisms concerning the effectiveness of SOCA and already doubts concerning the NCA, it is argued here that a robust national police agency response is necessary in the fluid world of organised crime previously described where organised criminals, especially those involved in drugs, will bamboozle policing based on forty-three police areas. This is especially the case where a National Intelligence Model already often artificially splits up organised crime groups into three levels, local, regional and national and international level, whereas in practice, middle market brokers and many others usually operate at all three levels (Gilmour, 2008; Silverstone, 2010).

Much more troubling has been the growth of pre-emptive criminalisation and the emergence of powers which blur the historic division between criminal and civil law, aptly described by John Lea, as 'a full frontal assault on due process'. This trend began with the Proceeds of Crime Act (POCA) in 2002,[14] and is most pronounced in the Serious Crime Bill 2014, where there are several completely new, or new additions to, existing initiatives which rely on the civil burden of proof to prosecute but then attract serious custodial sentences if not obeyed. These initiatives include: widening the scope of POCA to stop the hiding of assets with partners; increasing the scope of the Serious Crime Prevention Orders[15] by adding further trigger offences such as the cultivation of cannabis; increasing the use of its financial cousin the Financial Reporting Order; and the broadening of the scope of the gang injunction[16] in relation to a more expansive definition of a gang, to include the threat posed by organised crime.[17] Finally there is a proposed offence of 'participation in the activities of an organised crime group'. This deliberate attempt to imitate American RICO legislation needs elaborating in greater detail as 'the aim is to make it easier to prosecute those who support organised criminal activity but also those at the top of the organisation who attempt to detach themselves from the activities they control directly'.

There are two critical aspects to this new offence. First, as with the other initiatives concerned with organised crime, it is not considered necessary to prove the offence beyond reasonable doubt. Instead, as the Home Office outlines:

> Knowledge is considered the highest level (which the offence of 'conspiracy' requires) followed by recklessness, belief (which the 'encouraging and assisting' offence requires). Lower than belief is reasonable grounds to suspect and then suspicion at the lowest. The mental element of the new offence will be 'knowledge or reasonable grounds to suspect'. This means that the jury must be satisfied that the defendant at least had reasonable grounds to have suspected that they were involved in organised crime.
>
> (Home Office, 2014; 3)

The second significant aspect of this legislation is the broad definition of organised crime,[18] which omits to mention any specific motivation such as financial (as in previous definitions) and also omits any mention of a sustained endeavour, or of a formalised structure, let alone issues of corruption or the use of serious violence, seen in definitions used by law enforcement elsewhere.[19]

The cumulative effect of these changes could mean that those suspected of being members of organised crime groups could be subject to a barrage of powers—participatory offences, Serious Crime Prevention orders, Proceeds of Crime confiscation orders and Financial Reporting Orders, which could then lead to heavy prison sentences for people who have not committed any serious sexual or violent offence. Perhaps, these powers might be necessary if the UK was in the midst of takeover by violent monopolising 'Mafias', but in their absence it is much more likely that they will be used 'imaginatively', that is, to target the 'usual suspects', those purported criminals who reside in the UK and are therefore more vulnerable to traditional investigative measures. This is especially the case when many defendants are no longer able to automatically rely on skilled council because of the restrictions imposed by the Legal Aid, Sentencing and Punishment of Offenders Bill 2012. Ultimately, the punitive effects of the legislation are bound to be felt by those who are already subject to existing Gang Injunctions, joint enterprise and intelligence matrices, and it is argued that the combined weight of these initiatives could make the UK vulnerable in relation to its obligations to the Human Rights Act, where Article 6 states that we should not punish anyone without fair trial.

The Future: Structural Pathos or Liberal Agency

This exaggerated response to organised crime has been mirrored by an exaggerated critique of how organised crime has merged with the legitimate economy. It is tempting, as recent critics from the left have done, to argue that in post-industrial times, there has been a structural normalisation of organised crime: we need to face up to the fact that all too often it is not possible to disaggregate criminal and legal activities 'where the penetration of market forces into British society has enabled the normalization of individualistic and predatory relationships' (Hobbs, 2013; 234).

However, whilst accepting the core tenets of this thesis—that at a structural level, British society has become increasingly unequal; that policing frequently exacerbates this inequality and that consumerism has become one of our dominant ideologies—the evidence presented in this chapter cannot support the contention that there is no longer a distinction between organised crime and wider society (Wilkinson & Pickett, 2010; Reiner, 2012; Silverstone, 2013a and b). Instead, it is argued here, that collapsing the activities of organised criminals into a broader critique of a predatory system is too defeatist and does not do justice to either the existence of discrete pernicious organised crime groups or the inadequacies of the state's punitive response.

Although not an existential threat, it seems that currently, groups faced with punitive but ill-informed law enforcement not only exist but also can thrive. Take two examples from my recent work: In 2011 it was noted regarding Chinese smuggling that 'there are also several exam agencies offering applicants 100% confidence of passing the International English Language Testing system'(Silverstone, 2011; 66), whilst in 2014, an investigation by the BBC found 'systematic fraud' in the UK's student immigration system, with agencies offering to help applicants who could not speak English to pass the government's English test by arranging for someone fluent in English to take the oral English test and providing all the answers to the multiple choice test'. In relation to cannabis cultivation it was opined in 2010 that, without more representative and in-depth community policing engagement reform, 'existing criminal methods will be replicated by other emerging crime groups' (Silverstone, 2010; 9). By 2013, new criminal groups had moved into cannabis cultivation in a significant way and an increasing number of cannabis farms were being detected: '7,865 projected for 2011–12 compared with 6,866 in 2009–10 when the last problem profile was published' (ACPO, 2013; 1).

Therefore, it is argued that a far more effective response to the contemporary cosmopolitan threat from organised crime is to return to the types of pragmatic recommendations made in the Middle Market report. These reforms ought to have three broad strands which can be briefly outlined here. First, law enforcement must improve. This means addressing enduring issues of information hoarding and over-classification mentioned in the Introduction (Sheptycki, 2004; Stanier, 2013). Secondly, law enforcement must diversify and become more representative of the communities they represent. For the existing workforce tasked with confronting organised crime, there is an urgent need to mainstream language and/or cultural skills, and they can look to their counterparts in the diplomatic service for help with this. Thirdly, in relation to reforming our legislation, reformers need to urgently look across the pond. Here under Obama's stewardship, the United States, having already decriminalised prostitution in some states, has now decriminalised cannabis in others and has most recently offered (a limited) amnesty to illegal migrants and their offspring currently living there.

The fact that arguing for the decriminalisation of prostitution and cannabis and an amnesty for illegal migrants is seen as far from pragmatic is testament to how effective the bogeyman creation of organised crime currently is. Yet as the Home Secretary struggles with the apparition of 'modern slavery', the enormous bill from a failed Raytheon contract but still porous borders and a police service struggling to contain new methods of cultivating old drugs as well as the constant appearance of new ones, it is worth considering that American policy positions concerning the regulation of illegal markets are frequently followed (Andreas & Nadelmann, 2006). My guess is Geoff would have appreciated the irony.

Notes

1 Both Dutch and Italian scholars are able to draw on evidence gleaned from wire taps and investigations.
2 Although 'ephemeral' may well not be accurate, see Dorn et al., 2005 for a broader review of the literature in relation to drug trafficking. In the UK, it is accepted by most scholars of organised crime that some drug-dealing enterprises and individuals can operate for an extended period of time.
3 And was really exploration of the breadth and depth of organised crime.
4 Utilising case files and wire taps.
5 Silverstone & Whittle, 2015.
6 This is in direct contrast with the high levels of internecine violence at the lower levels of the drug market.
7 Also see Paoli et al. (2009; 205) 'In line with our analysis, several studies also point out that the success of criminal enterprises frequently rests on family ties and bonds of friendship or locality or, more rarely, common ethnicity'.
8 See, for example, Campana (2013), Morselli, Turcotte & Tenti (2011), Spapens (2011).
9 For example, it is estimated by the Greater London Authority that 'the number of irregular residents (i.e., migrants and their children) in the UK at the end of 2007 is 618,000, with a range of 417,000 to 863,000'. Many of the people in this group will

be in a precarious economic position, and some may struggle to earn a living in the legal economy. (GLA, 2009).

10 Currently estimated at £24 billion a year (Home Office, 2014).

11 Whilst in the academy, the fact that the cost from immigration crime can stay exactly the same for a two-year period from 2007 until 2009 must stretch the credibility of the figures.

12 As Levi (2007; 780) writes: "The key thing to note is that provided that criminals work over a 'prolonged' period of time – however long (or short) that is – "organised crime" can mean anything from major Italian syndicates in sharp suits or Sicilian peasant garb to three very menacing-looking burglars with a window cleaning business who differentiate their roles by having one act as lookout, another as a burglar and a third as a money launderer!"

13 The new offence will provide the National Crime Agency and the police with a further means to relentlessly pursue the known 36,600.

14 And has gained momentum since, despite the failure of the Asset Recovery Agency (a bespoke agency set up to reclaim the proceeds of crime).

15 As the Home Office guidance explains, 'The SCPO is a civil order; it is not the same as being investigated or convicted for a crime'. The FRO is also a civil order, but can only be imposed if the person has just been convicted of a qualifying offence (i.e., it is a 'post conviction' order). However, breach of an FRO is also a criminal offence and is punishable by up to six months in prison (HO, 2014; 3).

16 The gang injunction is granted on the balance of probabilities that the respondent has engaged in, or has encouraged or assisted, gang-related violence.

17 'Street level gangs are involved in drug dealing. This change will also enable areas to address the cross-over between urban street gangs and the lower levels of drug activity controlled at a higher level by organised crime groups' (Home Office, 2014; 1).

18 The definition of an organised crime group is three or more persons who act (or agree to act) together to further the carrying on of criminal activities. These criminal activities must attract a sentence of at least seven years for the participation offence to be applicable. This captures the various activities organised criminals are engaged in, including (but not limited to) drug trafficking, human trafficking, organised illegal immigration, firearms offences, fraud, child sexual exploitation and cybercrime.

19 Even the FBI defines organised crime more specifically: 'as any group having some manner of a formalized structure and whose primary objective is to obtain money through illegal activities. Such groups maintain their position through the use of actual or threatened violence, corrupt public officials, graft, or extortion, and generally have a significant impact on the people in their locales, region, or the country as a whole' (FBI website, 2013).

References

ACPO. (2013) *UK National Problem Profile. Commercial Cultivation of Cannabis 2012.* http://www.acpo.police.uk/documents/crime/2012/20120430CBACCofCPP.pdf [Accessed 1.1.2015]

Andreas, P. & Nadelmann, E. (2006) *Policing the Globe; Criminlization and Crime Control in International Relations*, Oxford: Oxford University Press.

Basel Institute on Governance. (2014) *Assets Recovery Agency (ARA)* http://www.assetrecovery.org/kc/node/0876cba2-a34b-11dc-bf1b-335d0754ba85.0;jsessionid=5FE5D29F17D2C522D239C7176CEFA9FD [Accessed 10.11.2014]

BBC News (2012) HSBC money laundering report: Key findings. http://www.bbc.co.uk/news/business-18880269

Bowling, B. & Ross, J. (2005) SOCA: the Serious and Organised Crime Agency. *Criminal Justice Matters*, 63 (1).

Campana, P. (2011) Eavesdropping on the Mob: the functional diversification of Mafia activities across territories. *European Journal of Criminology* 8(3), 213–228.

Campana, P. (2013) Understanding then Responding to Italian Organized Crime Operations Across Territories. *International Journal of Policing and Policy*, 7 (3), 316–325.

Campana, P. & Varese, F. (2012) Listening to the Wire: Criteria and Techniques for the Quantitative Analysis of Phone Intercepts. *Trends in Organized Crime*, 15 (1), 13–30.

CEOP (2011) The trafficking of women and children from Vietnam. CEOP. https://www.google.co.uk/#q=CEop+the+traffivking+of+women+2011

Chin, K. & Finckenauer, J. (2012) *Selling Sex Overseas; Chinese Women and the Realities of Prostitution and Global Sex Trafficking*, New York: New York University Press.

Dees, J. (2012) Claws of the Dragon; Chinese Organised Crime in the UK. *Papers From the British Criminology Conference*, 12, 61–78. http://britsoccrim.org/volume12/pbcc_2012_Dees.pdf [Accessed 1.1.205]

Dorn, N., Levi, M. & King, L. (2005) *Literature Review on Upper Level Drug Trafficking*, London: Home Office.

Dorn, N., Murji, K. & South, N. (1992) *Traffickers: Drug Markets and Law Enforcement*, London: Routledge.

Dubourg, R. & Prichard, S. (2007) *The Impact of Organised Crime in the UK: Revenues and Economic and Social Costs*, London: Home Office. https://www.gov.uk/government/uploads/system/uploads/attachment_data/file/99094/9886.pdf [Accessed 1.1.2014]

European Monitoring Centre for Drugs and Drugs Addiction. (2014) *European Drug Report; Trends and Developments.*

EMCDDA. (2014) *United Kingdom Drug Situation: Annual Report to the European Monitoring Centre for Drugs and Drug Addiction (EMCDDA) 2013 FBI—Glossary* (2015) www.fbi.gov [Accessed 1.1.2015]

The FBI Glossary of terms. https://www.fbi.gov/about-us/investigate/organizedcrime/glossary

Gilmour, S. (2008) Understanding Organized Crime: A Local Perspective. *Policing a Journal of Policy and Practice*, 2 (1): 18–27.

GLA (2009) *Economic Impact on the London and UK Economy of an Earned Regularisation of Irregular Migrants to the UK*. London: GLA. http://www.lse.ac.uk/geographyAndEnvironment/research/London/pdf/irregular%20migrants%20full%20report.pdf [Accessed 1.5.2016]

Hales, G., Lewis, C. & Silverstone, D. (2006) *Gun Crime: The Market in and Use of Illegal Firearms*. London: Home Office.

Hall, S. (2012) 'Consumer Culture and the Meaning of Urban Riots in England', in S. Hall & S. Winlow (Eds), pp 145–165. *New Directions in Criminological Theory.* London: Routledge.

Hallsworth, S. (2013) *The Gang and Beyond; Interpreting Violent Street Worlds*, Basingstoke, UK: Palgrave Macmillan.

Hallsworth, S. & Lea, J. (2011) Reconstructing Leviathan: Emerging Contours of the Security State. *Theoretical Criminology*, 15 (2) 141–157.

HM Government. (2011) *Local to Global: Reducing the Risk from Organised Crime.* London: HM Government. https://www.gov.uk/government/uploads/system/uploads/attachment_data/file/97823/organised-crime-strategy.pdf [Accessed 1.5.2016]

Harfield, C. (2006) SOCA: A Paradigm Shift in British Policing. *British Journal of Criminology*, 46: 743–761.

HM Government. (2013) *Serious and Organised Crime Strategy*. London: HM Government. https://www.gov.uk/government/uploads/system/uploads/attachment_data/file/248645/Serious_and_Organised_Crime_Strategy.pdf [Accessed 1.5.2016]

HMIC. (2005) *Closing the Gap: A Review of the Fitness for Purpose of the Current Structure of Policing in England & Wales*. London: Home Office. http://police.home-office.gov.un/news-and-publications/publication/police-reform/Closing the Gap 2005.pdf?view=Binary [Accessed 1.1.2015]

Hobbs, D. (2013) *Lush Life: Constructing Organized Crime in the UK*, Oxford: Oxford University Press.

Home Office. (2004) *One Step Ahead: A 21st Century Strategy to Defeat Organised Crime* http://www.archive2.official-documents.co.uk/document/cm61/6167/6167.pdf [Accessed 1.1.2014]

Home Office. (2014) *Amendments to Gang Injunctions*. https://www.gov.uk/government/uploads/system/uploads/attachment_data/file/317529/2014–06–03_signed_IA_Gang_injunctions.pdf [Accessed 1.1.2015]

Home Office. (2014) *Serious Crime Bill: Participation in Organised Crime*. Impact Assessment. https://www.gov.uk/government/uploads/system/uploads/attachment_data/file/317530/2014-06-03_signed_IA_Participation_Offence.pdf [Accessed 1.5.2016]

Lakhani, (2007) The Independent Saturday 22 September 2007. Children trafficked from Asia to UK to work in cannabis factories. http://www.independent.co.uk/news/uk/crime/children-trafficked-from-asia-to-uk-to-work-in-cannabis-factories-5329351.html.

Legal Aid, Sentencing and Punishment of Offenders Act 2012, http://www.legislation.gov.uk/ukpga/2012/10/contents/enacted [Accessed 1.1.2015]

Levi, M. (2007) Organized Crime and Terrorism in M. Mcguire, R. Morgan, & R. Reiner (Eds) *The Oxford Handbook of Criminology*. Oxford: Oxford University Press.

Matrix Knowledge Consultancy. (2007) *The Illicit Drug Trade in the United Kingdom*. London: Home Office. http://www.homeoffice.gov.uk/rds/pdfs07/rdsolr2007.pdf

May, T., Duffy, M., Few, B. & Hough, M. (2005) *Understanding Drug Selling in Communities: Insider or Outsider Trading*. The Joseph Rowntree Trust. http://www.jrf.org.uk/publications/understanding-drug-selling-local-communities [Accessed 1.1.2015]

Metropolitan Police (2005) Middle Market Drugs Project celebrates first anniversary. http://content.met.police.uk/News/Middle-Market-Drugs-Project-celebrates-first-anniversary/1260267637311/1257246745756 [Accessed 1.5.2016]

Morselli, C., Turcotte, M. & Tenti, V. (2010) *The Mobility of Criminal Groups*. Research and National Coordination Organized Crime Division Law Enforcement and Police Branch Public Safety Canada. http://publications.gc.ca/collections/collection_2012/sp-ps/PS4–91–2010-eng.pdf [Accessed 1.1.2014]

Morselli, C., Turcotte, M. & Tenti, M. (2011) The Mobility of Criminal Groups, *Global Crime*, 12, 165–188.

Paoli, L., Greenfield, V., & Reuter, P. (2009) *The World Heroin Market: Can Supply be Cut?* Oxford: Oxford University Press.

Pearson, G. (1987) *The New Heroin Users*, Oxford, UK: Blackwell Publishers.

Pearson, G. (2013) *An Ethnography of English Football Fans: Cans, Cops and Carnivals*. Manchester: Manchester University Press.

Pearson, G. & Hobbs, D. (2001) Middle Market Drug Distribution. Home Office Research Study 227. http://eprints.lse.ac.uk/13878/1/Middle_market_drug_distribution.pdf [Accessed 1.1.2015]

Reiner, R. (2012) 'Political Economy and Criminology: The Return of the Repressed', in S. Hall & S. Winlow (Eds), pp 30–52. *New Directions in Criminological Theory*. London; Routledge.

Schoenmakers, Y.M.M., Bremmers, B. & Kleemans, E.R. (2013) Strategic Versus Emergent Crime Groups: The Case of Vietnamese Cannabis Cultivation in the Netherlands. *Global Crime*, 14 (4), 321–340.

Sheptycki, J. (2004) Organizational Pathologies in Police Intelligence Systems: Some Contributions to the Lexicon of Intelligence-led Policing. *European Journal of Criminology*, 1 (3), 307–332.

Silverstone, D. (2003) The Ecstasy Of Consumption: The drug ecstasy as a mass commodity in a global market. PhD thesis. London: London School of Economics and Political Science.

Silverstone, D. (2010) The Policing of Vietnamese Organized Crime within the UK, *Policing a Journal of Policy and Practice*, 4 (2), 132–141.

Silverstone, D. (2011) A Response to; Morselli, C., Turcotte, M. and Tenti, V. (2010) The Mobility of Criminal Groups. *Global Crime*, 12 (3), 189–206.

Silverstone, D. (2013a) 'Globalisation and Criminology: The Case of Organised Crime in Britain', in F. Pakes (Ed), pp 27–45. *Globalisation and the Challenge to Criminology*. New York: Routledge.

Silverstone, D. (2013b) *Review of Lush Life: Constructing Organised Crime in the UK*. http://clcjbooks.rutgers.edu/books/lush_life.html [Accessed 1.1.2015]

Silverstone, D. (forthcoming) Turkish organized crime in the UK. *Trends in Organised Crime*.

Silverstone, D. & Crane (2015) 'Mapping and Conceptualising Organised Motor Cycle Gangs: The British, German and Spanish Experience', in A. Bain & M. Lauchs, (Eds) *International Perspectives of the OCMG*. Carolina Academic Press.

Silverstone, D. & Savage, S. (2010) Farmers, Factories and Funds: Organised Crime and Illicit Drugs Cultivation within the British Vietnamese Community. *Global Crime*, 11 (1), 16–33.

Silverstone, D. & Whittle, J. (2016) 'Forget it, Jake. It's Chinatown': The policing of Chinese organised crime in the UK. The Police Journal: Theory, Practice and Principles, 89 (1): 70–84.

Spapens, T. (2011) Interaction between Criminal Groups and Law Enforcement; the Case of Ecstasy in the Netherlands. *Global Crime*, 12 (1): 19–40.

Spapens, T. (2012) The Question of Regulating Illegal Markets: The Gambling and Cannabis Markets in the Netherlands GSTF. *Journal of Law and Social Sciences*, 2 (1), 30–37.

Sproat, P. (2014) 'Landscaping the Policing of Organised Crime: Some Designs and Reflections', in J. Brown (Ed), pp 252–268. *The Future of Policing*. London: Routledge.

Stanier, I. (2013) Contemporary Organisational Pathologies in Police Information Sharing: New Contributions to Sheptycki's Lexicon of Intelligence Led Policing. Unpublished Professional Doctorate Thesis.

Tzanetakis, M. (2013) *Added Value: Understanding the Organisation of an Upper Level Drug Dealing Network*. http://ecpr.eu/filestore/paperproposal/4b135ac5–30ec-4882–9b91-a86d6b21ec41.pdf

Wang, P. (2013) 'The Increasing Threat of Chinese Organised Crime: National, Regional and International Perspectives'. *The RUSI Journal* 158 (4), 6–18.

Wilkinson, R. & Pickett, K. (2010) *The Spirit Level: Why Equality is Better for Everyone*, London: Penguin.

Zhang, S. (2008) *Chinese Human Smuggling Organizations: Families, Social Networks, and Cultural Imperatives*. Stanford: Stanford University Press.

10 Fear and Loathing in a Dirty Old Town

Violent Notes from a Drug Ethnography

Brendan Marsh

Nobody wants the struggles, the problems and the fighting; it's bad for business. It just seems to happen anyway. Life and death becomes the dominating factor in your life, thinking about who you want to kill, making life and death decisions about other peoples' lives.

(Dano)

If you don't get shot, you are going to have to shoot someone. If you can't live with shooting someone then you are in trouble; if you can, you are going to have to shoot someone else because his family are going to shoot you. You are going to be killing people just to stay alive and then you are going to have to run a business at the same time, that's the reality of it.

(Barry)

The aim of this paper is to offer some insight into the world of the violent drug dealer in the higher echelons of Dublin's domestic drug trade, or, what Pearson and Hobbs (2001) refer to as the 'middle market'. Research into this economic and social arena was undertaken from 2011 to 2014, in which I endeavoured to investigate and understand the role of violence in illegal drug-dealing networks in Dublin City. Of the thirty-five people interviewed, thirty-one have experience of the illegal drug trade in their present or past lives, either as dealers or as customers, most as both. Seven of the participants were interviewed on multiple occasions, and additional informal discussions relating to the drug trade took place with some of these men and women during many hours spent together. Interviewees ranged in age from 18 to 64.

Emerging from the run-down areas of Dublin's inner city, as well as the sprawling concrete housing estates that have been described as 'something like national parks containing the potentially dangerous forces of the socially excluded' (Saris et al., 2002:186), are legions of emaciated addicts desperate for relief from the agonised reality of their internal landscape. Stumbling from one intoxicated episode to the next, they seek to drown out the shame and failure of their lives with chronic drug consumption (Pearson, 1987). At the other end of the scale, and usually emerging from the same social context, the dealer realises opportunities for great profit (Hobbs, 1997) in the endless demand for product from the army of addicts who cross his path, and the seemingly endless supply of drug-using youth who progress to replace the ranks. Despite the appearance, in the drug trade, of hardened professionals 'doing business', the line between business and personal is far from clear, and much conflict is due to interpersonal entanglements, petty jealousies and lingering resentments (Pearson and Hobbs, 2001). Some infractions elicit severe retaliatory and punitive violence; however, only a minority of individuals in the drug trade are willing and capable of inflicting such harm on others. Violence can therefore demonstrate both the nature of the transgression and the subjective violence of the perpetrator manifest in the objective violent act. The first section of the paper considers the moral acculturation to violence that the aspiring drug dealer must accept to make it into the 'big time'. Fear affects all actors in the drug trade, but the refusal of the dominant actor to be crippled by its power is also discussed. The paper then looks at the mindset of the violent drug dealer, as well as the role of paranoia and concern for reputation as causes of violence in the drug trade. The third section takes a closer look at the emasculating nature of much violence, particularly murder. Finally, the paper offers a brief account of an emerging typology of dominant actors in the illegal drug trade.

Brutal Evolution

In the illegal drug trade, more than most other areas of 'organised crime' (Von Lampe and Johansen, 2003), violence is an ever-present possibility. This possibility lurks in the background of every transaction and every relationship, and it is one of the features that define the structure of identifiable groups and status within extended trading networks. The illegal drug market is regulated by the use and threat of physical force, with often irrational cycles of conflict stemming from resentful and paranoid individuals with a heightened sensitivity to insult dealing with similar individuals over great sums of money (Hobbs, 2003). The committed dealer aligns his moral self with the necessities of his trade; of murder and torture, violent victimisation and the destruction of human bodies. The desire to be successful, to keep the money rolling in and maintain their position in the field, overrides moral objections to the 'systematic and effective use of violence' (Bourgois, 2003:24). For some, witnessing and inflicting violence proves too difficult, too visceral, and both the moral repulsion and survival instinct overpowers their desire for wealth and status. Jason was a drug user for twelve years during which time he made many forays into dealing, and, because of family connections in the trade, spent a considerable amount of time in the company of significant players:

> The bloke I sold for and his bodyguard brought me into a shed in a car yard where they had a bloke tied up. Your man tried to rip them and they kidnapped him and broke him up. They gave him a serious beating, they stabbed him and whacked him out of it with a baseball bat. . . . They kept

stopping to snort coke and then they'd torture him again. I actually start crying as I watched it, it was like it was happening in slow motion. The main bloke was definitely psychotic and the other guy kept laughing and slagging the bloke, who was nearly dead. I was terrified that they were going to kill him, I could hear his bones cracking, I knew if he died they would have to kill me too to cover themselves. Eventually we dumped him in a laneway; how the bloke lived I don't know.

(Jason)

As Jason's tolerance for brutality was found lacking, he stood at a moral cross-roads where he chose to scale down his activities to avoid such violence. His instinct that there was some kind of qualitative difference between him and the perpetrators of such violence was reaffirmed during another important incident:

I got arrested for a batch of coke and then they found cartridges off a shot-gun in my car. In the station the detective stared at me, right into my eyes, and told me I wasn't cut out for a criminal life. He saw right through me, saw through all the bullshit I was spinning them. He told me the people I was associating with are a different breed of people and as much as I was around them and doing business with them I didn't have what it took to be a criminal. I will never forget that, that really hit home with me and I got out of that life soon after.

(Jason)

The ambitious dealer who persists in the trade will reach a point where he will realise that his own life is in danger, or where he will have to consider taking the lives of others. Capacity for lethal violence, and willingness to run the risk of violent retaliation, are core attributes of successful dealers (Hobbs, 2003). Some actors, such as Jason, fail to suppress their own moral outrage, and indeed fear, and they seek an exit. For others, these existential and moral hazards prove little deterrent and they continue in their pursuit of financial reward. Their social position and economic status become inseparable from their violent tendencies (Winlow, 2001), and, as Gambetta (2009:78) states, 'while cunning can get one a long way, success in the underworld is often decided by violence, or by the credible threat of its use'. Barry operated as a middle-market supplier for many years, and, as such, he sourced substantial quantities of drugs on credit and passed them out to dealers around the city:

You have to be able to look after yourself. Sometimes you have to fucking punish, there's no two ways about it, doesn't matter how you feel about it at the time or how you feel about it afterwards, these things have to be done. There is no grey area in this, you can't pretend to give someone a beating and hide them away for a week. If someone says 'I want his finger' then you brought his finger, 'I want his arms broke' then you broke his arms, that's the way it works, if they say 'I want him killed' then you kill them, that's how it works.

(Barry)

For the aspiring 'gangster', the natural human response of fear in the face of danger must be overcome and frozen out, to be replaced with rage and intense fury. The adrenal response when faced by a man with a reputation for serious violence leads to an exchange of fear between the men, the weaker individual exudes fear and the stronger watches for the tell-tale signs. This signalling of fear happens through the body, through the movement towards and movement away, where the eyes look and how the head is held (Gilligan, 2006). When a man notorious for extreme violence presents himself there is an instant recognition of danger, followed by an instinctual urge to avoid and survive. Many men who pride themselves on their ability to stand their ground in the rough cultural context of urban working-class life opt for the humiliation of submission rather than clash with the serious criminal (Winlow & Hall, 2006). Fear must be suppressed by harnessing the energy of the adrenal response and directing it into potential for fury and savagery. Rage 'transforms humiliation so quickly and smoothly that talking and writing about the process can very easily become artificial and obfuscating' (Katz, 1988:23). Humiliation drains, it moves down the body and leaves one limp and lifeless. Rage fills the body, from the feet up, empowering and energising:

When you think your life is being threatened of course the fear comes up, and it's how you react that's important. My thing is instant anger, I will go from zero to 100 in a millisecond, just total wrath and rage comes in.

(Barry)

Fear is the active dynamic between all players, and to show that one is susceptible to fear can be a lethal mistake. Fear is an intolerable state that must be conquered and eliminated; fear corrodes the individual from the inside and human beings will go to great lengths to subdue its power. The serious criminals' greatest fear is the humiliation of being labelled as a coward, that is, being perceived to be a person whose actions and reactions, or lack of, are determined by the fear of others (Winlow & Hall, 2009). Therefore, the insult of being threatened is great as it is a threatened humiliation, and shame invites explosive reactions:

I don't give a bollox about comeback or about who you are or what family you're from. No one is going to put fear into me, who the fuck do they think they are. If I'm backed into a corner I will go at anyone; I've always stood up and I would never back down. I also know that if I need backup there's people I can ring, there are people there.

(Alan)

For the serious criminal, to see fear in another and exploit it is enjoyable; it brings excitement and a sense of achievement. Indeed, eliciting fear in others is how one advances in the world of the violent drug dealer; the actor hones his professional skills and reinforces the essential self-regard of the 'gangster' with the mixture of ego and emotion involved in intimidating others. Psychological violence has the purpose of dominating others through intimidation and fear and is 'aimed at the mind, the soul, the psyche of a person' (Imbush, 2003:23). The celebrity of notoriety affirms the self-narrative of the dominant criminal and communicates to all that there is something terrible and terrifying in the very essence of the individual:

> The invincibility of who you are, crime can give you power, crime instills power in you. I've often walked into a pub with my mates and people stand up and leave because they are afraid there's going to be trouble. I wouldn't be going in to start trouble, just to have a drink, and the barman would ask you to come in smaller groups because his customers are leaving. I had no control over other people perceptions of me but when I started getting powerful I noticed this. I could actually read it in people faces. It's like being a superstar walking around, people recognizing you, it's the same principle but it's with criminality.
>
> (Barry)

For the young men set on climbing the ladder in the illegal drug trade, determination to succeed at all costs becomes their defining characteristic. Not only must they cultivate a cold and heartless approach to their fellow human beings, but they must also develop a resistance to their own moral objections to violence. The craving for material wealth and personal power rests on their tolerance for violence and their ability to reduce human life to a means to an end.

Violent Professionals

Violent drug dealers demonstrate a commitment to a lifestyle that is inherently dangerous and dehumanising; they willingly accept 'the risks of hostility, violence and punishment that accompany crime, and a landscape littered with humiliated others who failed to make the grade' (Hall et al., 2008:193). Each individual develops a set of skills and a 'criminal mindset' as they negotiate their way through the difficult economic and social terrain of the drug trade. Indeed, he who achieves longevity in the violent world of the urban drug trade appears to command a calculated mastery of thought and action. After all, even with a gut full of rage and a mind racing with murderous intent, it can be necessary to smile and chat with one's object of hatred in order to achieve a 'set-up' or 'double cross'. Though 'rage searches for a target to extinguish itself'(Katz, 1988:29) it is also 'often coherent, disciplined action, cunning in its moral structure' (Katz, 1988:30). The successful criminal attempts to be adept at suspending his own emotions while at the same time reading the motives and agendas of others through their emotional cues. Gambetta (2009:xvii) writes that serious criminals 'are constantly afraid of being duped, while at the same time they are busy duping others'. The stakes of failure are very high and the consequences for making a mistake, such as overlooking a potential source of danger or not picking up on a double-cross situation, can be extreme. One such incident was recalled by Franner, a user dealer who has returned to drug use and crime after five years of desistance and recovery:

> Me and my so-called best mate were standing at the lane waiting to be picked up to go do a robbery, to take a fella's guns off him. Next thing a motor bike pulls up and the bloke gets off the back and starts shooting at me. I ran like fuck and got hit twice but I got away. The dirty bastard had set me up.
>
> (Franner)

Paranoia infects the market and the social system shared by participants. The intensity of the strained relationships between players, and simmering tension over real and imagined betrayal, creates potential for internecine conflict in criminal groups. Paranoia is induced by the illegality of the trade as well as the untrustworthy nature of the power-hungry criminal, and, as Gambetta (2009:x) states, 'the very fact of being a criminal makes one less trustworthy in the eyes of other criminals'. Moreover, the use of mind-altering substances exacerbates the potential for violence in these fraught and tense relationships (White, 2004). Franner was involved in many violent conflicts throughout his life and career as a drug dealer, which he accounts for by describing the suffocating nature of working within criminal groups staffed by violent, paranoid and substance-abusing people:

> One time we had organised for a decent batch of gear to be delivered by car. The car was stopped by the police and the gear was found. My mate went nuts; he start blaming people and falling out with people, calling people rats. So loyalties were compromised and we fractured into different little groups. There was this sense of imagined control over all things, a sense of untouchability, so if things go wrong it has to be because someone said something to someone. It ended with people taking out hits on each other, friends and allies becoming enemies, reputations sullied.
>
> (Franner)

Indeed, when similarly paranoid and dangerous others search for weakness with a predator's eye, peace of mind becomes a faint memory. Criminals know not to trust criminals; they know better than anyone the type of deceptive, manipulative and self-serving agendas that criminals pursue (Gambetta, 2009). They know intimately the type of determined ingenuity with which the criminal pursues his self interest, the callous indifference to the lives of others, and the thirst for power and unwillingness to forgive and forget. This knowledge serves to heighten their sense of insecurity and vulnerability, and dominant personalities in the drug trade often live in a state of constant paranoia and hostility:

> When you are around those lads you can smell the fear, there's a tangible sense of fear among them that their status will be challenged. When one of them is put on the spot the others watch for weakness; they watch every move and every facial expression for weakness. They can almost taste fear in the air; you see them trying to sense it. The pressure of losing weighs heavy on them; they can't show any chink of weakness because people are always looking for weakness.
>
> (Dano)

Conflict can become a public performance to be viewed and commented upon especially by the youth and the criminal fraternity. There is a careful eye cast upon how actions are received and the standing of one's reputation. Power, in this context, is the ability to coerce, to ensure compliance and maintain security. Demonstrations of power that leave no room for doubt are essential as the street is always watching, and always gossiping (Hobbs, 2013). Much violence is therefore moralistic in nature; it is to enact justice for being wronged. However, retribution is seldom proportionate to the offence as a key objective of retaliation is to 'deter future aggression' (Jacobs and Wright, 2006:41). Retaliation, therefore, has a strong pedagogical function and is always carried out with an eye to how it will be received among the watching criminal fraternity (Winlow & Hall, 2009). Concern for reputation as a serious force to be reckoned with is a crucial consideration for the serious criminal:

> The mindset is: he thinks I won't do it, it's a game and I won't do anything about it. People thinking that they are being taken for a fool is one of the biggest causes of violence.
>
> (Paul)

The conflict-oriented individual seeks revenge and will persist in the hatred for his adversary. The qualities of deviance are attached to the enemy in a kind of essentialism run riot and the deviant other is to be the target of justice through violent retribution, and, as Black (1993:xv) states, the individual 'called the victim by the criminologist is called the offender by the killer or assailant'. Criminal esteem and the protection of business interests demand consistent action, and failure to perform reveals a chink in the armour that can be fatal for a crew or an individual's place in a crew. Violent retaliation is often driven by the symbolic meaning of the original affront, and, therefore, by the symbolic meaning that the retaliatory violence delivers. Violations that could be considered as minor or inconsequential by objective observers can be experienced as profoundly damaging by the targets of such offences. Reputation and the identity of the individual can be deeply hurt and 'affronts attack ontological security rather than some economic or political utility' (Jacobs and Wright, 2006:46). When in that state of mind, even perceived slights can bring the force of violence down upon a victim (Winlow & Hall, 2009). Hostile and paranoid people can act out their state of mind at the least provocation:

> They can take the smallest things personally, they have a super sensitive attack mode. 'What did he mean by that? Is he insulting me here? Is he attacking me here?' It's not an issue wiping someone out or leaving them badly badly damaged, is not an issue.
>
> (Jamie)

Amidst the paranoia, suspicion and fear of retaliation, violent drug dealers cultivate a hardness of the heart and mind that becomes the armour of battle of everyday practice, the battle to maintain one's 'face' in an economic and social system consisting of like-minded people.

Violent Practice

Violence has an emasculating quality, and deliberately so. Designed to humili- ate, and to make the target and his people suffer not just physically but psycho- logically also (Gilligan, 2000; Finckenauer, 2005), the depth of shame inflicted on the opposing individual or group equates to the boost to the actor's ego and power. Violence is a shaming discourse, especially relating to on-going feuds, a battle of life and death where death is preferable to living with defeat. Fac- ing the humiliation of submission becomes a fate worse than death and an experience worse than killing, as 'the most negatively valued experience is shame (humiliation), and . . . the highest good is the opposite of shame, namely pride (Gilligan, 1976:151). The drive to viciously emasculate one's enemy is strong in the serious criminal, who demonstrates a violent intentionality and agentic ferocity that strikes fear into the hearts of many who cross his path. Alan grew up around active criminality as his immediate and extended family was involved in drug dealing and serious crime. From a young age violence was his method for resolving conflict and regulating his social relations; he is a dominant character who has impressed his vengeance upon others with savagery:

> A bloke that I had a lot of conflict with when I was into the drugs caused me a lot of hassle . . . (he) kept spreading rumours about me, saying hor- rible things about my girlfriend and daughter. . . . I followed him home one night and kicked in the door of his flat. I battered him, I booted him in the face, smashed him with my head, and savaged his face. . . . I danced on him; there was blood everywhere. I then stabbed his face and head with a blade . . . then I just rammed the blade into his back and left it there. I just wanted to hurt him more and more and I really could have killed him.

I didn't even think that he could die I didn't give a bollox; I just wanted
to cause him more and more pain. A few weeks later I saw him again and
tried to run him over in the jeep, chased him up the street.

(Alan)

The higher levels of the drug trade can be described as a criminal subculture
that dismisses the sanctity of life. In this subculture, as in many serious criminal fraternities, to kill is not morally wrong (Levi, 1981). Indeed, as a necessary
part of the occupation, it is to be embraced, practiced and perfected. The urban
capitalist soldier who dominates the drug trade is recognised and respected for
efficient killing, ruthless collection of debt and intolerance for personal insult.
He is judged by the swiftness and the severity of his violence, and violence
'sustains his identity as a man who . . . demands total respect (Hobbs, 1995:51).
In a business and social arena where murder is not uncommon, emphasis is
placed on not just who gets killed but also how professionally they are killed.
Taking life provides the scene to exhibit power and status; it demonstrates not
just cruelty but also how long the arm can reach. Dano was involved in using
and selling drugs for almost twenty years, and engaged in many violent rivalries with other drug-dealing groups. He emphasised the importance of creating
a reputation for utter ruthlessness as a method of maintaining his own security.
Reflecting on his own life, but also commenting on the radicalisation of violence in his community during his lifetime, he stated that:

Murder is the way to make a name for yourself but it's also how vicious
your murder is. A fella was telling me how he shot a guy and made sure
he disfigured the body so his family couldn't have an open casket. He did
that as a statement; he did that to make it as gruesome as possible and to
send the message to everyone that 'if you cross me this is what I will do'.
Murder is the means by which they make a statement; it's to gain status.

(Dano)

The killer is the most significant person in the life of the victim, the person who
has had a greater impact than any other. Family cannot think of the loved one
without thinking of the killer; they cannot reflect or reminisce on the living days
of the lost loved one without the name and the face of the perpetrator invading
their recollection. The perpetrator, as a central part of the death, is always present in the lives of those left behind. Death by violence is a tragedy of malicious
intent and the killer, whether alive or dead, incarcerated or free, stands over
the memory like a permanent haunting spectre. The one who takes life is not
unaware of these facts, and kills in the knowledge that revenge could be sought:

When I arrived at the hospital I saw my brother lying on a bed with a large
tube protruding from his mouth. The right side of his face was marked and
his neck was heavily bruised. His eyes were open and completely blank;
he was brain dead. The kid was only 18. It was really fucked up; my folks

were old and they were in bits. My sister and brothers there too. It's all a blur now, a painful and confused memory, but I remember very clearly I was staring at my brother and thinking that out there somewhere was the person who had done this to him, to us.

(Ben)

Killing, therefore, has a price; namely fear of retaliation and revenge. Actors will, of course, seek to minimise this possibility by avoiding such action where they believe there is a significant chance of revenge being sought. Taking action against a 'connected' criminal or against an indebted addict who is the wayward son of a powerful family, can backfire and cause endless hassle and conflict. According to Richie, who hails from a large extended family and was involved in various forms of 'organised crime', including drug dealing, for most of his adult life:

They do their homework on them to see if there will be a kickback, 'if I kill so and so what's going to happen, who are they, what's their background, what's their family'. If you kill a guy from a big family it can cause a lot of heartache for you; they have to look into who they are gona pop.

(Richie)

Nevertheless, because of the pressing desire to exact revenge for whatever unforgiveable public humiliation, whether it be financial indiscretion or personal attack, individuals will decide that their enemy must be taken out regardless of potential violent fallout. When ego, rage and hatred conquer the natural human self-preservation instinct, however temporarily, killing becomes possible (Gilligan, 2000). The violent drug dealer lives with the intimate knowledge of how practically difficult it can be to kill, yet how morally possible it is to take a life, and the ever-present anxiety that someone out there, known or unknown, possibly both, is plotting and planning in a determined fashion to end their existence by smashing lead through their skull (Jacobs and Wright, 2006). This knowledge and paranoia is incorporated into the conscious subjectivity of the individual and exerts a constant and intense pressure as he proceeds about his daily life in a calculated fashion. The 'gangster' watches every gesture and monitors every conversation from behind dishonest eyes as multiple and even competing agendas run through his mind as he interacts with friends, associates and rivals. This practice becomes second nature, and it is a system of personal thought and action that leaves little room for the softer emotions:

I was involved in some very serious violence, as serious as it gets; you can't go any further. That stuff weighs heavy on ye, it keeps coming back up inside ye. When you are living like that, being violent, you need to be frozen. Your real emotions; you can't have them near ye, they need to be pushed aside, frozen out.

(Dano)

For those who kill intentionally and repeatedly, accepting defeat, rather than taking life, becomes the line that must not be crossed. Particularly for those engaged in feud-related cycles of violence, 'combustible pockets of savagery that erupt with little warning every few years' (Hobbs, 1995:39), the elation of successfully killing an enemy represents not just the joy of destroying an object of contempt and hatred, but also of eliminating a threat to one's own life:

> I was outside a boozer having a smoke and a car pulled up and a bloke from the gang we were fighting with leaned out and took a photo of me on his phone. I was seething because that was a message, a photo is the same as a shot, the message was, 'you can be got'.

> (Dano)

Violence is, therefore, systemic in the drug trade because of the predatory nature of many dealers who persistently seek advantage over others. Moreover, the violent dispositions of actors, coupled with rampant ego, can create a perfect storm for interpersonal conflict between dealers and 'gangsters'. Killing an enemy fuels cyclical violence (Hobbs, 2003; Gambetta, 2009) and reinforces the violent ideology of the economic and social system that is the illegal drug trade. Especially in feud-related cycles of violence, murder becomes a catharsis of stress and fear, as well as a confirmation of the moral certainties and norms that the violent dealer and criminal lives with. Killing is the pinnacle of developmental success, a rite of passage and a justification of narrative.

The Main Men

A subsection of individuals present a nefarious presence in the drug trade and appear to lack any demonstration of good intentions. The psychopath exists as a real encountered persona in the cultural milieu of the serious criminal fraternity. He displays a commitment to violence that is unsurpassed by other actors and engages in acts so horrendous, malicious and cruel that it leaves little room for justification or redemption. Diagnosed primarily by the street, but also often by media, 'for a psychopath the chance to use violence is a pleasure rather than a cost' (Gambetta, 2009:35). Very few actors in the drug trade meet this description, but undoubtedly there are those who do. They display the tendencies of 'The Bully' in Hans Toch's typology of violent men, which offers the portrayal of this type as the:

> most unpleasant type of violent person . . . (he) goes out of his way to be unfair, unmerciful, and inhumane in his violence . . . he derives satisfaction from the suffering of others. . . . The Bully is the artisan of violence, for whom force is a tool or an instrument self-consciously employed to inspire terror and to increase pliability . . . the bully is really the man who enjoys the experience of exercising effective violence.

> (Toch, 1992:157–158).

Rumour and speculation presents the psychopath as someone for whom personal fear does not exist, and he therefore inspires great fear in others. Acting beyond the behavioural norms of the criminal fraternity, his predation is at times sexual in nature, and killing women and young people poses no moral dilemma. He will use violence when there seems little reason to do so, and 'gives no quarter, because lenience takes away the edge or full measure of his enjoyment' (Toch, 1992:157). Other actors in the trade suspect that he may be mentally ill, even evil. Joe was a user dealer who ran up considerable debts over many years because of his insatiable appetite for drugs, and ran out of options in his local area for sourcing drugs to sell on credit. He described his supplier of last resort in the following terms:

> One guy I used to sell for, he would give you drugs and want the money in a week. You knew if you didn't have the money in time you were going down and that's that. He had us all working for him out of fear. I've seen him doing horrendous things to people. He's sick and twisted, a total bully and an absolute dirtbird. He put the fear of God into everybody but he was the only one who would give it to us on tick.
>
> (Joe)

The psychopath is a violent anomaly, even in the brutal world of the illegal drug trade, and can therefore be very useful to dominant individuals or criminal crews who are willing to deal with him and put his talents to use. Serious violence, no matter how seemingly irrational, can lead to a reputation that will have commercial value, and 'the more irrational the level of violence that is utilised, the greater the transcendence of rationality and the more valuable the reputation' (Hobbs, 2003:681). The psychopath inspires such fear through his use of violence that his presence in a criminal crew is very useful for collecting money from sellers and addicts, and indeed for intimidating the opposition (Bovenkerk et al., 2003). Individuals, groups and indeed whole communities can be forced to submit to the will of a criminal group by the power of one individual's reputation for violence:

> There's a few guys I know who actually enjoy killing people, that's what they're good at, seriously that's what they are good at, they are happy to do it. . . . If you are in a crew and you happen to get a psychopath in your crew then in the drugs business you are half way there to having a good crew; that's the reality of it. People who have the intelligence will pick up on that and say 'get him in here'. . . . You get a psycho and get him to kill someone right in front of ye, bring him to a field and get him to kill someone, preferably someone he knows and even likes. After that you know you have him, he will do anything for ye.
>
> (Barry)

The psychopath represents an embrace of cruelty that indicates profound illness of the psyche. He is an individual who is 'irresistibly drawn to violence regardless of pecuniary consideration' (Hobbs, 1995:124). These tendencies, as with all the attributes of the dominant characters in the drug trade, exist on a continuum. The majority of the dominant personalities in the criminal 'underworld' could be described by the 'wildly pejorative designation' (Toch, 1992:151) of psychopath as they slash and shoot their way to wealth and status. In working-class communities, where the reputations of the men of violence hover like a dark mist, the special term of 'psychopath' is reserved for those individuals who exhibit a terrifying lack of human decency in their dealings with others. They are often cruel, often ruthless, and seem determined to bring their violent action further than their peers. To those they dominate with terror they appear barely human, a monstrosity of cruelty bearing down upon them with all human characteristics seemingly absent, like a supernatural entity from a horror film. The psychopath conducts his business 'with an aristocratic bearing that supports a self-confident association with terrible power' (Katz, 1988:128) and contributes greatly to the 'omnipresent threatening reality' (Bourgois, 2003:34) of the illegal drug trade.

The crew leader, or 'gang boss', is a powerful individual imbued with a variety of criminal competencies and skills that allow him to thrive in a criminal scene characterised by threat, deception and greed. To achieve and maintain this position, he appears 'committed to total physical domination' (Hobbs, 1995:123) of those in his inner circle and wider community, making him someone whom even the physically strong and the psychologically violent regard with a mixture of admiration and fear. The leader appears as a man of supreme confidence who possesses a sharp, alert and insightful mind (Bovenkerk, 2000). He demonstrates a distinct lack of empathy for the suffering of others and a callous disregard for the welfare of people outside of his own circle of family and friends. These individuals, who can be leaders of territorially based criminal groups or powerful individuals in networks of distribution, demonstrate an irresistible urge to dominate and a willingness to use whatever extremes of violence are necessary to secure their position. Exhibiting a proven track record in the use of cunning, determination and ruthlessness, there exists in those around him a perception that he is very well connected into circles of professional criminals. One research participant, who spent a great deal of time in the company of people who displayed these characteristics, spoke of the absolute dominance of key individuals over criminal groups with which he was familiar:

> There's two classic attributes that I often see in the lads I know who have made it big. First is to have a class A personality, be engaging, friendly, people will like him, have a top personality. Once you have that you have people looking up to you and wanting to be with you. Second, then you need to start directing a reign of terror; fear is a great thing to control. You control people around you, then you widen the circle and control the area around you, then keep widening the circle. . . . They are the ones who stand out, they stand out in any company, they have the balls to make it to

the top. The people I know who are on the top of the food chain are driven to succeed, they don't give a bollox.

(Jamie)

These 'upwardly mobile entrepreneurs of violence' (Hobbs, 2003:682) are judged to be reliable, dependable and competent, with problem-solving and income-generating abilities that are beyond question (Adler, 1993). In short, he is the boss for a reason and any thought of challenging his dominance must take into consideration both the consequences of failure and the backlash of success. Submission to his dominance is based on the recognition of his 'name', that is, the recognition of his reputation for application for lethal violence and ability to suppress the comeback. This type of personal ferocity lies not in the steroid-induced muscle of many pretenders, nor in the fighting competence of those who prove themselves on the street, nor even in the demonstrated bloodlust and cruelty of those called 'the psychopath'. Instead, it resides in the personality of the dominant professional criminal and the attributes he uses to stamp his authority on his economic and social sphere of influence (Hobbs, 2013).

To those they control with fear, those in their circle, they can appear paternal and even honourable. This fear-induced loyalty and friendship also has an economic rationale as he is the central figure in a networked system of local distribution. Put simply, his name brings in the cash and the goose that lays the golden egg must be protected at all costs. He is, in effect, the ultimate authoritarian father who, while encouraging aggression, strength and entrepreneurship from his cluster of sons and wider clan, will not tolerate any challenge to his control:

... you haven't got the freedom to go and do whatever you want; you must seek permission from above. If directions come from above they must be followed; there is homage paid to the leader ... one bloke is the top man. . . certain people do their own thing or have responsibility or give kickbacks.

(Jamie)

These 'bosses' inspire great admiration, envy and of course fear, as they strut about their housing estates pregnant with self-importance, seeking confirmation of their dominance through the currency of recognition; acknowledgement from peers and diverted stares. Many in the drug trade try to reach this much-admired position of authority and status; few succeed.

Conclusion

While the trade finds many customers in the night-time economy (Hobbs et al., 2003), it is the daily users and drug addicts who provide the solid customer base for the range of products on offer. Of course, most drugs cross social boundaries, and even heroin knows no class; however, both drug addiction and the trade in illegal narcotics are most visible in working-class areas (Pearson, 1987). Violent drug dealers often emerge from, and ply their trade in, communities suffering from structural inequality and economic marginalisation, and are therefore vulnerable to 'predatory criminal colonisation' (Hobbs et al., 2003:219). Arguably the most stigmatised profession, despised and feared by their host communities, drug dealing epitomises 'the brutal adaptability of those born at the back of the queue' (Hobbs, 2013:170). The (usually) men who rise to dominant positions in the illegal drug trade are very serious players; serious in their attitude to business, in the severity of their sanctions and in their commitment to violence to regulate their social and personal reputations. Indeed, the drug dealer demands 'disciplined responses from individuals whose very identities are inspired by disorder' (Hobbs, 1995:118), and uses the force of his violent reputation to enforce his demands. As involvement in drug dealing progresses from an earner to a nefarious enterprise, the dealer develops a narrative of self-indulgence that has at its core a self-centred and self-righteous view of everything (Gambetta, 2009). Driven by 'seductive visions of self-aggrandizement' (Hall, 2012:47), the individuals' moral reasoning evolves over time to encompass a range of serious criminal values. The violent drug dealer is effectively entirely separate from the bulk of society in how he thinks, his actions and his reactions, and there is little in the way of participation in any version of a prosocial consensus of values. Their practice communicates moral values that are beyond the boundaries shared by mainstream society, a criminal ideology that encourages the physical destruction of others in the pursuit of profit, security and esteem. Most of these men wear their 'limitless moral indifference' (Katz, 1988:234) as a second skin, and exert a consciously corrupt moral agency when they commit acts of horrendous violence for personal and financial gain.

Though it is true that many 'involved in successful, lucrative criminal activity such as drug brokerage at this level develop a sense of exaggerated personal power and invulnerability' (Pearson & Hobbs, 2001:15), there is some evidence to support their sense of 'being above the masses' (Bovenkerk, 2000). The criminological focus on those who run afoul of the criminal justice system, or are caught up in other 'services', belies the fact that a not insignificant proportion of high-level drug dealers, as well as other serious criminals, enjoy long and lucrative careers. Despite the personal and social consequences of being involved in serious violence, many of these individuals remain in their dominant position for decades. Because of their wealth, their control over many weaker individuals and their experience in their trade, they fit the description of the 'powerful offender' (Lea, 2005), and are extremely difficult to dislodge from their throne, either by violence or by force of law.

References

Adler, P. A. (1993) *Wheeling and Dealing: An Ethnography of an Upper-Level Drug Dealing and Smuggling Community*, Columbia University Press, New York.
Black, D. (1993) *The Social Structure of Right and Wrong*, Academic Press, San Diego.
Bourgois, P. (2003) *In Search of Respect: Selling Crack in El Barrio* (Vol. 10). Cambridge University Press, Cambridge.

Bovenkerk, F. (2000) "Wanted: Mafia Boss"–Essay on the Personology of Organized Crime. *Crime, Law and Social Change*, 33(3), 225–242.

Bovenkerk, F., Siegel, D., & Zaitch, D. (2003) Organized Crime and Ethnic Reputation Manipulation. *Crime, Law and Social Change*, 39(1), 23–38.

Finckenauer, J. (2005) Problems of Definition: What is Organized Crime?, *Trends in Organized Crime*, 8(3), 63–83.

Gambetta, D. (2009) *Codes of the Underworld: How Criminals Communicate*, Princeton University Press, Princeton, NJ.

Gilligan, J. (1976) 'Beyond Morality: Psychoanalytic Reflections on Shame, Guilt, and Love', in Lickona, T. (ed) *Moral Development and Behavior: Theory, Research, and Social Issues*, Holt, Reinhart and Winston, New York.

Gilligan, J. (2000) *Violence. Reflections on Our Deadliest Epidemic, Forensic Focus 18*, Jessica Kingsley Publishers, London.

Hall, S. (2012) *Theorizing Crime and Deviance: A New Perspective*, Sage, Thousand Oaks, CA.

Hall, S., Winlow, S., & Ancrum, C. (2008) *Criminal Identities Consumer Culture: Crime, Exclusion and the New Culture of Narcissm*, Routledge, Hoboken, NJ.

Hobbs, D. (1995) *Bad Business: Professional Crime in Modern Britain*, Oxford University Press, Oxford.

Hobbs, D. (1997) 'Criminal Collaboration: Youth Gangs, Subcultures, Professional Criminals, and Organized Crime', in Maguire, M., Morgan, R. & Reiner, R. (eds) *The Oxford Handbook of Criminology Ed 2*, pp 801–840, Oxford University Press, Oxford.

Hobbs, D. (2003) 'Organised Crime and Violence', in Heitmeyer, W. & Hagan, J. (eds) *International Handbook of Violence Research Vol 2*, Kluwer Academic Publishers, The Netherlands.

Hobbs, D. (2013) *Lush Life: Constructing Organised Crime in the UK*, Oxford University Press, Oxford, UK.

Hobbs, D., Hadfield, P., Lister, S., & Winlow, S. (2003) *Bouncers: Violence and Governance in the Night-Time Economy*, Oxford University Press, Oxford.

Imbush, P. (2003) 'The Concept of Violence', in Heitmeyer, W. & Hagan, J. (eds) *International Handbook of Violence Research Vol 2*, Kluwer Academic Publishers, The Netherlands.

Jacobs, B., & Wright, R. (2006) *Street Justice: Retaliation in the Criminal Underworld*, Cambridge University Press, New York.

Katz, J. (1988) *Seductions of Crime*, Basic Books, New York.

Lea, J. (2005) *Powerful Offenders and the Criminal Justice System*, Available from: http://www.bunker8.pwp.blueyonder.co.uk/cjs/powerful.htm [23 January 2015]

Levi, K. (1981) Becoming a Hit Man: Neutralization in a Very Deviant Career. *Journal of Contemporary Ethnography*, 10(1), 47–63.

Pearson, G. (1987) *The New Heroin Users*, Blackwell, Oxford, UK.

Pearson, G., & Hobbs, D. (2001) Middle Market Drug Distribution, *Home Office Research Study*, 227.

Saris, A. J., Bartley, B., Kierans, C., Walsh, C., & McCormack, P. (2002) Culture and the State: Institutionalizing 'the Underclass' in the New Ireland. *City*, 6(2), 173–191.

Toch, H. (1992) *Violent Men: An Inquiry Into The Psychology of Violence*, American Psychological Association, Washington, DC.

Von Lampe, K., & Johansen, P. (2003) *Criminal Networks and Trust*, Paper Presented at the 3rd Annual Meeting of the European Society of Criminology (ESC), Helsinki, Finland, Available from: http://www.organized-crime.de/criminalnetworkstrust.htm

White, W. (2004) Substance Use and Violence: A Brief Primer for Addiction Professionals. *Addiction Professional*, 2(1), 13–19.

Winlow, S. (2001) *Badfellas: Crime, Tradition and New Masculinities*, Berg, Oxford, UK.

Winlow, S., & Hall, S. (2006) *Violent Night: Urban Leisure and Contemporary Culture*, Berg, Oxford, UK.

Winlow, S., & Hall, S. (2009) Retaliate First: Memory, Humiliation and Male Violence. *Crime, Media, Culture*, 5(3), 285-304.

11 Drug Markets, Ethnography and Geoff Pearson

A Tribute to the Man of the People

Daniel Briggs

Introduction

I sit in *The Railway* pub in Blackheath, looking out of the window, only able to shake my head at the supposed 'heatwave summer' we have been predicted in 2013 for it is a blustery March day in London and that is enough confirmation for me that we will be lucky to see the sun three consecutive days without it raining. I sit already sipping at my pint, eager to discuss my new ideas with my colleague, who has said he 'doesn't normally come this far out' but would enjoy the change. As he ambles in slowly, he looks around in the poorly lit pub and, when he sees me, his smile broadens and his bushy eyebrows follow suit. He goes to buy a Guinness and returns, sipping slowly and turning the glass around with both hands. He recounts experiences from his recent excursion in Egypt where he was following his passion for archeology and ancient civilizations. I recount what I can from my little experience of the country, but mostly listen to him. We get on to the subject of criminology, and he starts to give me some feedback on my work on the deviant and risk behaviours of young Brits (Briggs, 2013). He said he liked it but when it got to some of my fieldnotes documenting what the young people did, he said, he tells me 'sorry, mate, I don't get it' and laughs heartily. I ask him if he would be interested in collaborating on a writing project, something which could follow up my work on crack cocaine use and distribution and his on the development of drug markets over the past thirty years. He looks disinterested but proposes instead that I might be interested in a project for the Red Cross, researching the immigration experience.[1] He tells me he will talk to his wife, Marylin, who works there, to set things up for me.

   Unfortunately, this didn't happen. For a few weeks later, as I walked out of the University of East London campus into the surrounding grey and constant of the traffic, I received a call from Dick Hobbs. To my sadness, it is to tell me that this man, Geoff Pearson, had died. For a minute, I stop in my stride, finding it difficult to comprehend this. It's like one of those moments which happens to someone else and you struggle to deal with its significance. Suddenly, my mind sifts through our meetings and through the conversations about my work. I did not know Geoff as well as some, by no means, but was certainly extremely grateful for the open and constructive guidance he gave me during my PhD and with the publication of *Crack Cocaine Users: High Society and Low Life in South London* (Briggs, 2012). More than anything, Geoff believed in me, probably at a time when I was doubted by others and needed guidance as an early-career academic. So Geoff has been someone integral in my career, both in a professional and personal capacity.

In memory of him as much as to honour my suggestion of writing together, I have put this chapter together around the development of drug markets in the UK. While Geoff was an expert in many areas, here I want to point out the influence of his work, predominantly, *The New Heroin Users* (Pearson, 1989) and his work on middle-market distribution, and the importance he placed on immersion in the field. In this respect, the first part of the chapter draws on his work on drug markets and places it in the political era of the 1980s when increased social control was imposed on drug users, and the reduction of welfare support. Thereafter, the chapter shows how this work laid the foundation for further studies which continued to draw attention to the experiences of drug dealing and drug use in marginal urban areas. The chapter concludes with a reminder that, in undertaking these works, Geoff advocated qualitative methodologies, in particular ethnography, and why it is important to retain this approach in a time of the dumbing down of social sciences if we are to take seriously drug harms in a postmodern context.

Geoff and His Work on Drug Markets

Geoff's main contribution to the study of drug markets, deprivation and drug use came about during the 1980s when Britain started to develop significant problems of heroin. Before this, there had been almost no real issue of problematic drug use; however, at the beginning of the 1980s, heroin use had spread to other cities across the UK such as Liverpool, Manchester and Glasgow. Researchers in the United States had already started to identify similar patterns of drug use with the advent of crack cocaine and how the deterioration of U.S. urban inner cities, where crack flourished, was set against the decline of urban manufacturing industries, weakening welfare support services and widening income disparities (Agar, 2003) which saw a 'collapse of the official economy corresponding to the vertiginous growth of the informal economy, and especially the drug trade' (Wacquant, 2004: 103).

This certainly seemed to be the case for the UK as well. Geoff, among others (Parker et al., 1987), was among the first to follow this trend. In *The New Heroin Users* (Pearson, 1989), Geoff examined the relationship between this new heroin epidemic and marginality—the experience of poverty, unemployment, poor housing conditions and other social disadvantages. The profile of these new drug users using heroin were white working-class unemployed, socially excluded young people and thereafter further connections were made with prostitution and acquisitive crime. Geoff pointed out that the experience of heroin use compounded the brazen elements of social exclusion—poverty, deprivation, living in substandard conditions—and exacerbated these experiences.

These were important contributions to the literature and wider policy audiences, especially because at the time governmental responses tended to increase penalties for drug use/possession and lambast the 'poor' decision-making of the people using the drugs (Reinarman and Levine, 1997). Equally misrepresented in social policy, media institutions and even some researchers at the time were conceptions that the 'effects' and 'consequences' of heroin use were something representative of the 'drug-doing-the-damage-to-the-user' which enabled widespread political rhetoric to be exercised on this group of people, and was thereafter reflected in moralizing social policies which sought to make people responsible for their own drug use. Someone who had succumbed to heroin use, had made poor life choices, could not look after themselves like a 'normal person', and was on the slippery slope to homelessness and destitution (see Briggs, 2012a for the summary of the argument). Geoff didn't go too much into this per se but didn't let the significance of his research findings disappear, and in countless publications thereafter Geoff persisted with highlighting the various injustices attached to these young peoples' circumstances: the lack of adequate healthcare, the increased law enforcement which perpetuated their criminality and the policy shortfalls of failing to investigate the issue with depth.

Indeed, writing in the mid-1990s, he drew up a history of the relationship between deprivation and harmful drug use, touching on the classical studies of the Chicago School and ethnographic post-war efforts to conceptualise how drug epidemics seem to flourish with greater intensity in marginal areas (Pearson, 1996). This was to add greater strength to his previous arguments. Importantly, he questioned the way in which many of the other studies set out to explore the issue of drugs and social exclusion but instead ended up securing the association between 'drugs' and 'the poor'. He was equally critical that 'unemployment equated to problematic drug use' as he countered claims that people equipped with 'addictive personalities' were more prone to damaging levels of drug use.

Geoff also seemed to mix his social work background with other aspects of drug use. For example, during the summer of 2000, 'Substance Abuse and the Family' was published in *Current Opinion in Psychiatry*. In the paper, Geoff attempts to explore the micro interactions which take place where children grew up in substance-using families, and how as a consequence, this experience negatively affected children. Geoff seemed unmoved by the potential empirical territory he could research, which is why, by the time Geoff had published with Dick Hobbs on middle-market distribution for the Home Office (Pearson, et al., 2001), their place in history in terms of drug markets was already firmly established, while I, on the other hand, was just finishing my first degree in criminology.

Yet the work undertaken by Geoff and Dick at the turn of the twenty-first century continued to produce publications (Pearson and Hobbs, 2003) predominantly concerned with exploring the way in which drug distribution occurred in local, regional, national and, in some cases, international contexts. Yet Geoff's involvement in exposing significant issues related to attitudes to drug use, the damaging use of drugs and the way in which systemic circumstances often altered 'drug careers' quite significantly. For example, in partnership with Dr Michael Shiner, he published on the attitudes to different drugs among young people and adults, the research being one of the few contemporary studies which has considered how place and meaning of 'illicit drugs' is interpreted by different cohorts. In *One Problem Among Many* (Ward et al., 2003), a Home Office study dedicated to understanding the pressures to use drugs among care leavers, Geoff's involvement in the mixed-methods research was able to emphasise the risk of increased drug use young people faced when in temporary-housing contexts, highlighting, once again, the policy shortfalls of a lack of service provision for this cohort.

The New Problem of Crack Cocaine

In some papers, Geoff drew on the problem of crack cocaine which developed in similar deprived areas of the UK from the mid-1990s onwards, and like Howard Parker, he also wrote at some length about these new issues, although not to the same degree or to the same depth as he had done on heroin. Cocaine's expansion to Europe gathered momentum following the U.S. 'crackdown policies' ('War on Drugs'), which diversified market opportunities. Indeed, increases in cocaine prevalence rates were seen across Europe in the 1980s and 1990s, although they didn't reach the same levels as in the U.S. The UK was not exempt from this expansion. Cocaine use and heroin use also steadily increased from 1975 and this was augmented in the mid- to late 1990s by the advent of crack use in the UK (EMCDDA, 2007; Shifano and Corkery, 2008). Very soon, as in the U.S., similar social and economic repercussions became evident. Research found that crack markets had evolved in 'urban disadvantaged communities', which, some suggest, resulted in increased neighbourhood crime and vandalism, drug dealing, family breakdown, poor educational attainment and disaffected young people (Child et al., 2002; Lupton et al., 2002; May et al., 2007). Yet most of these communities were already socially excluded (Parker et al., 1998) as Geoff had previously identified (Pearson, 1989; 1992). Already vulnerable populations such as sex workers, heroin users and marginalised minority ethnic populations seemed to be worst affected (Parker et al., 1998).

The advent of crack cocaine compounded not only the areas where heroin markets were prevalent but also the circumstances of heroin users. In 2008, at least one in eight arrestees (or 125,000 people) in England and Wales were estimated to be 'problematic' crack and/or heroin users, and between one third and half of new receptions to prison were problematic drug users (crack or/and heroin users)—equivalent to between 45,000 and 65,000 prisoners in England and Wales (UKDPC, 2008). This had high social and economic costs for society because enforcing UK drug policies through various agencies such as the police, courts, probation and the prison service has been estimated to cost £13.5 billion in England and Wales (Hay et al., 2006). There then followed an ambitious campaign to get drug users into treatment. For example, the number of problematic drug users in treatment increased from approximately 88,000 in 1998 to 195,000 in 2006–7 (NTA, 2007). However, despite rhetorical commitments to rebalance UK drug policy spending towards treatment, the bulk of public expenditure remains devoted to criminal justice measures (Stimson, 2000; Reuter and Stevens, 2008). Some suggest there was a shift in the NTA's accountability from the practical matters of recovery such as housing, social care and benefit support, to an 'overemphasis on the treatment of addiction' (Audit Commission, 2004; Fox et al., 2005) at the expense of other key areas of drug policy, such as the prevention of drug-related deaths, viral infections and/or reducing the social exclusion of drug users (Reuter and Stevens, 2008). And it was into all this that I was about to step after graduating with my Masters in Criminology.

My Avenue into Criminology and Thereafter into Crack Dens

My A level results were not as I or my parents had expected so after spending a year out working in the retail industry, and seeing my fair share of fraudulent activity among the staff, I went through the process of university clearing, hoping to get a degree in something. Such was my poor performance that only one university was prepared to admit me and could not offer my desired programme of study, yet had a place on a criminology degree. It sounded interesting so I accepted. Middlesex University, it turned out at the time, was well known for criminology as it was the stomping ground of some of the true greats such as Professors Jock Young, John Lea, Roger Matthews and Vincenzo Ruggiero. I was a slow starter at university as I found it difficult to write, only flourishing in my last two years of study. In my third year, I had managed to get some hourly paid work at the Institute of Psychiatry (we all start somewhere, right?!) and my contract was shortly to expire. In a fluster to get something and find some life direction, I sent my CV to members of the department just before the advent of the summer of 2001.

To my luck, a week later, someone in Imperial College contacted me about an unexpected vacancy on a project interviewing drug-using prisoners. I went along for a brief interview and was researching in prisons the following week. Some of these early memories still remain clear in my head (Briggs, 2011: 33):

> The Victorian prisons really evoke a sense of history for me. Although quite depressing and dirty, there is something oddly intimate about them— especially about HMP Brixton. Once again, I am interviewing drug users with offending histories—or vice versa. For some reason, the medical officer cannot locate the correct person for me to interview. I follow him around the packed wing, weaving in and out of large men who look at me as I walk past. He shows me where I am to be undertaking the interviews and tells me to stay on the wing while he goes to see where the prisoner

has been put/transferred. I get talking to a couple of chaps who hang over the staircase with long brooms in their hands. When a guard walks past, they suddenly get a little more active with their brushes. I get a little bored standing there and since I have no one to talk to, I go for a walk. A young man called Steve offers me a tour. He introduces me to "Chuck, Babs, Pablo"; however, as I stroll along, I hear a crunch under my shoe. Thinking whatever it is will dislodge itself with another step, I continue. However, the crunch becomes an awkward scratch under my shoe with each step I take. It grates on me—like eating sand in a sandwich or scraping nails down a blackboard. I stop and look under my shoe where there is, embedded between the rubber, a whole tooth (including root). Steve starts to smile as I attempt to pick it out with my fingernail.

(Field notes)

What made the biggest impact on me were the testimonies of suffering and how, in the process of undertaking a research project for the Home Office, we ended up asking the right people the wrong questions; it seemed to be all about 'what drugs', 'how many drugs' and 'drug expenditure' rather than why the offenders were taking drugs. Perhaps Geoff had questioned what he had undertaken for the government, which was why he published extensively elsewhere: to be able to explore the central issues in more depth. The surveys we had to use at the time seemed to me to be more about finding out how much drugs the prisoners were using rather than for any use connected with improving prison programmes. I felt uncomfortable with this because part of the research blurb we read to each participant promised to improve their conditions but it was difficult to see how as very few questions were attached to their experience about drug services. It was more about their profile, how long they had used drugs, which drugs they had tried, how much they consumed, what they consumed, how much they spent on drugs, etc. I interviewed well over 150 people in around twenty-five different prisons and got very tired of trying to fit their experience into the box answers (yes/no answers). Very often they were saying things which either contradicted what would fit in the box or I had to try to cut them off mid-response and guide them to answer the question according to my available answers. The research team was given only forty minutes to complete the interview and very often personal questions were put at the beginning of the survey, which to me seemed to put many off from feeling comfortable. In short, the interviews were often rushed, the questions were impersonal and ill-designed and there was little place for deviation. To me, we were not doing justice to the participants of the research.

I was certainly motivated to learn more and enrolled in a Criminology Master programme where I ended up working with the very experts who had taught me my undergraduate in the Centre for Criminology. Of key importance during those years were three main texts: *The Drugtakers* (Young, 1971); *In Search of Respect: Selling Crack in El Barrio* (Bourgois, 1995); and *Doing Time* (Matthews, 1999), probably because they pried open my interest in both drugs, incarceration and ethnography, while at the same time exposed me to the way power relations and structural violence operate through different social institutions. I also worked part time on projects examining jurors' experience of the justice process and fear of crime in a council estate while undertaking freelance work for a private drug and alcohol company which had accumulated several Home Office and Youth Justice Board research projects. By the time my Masters programme had finished, I had research experience, had solidified my interest in drugs and turned my attention to the use of crack cocaine: I wanted to know why the drug was associated with such chaotic use, why it was associated with the highest amounts of crime and why crack cocaine users were among the drug users most marginalized and with the most significant health problems.

At the time, only Howard Parker and colleagues, and to some degree Geoff, had devoted time to this area but many of the Home Office studies seemed more about making a case for more law enforcement around the drug distribution of crack markets and reducing welfare support than anything else, something that Geoff had identified with heroin markets in the 1980s. I took a full-time position at the private drug and alcohol company, and from time to time working with Howard Parker, and started to try to write an ethnographic proposal to study crack use in London. While almost every London borough at the time had a severe crack cocaine problem, it was sad that I had to approach eight different Drug Action Teams with the idea before I was awarded funding from one. Even then, they would only allow me the funding if I signed an insurance liability waiver so I was responsible for myself. I had never really undertaken an ethnographic project before though; probably what I had been doing in numerous prisons around the country seemed similar in the way I wrote about my encounters. I liked the idea of documenting what went on around my interviews in prison (Briggs, 2011: 32–33):

> This time, I am visiting different young offender institutions. Looking back, I think this was certainly more difficult for me, as someone still quite young interviewing people not much younger than me. By now I am used to the potential problems of getting into the prisons. On this study, I make a pointless journey up to HMP Wakefield only to return the same day when the prison guards on reception said they had 'no paperwork' for my visit. I am also used to the jingling noise of the keys, the thick heavy doors, which have to be opened every few seconds, and the odd banter between offenders and the 'screws'. This time I am in a YOI New Hall for young girls. Once again, I have no interview room available and my confidential interviews about drugs, alcohol and service provision threaten to echo around the wing. Once again, I am led in. The wing has several levels and I am led around to what looks a leisure area; there is a TV, books and various magazines. Everyone else is on 'activity' or 'education' so there is hardly anyone on the wing. As I wait, I am approached by Deanne, who is 17 and has already been in prison four times for various violent offences.

Indeed, she walks aggressively and carries the image of her offences. I feel guilty about the information I am collecting because the way in which she answers makes me feels like she has told so many people the same thing so many times. I also feel she is quite selective with me. She gives me short answers, will not expand on anything and the interview lasts only 20 minutes. 'You done yet, mister?' she mumbles. I close my notes and she shuffles off ahead of me. The guard then comes over to officially chaperone her away; she scuffs the floor with her flip-flops, each step awkward and tired. While the guard tells Deanne to go to her cell, I ambled towards the wing exit. There is then a flurry of exchanges on the guard's radio and she tells me there is a prison lockdown (which means no one can move from wing to wing, including me). I stand around looking for things to entertain me. Deanne lingers on the second floor and looks down at me for a minute or two. She shouts down, 'Oi mister, you wanna see my cell'. I ask the guard if this is possible. The guard nods her head and I bound up the two levels of stairs, while the guard rolls her eyes and slowly follows. As I walk into Deanne's cell, I am completely blown away. Deanne jumps on the bed. 'Look, this is my mum and my sister', and childishly waves a picture of her family at me. As I smile looking at the picture, my eye is diverted to the damp and mouldy wall which is littered with drawings, poems, letters; they come alive in the breeze as do the cut-out paper angels flapping from one of the prison bars. She continues to jump around, showing me moments from her life. She grabs a letter from her mum and shoves it in my hand: 'Dis one is my favourite': 'We will always love you. Come home soon', it reads.

(Field notes)

So by the time I started to hang around with crack cocaine users in south London, I was into the swing of documenting experiences. The startling reality which was to come across was totally alien for me; the personal deprivations into which people had descended; the internalized self-abuse of damaging drug-consumption practices; the raw smell of bodies in crack houses. There was just no end to the exposure to numerous broken and damaged lives and the sheer brutality of some of the drug-using environments (Briggs, 2010: 38–9):

We [Blood and I] had to climb a wall near an old train bridge under some barbed wire and then almost jump down into what used to be a garage (I think). It was slippery because it had been raining. I nearly fell by slipping on the bricks and wood. In the yard, there were old tires. There were flies buzzing around, and there was a strong smell of piss and shit. As we walked into the downstairs room, over the broken bricks and wood, there was a mattress in the corner and loads of fag butts on the floor. We went upstairs or tried to as there were stairs missing and you had to almost jump up, but there was a rope to hold on to. Blood warned me to watch where I stood, as there were needles and syringes everywhere. It was so dark,

I could hardly see where I was going. We pulled ourselves to the top of the stairs, where there was a hole in the roof. A bird flew out. I looked to my left and there was what looked like a bedroom, couple of mattresses and sofas—half upturned, half torn. The piss and shit smell became stronger. We walked through a narrow corridor to the right and came into what looked like the main room. There was piss, shit, syringes, semen stains all over the mattresses and sofas. Under each step I took, I could hear the crunch of syringes. I was glad I was wearing my heavy-duty boots. I was invited to sit down by Biker, a squat regular who was well practiced in the art of bike theft. I looked at the sofa, and carefully perched on the arm. The place lacked everything—light, water, electricity, warmth, and it was right under the railway so I reckon no one slept. Blood had spent the last two nights there and now he had lice.

(Field notes)

To this day, if I close my eyes, I can relive these moments in my head, which is why the experience burnt me emotionally (Briggs, 2012b); I got too close to the field and promised myself that immersion could never develop like that again. My difficulty with coming out of the field, in fact, was reflected in my early attempts to write my PhD for, in my appreciation of the drug users circumstances, I struggled to conceptualise their experience; having gotten too close to them I could only see them as systemic victims rather than both victims and perpetrators of their own misery (see Bourgois, 1995). In hindsight, my analysis was too deterministic, and it took me several years to fully withdraw myself from the fieldwork experience before I could separate my emotions from what I needed to write.

Geoff and His Direction on My Work

It was after my revised manuscript was submitted at viva that my first contact with Geoff was made, for he was to be pivotal in the direction of my work and in the guidance of the publication *Crack Cocaine Users: High Society and Low Life in South London* (Briggs, 2012a). Relatively speaking, our lives probably crossed late on; Geoff had retired but was still actively writing and editing the collection *Routledge Advances in Ethnography*. It would have been easy for me to have published my thesis as it was, with the chapters copied and pasted, with some small adjustment to the titles, but Geoff insisted I make it more 'reader friendly' and more generally accessible. This was fine by me because I had always found academic writing to be style restrictive and often unfriendly to flair and creativity; some papers I had read were quite abstract and seemed deliberate in their construction of vocabularies which spoke just to others who were similar in their knowledge of them.

Although Dick was involved, it was mostly Geoff who guided me in revising my book structure. I was to separate a section on the crack house and cut down the referencing quite significantly; Geoff was critical that it would put off readers if they started the book and had to immediately engage with a heavy section dedicated to a literature review. After revising a few chapters, he asked to meet to give me the copies with his comments as the computer he was using wouldn't let him 'save comments on the page', he said. I was struck by Geoff's friendliness when we first met in a pub in London Bridge. When he handed me the paper copies of my chapters, there were only a few notes on it; he neither berated it nor sung its praise. It was 'quite good', he said. After going through several other chapters and meeting up, we spent less time talking about the manuscript and criminology and instead talked about places we had been and fond memories we had. He always made me envious with the number of trips he had planned to exotic destinations to swim with tropical fish, a passion of mine as well.

But Geoff went above all this when I called him one day wanting some advice. One of the most challenging things for me had been to start work in an institution where very little publishing and research took place, and one consequence of this was that some colleagues weren't too welcoming to new staff with different attitudes to these areas. Perhaps this was credit and due reflection of the type of person he was, someone friendly and always looking to support people in difficult circumstances, for it was during a difficult period for me at a former university, that he was there to impart his knowledge and experience. I remember clearly two conversations I had with Geoff on the phone, at some length, about how I could navigate myself through these conflictive situations . . . and there he was, giving me grounded advice on how to work through the problems. In hindsight, I think I could have gotten quite quickly disoriented with the discipline and the university but Geoff was one of those people who helped me refocus and maintain a steady course. My work continued, not only in drugs and social exclusion but also in other areas, and to this day I am grateful for his direction.

In Memory of Geoff: An Ethnography for the Future

I have learned many things for a man I met only half a dozen times; some things I sort of knew which, in the process of having known Geoff, have been confirmed while others have really helped me see clearly through the academic haze. Firstly, in the consideration, and the evaluation (perhaps more importantly), of the implementation of drug policies, there could be nothing more important than to actually consult the person or people who are using the drugs, something which Geoff always canvassed as an expert with decades of experience in the field of drug markets. It's fairly commonplace for drug policy to be broadly designed by policymakers willy nilly in the form of 'shock campaigns' or 'educational programmes' in the hope that the more unappealing drugs are made or the more people 'know' about them will be enough to deter the potential to make 'free will' decisions to consume them. It is a long story told by Geoff (Pearson, 1989; 1992) as well as myself in other works (Briggs, 2012a; 2012b). But, perhaps more alarmingly, drug policy is often poorly designed for reasons connected with our approach as social life researchers. Increasingly, when university departments or private research companies report on drug problems, they either offer statistical accounts of the realities of the drug users' world or deconstruct the drug users' experience into variables otherwise known as 'risk factors'. The complexity of social life does not deserve to appear as complex regressions or even be dismantled into a series of digestible categories but rather appreciated, even if it may seem messy.

The mistakes made in this process seem to do with a) the way research is designed; b) the lack of appreciation of social context of the drug user's world; and c) the way the people under investigation are probed about their behaviour. When designing research, very often the questions can limit the response of the participant, thereby restricting the construction and understanding of subjective realities. The immediate consequence of this is that the full and rich experience of the drug user is almost immediately sidelined. Secondly, much drug research is undertaken in clinical conditions or, perhaps better said, in contexts which are not those where the drug use takes place. In these instances, the physical and structural context of the interview can often skew the responses of the participants, perhaps as they either become fearful that their responses may not be treated with confidence or cannot articulate accounts/rationale for their drug use as they might be able to otherwise if they were using drugs in their natural setting. Lastly, without careful interview guile, there is also the danger that the epistemological elements of the interview can wobble if researchers do not manage the discussion, placing an emphasis on the experience of the person they are interviewing, for example, to avoid patronizing, moralizing them, self-telling (using accounts of themselves, thereby squashing the narrative of the participant) or failing to recognize the importance of particular issues connected with their drug use. A major error in this respect is to confine drug use to rationale choice and to discount cultural, structural, social, situational and subjective elements which influence attitudes and decisions to use drugs.

I have continually canvassed for an ethnographic approach to researching social problems because I believe that getting close to drug users, untangling the complexity of their situations and analyzing their discourses, being critical to their narratives but at the same time allowing them to speak openly about their experiences, is one of, if not the, most important key to forming policy. For example, the reflections made by drug addicts in *Crack Cocaine Users* (Briggs, 2012) are not only key moments in the construction of the drug users' realities but in the research process. In this way, it is important to 'live' their realities in some way so you can feel the data, know how it feels. Geoff Pearson canvassed all these things, and above everything, was a man who believed in people rather than the criminal convictions attached to their actions; who could represent honestly and neutrally about people and problems without letting their stereotype dominate; who was relentless in writing and committed to ensuring that the people he was researching were adequately represented. This was one among many reasons why he wrote so extensively on drugs as well as numerous other pressing issues. To me, he was humble enough to downplay his own achievements which made him always approachable, instead setting the agenda for the next generation by being their inspiration: he was a man for the people he researched as he was for those developing as researchers. His philosophy lives on in my work.

Note

1 Something for which I was to write about in 2014. See Briggs and Dobre (2014) for an analysis of the migration experience for Romanian workers in London.

References

Agar, M. (2003) 'The Story of Crack: Towards a Theory of Illicit Drug Trends' in *Addiction, Research and Theory*, Vol 11 (1): 3–29.

Audit Commission. (2004) *Drug Misuse 2004—Reducing the Local Impact*, London: Audit Commission.

Bourgois, P. (1995) *In search of respect: Selling crack en el barrio*, Cambridge: Cambridge University Press.

Briggs, D. (2010) 'Crack Houses in the UK: Some Notes on their Operations' in *Drugs and Alcohol Today*, Vol 10 (4): 33–42.

Briggs, D. (2011) 'Tales from Prison: Reflections on a Decade of Offender Research' in *Safer Communities*, Vol 10 (4): 31–36.

Briggs, D. (2012) *Crack Cocaine Users: High Society and Low Life in South London*, London: Routledge.

Briggs, D. (2013) *Deviance and Risk on Holiday: An ethnography of British tourists in Ibiza*. London: Palgrave MacMillan.

Briggs, D., and Dobre, D. (2014) *Culture and immigration in context: An ethnography with Romanian migrants workers in London*, London: Palgrave MacMillan.

Child, P., Edmunds, M., and Joseph, I. (2002) *Substance Misuse Treatment Needs in a London Borough*, London: Rivertown DAT.

EMCDDA (2007) *Annual report 2007: The State of the Drugs Problem in Europe*. Luxembourg: Office for Official Publications of the European Communities.

Fox, A., Khan, L., Briggs, D., Rees-Jones, N., Thompson, Z., and Owens, J. (2005) *Throughcare and Aftercare: Approaches and Promising Practice in Service Delivery for Clients Released from Prison or Leaving Residential Rehabilitation*, Home Office Online Report, London: Home Office.

Hay, G., Gannon, M., MacDougall, J., Millar, T., Eastwood, C., and McKeganey, N. (2006) *Estimates of the Prevalence of Opiate Use and/or Crack Cocaine Use (2004/05) for the London Region*, London: Home Office.

Lupton, R., Wilson, A., May, T., Warburn, H., and Turnbull, P. (2002) *Drug Markets in Deprived Neighbourhoods, Research Findings 167*, London: Home Office.

Matthews, R. (1999) *Doing time: An introduction to the sociology of imprisonment*, London: Palgrave MacMillan.

May, T., Cossalter, S., Boyce, I., and Hearnden, I. (2007) *Drug Dealing in Brixton Town Centre*, London: Lambeth DAT.

NTA. (2007) *Statistics for Drug Treatment Activity in England 2006/07: National Drug Treatment Monitoring System*, London: National Treatment Agency for Substance Misuse.

Parker, H., Bakx, K., and Newcombe, R. (1987) *Living with Heroin: The Impact of a Drugs Epidemic on an English Community*, Milton Keynes: Open University Press.

Parker, H., Eggington, R., and Bury, C. (1998) *New Heroin Outbreaks Amongst Young People in England and Wales*, Crime Detection and Prevention Series, London: Home Office.

Pearson, G. (1989) *The New Heroin Users*, Oxford: Blackwell.

Pearson, G. (1992) 'Drugs and Criminal Justice' in E. Buning, E. Drucker, A. Matthews, R. O'Hare, and R. Newcombe (Eds) *The Reduction of Drug-Related Harm*, London: Routledge.

Pearson, G. (1996) 'Drugs and Deprivation' in *Royal Society for Public Health*, Vol 116: 113–117.

Pearson, G. (2000) 'Substance Abuse and the Family' in *Current Opinion in Psychiatry*, Vol 13 (3): 305–308.

Pearson, G., and Hobbs, R. (2003) ' "E" is for Enterprise: Middle Level Drug Markets in Ecstasy and Stimulants' in *Addiction, Research and Theory*, Vol 12 (6): 565–576.

Reinarman, C., and Levine, H. (Eds.) (1997) *Crack in America: Demon Drugs and Social Justice*, Berkeley: University of California Press.

Reuter, P., and Stevens, A. (2008) 'Assessing UK Drug Policy from a Crime Control Perspective' in *Criminology and Criminal Justice*, Vol 8: 461–482.

Shifano, F., and Corkery, J. (2008) 'Cocaine/Crack Cocaine Consumption, Treatment Demand, Seizures, Related Offences, Prices, Average Purity Levels and Deaths in the UK (1990–2004)' in *Journal of Psychopharmacology*, Vol 22: 71–79.

Stimson, G. (2000) 'Blair Declares War': The Unhealthy State of British Drug Policy' in *International Journal of Drug Policy*, Vol 11: 259–264.

UK Drug Policy Commission (UKDPC) (2008) *Reducing Drug Use, Reducing Re-offending*, London: UKDPC.

Wacquant, L. (2004) 'Decivilizing and Demonizing: The Social and Symbolic Remaking of the Black Ghetto and Elias in the Dark Ghetto' in S. Loyal and S. Quilley (Eds) *The Sociology of Norbert Elias*, Cambridge: Cambridge University Press.

Ward, J., Henderson, Z., and Pearson, G. (2003) *One Problem Among Many: Drug Use Among Care Leavers in Transition to Independent Living*, London: Home Office.

Young, J. (1971) *The Drugtakers: The Social Meaning of Drug Use*, London: Judson, McGibbon and Kee.

12 'Ethiopia or Utopia?'

Reflections on the
New Heroin Users

Mark Gilman

It's a cliché because it's true. I am where I am today because of Geoff Pearson. When I met Geoff I was a mature student aged 25, with dubious motives for being in higher education. Had I not contracted dysentery in India in 1980 I would have carried on travelling round the world seeing Jack Kerouac looking back at me from the mirror. Dysentery introduced me to people who suggested I should 'go to college or university' (it's a long story involving tropical medicine waiting rooms). No one had ever suggested I should or could go to higher education. I knew lots of people who had been to prison and a few who had been admitted into psychiatric institutions but I didn't know anyone who had gone to university. When I asked my dysentery friends why I should go to university, they said, 'because you read books, the student grant is twice as much as the dole and you can stay in bed all day'. So, in September 1981, I found myself in Bradford, West Yorkshire. I had chosen Bradford & Ilkley Community College because their advert showed a backdrop of the recent inner-city riots (or 'uprisings'), the beer was good, the cheap and cheerful curry houses were a revelation and it was less than one hour's drive from my mum's newsagents in Bury, Greater Manchester.

I started out on an education degree to become a teacher in primary schools because there was a shortage of men in primary schools. I enjoyed the teaching practice with the children in the classroom, but the staff room alienated me completely. I had nothing in common with the other teachers. I hadn't enjoyed school and had left at 15 with few qualifications, and couldn't ever imagine spending a lifetime with those people in that environment. So, I switched to a BA (Hons) in Organisation Studies. Growing up in a newsagents shop and working on market stalls in working-class communities in Greater Manchester I had known quite a few people who had drifted into acquisitive crime as a kind of career option. So, I fancied that one day I might eventually put these two elements together and study organised crime (this is still on my list of things to do).

I think I first met Geoff Pearson towards the end of my first degree in Organisation Studies in The Mannville Arms in Bradford. I am pretty sure that our first barroom conversations were prompted when Geoff heard my strong Bury accent and we started to talk about our shared passion in Manchester United

Football Club. I was a season ticket holder and went to all the home games and quite a few away matches. I didn't really know who Geoff was until I saw the advert for a research assistant on a project called 'Young People and Heroin in the North of England' (Pearson et al., 1986). I asked around and realised that this really nice bloke and passionate United supporter was a proper academic. Moreover, one of his books was called *Hooligans: A History of Respectable Fears* (Pearson, 1983). Having followed Manchester United home and away throughout the 1970s I had a close anthropological proximity to football hooliganism as well as regular crime and ordinary criminals.

When I was appointed as a research assistant to work with Geoff Pearson and Shirley McIvor on a study of young people and heroin in the North of England, it really did feel like I had won the lottery. My life changed from that moment on and everything I have done since then is pretty much down to Geoff giving me a chance to prove that I could do something with my life that would pay the bills and keep me interested. To this day my passion is still with addiction; crime and social policy and I have had the privilege of working in research, policy and practice for universities, government departments and charitable organisations.

Geoff understood the importance of social class in British society. He was one of very few academics who genuinely understood the world view that emanates from the housing estates and marginalised communities of the UK. We shared several demographic features. We were white men from working-class backgrounds who, via education, had found a home in middle-class England. He was always prepared to listen when I said that I never felt like I fitted in anywhere now. You couldn't really be middle class because your accent and your bad teeth betray your roots, and the working class become ever more suspicious as you move up the road to the posh houses. The fieldwork for the Young People and Heroin research took place at the same time as the miners' strike came to an end. People were coming to terms with the political implications of the end of the kind of class politics that had dominated the post-war period. Identity politics began to replace class politics and much of my interest in politics went the same way as my interest in being a schoolteacher or a full-time academic. The truth is that I have never really been a part of the working-class world occupied by coal miners or factory workers. I lived amongst the working class but I lived in the paper shop, and I passed my eleven plus (but didn't make it to a proper grammar school) and left school at 15 with four poor 'O Levels'. Geoff and I used to talk about the plunder of biography in the pursuit of ethnography, and I wrote about this in 1994 in relation to football fans and drug use (Gilman, 1994).

Between leaving school and going to Bradford I was engaged in all kinds of casual work and travelled extensively. I had thought these were my 'wasted years', but in conversations with Geoff I realised that the experiences of these ten years could be useful in anthropology and ethnography. I had spent ten years (1972 to 1981) rubbing shoulders with a very particular kind of people. These were people who exist in that grey area between the licit and illicit economies—not heavy-duty criminals in the main but people who are 'chancers', 'spivs' and 'wheelers and dealers'. These people came from working-class backgrounds but for one reason or another had rejected, or been rejected by the kind of honest toil associated with heavy industry and manufacturing. Instead they hustled around in the quest for a fast buck and a few quid on the side. Many of them were officially unemployed and 'signed on' (for state welfare benefits) until it became too much trouble, at which point they disappeared from official records until the organs of the state finally caught up with them. One of Geoff's contemporaries, Laurie Taylor, talked about attending a funeral of a hedonistic entrepreneur and in describing the mourners he reminded me of a great many of the people I grew up with:

> They were mostly men of about 25. But men who'd probably been men since the age of 14, when they decided that school was a wank and that, rather than hanging around waiting for a dead end job, they'd go out and find their own way to make a living. A bit of wheeling and dealing. A little ducking and diving. What was new was their confidence, their solidarity. As soon as they began to talk, you realised that this was not a diffuse collection of misfits, suitable cases for treatment or counselling. This was a small unapologetic army of working class entrepreneurs equipped with a defiant sense of moral righteousness and an absolute certainty that those like themselves who made money from their wits were the winners, the top men.
>
> (Taylor, 1992, p. 11)

It was precisely these kinds of working-class men who were the early adopters of heroin smoking in Merseyside and Greater Manchester in the first wave of brown powder heroin epidemics. Colin Blaney gives an excellent introduction to this world in two of his books *Grafters* (Blaney, 2006) and *Undesirables* (Blaney, 2014).

For the practicalities of the Young People and Heroin study it was decided that we would divide up the North of England between me and Shirley. I concentrated on Lancashire and Cumbria, Greater Manchester and parts of Merseyside with occasional forays into South Yorkshire. We were assisted by Susan Noble, an American who had the unenviable task of transcribing tape-recorded interviews between me, with a strong Bury accent, and the interviewees whose accents ranged from deep Liverpudlian 'scouse' to the broadest South Yorkshire. The wide range of accents and terminologies was something that intrigued and amused us and made the work so much fun. But, it was the stories that mattered most. Geoff insisted that we let the respondents tell their stories as naturally as possible. Having interviewed one person I asked if they knew anyone else who would be prepared to speak to us. This 'snowballing' technique is now widely used. At the time I remember asking Geoff when we would know that we had interviewed enough people in one area—'When you start hearing the same story, then I suppose that particular snowball has melted'. Geoff was a populist. He wanted people to understand and engage with the research process. He was a natural scholar who could explain the most complex sociological and criminological theories in ways that the man at the bar understood.

I remember being challenged at a meeting when I was talking about our study by a prominent research psychologist who said that our study was interesting but the methodology was no more robust than one might expect from a well-researched magazine article. I took exception to this and asked Geoff how we should respond. It was Geoff's response to this incident that steered me away from any serious aspirations to be a career academic. He said something along the lines of the best qualitative research needing to be a good read and, in fact, the best ethnographies should read like a novel, so I should take this as a compliment. Over the subsequent years we shared a passion for anthropology and ethnography, and I came to appreciate that the best of them do indeed read like good novels. They tell a story based on the evidence. Some of our most intense and enjoyable conversations over the last few years were about my obsession (which I think Geoff shared) with research about the lives of inner-city American 'addicts'. We now have a standard to aspire to. *The Corner: A Year in the Life of an Inner City Neighbourhood* introduced the world to the realities of life on a couple of streets in Baltimore, Maryland, United States, and was dramatized for television (Simon and Burns, 2009). This groundbreaking ethnographic work was to find popular expression in the seminal television series 'The Wire'. Just like David Simon and Ed Burns, Geoff Pearson was always interested in giving a voice to the outsider.

Geoff retained a steadfast academic regard for quantitative data but was always looking to find the human beings inside those data. One can respect quantitative data whilst simultaneously tasting the salty tears of the human beings whose lives might be hidden by the bald statistics of epidemiology. Alarm bells of caution ring every time I hear policy and practice decisions being made in absolute confidence because they are based on 'evidence' derived from randomised controlled trials, meta analyses and systematic reviews where, so often, there is no sense whatsoever of the lives of the people who will be affected.

Over the past few years I have become interested in the public health research on social contagion and notions of 'homophilly'. In other words, like attracts like. We tend to be attracted to people like ourselves. The Framingham Study has shown how smoking cessation and divorce are contagious and that our fat friends make us fat (Christakis and Fowler, 2007). In our research on heroin in the North of England, we soon realised that heroin use and heroin problems were features of urban clustering. We looked at a small town in Greater Manchester with a population of approximately 25,000 people that had a reputation for being home to significant numbers of heroin addicts. When we looked we found that most of them were clustered in a few streets on a particular estate. Housing policy and friendship networks had seen heroin use become socially contagious. But to be infected you had to be nearby in terms of geography (housing policy) and/or friendship networks. This is when we debunked the idea of there being a Mr Big heroin dealer giving away free samples at the ice cream van. Instead what we found were local friendship-based, heroin-using networks being supplied by one of their own peers. Tragically for them and their families, when one of these guys got caught they were cast in the role of the evil heroin dealer, a folk devil who duly received harsh custodial sentences to satisfy the blood lust created by the moral panic.

When our fieldwork began in the spring of 1985, most heroin users bought their heroin from someone they knew who also used heroin—a 'user dealer'. Typically, this would be someone who would buy about £300 worth of heroin (or have it 'laid on'—loaned in lieu of payment) and take out enough for their own habit and then sell the rest to recoup the original £300. Obviously, this same system could operate at higher and lower levels and amounts. By the end of our fieldwork (late summer 1985) much of the heroin in Greater Manchester and Lancashire was distributed via a relatively open street market in south central Manchester (Gilman, 2000). The centralisation of heroin distribution was a result of successful actions against user dealers who were very easy to arrest and charge with supply. The primary purpose of the user dealer's market activity is to get enough drugs for themselves. Unlike the person who is involved in heroin distribution solely for the money—a 'bread head'—the user dealer spends a lot of time intoxicated. The user dealer often doesn't take anti-surveillance measures and doesn't really know whether it's New York or New Year, and catching them is like shooting fish in a barrel. Police actions against user dealers on white working-class housing estates could usually count on good information from local residents. Why does Tommy have taxis pulling up outside his house at all hours of the day and night? He's up to no good. I bet it's the same people who robbed the fishing tackle out of my brother's garden shed. I'm phoning the police. This wasn't the same in south central Manchester where sections of the community still held strong anti-police attitudes after the riots or 'uprisings' of 1981. The site of the open air market was a shopping precinct and not primarily houses and flats. Rivalry over market share as well as the usual things that young men argue over (girls and respect) led to Manchester becoming 'Gunchester' and several young men lost their lives in the crossfire that ensued (Walsh, 2005).

In later years I became friendly with one of the most prolific arresting officers in many of these cases (known to the heroin users of Greater Manchester as 'Bad Ron'), and he asked me if I would send his apologies to one of the men who had served one of these long sentences. I duly obliged but I am afraid to say the apology was not accepted. Some years later, Bad Ron was featured on the front page of the Manchester Evening News where he issued a public apology to all the people he had arrested as he had come to realise the futility of the war on drugs. In recent years the user dealer has made something of a comeback. Packages of heroin and crack cocaine can be 'laid on' to user dealers by 'bread heads'. This might involve pre-packaged bundles of, say, fifty-five £20 'deals', with each deal consisting of two brown (heroin) and one white (crack) or any other variation. The bread head lays on these fifty-five £20 'deals' for £1,000. So, when the user dealer has sold fifty at £20 each, they have the £1,000 and five deals, or £100 profit. If the user dealer sells out and has the £1,000 ready for lunchtime there may be no chance of a 're-up' (e.g., another 55 deals). The bread heads don't want any user dealer to get too big, and bitter experience has taught that giving more drugs to a using addict is like giving strawberries to a donkey. All too often the second lot of fifty-five deals doesn't raise £1,000 as users consume too much themselves. Then they are in debt, and the bread head may have to punish them and violence is bad for business.

Quite early in our research we hit upon the idea of the 'normalisation' of heroin use. At the outset of our fieldwork we had expected to find a dishevelled and dispirited bunch of people using heroin in darkened rooms as an act of retreat from the harsh realities of Thatcher's Britain. Instead, we found that most of those who got caught up in smoking brown powder heroin in the mid-1980s were pretty normal young men and women. They didn't appear to be particularly deviant or sick or diseased. They weren't committed to any notion of bohemia or hippydom, and they wouldn't have known William Burroughs from William Hill. They happened to live in a place with a group of friends where heroin appeared as a commodity. It didn't have to be injected, it could be smoked, it was relatively cheap and it got you wasted. During the Industrial Revolution there was a saying that 'the quickest way out of Manchester is a bottle of gin'. Brown powder heroin did exactly the same for unemployed youths in the North of England in the 1980s. Mass unemployment provided part of the answer to the questions: Why heroin? Why here? Why now?

If there had been jobs to go on Monday morning, then many of those who experimented with heroin and went on to become full-blown heroin addicts might not have. We know that heroin can be used as a recreational drug. It's probably not a great idea to try this but it can be done and Norman Zinberg had told us about his 'chippers', who used heroin only on specific occasions and managed to maintain a recreational relationship with heroin by restricting its use within tight parameters (Zinberg, 1984). What we were seeing was time and structure (time discipline) being eroded by mass unemployment. Sadly, many of these otherwise normal heroin users became heroin addicts by default. They didn't have jobs. Rather they existed within the time vacuums that are created by unemployment. In these circumstances there is no difference between weekends and weekdays. Once physically dependent on heroin the time vacuum is immediately filled by the need to get up and get some money to get some more heroin to stave off withdrawals. Another way of making a bag of heroin go further is to inject it. Very quickly our normal unemployed heroin addicts were committing crime to get the money to buy heroin and sharing equipment to inject it.

Very quickly these new heroin users found themselves in a new kind of hell characterised by the monotony of Beezley Street's groundhog days where, as John Cooper Clarke said so well, 'it's a sociologists' paradise, each days repeats' (Clarke, 1983, p. 83). The Clash also provided a fitting soundtrack in 'Straight to Hell', . . . 'the steel mills rust there ain't no need for ya—Go straight to hell boys' (The Clash, 1982). This particular hell consisted of a relentless groundhog day where each day consisted of the same thing: get the money; get the gear, day in and day out.

The spectre of young working-class people getting addicted to a drug they couldn't afford and stealing to raise the money to buy it gave birth to 'fear driven funding'. Drug charities like The Lifeline Project in Manchester had been struggling along on a shoestring for more than ten years (Yates, 1992). The fear of heroin driven acquisitive crime (particularly domestic burglary) saw an unprecedented injection of funding into the expansion of community drug treatment services. The Central Funding Initiative of some £18 million was the beginning of an investment that was to reach almost £1 billion in 2010 (Maremmani et al., 2014). The Lifeline Project now has a considerable share of the UK drug treatment provider market and has an annual turnover well in excess of that original £18 million. Fear has funded the growth of a British addiction treatment industry.

The fear of heroin-driven crime was soon followed by a fear of heroin-driven injection practices that included the sharing of needles and syringes that could lead to an epidemic of HIV and AIDS. This fear soon dictated that the practice of harm reduction should become the dominant organising principle. The behaviour of these new heroin addicts needed to be contained and controlled to protect the public's health and safety. Heroin-driven acquisitive crime was (and still is) successfully reduced by providing wholesale provision of opioid substitution treatment (OST), and methadone maintenance quickly became the treatment of choice in community drug services. Needle and syringe programmes (NSP) to prevent the spread of blood-borne viruses (BBV; e.g., HIV) from this high-risk group (injecting drug users) to the general population followed in tandem. OST and NSP became the fish and chips of British drug treatment. Somewhere in there I worry that we may have lost sight of the human beings who were reduced to numbers on a spreadsheet to be manipulated, massaged and fought over in ideological and financial drug treatment wars and funding bids.

The contemporary UK recovery movement is, in part, a working-class backlash against the marginalisation of the individual addict who was subject to policies and practices that were designed for the benefit of the public's health and safety and not theirs. In societal harm reduction terms, policies and practices can be successful if they reduce crime and BBV transmission at the same time as the individual addict's health and welfare deteriorates. I was involved in establishing harm reduction in the 1980s, and I remain a committed harm reductionist whilst accepting that the health and welfare of some individual addicts has been sacrificed on the altar of societal harm reduction.

I have also been a student and friend of the UK Recovery Movement since 2005. In our last few conversations, Geoff was starting to develop an interest in the overlaps between the process of recovery from addiction and the process of desisting from crime. Of particular interest is the role of stories and storytelling and how people in recovery and in desistance construct stories ('the redemptive scripts') about their lives wherein they are not responsible for their problems but they are responsible for the solutions to their problems. In Alcoholics Anonymous meetings, stories are shared that tell the newcomer what it was like, what happened, and what it is like now. Jesse Jackson famously said, 'You are not responsible for being down but you are responsible for getting up. Sweat and tears are both wet and salty. Tears will get you sympathy; sweat will get you change' (Maruna, 2008, p. 148).

Recovery stories are often the flip side of addiction stories. This is how I got into addiction and this is how I got out of it. In the first wave of brown powder heroin use a lot of the working-class 'addicts' had been introduced to heroin by way of close proximity and easy access. They didn't appear to have had particularly traumatic childhoods, and we knew next to nothing about their genetic heritage. Looking back down the years I do wonder if they were as normal as they seemed at the time. I say this because some of those who developed a taste for heroin steered themselves away once they saw where this road led. Like the distinctions made in Alcoholics Anonymous between problem drinkers and alcoholics, some of these heroin users were able to stop in the face of ill health, divorce and parental pressure. The 'addicts', however, were in for the long haul and for them the years ahead were to be characterised by hospitals, institutions and prisons.

Their heroin use was forged in a context of mass unemployment, and their addictions were developed and consolidated by welfare benefit dependency. When methadone maintenance first hit the streets of the East Coast of America there was hope that unemployed heroin addicts would go to work and spend the money they would have spent on heroin on something legitimate. Unfortunately, some of them (a lot of them?) spent their heroin money on alcohol and stayed on welfare. This led to the term 'Methadone, Wine and Welfare' (Preble and Miller, 1977). The UK version of this is Methadone, Booze, Benzos, Benefits and Daytime TV. Today's heroin addicts are now trapped in lives where complex dependency is the norm. What was once a heroin habit is now a heroin habit plus a methadone dependency multiplied by an alcohol problem and divided by an insatiable desire for crack cocaine and doughnuts. The treatment industry's methadone and needles have reduced criminal activity and the spread of HIV. Heroin addicts are kept alive long enough to hear the recovery message or die prematurely from a chronic lifestyle-related illness such as liver disease (alcohol) or lung cancer (smoking). Failure to uncritically sing the praises of harm reduction is to risk condemnation and be cast as an abstentionist conservative or an abstinence-based conservative (even though harm reduction came of age under conservative governments).

As ever in Britain, class confuses everything. Addiction is often said to be an equal opportunities condition that doesn't respect class, race or gender. The most extreme forms of addiction are products of a perfect storm of genetics, childhood trauma and early exposure to drink and drugs. If addiction is in your family history, then you need to be hyper vigilant in respect of your relationship with drink and drugs. If you experienced childhood trauma, then you are at higher risk of addiction. If you grew up in a family or a community within which drink and drugs were easily available and their use normalised, then your risk profile cranks up another couple of notches. The trauma can vary on a continuum from extreme acts of physical and sexual abuse at one end and the emotional neglect of a distant parent at the other. 'It's Friday, it's five to five . . . It's Crackerjack!' For a couple of generations this introduction to the popular children's BBC TV show signalled the start of the weekend and was a joyous sound. However, for the children of alcoholic fathers this was an anxiety-provoking sound. If your dad had a drink problem and got paid on Friday lunchtime and went straight to the pub, then Friday night could go one of two ways: sloppy kisses, hugs and pie and chips all round or a slap round the head and straight to bed. In trauma terms it doesn't really matter which one it was (though the pie and chips were obviously preferred) as it's the unknowing and the uncertainty that matters. To be in such a high state of neurological arousal and anxiety as a child and to have to worry about the behaviour of the person who is supposed to love and look after you isn't normal—it's traumatic. Eventually though the traumatised child discovers drink and drugs for him- or herself and now it really doesn't matter which father comes home or whether he comes home at all. Now you have your own medicine and can treat your anxiety with something that, unlike adults, is reliable and honest. Young people who develop the most serious substance use problems tend to become detached from people and attached to substances. This is not surprising given the behaviour of so many of the adults in their lives.

A can of strong alcohol or a joint of skunk will never lie. It does what it says on the tin—every time, guaranteed. White cider doesn't promise you a bike for Christmas and then drink all the money. A £10 bag of skunkweed doesn't promise to take you on holiday and then blow the holiday money on its own heroin habit. Of course, the perfect storms of addiction also blow into the lives of the rich and famous. But, if all this is being played out against a wider backdrop of multiple disadvantage and complex dependencies, the prognosis is bleak and it's not long before heroin arrives as the ultimate in self-medication and starts to solve problems you never even knew you had. Crack cocaine is now twinned with heroin in most retail distribution systems. It's virtually impossible to buy just 'brown' (heroin) on its own. Most of the lowest-level sales are for brown and 'white' (crack cocaine). Gone are the days of the single-substance heroin devotee. The opiophile has been replaced by the addict alcoholic who enters treatment services using opioids, benzodiazepines, alcohol and crack cocaine.

Addiction may be an equal opportunity problem but treatment for addiction is heavily class biased. If you can afford to buy your heroin or you can acquire your opioid medications without recourse to theft from shops, cars and houses or prostitution and soliciting, then you *have* a problem. If you steal to buy your drugs of addiction, then you *are* a problem. If you *have* a problem, you can get treated for that problem. You (or your insurance company) may have to pay for that treatment but it will look like treatment. You will be detoxified and treated in a residential centre, the treatment goal will usually be abstinence from all drugs (including alcohol) and your aftercare will consist of attending meetings of Alcoholics Anonymous (AA), Narcotics Anonymous (NA) or Cocaine Anonymous (CA). On the other hand, if you *are* a problem, you are most likely enrolled onto the evidence-based frontline treatment of Opioid Substitution Treatment (OST). The treatment goal will be to keep you alive by giving you more opioid drugs to raise your tolerance to opioids, manage your behaviour so that you reduce the amount of crime you commit (and the victims you create) and keep you free from HIV (and other BBVs) so that you don't spread those diseases to the wider population. To the person on the Clapham omnibus this doesn't look like treatment but the social message is clear: all addicts are equal but some are more equal than others.

In criminological theory, Left Realism assisted in paving the way for an acceptance of this utilitarian harm-reduction approach. Working-class people are often the most victimised by the behaviour of heroin addicts in their communities. It's their houses, sheds and cars that get robbed first. OST reduces the number of working-class victims of drug-driven crime and alongside Needle and Syringe programmes they rightly make up the basic building blocks of the current British treatment system. The inequity arises when that's all you get in the name of treatment. The contemporary UK recovery movement is an attempt to rectify this and is, at its heart, a movement for social justice, with its roots in the self-help and self-improvement movements of the nineteenth and twentieth centuries, including trade unions, friendly societies, the co-op and the workers educational association.

Middle-class addicts such as doctors, dentists, lawyers and pilots don't tend to end up on methadone maintenance programmes. Rather, they go to abstinence-based residential treatment centres and get aftercare support from AA, NA and CA. The contemporary British drug treatment system is not unlike the British education system. You get what you're given unless you can afford to pay, get a scholarship or sponsorship or someone you know can show you and your family how to work the system. Develop a religious habit, start attending church and get your kids into the local church schools. Buy a house in the middle-class catchment area of the most successful comprehensive school whose pupils have parents in good jobs and professions. Take a couple of weeks off work and detoxify yourself at home and get to AA, NA or CA and do ninety meetings in ninety days. You will save yourself a fortune. There are no waiting lists. Your chances of life insurance will be unaffected as no one in authority will ever know and you will be getting the same support as someone who has spent £30,000 on a detox and some state-of-the-art talking therapies. The most expensive treatment services send their patients and clients to AA and NA and CA anyway, so cut out the middle man and go straight to the source of long-term recovery where everything is completely free. It must come as a shock to realise that, in effect, you have spent £30,000 (or much more in some cases) on a Big Book of Alcoholics Anonymous. In 1985, drug treatment services were coming to grips with the £18 million that was invested by the Central Funding Initiative. Organisations such as The Lifeline Project in Manchester and The Bridge Project in Bradford were used to making do and mending. Much of what they did was based on what had worked for the people who set these organisations up. The Blenheim Project in London produced booklets on Do It Yourself (DIY) detox. People who had developed a heroin dependency could be found using the cold water extraction method on a box of paracetemol and codeine tablets. Once the paracetemol was extracted the codeine was used as part of a DIY detox. Another favourite in Manchester and Liverpool was the "desert detox". This involved getting to somewhere like Egypt or Israel (or even Spain) with a green soda pop bottle full of methadone and weaning yourself off whilst walking in the desert or along the beach. After billions of pounds worth of investment the contemporary UK recovery movement is rediscovering this DIY approach to treatment. It's always been true that 'getting off is easy but staying off is hard'. Thanks to the newfound interest in mutual aid the staying off is getting easier and it gets easier with every person that does it. Narcotics Anonymous has seen unprecedented growth in Liverpool, Birmingham, Manchester and Lancashire. The growth of NA in working-class communities of the UK has echoes of the situation in Iran where NA's growth is unprecedented (Lavitt, 2014). This success has seen alternative forms of mutual aid emerge as well. Some of these are based on ideas of cognitive behavioural therapy or extensions of faith-based organisations. But, it's the growth of the 12-step fellowships amongst working-class addicts and alcoholics that is most interesting because this growth has happened in the face of wholesale opposition. AA and NA and CA with their talk of God, spirituality and higher powers are an anathema to the secular liberals that dominate in the worlds of academia, commissioning services and providing services. It is even more frustrating for commissioners and providers because the 12-step fellowships cannot be bought in and co-opted to do their bidding. A fundamental principle of 12-step fellowships is that they are totally self-financing. The only money they have is that which they raise by passing the hat or the pot in line with their Tradition Seven ('we are totally self-financing'). The 12-step fellowships have proved particularly popular with the people who were criminally active before ever they became heroin addicts. It seems that they respond well to the simplicity of the programme and the uncompromising way that peer support works in these fellowships. There is none of the baffling existentialism inherent in so many other talking therapies. Take non-directive Rogerian counselling, for example. You go for help (having been coerced to seek that help by family and/or the criminal justice system) and you explain your situation to the counsellor, who then says "and how do you feel about that?" When you look baffled, the counsellor explains that you already have the solutions to your own problems and all they will do is help you find your own solutions. Moreover, the counsellor will have no personal experience of addiction or if they do they will not be able to disclose this because it's unprofessional. Compare this to what happens in 12-step fellowships. You get there via attraction, not promotion. You hear that so and so who you used to be in prison with is 'in recovery'. He or she no longer uses drugs and has a house, a regular job, a family and a whole network of new friends. So, you make enquiries and you get to a meeting. In this meeting you hear stories of people who were just like you. They used drugs and drank alcohol like you, they 'grafted (committed crimes) like you and they had been in all the same institutions as you. The same approved schools, the same borstals, the same Young Offenders, the same adult prisons, the same detox and rehabilitation centres and the same methadone clinics. As they share their stories in the meetings you sit there with the same three words rattling round your head—'yeah me too!' This creates the identification necessary to embrace the 12-step programme. There are no existential grey areas in those rooms. It's very simple—if you want what we've got (jobs, homes and friends), you just need to do what we've done. ***Doing*** is what it's all about. It's not about thinking or feeling or any of that middle-class therapeutic indulgence. It's a programme of action. Cognitive approaches can suggest that you can think your way to right living. The 12-step fellowships say that by your actions you can live your way to right thinking. The other thing is that the 12-step fellowships offer you a different gang to join. In fact, in Liverpool and Manchester, people in 12-step recovery will often refer to themselves as 'being in the firm'. In Lancashire, people say they are part of the 'odd squad'—'we are here because we are not all there'. The humour in the rooms is fierce and deeply dark. Someone will tell a story that would make 'civilians' recoil in disgust and horror and those on the firm, the odd squad all start howling with laughter. You woke up in your mother-in-law's bed caked in vomit, feces and urine—yeah me too. What a laugh. You just don't get that in a counselling session with Richard. The rooms are not for the faint-hearted though as the advice can be brutal: 'Take the cotton wool out of your ears and stuff it in your mouth. You might just hear something that will save your life'. Recovery in the rooms can be especially challenging for the highly educated: 'I have a degree you know'. 'Good, thermometers have degrees and you know where they shove them, don't you?' At the end of 12-step meetings, after the serenity prayer and whilst people are still holding hands, there is a saying that is often recited: 'It works if you work it so work it because you're worth it'. They could add it doesn't work because you *know* it or because you *feel* it. There is also no place for victims in the 12-step rooms. 'Victimese' might be the lingua franca of treatment but it's not spoken in 12-step rooms as they know how it goes: 'Poor me, poor me, pour me a drink!' Recovery with your peers in the 12-step rooms is about a programme of action that takes place in the present and requires presence. People come into the rooms with horrific stories of abuse and neglect only to be told that yesterday is history and tomorrow is a mystery. All we have and will ever have is today, this moment right here and right now, and we choose to do the right thing, right now. This is sometimes put in a little bit more prosaic and pithy way: 'If you have one foot in the past and one foot in the future, you are pissing on the present!' This is all done with the most intense sense of love and does make you start to believe that the Beatles were right all along and all you need is love (although the £1 billion has helped).

Given our passion for stories I have to end with the story that made us cry with laughter. I went to a small end-terraced house in South Yorkshire to record an interview with a young man and his wife about their heroin use. When I got there a young baby lay asleep on a scatter cushion and the wife was nodding in and out of sleep or was heavily intoxicated. This was at the time of Band Aid and famine relief. I asked the husband how he and his wife had got into heroin. 'Well, we used to just use amphetamines and then last winter the chimney fell through the glass outhouse and we all had to move into this front room with the baby and it was freezing and you don't want to be freezing and speeding, do you. So, we tried some heroin and that were it.' I then said that this explained how they had started to experiment and asked how it became a regular thing, a habit? The husband said he just liked it but at this moment the wife woke up and said, 'It sends you to Ethiopia'. The husband looked at me, gave a resigned sigh, then said, "She means Utopia, the silly cow!' I hope and yes, I pray, that that guy and his wife made it to tell that story in the rooms of Narcotics Anonymous and that that baby is now a successful 30-year-old with a job, a home and friends, and not living the dream of methadone, booze, benzos, benefits and daytime TV.

References

Blaney, C. (2006) *Grafters: The Inside Story of the Wide Awake Firm, Europe's Most Prolific Sneak Thieves*, Maverick House.

Blaney, C. (2014) *Undesirables: The Inside Story of the Inter City Jibbers*, John Blake Publishing.

Christakis, N. A. and Fowler, J. H. (2007) The Spread of Obesity in a Large Social Network Over 32 Years. *New England Journal of Medicine* 357(4): 370–379.

Clarke, J. C. (1983) *Ten Years in an Open Necked Shirt—and Other Poems*, Arrow/Arena Books.

Gilman, M. (1994) Football and Drugs: Two Cultures Clash. *The International Journal of Drug Policy*, 5(1): 40–51.

Gilman, M. (2000) "A Qualitative View of Drugs Policing: Heroin Markets in Greater Manchester, UK." In: Greenwood, G. and Robertson, K., eds. *Understanding and Responding to Drug Use: The Role of Qualitative Research*, pp. 203–209. EMCDDA.

Lavitt, J. (2014) The Crescent and the Needle: The Remarkable Rise of NA in Iran, *The Fix*.

Maremmani, I., Hill, D., Gilman, M. and Littlewood, R. (2014) Increasing Importance of Measuring Outcomes in Opioid Dependence Care: What Matters now and in the Future? *Heroin Addiction Related Clinical Problems* 16(4): 71–78.

Maruna, S. (2008) *Making Good: How Ex-Convicts Reform*, American Psychological Association.

Pearson, G. (1983) *Hooligans: A History of Respectable Fears*, London: MacMillan.

Pearson, G., Gilman, M. and McIver, S. (1986) *Young People and Heroin: An Examination of Heroin Use in the North of England*, London: Health Education Council.

Preble, E. and Miller, T. (1977) "Methadone, Wine and Welfare." In: Weppner R.S. ed. *Street Ethnography*, Los Angeles: Sage.

Simon, D. and Burrs, E. (2005) *The Corner: A Year in the Life of an Inner-City Neighbourhood*, Canongate Books.

Taylor, L. (1992). When the Music's Over. New Statesman and Society, 24 April.

The Clash. (1982) *Straight to Hell*, on Combat Rock CBS Records.

Walsh, P. (2005) *Gang War: The Inside Story of the Manchester Gangs*, Milo Books.

Yates, R. (1992) *If it Weren't for the Alligators*, A Lifeline Publication.

Zinberg, N. E. (1984) *Drug, Set and Setting; The Basis for Controlled Intoxicant Use*, Yale University Press.

Section Four

Geoff's Final Publication

13 Drugs, Care and Sex Work

Sex and Survival

Jenni Ward and Geoffrey Pearson

Introduction

This chapter on young people growing up in state care, vulnerability and sex work draws on research I was involved in with Professors Geoffrey Pearson and Tim Newburn in the late 1990s into the early years of the new millennium. The research was carried out as one of a handful of studies on the Economic and Social Research Council's (ESRC) 'Youth, Citizenship and Social Change' programme titled, *'The Scale and Meaning of Drugs in the Lives of Young People Growing up in State Care'*. The study surveyed 400 young people living in residential or foster care and a small number of 'care leavers' across different English towns and cities, and thirty participated in a life history interview. Many of the young people had experienced multiple and disrupted care placements, backgrounds of drug- and/or alcohol-addicted parents, and some described teenage lifestyles that incorporated early and exploitative sexual relationships. This chapter draws to the fore some of the findings from this earlier research to contribute to the current debates and calls for improvements in responding to this problem (Jago et al., 2011; APPG, 2012; House of Commons Education Committee, 2014). Importantly, it is a tribute to Geoff's work on the study.

It was just a few months before Geoff's unexpected passing in April 2013, over one of our restaurant lunches that Geoff was reflecting on the failings found to have occurred across a range of social and health care services in the case of the six young women drawn into the 'sex grooming' ring in Rochdale (RBSCB, 2013). He commented what we had found in our earlier ESRC study was as relevant today as it was then, and moreover was useful for an understanding of the circumstances in which some young people end up in these sexually exploitative relationships. He was interested in returning to this earlier research to publish some of the detail from the life history interviews. The accounts and trajectories we recorded could shed light on how some growing-up pathways unfold into those of street survival, sexual exploitation and drug and alcohol addiction as alternative care and nurture is sought away from family problems and breakdown in state childcare arrangements.

Being invited to write this chapter has been an opportunity to revisit this work and to provide commentary on the need for Social Services and other adolescent social care and health services to become more attentive and responsive to the early warning signs young people and families 'in need' occasionally call for (*cf.* Coy, 2008; Pearce, 2010; Warrington, 2010 among others). This is highly important in this era of fragmentation and partial privatisation of children's Social Services and where good leadership, responsibility and accountability are paramount. I am proud to have been asked to represent this area of Geoff's working interest and concern. He felt irritated by the institutional failings that continue to blight the lives of some young people in the UK. Geoff and I had discussed penning some words.

This chapter connects our earlier study to the wider body of research and commentary which has been raising various questions regarding the inadequate listening to young people's voices so that appropriate and real interventions can occur when they should.

Background and Context

Although commentators and campaigners have been writing on the issue of youth sexual exploitation and youth prostitution for some time, highlighting its nature and extent, and raising concerns about its hidden form, and consequent difficulties in protecting victims and prosecuting perpetrators (2002, 2010; Cusick, 2002; Coy, 2008, 2009; Ward and Patel, 2006; Melrose, 2010; Phoenix, 2010; Warrington, 2010; Howard League for Penal Reform, 2013 among others), the wide publicity of the 'Rochdale case' and now subsequent cases[1] crystallised attention to this style of youth 'sexual exploitation' in the UK.

Empirical research carried out with young people experiencing 'sexual exploitation', as well as first-hand evidence that emerges from children's charities and voluntary organisations supporting vulnerable young people (e.g., National Society for the Prevention of Cruelty to Children and Barnardos), highlights correlations between troubled family lives and breakdown, running away and/or going missing from care, and youth drug and alcohol misuse (Biehal and Wade, 2000; Cusick, 2002; Coy, 2008, 2009; Ward and Patel, 2006; Brodie et al., 2011; Smeaton, 2013 among others). Indeed, the Serious Case Review that followed the failings emerging out of the Rochdale case provided indication that most of the six young women had disconnected family ties, had been in state care and had various other vulnerabilities such as educational learning needs (RBSCB, 2012:20).

Given the sensitivities and difficulties with researching this group it is not surprising there is little research of this nature, but studies that come from a different angle can shed light. For example, studies of young people growing up in 'care' such as ours, studies of 'care leavers' (see Ward et al., 2003;

Coy, 2008, 2009), studies cf young people who go missing from home, etc. (Rees, 2011) are examples. The latest findings from the third wave of the national study on 'young runaways' states that little seems to have changed in the scale of running away since the first survey in 1999 when it was estimated more than 100,000 young people under the age of 16 were 'running away', or were forced to leave home in the UK each year (Rees, 2011). The third survey carried out with 7,349 secondary school children reports that young people are at heightened risk of danger and being harmed while they are missing from home. For instance, the report found a number had slept rough, or with someone they had just met while they were away from home (ibid.: 16.).

The following section draws on data from our earlier study and provides information from the life history interviews to illuminate the nuanced way in which disrupted families, entry into state care and the seeking of alternative care and nurture among older-aged peers and at the street-level can interact. This material provides a real backdrop to the circumstances that some young people live with and which places them at risk of drug misuse and risky sexual encounters. The stories provide understanding of the complex nature and formation of sexual relationships as they occur among some vulnerable young women and the way in which drug use intertwines.

The Young People in Care Study

Our ESRC study was carried out between January 1999 and February 2001. The 400 young people who took part were recruited from across twenty-two English Local Authority Social Services Departments and lived within residential children's homes (n=68), foster family placements, and as care leavers.[2] A sample of residential children's home staff, managers and foster carers (n=30) were also interviewed.

The young people ranged in age from 10 to 23 years, with an average age of 15.4 years. Just under half were young women (46%: n=185). Table 13.1 shows a breakdown of the sample by the care status at the time of the interview. Table 13.2 illustrates the number of care placement moves the young people had so far encountered while living in care.

Table 13.1 Sample by Accommodation Type

Type of accommodation	Per cent	N
Residential care	46	185
Foster care	42	168
Care leaver	9	35
Secure unit	3	12
Total	100	400

Table 13.2 Number of Placement Moves

Number of placement moves	Per cent	N
1–2	34	136
3–5	30	118
6–8	18	71
More than 8	14	54
Total	96	379

State Care History

To obtain knowledge of the young people's care histories we asked how long they had been living in state care, and how many residential children's homes and foster families they had lived in since coming into care. A continuing concern in relation to the state care population is the extent to which some young people are moved from one care placement to another. Continuity in care is found to be closely correlated with improved outcomes (House of Commons Education Committee, 2014). Just under half of the young people (42%; n=170) had been in care for two years or less. A total of 23 per cent (n=91) had been in care for eight years or more, and the remainder between two and eight years. Based on the average age of 15 years, this indicated a fairly high number entered state care in their early teen years. Our life history interviews typically verified that tensions within families could arise alongside emergent and challenging adolescent behaviors, which for some resulted in entry into care.

As Table 13.2 illustrates, a third (34%; n=136) had experienced one to two placement moves, but 14 per cent (n=54) had experienced upwards of eight different moves involving placements in both foster families and in residential units. Not surprisingly, young people found this aspect of being in care to be particularly unsettling.

Interviewer: How is it all that moving about?
  It was really stressful, 'cause when you move in you make a group of friends and you start to settle down; you start getting to know the foster parents, start trusting them a little bit, then all of a sudden you have got to move, and then you have got to start all over again and start building up more trust; you feel like you are always watched all the time.

(Male, 21, care leaver)

It was a common understanding among state childcare professionals that the greater the degree of anti-social behaviour a young person displayed, the higher the number of care placements they were likely to experience.

Residential children's home staff pointed to this becoming self-perpetuating where the more placements a young person experiences, the greater the propensity towards anti-social behaviour. It was often noted by residential children's home staff that working in residential units was becoming increasingly difficult since their day-to-day work involved primarily containing the most challenging young people. Further, the more anti-social a young person became, the opportunities to be accommodated within a foster family situation were reduced. Foster family placements, if indeed they go well, are considered to provide the important stability a young person needs to go on and succeed in life.

A fifth of the sample (21%; n=80) had only ever been accommodated in a foster family home, reflecting the growing trend over the decades to utilise foster care or kinship care wherever possible, rather than residential group care home living. Despite an understanding that residential care is necessary for some young people, it is commonly regarded that young people are best looked after in a family environment (Boddy, 2013; The Care Inquiry, 2013).

Family Background

We asked young people which members of family they had last lived with before coming into care. One fifth (20%; n=78) had been living in a household headed by both parents. Eight per cent had been living with their mother and a stepfather. Owing to the sensitivity of some young people's entry into care we did not ask explicitly why they had been taken into care, but from the life history interviews it was apparent a few of them had begun experiencing conflictual relations and problems with their mother and her 'new partner'. The large-scale study by Bebbington and Miles (1989) into the backgrounds of 2,500 young people admitted into care found family composition such as growing up in a single-parent household and growing up with a mother's live-in partner to be a risk factor relating to entry into care. Three quarters of their sample were living in a one-parent family before entry into care.

Drug Histories

Because our study was centrally interested in the place and meaning of drugs in the lives of these young people, we asked them whether they had ever used drugs, how recently and how frequently they used drugs. A sizable number had 'tried' a range of drugs, yet cannabis was the only substance which could be defined as being used regularly. Figure 13.1 illustrates more than a third (38%) had smoked cannabis in the past month and 15 per cent (n=62) said they smoked cannabis 'most days'. Between 3 and 7 per cent had used other drugs, including cocaine, crack and heroin. These findings indicated a considerable proportion of the care sample used drugs regularly. Most drugs had been used

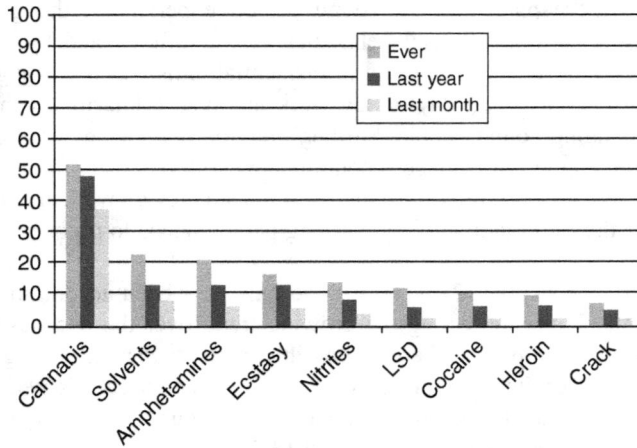

Figure 13.1 Frequency of drug use among a sample of young people living in state care.

by a larger proportion of the sample than other surveys of young people at that time reported (Parker et al., 1998; Ramsay et al., 1999). There is little more recent research to which we can refer, to verify whether a similar trend exists today. Given drug use among young people is reportedly on the decline, it may be that this is similarly the case among young people in care, but McCrystal et al.'s research (2008) found levels of drug use among young people in care to be similar to ours, thus warranting continued attention and investment in appropriate responses and services.

Are Drugs a Problem for Young People in Care?

We were interested in whether any of the young people who had used, or were still using drugs, had experienced problems relating to their drug use, and if so what type of problems. A significant minority (21%) of those who had used drugs (n=255) viewed themselves as having experienced some form of life-style and/or health problem. Put another way, one in seven of the total sample (14%) reported having experienced problems. For the majority, such problems generally centred around disciplinary issues such as school exclusion, sanctions within care homes or police action. Some were experiencing more serious health-related issues such as drug addiction, or a general downward spiral which was negatively affecting day-to-day functioning. Five per cent (n=14) of those who had ever used or 3 per cent of the total sample reported having been, or being drug addicted at the time of the interview and some were battling to control addiction. Four per cent (n=17) of respondents reported having injected either heroin or amphetamines at some point in their lives. As stated previously, it is difficult to verify whether this situation is the same today because of a lack of systematic studies exploring these details, but it can be assumed that the problem drug user population that exists in the UK today comprises some young people who are living in state care, care leavers and/or young people who have gone missing from care. The consequent specialist health needs, both physical and mental, of these young people is therefore highlighted and necessarily worth consideration.

Sex Work and Care

Our survey asked many lifestyle questions, including exploring connections to youthful commercial 'sexual exploitation'. We specifically phrased the question 'have you ever received money from someone you have had sex with?' Three per cent (n=12) of the young people reported they had. Table 13.3 illustrates their characteristics. Ten were young women and almost half (n=5) had used heroin, crack cocaine and/or powder cocaine. This had commonly involved periods of heavy dependence. To some extent the findings of our study make apparent the risk towards sexual exploitation that is found among this population.

In the discussion that now follows, we focus on the experiences drawn from some of the life history interviews with young women in our study. From their detailed accounts we can draw some knowledge on how young people in care, or who are experiencing conflictual family relations, fall through the net and end up fending for themselves at an early age.

Before providing this detail, we engage in a brief discussion of terminology because in contemporary debates of youthful sexual exploitation space is generally given over to the use of terms and how adequately, or indeed inadequately, they represent the dynamics of youthful sexual relations, some of which have exploitation at their core (Pearce, 2010; Phoenix, 2010; Melrose, 2010).

Table 13.3 Young People in Care Who Had Received Money in Exchange for Sex

Gender	Ethnicity	Age (average)	Care status	Ever used drugs	Main drug use
Female, 10 Male, 2	White, 11 Non-white, 1	14–19 yrs (16 yrs)	Residential care, 4 Foster care, 3 Secure unit, 2 Care leaver, 3	Yes, 11 No, 1	Cannabis, 10 Heroin, 5 Crack, 4 Cocaine, 4

'Care status' refers to the type of accommodation respondents were living in at the time of the interview. Yet, this factor means little in terms of correlation to commercial sex since the young people had generally lived in residential as well as foster care.

Defining the Terms

The terminology surrounding the sale of sex has been extensively discussed (Cusick et al., 2003; Chase and Statham, 2005; Melrose, 2010; Pearce, 2010; Phoenix, 2010) and is indeed a contested term, with some commentators insisting on the term 'sexual exploitation' and others seeing it as being too reductive, assigning young people to victims of abuse and denying their sense of agency in sexual relations (*cf.* Pearce, 2010). Others see underage sexual relations that are underpinned by manipulation as nothing other than sexual exploitation and child abuse. This is certainly a way it can be defined, and it is argued this representation has been useful for mobilising policy responses that treat those young people involved in street-level prostitution as victims rather than offenders (Pearce, 2010). The question does remain, however, whether this terminology is helpful for all understandings and discussions of this issue and the varied points at which interventions among those affected need to occur? I return to this point in the conclusion. Some earlier American literature refers to relationships of this type as 'survival sex' ties. Greene et al. (1999) state "survival sex" refers to selling sex to meet subsistence needs. It includes the exchange of sex for shelter, food, drugs or money' (ibid.: 1406). This term seems appropriate for the young women we write about here. In the main, the relationships they described were underpinned by early independence, and in the absence of family and formal institutional support, older-aged and already independent adults were latched onto to provide shelter, care and nurture.

Family and State Care Placement Breakdown

A common scenario among the young people we interviewed was the breakdown of natural family and foster family relationships in the mid-teen years. Often in these circumstances, rather than rely on the responsibilities of statutory Social Services departments to find replacement care provision, they had opted to draw upon already established relationships with friends, friend's families, boyfriends and others for their physical shelter and emotional protection and needs.

Many described their growing up as involving multiple care placements in both foster families and residential care units, as well as receiving interventions by various professionals and Social Services, something in their mid-teens some now wanted to avoid. During this point of transition and indeed vulnerability, girls often referred to forming relationships with men who were 'quite a bit older' than themselves.

Broadly, we found the relationship types of the girls we centred on could be differentiated from each other in two ways. There were those who were highly vulnerable, and who, during the period of transition from care to self-reliance, were naively drawn into dependent drug/sex relationships, who experienced severe exploitation and whose stories resembled the horror stories occasionally read about in the media. In contrast, there were young women able to remain in control of both the relationship and their drug use, ceasing either, or both in favour of their health and/or dignity. These young women recognised the point at which the dynamics of the relationship were changing, where more was expected of them than when the relationship had started out, and were able to curtail contact with their 'friend/boyfriend' from that point. To some degree, these young women used the relationship to their benefit, in the way it provided easy access to drugs and important company in recreational leisure time drug consumption.

Below is the case study of Leyla which illustrates her route into state care, but the way an alternative care arrangement was opted for in the face of the loneliness and stresses caused through being in care, Social Services placement decisions and quite likely the presence of childhood trauma.

Leyla: Security and Exploitation

At the time of the interview, Leyla was 17 and had recently exited from a two-year period during which she had been selling sex to provide for her, and her 'exploiter's' drug addiction. The two-year period involved varied sex work experiences, including sexual relations with him, working the streets with a number of clients, and at another time depending on a single wealthy client who monetarily provided for her.

At age 13 Leyla and her siblings were placed in local authority care following years of disruptive and chaotic parenting. Both parents were alcoholics. Leyla described her growing up as that where she and her brother and sister had looked after themselves and taken on the day-to-day care of their baby brother. Because of this responsibility Leyla's attendance at school was erratic and eventually ceased by age 13/14. Leyla began smoking cannabis with her older brother and other local street youth at age 12/13. Social Services eventually intervened in the family, removing Leyla and placing her in a residential children's home, while at the same time separating her from her twin sister, who was put in a children's home in a town 30 miles away. After a brief period of living in the residential unit Leyla was accommodated in a foster family placement but described not being able to settle, saying:

> You don't feel right at somebody's house and you don't want to settle down cos you get hurt and you got to move cos if you really like staying in foster care and you get kicked out, then it hurts, cos you get close to that person and you got to change again.

She described never being at the foster home, instead returning to her local area where she stayed wherever she could and with whoever would have her— 'when you got nowhere to stay you just doss at anybody's houses, who's going to let you stay there'. From that point, it can be said the care placement had dissolved and Social Services lost contact with her. Leyla was now living a free-wheeling lifestyle which brought her in contact with other young people in similar positions to herself. One of these was a group of differently aged people with whom she began shoplifting and taking harder drugs, including heroin. Leyla was aged 14 at this point.

One night, an older-aged male member of the group from whom the rest of them were buying their drugs, offered to have Leyla stay at his place. Gal was 35 years old and had been using heroin for ten years. This was the beginning of a two-year period in which Leyla became trapped in a mutually dependent relationship with him, becoming heavily addicted to heroin and 'crack' cocaine and selling sex to cover the costs.

At first, Leyla described a supportive relationship in which Gal had given her heroin at no cost, and provided for her in other ways. The relationship seemed genuine and caring and there was no pressure for her to give anything in return. At the time of interview Leyla reflected on this period of her life, as one of naivety:

> At the time I thought he was doing it to help me, he was helping me, he let me stay there, and he was doing it because he was trying to be nice but then I realised he was doing it for a reason. You ain't going to give something for nothing, are you, unless you want something in return.

The manipulation she went on to face in exchange for a roof over her head is expressed in the following comment:

> I couldn't go out when I wanted . . . Gal kept me in his home, he was saying take this, take that and because I was so young and I was in his house, I couldn't do nothing and cos I needed to stay at his house, I had nowhere else to stay, I would have took anything anyway, just to stay in his house and just to keep him happy.

After Leyla had been staying with Gal for some time, the car break-ins he was involved in landed him in trouble with the law, and he went to prison. The sudden cut-off of Leyla's routine drug supply through him generated problems, and in the lack of any other kind of support she began to 'work the streets' to pay for what had become a physical dependence on heroin. At this point she was aged 15.

At the time of the interview Leyla described trying hard to manage her heroin addiction and the drug treatment programme she was on, as well as having to learn how to have a normal girlfriend/boyfriend relationship:

> We don't know what a proper relationship is, all we know of a relationship is getting money off men and going home and spending their money, we're trying to get into like a relationship with somebody we like, get other things normal people do, but with somebody we like, it's like really hard to get into a relationship, we think they're going to hurt us or something, it's like, I don't know it's weird.

Leyla's twin sister, Penny, similarly described a dreadful experience of street-level prostitution, homelessness, drug addiction and ill health. She had effectively been rescued off the streets by a voluntary sector agency doing outreach work with sex workers. At the time of the interview she too was trying hard to stay off drugs, but admitted to sometimes selling sex, for financial purposes:

> Every now and again, only when I need money like, I don't do it, like all the time, I only go out, because £20 now will last me ages, £20 for food will last me a couple of days, if I was doing gear [heroin] it would have just gone like that, but now I save my money and I buy clothes and that, try to be normal.

Wherein, these scenarios describe severe cases in terms of being lured into drug/sex relationships driven by coercion, exploitation and gain, other girls found themselves on the fringes of commercial sexual relations through the friendships and leisure-time drug-using circles they were a part of. Carla was one of these.

Carla: A Close Encounter

At the time of the interview Carla was aged 18. She was seven months pregnant by her husband, who was slightly older at age 19. Carla was finding the relationship had different stresses to her previous ones, which had been with men some years older than herself. Carla grew up in South Africa until the age of 11 and had lived with her mother and her mother's boyfriend from the age of six. She found herself on her own following episodes of running away because of problems and volatility in the relationship with her mother. But, as has sometimes been found in circumstances such as these, young people are returned to live within the family environment in which they have been encountering problems and from which they have been running. This was the case with Carla but the relationship between her and her mother finally broke down at the age of 15. At first Carla tried to avoid Social Services assistance in the form of accommodation and support, instead relying on friends and boyfriends. But because of her young age and the struggle she was facing in managing this, she was compelled to move into a foster family arrangement.

The period after Carla left home was a combination of socialising and staying at friends' places, as well as being fostered into the family of a friend, but this did not work out and she left just after her sixteenth birthday. Carla described meeting a boyfriend who at age 28 was twelve years her senior, who along with him and her friends they lived a busy social life:

> Just used to hang about all night. I had so many friends who like either had their own flat or more or less were up all night, . . ., and we just used to wander around, mess about, drink and just go and see boyfriends I suppose. . . . It wasn't long after I left my mum's that I actually found a

boyfriend; he was quite a bit older than me, but I used to spend most of my time with him, so I was quite happy there. Going out with him in the car, going for a drive, going to the cinema.

Carla studied for her school exams and worked to survive financially and as well went on to attend college and gain further qualifications. She had smoked cannabis from the age of 12/13, saying 'it was easy to get hold of' and it was a part of the social scene she had joined as an older-aged teen: 'Everyone else was doing it, you were doing it; it was just part of the scene I suppose'.

In these older teen months, her main social space was a local pub where she described meeting lots of drug-experienced people such as heroin and cocaine users, and out of curiosity one day through a friend Carla tried out smoking crack cocaine. From there she described a controlled but ritualistic period of smoking crack and drinking. This style of recreational drug using involved relationships with two older-aged men who it appeared were attempting to seize an opportunity to engage Carla sexually, but she was able to read the situation and with the level of self-sufficiency and social capital she had acquired up to this point, she drew away and ended the relationships.

She describes one drug-using acquaintance she got close to whom she knew, through a previous dealer friend, had sexual feelings towards her, but were not reciprocated by her. For a time, he had respected the situation, but at a certain point Carla sensed the shift and cut the links:

> I said I don't want you round my flat no more, I've thrown your number away, it's off my phone, I don't want you coming round no more . . . and I just looked at him, I said, 'What do you think I am—stupid? This is my way, at the end of the day, I ain't never going to work for you, that's one thing you will not do.' I think as far as anyone's concerned sex is sacred, know what I mean, and I said that to the bloke, I just said you don't do it, you do not do it for money, you do not do it for someone else to get their money, know what I mean, you do it for love, and that's it.

Despite his persistence, she says:

> . . . he phoned me up a few times and said, 'Oh, do you want to go out for a drink?' I said, look I'm busy, bye and put the phone down and it was the hardest thing to do when I'd had a really bad day and he'd phone me up and I know that there's one [rock of crack cocaine] on the other end of the phone, there's a few on the other end of the phone and I just thought I can't do it any more, I just couldn't do it. . .

A common and disturbing feature of how these young women became drawn into exploitative sexual relationships with often older men, and into the drugs/sex link, was that it was a direct consequence of their efforts to deal with some of the experiences of being in care, and/or coping with troubled family environments that were chaotic, abusive and/or non-existent. Being in 'care' was supposed to be a solution to these difficulties. However, in many cases the experience of care seemed to mirror and amplify earlier experiences of chaos, rejection and hurt.

It is not enough to view the way these girls found themselves in risky sexual encounters as a result of misguided relationships, youthful naivety, helplessness and desperation. We must also reach for an alternative interpretation which understands the specific life transitions through which these young people pass, and to fashion systems of public response which are more appropriate to their complex needs—which combine childhood dependence with adult precocity—and which do not expose them to even greater degrees of risk than those to which they have already been exposed.

Discussion and Conclusion

It has been some time since this research was carried out, but it is fair to claim that for some young people growing up in the state childcare system today, or young people defined as 'children in need' and young 'care leavers' will invariably be facing the same, or similar sets, of circumstances to the young people written about here. It is well known that many young teenagers accommodated in state care come from troubled childhood backgrounds that in themselves cause long-lasting emotional and behavioural issues, and that once in care they can experience multiple placement moves and placement breakdowns, being accommodated in residential care units far from the areas in which they have been growing up and where family members and contacts reside, etc., all of which can lead to, or at least contribute to, young people seeking solace and nurture wherever they can find it. This is sometimes in inappropriate and exploitative relationships with older-aged men.

According to the Department for Education's annual statistics (DfE, 2013) there was a total of 68,110 looked-after young people between the ages of 0 and 16 in England at the end of April 2013. This was a 2 per cent increase on the previous year and a 12 per cent increase since 2009. In fact, it is reported that the total number accommodated is the highest than at any point since 1985. There was an increase in the number of 16-year-olds who came to be 'looked after' in this time period. This is put down to the Legal Aid, Sentencing and Punishment of Offenders Act (2012), which became statute in December 2013 (ibid.: 3). The act makes it law that any young person remanded in prison or remanded in the community by the courts is to become a looked-after young person and these young people will be supported by a social worker. A young person in the courts is anyone under 17 years of age. This legislative alteration could be a welcome arrival for some young people such as those I have just been writing about, since it could provide the vital lifeline support they have been looking for, but whose life circumstances have brought them into contact with marginal characters and activities bounded by criminal law. In the same way that some drug addicts find themselves receiving much needed dependency health treatment by coming through the criminal justice system, the same might be the case for these young people. The illegality of the street-level behaviours they have been forced into brings them into contact with the police and criminal prosecutions, but at the same time the necessary social care and welfare sources they desperately need can be mobilised at this point. It is therefore vitally important these specialist services need investment, decent resourcing and highly skilled empathetic staffing. However, it must be noted that critics sometimes refer to the pathway into help services through the criminal justice system as the criminalisation of social policy (*cf.* Howard League for Penal Reform, 2013).

There appears to be a real desire for change and reform of the state childcare system. This is evidenced in the current House of Commons All Party Parliamentary Group (APPG), which lays out a continued commitment to acknowledge the importance of placement stability in order to arrive at positive outcomes for those living in state care and to take on board what contributes to placement breakdowns as well as doing as much as reasonably possible to break the link between care and sexual exploitation (Department for Children Schools and Families, 2009; Department for Education, 2011; House of Commons, 2013).

Coy (2008) notes the string of policy documents and the central principles of childcare law that foreground the importance of young people's participation in placement decision-making (ibid., 2008: 260). This is rooted in the findings from research highlighting the single most negative aspect of state care as appraised by young people: the instability and insecurity caused from multiple placement moves and changes. At their core, the guidance in these policy documents is to limit the number of placement changes a young person experiences, but vitally to consult with them and hear their views. Coy reiterates 'a significant element of placement stability is the young person's commitment to the placement and motivation to make it succeed' (ibid., 260).

It has given me great satisfaction to return to, and make use of, the material we collected as a part of our study since it retains value in the way these real experiences that were reported to us reveal the complex ways some young people's existence comes to be lived out on the margins of society and among society's marginalised. I am not by any means excusing perpetrators of sexual exploitation by referring to them as society's marginalised, thus conjuring images of disadvantaged, needy characters who in themselves are troubled and neglected and who deserve support. But, from our research it was evident the men these young women had become entangled with were themselves 'hard' drug addicts, possibly also with lifetimes of disadvantage and well-practiced street survival skills. It is enough to say, in our attempts to provide rescue packages for young women and young men experiencing sexually exploitative relationships, that we make efforts to understand the multi and complex layers of dependent friendship relationships (*cf.* Pearce, 2010) as well as the power dynamics that underpin street survival, so that we can provide strong and meaningful messages and guidance for people to make their exit when they are indeed ready to.

Some of the work that is going on in the UK centres strongly on the notion of victims, victimisation and sexual exploitation, which indeed it is, but it is important to recognise the way, for a time at least, these relationships feel to the young person to be one of mutual love and care in a space of desperation and survival. It is fundamentally important to acknowledge and respect this stage since crackdowns and criminalising discourses at this juncture are likely to send all parties underground.

Notes

1 Since the Rochdale case other high-profile cases of sexual exploitation have emerged, the most recent being the revelation that approximately 1,400 young people were sexually exploited in Rotherham between the years 1997 and 2013 (Jay, 2014).

2 Young people are moved from the care system to their own accommodation between the ages of 16 and 18. From this point they are classified as 'care leavers'. Social Services are obliged to retain contact and provide support to them up to the age of 21, and older for some young people (HM Government, 2000). Because of this, age 21 became our upper age for inclusion, but one 23-year-old was also included in the study.

References

All Party Parliamentary Group. (2012) *Report From the Joint Inquiry into Children Who Go Missing from Care*. London: House of Commons.

Barnardos. (2014) *Report of the Parliamentary Inquiry into the Effectiveness of Legislation for Tackling Child Sexual Exploitation and Trafficking within the UK*. London: Barnardos. www.barnardos.org.uk

Bebbington, A. and Miles, J. (1989) The Background of Children who Enter Local Authority Care. *British Journal of Social Work*, 19, 349–368.

Biehal, N., Clayden, J. Stein, M. and Wade, J. (1995) *Moving On: Young People and Leaving Care Schemes*. London: HMSO.

Boddy, J. (2013) *Understanding Permanence for Looked After Children: A Review of Research for the Care Inquiry*. www.fostering.net

Brodie, I. with Melrose, M., Pearce, J. and Warrington, C. (2011) *Providing Safer and Supported Accommodation for Young People Who Are in the Care System and Who Are at Risk of, or Experiencing Sexual Exploitation or Trafficking for Sexual Exploitation*. University of Bedford and the NSPCC. www.beds.ac.uk [accessed 25 July 2014].

The Care Inquiry. (2013) *Making Not Breaking: Building Relationships for our Most Vulnerable Children*. The Care Inquiry, UK. www.frg.org [accessed 25 July 2014]

Chase, E. and Statham, J. (2004) *The Commercial Sexual Exploitation of Children and Young People: An Overview of Key Literature and Data*. Thomas Coram Research Unit, Institute of Education: University of London.

Chase, E. and Statham, J. (2005) Commercial and Sexual Exploitation of Children and Young People in the UK: A Review. *Child Abuse Review*, 14, 4–25.

Coy, M. (2008) Young Women, Local Authority Care and Selling Sex. *British Journal of Social Work*, 38, 7, 1408–1424.

Coy, M. (2009) Moved Around Like Bags of Rubbish Nobody Wants: How Multiple Placement Moves Can Make Young Women Vulnerable to Sexual Exploitation. *Child Abuse Review*, 18, 4, 254–266.

Cusick, L. (2002) Youth Prostitution: A Literature Review. *Child Abuse Review*, 11, 4, 230–251.

Cusick, L., Martin, A. and May, T. (2003) *Vulnerability and Involvement in Drug Use and Sex Work*. Home Office Research Study 268. London: Home Office.

Department for Children Schools and Families. (2009) *Safeguarding Children and Young People from Sexual Exploitation: Supplementary Guidance to Working Together to Safeguard Children*. www.education.gov.uk

Department for Education. (2011) *Tackling Child Exploitation: Action Plan*. www.education.gov.uk

Department for Education. (2013) *Children Looked After in England (Including Adoption and Careleavers) Year Ending 31 March 2013*. www.gov.uk [accessed 26 July 2014].

Greene, J. M., Ennet, S. T. and Ringwalt, C. L. (1999) Prevalence and Correlates of Survival Sex among Runaways and Homeless Youth. *American Journal of Public Health*, 89, 9, 1406–1409.

H. M. Government. (2000) *Children (Leaving Care) Act*. UK: The Stationary Office.

H. M. Government. (2004) *Every Child Matters: Change for Children*. Department for Education and Skills. www.education.gov.uk/publications

H. M. Government. (2012) *Legal Aid, Sentencing and Punishment of Offenders Act*. UK: The Stationery Office.

House of Commons. (2013) *Child Sexual Exploitation and the Response to Localised Grooming*. Home Affairs Committee. www.parliament.uk [accessed 24 July 2014]

House of Commons Education Committee. (2014) *Residential Children's Homes: Sixth Report of Session 2013–14*. House of Commons, London: TSO.

Howard League for Penal Reform. (2013) *The Policing and Criminalisation of Sexually Exploited Girls and Young Women: Summary*. www.howardleague.or.uk

Jago, S., Arocha, L., Brodie, I., Melrose, M., Pearce, J. and Warrington, C. (2011) *What's Going on to Safeguard Children and Young People from Sexual Exploitation*. University of Bedfordshire. www.beds.ac.uk

Jay, A. (2014) *Independent Inquiry into Child Sexual Exploitation in Rotherham (1997–2013)*. www.rotherham.gov.uk [accessed 17 September 2014].

McCrystal, P., Percy, A. and Higgins, K. (2008) Substance Use Among Young People Living in Residential State Care. *Child Care in Practice*, 14, 2, 181–192.

Melrose, M. (2010) What's Love Got to do With It? Theorising Young Peoples Involvement in Prostitution. *Youth and Policy*, 104, 12–32.

Melrose, M. and Pearce, J. (Eds.) (2013) *Critical Perspectives on Child Sexual Exploitation and Related Trafficking*. Basingstoke, UK: Palgrave Macmillan.

The Office of the Children's Commissioner. (2012) *I Thought I was the Only One. The Only One in the World*. Interim Report.

Parker, H., Aldridge, J. and Measham, F. (1998) *Illegal Leisure: The Normalisation of Adolescent Recreational Drug Use*. London: Routledge.

Pearce, J. J. (2002) *It's Someone Taking a Part of You: A Study of Young Women and Sexual Exploitation*. London: National Children's Bureau.

Pearce, J. J. (2010) Safeguarding Young People From Sexual Exploitation and From Being Trafficked: Tensions within Contemporary Policy and Practice. *Youth and Policy*, 104, 1–12.

Phoenix, J. (2010) Living and Working on the Cusp of Contradiction: Consumerism, Justice and Closed Discourses. *Youth and Policy*, 104, 32–46.

Ramsay, M. and Partridge, S. (1999) *Drug Misuse Declared: Results of the 1998 British Crime Survey.* London: Home Office.

Rees, G. (2011) *Still Running 3: Early Findings from our Third National Survey of Young Runaways.* The Children's Society. www.makerunawaysafe.org.uk [accessed 29 July 2014].

The Rochdale Borough Safeguarding Children Board. (2012) *Child Sexual Exploitation Themed Review.* www.rbscb.org

The Rochdale Borough Safeguarding Children Board. (2013) *The Overview Report of the Serious Case Review in Respect of Young People 1, 2, 3, 4, 5, & 6.* Rochdale Borough Safeguarding Children Board. www.rochdaleonline.org.uk

Smeaton, E. (2013) *Running Away From Hate to What You Think is Love.* Barnardos. www.barnardos.org.uk

Ward, J. with Patel, N. (2006) Broadening the Discussion on Sexual Exploitation: Ethnicity, Sexual Exploitation and Young People. *Child Abuse Review*, 15, 5, 341–350.

Ward, J., Henderson, Z. and Pearson, G. (2003) *One Problem Among Many: Drug Use Among Care Leavers in Transition to Independent Living.* Home Office Research Study 260. London: Home Office.

Warrington, C. (2010) From Less Harm to More Good: The Role of Children and Young People's Participation in Relation to Sexual Exploitation. *Youth and Policy*, 14, 62–80.

Index

248   *Index*

For Product Safety Concerns and Information please contact our EU
representative GPSR@taylorandfrancis.com
Taylor & Francis Verlag GmbH, Kaufingerstraße 24, 80331 München, Germany

www.ingramcontent.com/pod-product-compliance
Lightning Source LLC
Chambersburg PA
CBHW071848270326
41929CB00013B/2140

9780367371098